# TRANSFIGURING THE ARTS AND SCIENCES

In this important and innovative study Jon Klancher shows how the Romantic age produced a new discourse of the "Arts and Sciences" by reconfiguring the Enlightenment's idea of knowledge and by creating new kinds of cultural institutions with unprecedented public impact. He investigates the work of poets, lecturers, moral philosophers, scientists, and literary critics – including Coleridge, Godwin, Bentham, Davy, Wordsworth, Robinson, Shelley, and Hunt – and traces their response to book collectors and bibliographers, arts-and-sciences administrators, painters, engravers, natural philosophers, radical journalists, editors, and reviewers. Taking a historical and cross-disciplinary approach, he opens up Romantic literary and critical writing to transformations in the history of science, history of the book, art history, and the little-known history of arts-and-sciences administration that linked early modern projects to nineteenth- and twentieth-century modes of organizing "knowledges." His conclusions transform the ways we think about knowledge, both in the Romantic period and in our own.

JON KLANCHER is Professor of English at Carnegie Mellon University. His areas of research include Romantic and Victorian studies, history of books and reading, and the sociology of cultural fields. He is editor of *A Concise Companion to the Romantic Age* (2009).

CAMBRIDGE STUDIES IN ROMANTICISM

*Founding editor*
PROFESSOR MARILYN BUTLER, *University of Oxford*

*General editor*
PROFESSOR JAMES CHANDLER, *University of Chicago*

*Editorial Board*
JOHN BARRELL, *University of York*,
PAUL HAMILTON, *University of London*,
MARY JACOBUS, *University of Cambridge*,
CLAUDIA JOHNSON, *Princeton University*,
ALAN LIU, *University of California, Santa Barbara*,
JEROME MCGANN, *University of Virginia*,
SUSAN MANNING, *University of Edinburgh*,
DAVID SIMPSON, *University of California, Davis*

This series aims to foster the best new work in one of the most challenging fields within English literary studies. From the early 1780s to the early 1830s a formidable array of talented men and women took to literary composition, not just in poetry, which some of them famously transformed, but in many modes of writing. The expansion of publishing created new opportunities for writers, and the political stakes of what they wrote were raised again by what Wordsworth called those "great national events" that were "almost daily taking place": the French Revolution, the Napoleonic and American wars, urbanization, industrialization, religious revival, an expanded empire abroad, and the reform movement at home. This was an enormous ambition, even when it pretended otherwise. The relations between science, philosophy, religion, and literature were reworked in texts such as *Frankenstein* and *Biographia Literaria*; gender relations in *A Vindication of the Rights of Woman* and *Don Juan*; journalism by Cobbett and Hazlitt; poetic form, content, and style by the Lake School and the Cockney School. Outside Shakespeare studies, probably no body of writing has produced such a wealth of comment or done so much to shape the responses of modern criticism. This indeed is the period that saw the emergence of those notions of "literature" and of literary history, especially national literary history, on which modern scholarship in English has been founded.

The categories produced by Romanticism have also been challenged by recent historicist arguments. The task of the series is to engage both with a challenging corpus of Romantic writings and with the changing field of criticism they have helped to shape. As with other literary series published by Cambridge, this one will represent the work of both younger and more established scholars, on either side of the Atlantic and elsewhere.

*For a complete list of titles published see end of book.*

# TRANSFIGURING THE ARTS AND SCIENCES

*Knowledge and Cultural Institutions in the Romantic Age*

JON KLANCHER

# CAMBRIDGE
## UNIVERSITY PRESS

University Printing House, Cambridge CB2 8BS, United Kingdom

Published in the United States of America by Cambridge University Press, New York

Cambridge University Press is part of the University of Cambridge.

It furthers the University's mission by disseminating knowledge in the pursuit of education, learning and research at the highest international levels of excellence.

www.cambridge.org
Information on this title: www.cambridge.org/9781107029101

© Jon Klancher 2013

This publication is in copyright. Subject to statutory exception and to the provisions of relevant collective licensing agreements, no reproduction of any part may take place without the written permission of Cambridge University Press.

First published 2013

Printed in the United Kingdom by CPI Group Ltd, Croydon CR0 4YY

*A catalogue record for this publication is available from the British Library*

Library of Congress Cataloging-in-Publication Data
Klancher, Jon P.
Transfiguring the arts and sciences : knowledge and cultural institutions in the Romantic age / Jon Klancher, under contract to Cambridge University Press.
   pages   cm. – (Cambridge Studies in Romanticism)
Includes bibliographical references.
ISBN 978-1-107-02910-1 (Hardback)
1. Knowledge, Theory of–England–History–19th century.   2. Romanticism–England.
3. Science and the humanities–Great Britain–History–19th century.   4. Associations, institutions, etc.–England–History.   5. Books and reading–England–History–19th century.
6. London (England)–Intellectual life–19th century.   I. Title.
PR468.K56K48 2013
820.9'008–dc23   2013015317

ISBN 978-1-107-02910-1 Hardback

Cambridge University Press has no responsibility for the persistence or accuracy of URLs for external or third-party internet websites referred to in this publication, and does not guarantee that any content on such websites is, or will remain, accurate or appropriate.

*For Joan,
and my daughters Emily, Sophia, and Maya*

# Contents

| | |
|---|---|
| *List of tables* | *page* viii |
| *Acknowledgements* | ix |
| Introduction | 1 |

PART I  QUESTIONS OF THE ARTS AND SCIENCES

| | |
|---|---|
| 1  From the age of projects to the age of institutions | 27 |
| 2  The administrator as cultural producer: restructuring the arts and sciences | 51 |
| 3  Wild bibliography: the rise and fall of book history in the nineteenth century | 85 |
| 4  Print and institution in the making of art controversy | 107 |
| 5  History and organization in the Romantic-age sciences | 125 |

PART II  QUESTIONS OF THE LITERARY

| | |
|---|---|
| 6  The Coleridge Institution | 153 |
| 7  Dissenting from the "arts and sciences" | 182 |
| Epilogue: Transatlantic crossings | 223 |
| *Notes* | 232 |
| *Bibliography* | 274 |
| *Index* | 295 |

*Tables*

1  Royal Institution lecture series in seasons 1805–7         73

# *Acknowledgements*

This book has taken a long time to write and I have many people and institutions to thank. I would never have finished it without colleagues and friends who read parts of the manuscript, responded to talks, or discussed ideas from the book with me: Luisa Calé, Adriana Craciun, Simon During, Angela Esterhammer, Ina Ferris, Neil Fraistat, Sean Franzel, Kevin Gilmartin, Noah Heringman, Sonia Hofkosh, Anne Janowitz, Paul Keen, Alan Liu, Deidre Lynch, Jerry McGann, Michael Witmore, Bob Maniquis, Peter Manning, Leah Price, Tilottama Rajan, David Simpson, and Orrin Wang. I owe a special thanks to Jim Chandler for his timely interventions and unfailingly generous support of this project as it developed toward completion, as well as to Linda Bree's dedicated shepherding of the project through Cambridge University Press. Two anonymous press readers buoyed me with their enthusiasm for the project and gave immensely helpful critical advice on the work yet to be done.

At Carnegie Mellon I want to thank, for immensely helpful readings of chapters or other kindnesses, my colleagues Andreea Ritivoi, Peggy Knapp, Marian Aguiar, Kristina Straub, Jeffrey Williams, Kathy Newman, Rich Purcell, David Shumway, and Chris Warren; department heads David Kaufer and Christine Neuwirth provided timely leaves and other support to help this project toward completion. Over many years my Boston colleagues Susan Mizruchi and David Suchoff provided intellectual inspiration, constant friendship and practical help to move this book along through thick and thin. The especially kind offices of David Wagenknecht and Sacvan Bercovitch gave this project unexpected help at critical moments. Among past and present students whose ideas and creative thinking helped stimulate this project, I owe a special debt to Thora Brylowe, whose incomparable knowledge of the visual arts has taught the teacher in some key parts of this book; to Michael Rectenwald for history-of-science advice I hope I've put to good use; and to the many stimulating exchanges in seminars with D. J. Schuldt, David Haeselin,

Rebecca May, Tom Bondra, Corinna Parker, Miranda Burgess, Michael Hamburger, and Colin Harris.

In early phases of research the John Simon Guggenheim Foundation and the National Endowment for the Humanities provided important support for research leaves. At a crucial turning point in the evolution of this book, Bill Keach and Nancy Armstrong made possible a visiting professorship at Brown University that gave me a rich intellectual environment, remarkable students, and the best imaginable archives for work on the history of the book. I also want to thank librarians at the John Carter Brown and John Hay libraries at Brown University, the Houghton Library at Harvard University, the Cambridge University Library and the British Library, the Dibner Science Library at MIT, the archives of the Royal Institution, the Clement Library at the University of Michigan, the Yale Center for British Art, and the Special Collections at Hunt Library and the Hunt Botanical Library at Carnegie Mellon. Special thanks to Richard Noble and Mary Kay Johnsen for their invaluable archival help.

Above all I am immeasurably grateful for the love, support, and inspiration of my wife Joan Cucinotta. She has sustained me through the long work of the project with her sharp editorial eye and her steadfast belief that it would come to fruition. This book is dedicated to her, and to my daughters Emily, Sophia, and Maya, who have filled my world with love and surprise at every turn.

Revised versions of earlier essays appear as chapters 3 and 4 in this book, and I am grateful to the editors and publishers for permission to reprint material from my chapters in *Bookish Histories: Books, Literature, and Commercial Modernity, 1700–1900*, ed. Ina Ferris and Paul Keen (Basingstoke: Palgrave-Macmillan, 2009): 19–41; and *Outrage: Art, Controversy, and Society*, ed. Richard Howells, Andreea Ritivoi, and Judith Schachter (Basingstoke: Palgrave-Macmillan, 2012): 239–61. Brief parts of chapter 7 have been adapted from my essays "Discriminations, or Romantic cosmopolitanism in London," appearing in *Romantic Metropolis: The Urban Scene of British Culture, 1780–1840*, ed. James Chandler and Kevin Gilmartin (Cambridge University Press, 2005), and "Godwin and the Genre Reformers: On Necessity and Contingency in Romantic Narrative Theory," appearing in *Romanticism, History, and the Possibilities of Genre: Reforming Literature, 1789–1837*, ed. Tilottama Rajan and Julia Wright (Cambridge University Press, 1998).

# *Introduction*

This book investigates an enabling framework of modern literary and cultural studies, the "Arts and Sciences," by returning to a little-understood sphere of British Romantic culture – the emergence of new arts-and-sciences institutions in London that would generate both excitement and controversy in the metropolis, spread far and wide to the provinces, then migrate to the American lyceums and lecturing platforms of the nineteenth century. They would even have an impact, more indirectly, on the history of university disciplines or knowledge fields, some of them (like book history) still being constructed today. To grasp this Romantic turn in the history of the modern category "arts and sciences," I shall try to overcome the disciplinary divide between various kinds of knowledge-history (those of the sciences, visual arts, print, and the literary) to see how this matrix of arts-and-sciences institutions formed a response to the crisis, as well as a remediation, of the early modern Republic of Letters. One result was to help produce much of the literary writing we now call Romantic criticism. A related aim of this book is to grasp the discourse about institutions as a cornerstone discourse of modernity largely invented by the Enlightenment, but given perhaps its richest and most contradictory articulations in the Romantic age. This book does not try to resolve the status of "literature" at the end of the Romantic age, but it will offer reasons to believe that literature could only become a specialized world in its own right, from the nineteenth to the twentieth centuries, by simultaneously resisting and incorporating the increasingly disciplined domain called the "arts and sciences."

I shall first be concerned, in Part I of this book, with a historic invention at the turn of the nineteenth century, what contemporaries called, with a capital *I*, "Institutions" of the sciences, the arts, and many knowledges or practices in between: the Royal Institution (opened in 1800), the British Institution (1805), the London Institution (1806), as well as the Surrey (1808), Russell (1808), and Metropolitan (1823) Institutions among others.[1]

Founded in the midst of political struggle and commercial competition, they often began as risky, speculative projects – in the sense Defoe or Swift might have recognized in the early modern "age of projects" – yet they worked to turn these projects into powerful, often durable patterns of knowledge production, circulation, and cultural organizing that we would more customarily associate with "institutions" *sui generis*. These Institutions invented new methods of cultural transmission and defined new roles for the "artist," the "scientist," the "literary" writer and, not least, the "director," or what we would now call the "administrator." When we enter the world of these Institutions, we also find the more familiar kinds of cultural producer – poets, critics, novelists, editors, playwrights, natural philosophers, painters, architects, and lecturers – working hand-in-hand with those rather different kinds of knowledge producer I shall be emphasizing in this book: projectors, collectors, directors, and institutors.

Despite the relatively short lifespan these Institutions enjoyed in Britain (most were gone by 1900), their wider impact was arguably immense, both for the future of the "arts and sciences" as a modern category and for the way they helped to reconfigure the cultural past. Much of our own reflection on modernity's changing conditions for knowledge production and transmission has focused on the institution of the University, its current transformations and its longer historical role. Yet beyond a university genealogy, where the new learning Institutions of the early nineteenth century will require us to go, we find an altered scenario to think about. Unlike the German university's provenance for this spacious framework called Arts and Sciences, which moved into American university structures as the name of an emerging disciplinary research system in the later nineteenth century, the British discourse and practices of the arts and sciences around 1800 were notably more chaotic. These new Institutions of arts and sciences did not reach out from a secure institutional framework toward a public sphere, nor did they find pathways for scholars and students to become, through a strenuous outreach, "public intellectuals." Instead, such Institutions *began* there, in the realm of public controversy in the metropolis, diverse markets, political debate, and colonial rule. They made their impact on public knowledge and on forms of communication in ways that would, in the long term, have a striking if sometimes an oblique effect upon university knowledges and institutional continuity. These Institutions were subject to the powers of commercial society and particular markets of cultural production, and in a period of hotly contested political reaction, the writers, lecturers, and administrators who will appear in this book – among them, Samuel Coleridge, William Hazlitt,

Humphry Davy, Leigh Hunt, Jeremy Bentham, Charles Lyell, Percy Shelley, Thomas Bernard, Count Benjamin Rumford, Mary Robinson, Thomas Dibdin, Richard Carlile, and others – could very well grasp the feel and the moment-to-moment volatility of what a "conservative revolution" means and how it acts.[2]

These arts-and-sciences Institutions had a complex and lasting effect upon discipline formation, British print media, and what we may call learning-publics, the English audiences variously fascinated, taught, or repelled by the lectures and exhibitions coming their way. "The arts and sciences are now taught in lectures to fashionable audiences of both sexes," reported Robert Southey with some surprise and skepticism in 1807.[3] Women and Dissenters in particular could find what they would never be admitted to Oxford or Cambridge University to learn. Constructing a cross-class and mixed-gender constituency in London and then the provinces, the Institutions became distinctive for the social makeup of their spectators – the Royal claimed its "fashionables," the Surrey and London had their Dissenters of all kinds, the Russell drew in its more professional audience. No less visible were the intellectuals: Byron, Godwin, Lamb, Coleridge, Keats, Hazlitt, Crabb Robinson, Thomas Talfourd, Samuel Rogers, Thomas Campbell, Joseph Banks, or Jeremy Bentham, to name only a dozen among many.

While the Royal Institution and others became famous for scientific lectures and sometimes spectacularly staged experiments, they simultaneously pursued a more ambitious (to use our word) multidisciplinary agenda: instruction on moral philosophy, literary and book history, poetry and drama, the histories of commerce and technologies, the arts of printing and engraving, as well as the "fine arts" of poetry, music, painting, architecture, and aesthetics. Our knowledge of this lecturing, research, and publishing world has thus far been fragmentary, in part because of the highly unreliable paper trail scholars have had to follow (only the Royal Institution has left a substantial archive of its productivity), but also because of the very separation of disciplinary perspectives which those institutions ultimately, though not always intentionally, helped produce. Some of these Institutions began to be studied as "scientific lecturing institutions" by social historians of science in the 1970s, an early case study in what would become the wider cultural studies and history of the sciences. Others have been studied as "art institutions" by art historians since the 1980s and 1990s, while literary historians know them mainly for their sponsorship of literary lecturing by Coleridge or Hazlitt. These separate disciplinary histories of "art," "science," and "literature" respectively have tended to obscure the most novel innovation of early nineteenth-century cultural organizing in Britain – the emergence of a new complex of arts *and* sciences institutions going by the name of *Institutions* rather than the earlier nomenclature of learned "societies" or "academies." Societies and academies had played a fundamental part in building European knowledge since the mid seventeenth century across the Continent and in Britain. The new arts-and-sciences Institutions did not replace them – many new scientific societies appeared in Britain after 1800, in fact – but they created a very different kind of knowledge production and circulation with a far greater public impact than the earlier organizational forms had ever attempted or achieved.

These ventures in public scholarship afforded their audiences a combination of both disciplinary and, perhaps more revealingly, extra- and pre-disciplinary kinds of knowledge. Emerging work on the history of modern disciplines has increasingly opened the way to think more skeptically about assuming their long-term stability in light of what Luisa Calé and Adriana Craciun have suggestively called, with an ironic nod to Foucault, "the disorder of things."[4] At issue are not only formal disciplines but also "indisciplines" and "predisciplinary" knowledge formations that were often resistant to becoming incorporated into the later system of disciplined university subjects. Some became formal, important disciplines of modern knowledge (chemistry and geology, for example); others began to build "fields of study," such as historical bibliography or the history of books, only to be undone by contradictory forces at work in the very realm that was helping create them. Still others, like natural history, would prove so diverse and complex they would resist the disciplining of their knowledge entirely.[5] In what follows I shall treat these domains as "knowledge fields," a term I adapt freehandedly from the sociology of culture's theory of modern "fields of cultural production."[6] By using this expression I shall not mean that all fields can count what they produce as "knowledge" in the same way. If anything it is the opposite: fields like the literary, the artistic, the scientific, or the economic emerged from the early nineteenth century with dramatically uneven criteria of what counts as "knowledge" and which of these fields could most strongly lay claim to it. Questions of "arts" and "practices" complicated this matter of assessing knowledge enough that it will be useful to look into both the more highly organized fields of knowledge production and those more disorderly fields of inquiry that never became formal disciplines.

Such fields will also pertain to what many now call the "second scientific revolution" of the Romantic age, a recent periodizing of modern knowledge that has driven a good deal of innovative work since the 1990s, in Romantic studies as elsewhere, while it poses new problems and possibilities for grasping the interplay of humanities and scientific researches. The concept of a second scientific revolution in the Romantic age, for instance, has encouraged the assumption that "the order of disciplines," as Simon Schaffer puts it, amounts in historical perspective to "a utilitarian division of intellectual labour set up in the early nineteenth century."[7] In the following chapters I hope to complicate that picture by addressing problems of inter-, pre-, and in-disciplinarity in terms, not only of the new cultural Institutions of early nineteenth-century Britain, but also of the ongoing problem of the differentiation of cultural fields and disciplinary domains that still seems to me a key question and challenge to be met by any historical sociology of the literary or the cultural. For these reasons, I want to grasp the expression "arts and sciences" both in light of the dialectic it encompasses and to locate the historically shifting meanings of the "*and*" that both conjoins and separates its key terms.

Since the Royal, Surrey, and other Institutions would become most famous for their public lecturers, I should explain why this is not mainly a book about Romantic-period lecturing. Lecturing was a long-honored European practice both in and sometimes outside schools, universities, or academies; in late eighteenth-century Germany, Romantic lecturing became a remarkably prominent and complex medium of communicating knowledge in its own right, as Sean Franzel reveals in an incisive new study of its media, methods, and pedagogy.[8] But Germany's state-supported universities fostered lectures as a regular and largely academic form of inquiry and public scholarship that could have no counterpart in commercial London, where the state consistently refused to be patron to either arts or sciences. Instead, celebrity, charismatic authority, and sheer performative energy made Romantic lecturing a hot-ticket phenomenon in London from 1800, when the Royal opened what some called its "noon-day opera house," to 1823, when the Surrey Institution suffered financial collapse and when the vibrant arts-and-sciences Institution world, though still widely celebrated, also began to appear increasingly unequal to the knowledge-proliferation it had done so much to stimulate.

Along with lecturing, these arts-and-sciences Institutions put an equal and a surprisingly public emphasis on their forms of *administration*: how they were governed and financed, as well as how individual managers or directors hailed from particular professional or social origins and were perceived to have certain designs or commitments regarding how the new Institutions were to function. There was a wide public preoccupation with what kinds of authority were at work in administering these Institutions' arts-and-sciences agendas, and many observers who learned about their construction and aims also knew whether those agents were improving aristocratic landholders, bankers and investors, wealthy merchants, legal and medical professionals, MPs, Whigs and Tories, leading-periodical founders, or members of specialist scientific societies as well as art collectors and connoisseurs.[9]

Along with lecturing and administrating, this book will investigate the print media that engaged with these arts-and-sciences Institutions and with their least-known objective today, the building of ambitious print libraries, reading rooms, and bibliographical researches. Libraries, archives, and the belated English pursuit of bibliography and early modern book history became a key part of the Institutions' public mission. Meanwhile, print media, from quarterly reviews to monthly magazines to newspapers, became frequently and sometimes polemically entwined with the arts-and-sciences Institutions. It's important to see that print media have been mainly understood, since the rise of print and reading history, as produced in the markets of civil society, while "institutions" have been grasped as a separate realm, largely distinct from civil society (the state or the established church). But the early nineteenth-century British arts-and-sciences Institutions became adept at cross-hatching the mediatic with the institutional, and they did so in ways keenly responsive to the political, economic, and cultural pressures of the times. They used print media variously and opportunely – sometimes generating weekly or quarterly journals about the "arts and sciences" of a distinctively new type – while the British periodicals, no longer merely speculating *about* the possible relationships of "arts and sciences," would now become more actively engaged in organizing, criticizing, or advocating these new English institutions of knowledge production.

This was not yet an age of specialist scientific journals, but rather of publications like Thomas Bernard's the *Director* (1807), a weekly journal that set out to "promote, improve, and refine, the arts and sciences in the British empire" by networking in a single publication England's newest Institutions of knowledge with the older societies and academies (the Royal Society, Royal Academy, the Society of Antiquaries).[10] The *Director* sounded a theme of the moment – "In this country, nothing of a public nature can be effected but by clubs, societies, or institutions" – but the *Director* itself would become a case of print culture playing a critical part in mediating this institutional domain.[11] The same period saw a remarkable rise of the art-critical press, from the *Artist* (1807) and *Examiner* (1808) to

*Annals of the Fine Arts* (1816), and there was likewise a palpable turn in scientific writing, from those still using an older vocabulary for the sciences, such as the *Philosophical Magazine* (1798), to those articulating the new knowledges and idioms as signaled in titles like the *Quarterly Journal of Science and the Arts* (1816). The most powerful and distinguished print media in Britain sooner or later became imbricated in the emerging arts-and-sciences world. The *Edinburgh Review* entered complicated relations with the London phenomenon, from hostile reviewing to collaborative building; the *Quarterly Review*, not especially known for its secularizing interests since its founding in 1809, would take a notable scientific turn in the mid 1820s by depicting an institutional revolution occurring in the British sciences since the end of the eighteenth century. The *Anti-Jacobin Review* (1798), *British Critic* (1793), Leigh Hunt's *Examiner* (1808), and other politically focused journals took variously critical stances toward the lecturers, programs, or Institutions themselves. As Chapters 6 and 7 will explore, the more philosophical and political Romantic-age writers registered their impact in books ranging from *Biographia Literaria*, *Theory of Life*, and *The Friend* to *Chrestomathia*, *The Plain Speaker*, and *The Spirit of the Age*.

In Part II of this book I turn to Romantic literary writing and cultural criticism that grappled with the altered shape of the "arts and sciences" these Institutions were helping to produce. Their new kinds of cultural invention arose in part from the instability of what early moderns had long called the Republic of Letters. According to recent historical scholarship, this early modern framework of a "commonwealth of learning," which sustained the communicating and making of knowledges for two centuries, was by the end of the eighteenth century entering a state of crisis that would diminish its power as a normative world of knowledge production and scholarly/commercial exchange. The new arts-and-sciences Institutions of the early nineteenth century will show every sign of departing from that existing framework of educated knowledges. Still, if there was a crisis and collapse of the Republic's conceptual unity by the 1790s, as Ian Duncan, Paul Keen, and others have compellingly shown, this notional collapse was by no means the terminus of the intellectual field the literary republic had helped structure for nearly two centuries.[12] Instead, a mutation of that wider field was underway – both a differentiation of its knowledge genres in some ways, and a convergence of such knowledges in others.

Was this still Enlightenment? In their ordering and disordering of knowledges, the Institution world and its many participants could adapt the Enlightenment legacy only by transforming its matrix of disciplines, media, and modes of public outreach into a wholly renegotiated landscape of Romantic-age practices and spaces. To define such spaces, I shall attend throughout the book to key controversies that crystallized in or through the new learning organizations and their public impact. Institutions often arise out of controversy – indeed the history of religious and political struggle suggests they nearly always have done so – even as they generate new controversies to come. This is why institutions can appear as both stable and unstable, long lasting in one sense, yet remarkably volatile, contingently grounded, and prone to sudden change in another. Within a good many interlocking controversies at issue in the pages that follow, I focus mainly on those that concern questions of arts, sciences, belief systems, material interests, and philosophical dispute. Painters and architects stimulated controversy over the state of the British art field, through the Institutions and their print media, well before these struggles crystallized in the great Elgin Marbles debate. Critics of the Institutions' scientific powers opened territories of political dispute by challenging the scientific discipline-formation under way on various political, economic, and philosophical fronts. As the only major European capital without a university, London became a city especially open both to political struggles over who should have access to what kinds of knowledge, and to the commercial context that put into question whether this or that discourse could count as knowledge at all. Religious controversy also, to a perhaps surprising degree, entered the presumptively secular realm of producing "arts and sciences": Anglicans, evangelicals, rational Dissenters, Deists, Methodists, and atheists can all be found working to configure the early nineteenth-century public learning spaces, while High-Church Anglicans and anti-Jacobin writers often took every chance to oppose them. The secularity of the "arts and sciences" we now tend to take for granted was by no means the assumption guiding writers and organizers in the Romantic age.

If the formation called "arts and sciences" has been somehow less visible to us in the Romantic period than in the encyclopedic eighteenth century, it is in part because Romantic writers themselves often took a skeptical stance toward this rapidly proliferating discourse. Byron's "Parenthetical Address" (1812) mocked a version of its language by having his fictive "Dr. Plagiary" mindlessly rehearse what had become a national trope: "'In arts and sciences our isle hath shone' (This deep discovery is mine alone)."[13] In a time of cross-European war, the "arts and sciences" were becoming a key stake in the competition between French, German, British, and other national cultures or political visions which deployed them as arms in an international struggle. At the same time, Romantic writers could react to the discourse as if it were an obstacle rather than a stimulus to thinking or doing anything new. "We are so far advanced in the Arts and Sciences," Hazlitt demurred in *The Spirit of the Age* (1825), "that we live in retrospect, and doat on past achievements."[14] Leigh Hunt's *Reflector* (1810–11) warned English reformers that "the arts and sciences, which should have been primary planets and fixed stars in the parliamentary system," have instead become "the vortices in which we are whirling to destruction."[15] Nor have readers of Coleridge been quite sure of what he meant in his last published work by referring ambiguously to "the so called liberal arts and sciences" in a text on Church and State where the stakes of his meaning were surely very high.[16] These and other cases suggest that the intellectuals we have regarded as major Romantic writers took a questioning distance from the wider discourse on "arts and sciences," yet made a most active and complex engagement in what it does or should mean. They pushed and pulled, contested and absorbed, struggled with and sometimes capitalized upon the discourse of "arts and sciences" in ways not foreseeable from its early modern usage.

### Romanticism and the contingency of institutions

Romanticism has become culturally famous for generating powerful anti-institutional postures, or for vigorously pro-institutional defenses. Among the most important of these we would have to include Godwin's philosophical indictments of the "positive institutions" called government, Shelley's critique of religious and political institutions in his poetry and prose, Hazlitt's stinging assessment of "corporate bodies," Blake's exposing of those exploitive cathedrals in "Holy Thursday" or his fictional creation of that most anthropomorphic figure of institutions, the god Urizen. Edmund Burke furnished counterrevolutionary writers an idiom in which to defend Britain's great "immemorial" institutions that were now at risk in the wake of the French Revolution, and in a paradigmatic case, former radical critics of British institutional powers would convert, with Coleridge, Southey, and Wordsworth, to their most literary and polemical apologists.[17]

But while such critical or defensive postures have been important to grasping the Romantic period's most profound disagreements, they have tended also to obscure the extent to which the Romantic age was an extraordinarily active age of *instituting* in its own right. On the one hand, many could imagine or experiment with radically different kinds of instituting than had happened in the past. On the other, they could take old power structures and rethink them in a very modern way under the rubric "institutions" itself, as fascinated with what they could *do* as well as with how they worked and who was building them. "Institutions can new model our nature," enthused Robert Southey after reading a book of Quaker history in 1806, and many of his contemporaries, whether radical, Whig, or Tory, were working by that intuition as well.[18] The myriad forms such instituting could take are impressive when seen as a whole – scientific, artistic, welfare-shaping, punitive, rights-protective, print-cultural, culture-collecting, managerial or administrative, and so forth. In the following chapters I shall try to show what made this instituting process, and the language in which it was undertaken, *modern* as opposed to customary or even "early modern."[19] Thus I shall accentuate the recentness, the worked-up and modernizing character of this discourse of "institution," which, though it has tended to rear-project a social history measured in millennia, is itself no more than 300 years old. For late eighteenth- and early nineteenth-century writers, the discourse on modern institutions was still a *new* language even though it was drawing upon its early modern roots in the various verbs and participles *to institute* and acts of *institution* such as founding, educating, transmitting an inheritance, law-making, or declaring authority.[20] And whether we credit the emerging conceptuality of institutions to the Scottish, French, English, German, or Italian enlightenments, the modern discourse on institution was to be an invention of both magnificent intellectual skill and sometimes treacherous rhetorical powers.

Forged as a generalized noun gradually through the eighteenth century, *institutions* became a word uniquely capable of lengthening into a vast historical process, engaging its users in a fundamental anachronism whereby the distant past came suddenly closer and remarkably more familiar since it too, like we moderns, knew its own "institutions" of kingship or kinship, marriage or slavery, church or state. Human institutions have led a life of 20,000 years, sociologists tell us today, without blinking at the conceptual device devised by the eighteenth century that put modern social-scientific instruments to so sweeping a use for grasping all sociocultural pasts.[21] Such anachronism has thus tended to obscure the discourse on institutions' more effective Enlightenment invention as a cornerstone – or what Peter de Bolla would call a "load-bearing concept" – for thinking and writing about modernity itself.[22] In this light we can recall that the first consistently analytical deployment of the British discourse on institutions occurred in the Scottish Enlightenment, especially in the work of John Millar, Adam Ferguson, and Adam Smith. But the broader rhetoric of *institution* perhaps nowhere so tellingly assumed a modern shape than in the tumultuous dialogues of the Romantic age, whose writers would diversify, help stabilize, and also contradict this new discourse on modern institutions. In so doing, such writers thereby extended it to a wide range of nineteenth- and twentieth-century meanings – influencing Europe as well as Britain and the United States. To stand in momentarily for a wide range of these Romantic articulations, few could be more paradoxical than Percy Shelley's figure of the poet as "institutor" of laws, nations, and, not least, the "arts and sciences."

By the later nineteenth century, the conceptuality of institutions put to work by the Enlightenment would demonstrate its powers to help organize the disciplines of knowledge – anthropology, sociology, historiography, economics, or the various natural sciences – and, ultimately, the discipline of literary study itself. By 1895, this modern concept had a sufficient and various enough history of usage as to become the key focus of Émile Durkheim's *Rules of Sociological Method*, where he argued, against his own new discipline's many nineteenth-century critics, that sociology has a unique object of study as the "science of institutions."[23] On such social-scientific grounds, Anglo-American sociologists would command the theoretical and empirical study of institutions through much of the twentieth century, most prominently in the work of Talcott Parsons, where they put institutions at the center of modernity's differentiating "functions" or systems, consistent with a model of disciplines of knowledge as an orderly system, homologous from one to another and corresponding roughly to the disciplinary system installed in American universities since the 1870s.[24]

But what Durkheim did not then foresee was the convertibility of his claim – how an object of scientific and disciplinary study could later become a powerful critical and investigatory device for grasping the historicity, the social and political character of modern knowledges and the "arts and sciences" themselves. This important change from a proto-scientific status for the concept of "institution" to its more recent critical and historicist usage in social theory, cultural history, or literary and cultural studies can be traced to theoretical debates of the mid twentieth century, and it is itself an important transformation in the historicity of this modern concept. From the 1950s forward, a range of new intellectual projects launched from disparate directions – philosophy, anthropology, history of the sciences, linguistics, Marxism, historiography, and eventually literary study – would forge a wave of theoretical, cross-disciplinary, and methodological transformations that we have since come to call the linguistic, historical, and cultural "turns." We are still thinking through the implications of those institutional, historical, and indeed disciplinary questions that were crystallizing, between roughly 1958 and 1966, in the work of Habermas, Lévi-Strauss, Sartre, Fanon, Foucault, late Adorno, Williams, Kuhn, Bourdieu, Derrida, and Althusser – to name only most widely debated sources of argument and critical thinking of capitalist modernity over the next half-century.[25] One purpose in this book is to use the institution-concept's mutation – the point at which we might call the linguistic, historical, and cultural turns a more broadly "institutional turn" in late twentieth-century critical theory and cultural analysis – as a means to look into the origins of this great modern concept and discourse in the age of revolutions.

I take this transformation to help explain why, in an era of anti-foundationalist or constructivist literary and cultural studies over the past three decades, we have been using the notion of "institution" historically and theoretically as perhaps our most foundational concept. It has grounded the way we explain histories of culture, gender, nations and nationalism, literature, science, disciplines, and criticism itself. Literary historicism and cultural studies since the early 1980s have indeed so routinely invoked, studied, and grounded their arguments and assumptions in the concept and language of *institutions* that it's well-nigh impossible to imagine stripping such language out of recent literary and cultural criticism and find it still standing.[26] When such-and-such "became an institution," we now say, it acquired that modern authority, that persuasive claim for legitimacy, and that extraordinary power over public and personal lives against which we now try to map histories of power, of resistance, of empire (and writing back to empire), of social reproduction and crises of the same.

Yet, this book will argue, such foundational usages of the concept "institution" do not serve as well wherever we confront the social and cultural work of actual institutions that can flash or fail depending on historical circumstances and human actions. Institutions succeed or falter because of a host of competing contingencies. I shall accentuate the *contingent* character of institutions especially when, in an institution-building age like the Romantic, such constructs are fashioned in the most volatile circumstances, and where the term *institution* itself is invoked to suggest a historical authority and durability that we cannot find in real historical practice. So I shall be asking what made the language of institution – its *words* in public print media and in intellectual debate – newly and more decisively available to British writers at the turn of the nineteenth century; and what new, practical change in the urban landscape of institution-making in this period drove such writers to both diversify and challenge that language. I want to raise such questions in light of a relationship that has always been pivotal to the humanities – as expressed in the phrase "arts and sciences" that featured prominently throughout eighteenth-century print culture and then received a fundamental redefinition at the turn of the nineteenth century.

## Transfiguring the "arts and sciences"

In the seventeenth century, the terms *arts* and *sciences* could still often seem difficult to tell apart, if not wholly interchangeable. Cultural historians have attributed something more definite to this relationship with the emergence of scientific societies after 1660 and the Quarrel of the Ancients and the Moderns, when, according to David Spadafora and others, ancient science came to look unfit for modern tests of what constitutes knowledge, and modern experimental science or "natural philosophy" far more capable; at the same time, ancient literary epics and oratory looked victorious by any competitive comparison with any of the moderns.[27] The well-known outcome of this long controversy (by about 1720 in Britain) was in one sense a *narrative* one: the sciences "progress," yet the arts do not. Still, although this key differentiation of arts and sciences would hold in the *long* run of the next three centuries, it remained highly unsettled in the eighteenth and early nineteenth centuries. The rise of art academies and scientific societies from 1660 to 1800 could provoke, not a further solidifying of this division, but at times an effort to overcome it – to "improve" the fine arts, as the Royal Academy was teaching its students to attempt from its founding in 1768, to make the fine arts a modernizing domain of practices and knowledge. Against the Academy's attempt to bring the backward English art field into a knowledge-producing modernity by teaching the English how to advance the arts, Romantic writers like William Hazlitt would have to reassert the Quarrel's key principle in such writings as "Why the Arts are not Progressive?"[28]

At the same time, the phrase "arts and sciences" had been appearing widely in genres of print culture – encyclopedias, dictionaries of arts and sciences, magazines, and essays. What the expression really designated remained elusive: "if the words Arts and Sciences are found in their title pages," said Benjamin Martin of these print guides in 1755, "you seek in vain for the things themselves."[29] While Martin looked for "things," other contemporaries grasped a fundamental change in emerging *relationships*. For the Quarrel of Ancients and Moderns had not yet addressed the tangled middle-ground of the division between art and science – that is, the craft or artisanal, and the mechanical or technological "arts," where the real difficulty could lie. A vast range of customary crafts, artisan skills, and other "hidden arts," as the enyclopedist Ephraim Chambers called them in 1729, eluded systematic forms of knowledge production or being registered in print. Part of Chambers' promise to future encyclopedists was to vow that his enterprise could potentially unearth knowledge that lay obscurely in material practices and other as yet unknown places: "Numerous Things" were "not extant in Books, Libraries, or the Cabinets of Virtuosi," but rather "hid in Shops, Garrets, Cellars, Mines, and other obscure Places, where Men of Learning rarely penetrate: Rich Fields of Science lie thus neglected under Ground."[30] It remained a question where sciences stopped, where the arts began, and how many "hidden" practices of knowledge still lay untapped or inarticulate beyond the reach of experiment or print, learned societies or elite academies. Richard Yeo's valuable work on such encyclopedias reveals how those print projects aimed to join "manual and craft knowledge with natural philosophy and other 'liberal sciences'" in the eighteenth century. But in so doing, they were in fact "entering an old and still-unresolved demarcation dispute."[31] Meanwhile, as the arts-and-sciences dictionaries of the eighteenth century sought out these kinds of "arts," what Paul Oskar Kristeller called in a classic essay "the modern system of the arts" – meaning the *fine arts* – would crystallize as a distinctive category by the mid eighteenth century, yet remain largely distinct from what was usually meant by "arts and sciences," even by 1800.[32]

Thus the meaning and range of *arts* in both "liberal" and "practical" senses of the term was becoming an especially vexed question. The encyclopedist's problem of ferreting out the "hidden" knowledges that were still buried in skilled and customary practices, and not yet available to analytical or experimental discourse, would reappear in the late twentieth-century emergence of what Michel de Certeau (and Henri Lefebvre before him) called more theoretically the "practices of everyday life." For de Certeau, the eighteenth-century phrase "arts and sciences" designated a distinction between "practices articulated by discourse" (science) and those practices "that are not (yet) articulated by it":

> From Bacon to Christian Wolff or Jean Beckmann, a gigantic effort is made to colonize this immense reserve of "arts" and "crafts" which, although they cannot yet be articulated in a science, can already be introduced into language through a *"Description"* and, in consequence, brought to a greater *"perfection"* ... [Hence] the position of the "arts" is fixed, neighboring on but outside the field of science ... Art [as depicted in Diderot's *Encyclopedie*, for example] is thus a kind of knowledge that operates outside the enlightened

discourse which it lacks. More importantly, this *know-how* surpasses, in its complexity, enlightened science ... A problematics of lag or delay is introduced into the relation between science and the arts. A *temporal handicap* separates the various kinds of know-how from their gradual elucidation by *epistemologically superior sciences* [emphasis in original].[33]

De Certeau pictures the "arts" stretching beyond the sciences as a complex, unfathomable swarm of practices. But he also makes two further and I think critical points. The "lag or delay" between science and the practical arts is not the lag we usually think about when we regard science as modernity's cutting edge of knowledge, departing ever further from traditional arts and crafts from the past. It is rather a picture of the practical arts *outrunning* the discourse called science (or "natural philosophy" in the period described above); the "temporal handicap" thus belongs to science rather than to the still-uncaptured "kinds of know-how." Second, and as important, de Certeau accentuates the sense in which this *know-how* surpasses science by virtue of its greater complexity. As a modern system of discourse, science necessarily simplifies as it conceptualizes, even while its own internal operations become ever more complex by introducing into themselves the increasingly intricate boundaries between science and the surrounding, bafflingly complex world of practices and know-how that we are here calling "arts."[34] Perhaps the beauty in de Certeau's scenario is less in the distinction between "discursive" sciences and "non-discursive" arts (a less certain theoretical line to draw now, perhaps, than it was twenty-five years ago) than in the unsettling of scientific claims to being ahead of practices not yet rationalized, as if the "old" were somehow outrunning the "new" in both complexity and generativity.

Since early modern science depended so extensively upon the printed page or the book, it also required that the realm of "practical arts" be subject to representation in print in order to be articulated by a discourse. The sequential character of print and argument could thus be very much at odds with the three-dimensional density of the practical arts, providing a kind of material counterpart to more impalpable "delay" between sciences and arts. Diderot's *Encyclopedie* tended (brilliantly) to finesse this gap by way of the modern printed book's concession to the three-dimensional – the printing of illustrations – and to incorporate a great many images that seemed to represent to Enlightenment readers the integration of "sciences and arts" in just the sense that de Certeau reminds us they could not really be bridged. Surely they were not bridged in British encyclopedias (where illustrations were scarce) that formed the main print genre for displaying the "arts and sciences" in the eighteenth century.

Meanwhile, if Kristeller's "system of fine arts" did not figure very clearly into this early modern picture of "arts and sciences," as either de Certeau or the eighteenth-century encyclopedias represented it, it nevertheless had its own versions of the lag between discourse and practices or between "liberal" arts and their "mechanical" modes of execution. Students of Romanticism know that invidious distinction primarily through Blake's intransigent campaigns against Joshua Reynolds and the Royal Academy where Blake insisted on the unity of design and execution in painting or engraving while the Academy divided them, employing artisan "painters" to realize the formal designs created by Reynolds in one case, or excluding engravers like Blake or John Landseer from the Academy as mere mechanics in another.[35] These issues go to the heart of what came to be at stake in the "arts and sciences" debates and Institutional displays in Romantic-period England. They concern, first, the problem of the relative autonomy of "art" and "science" themselves – since a historical process of winning or losing key measures of such autonomy was entailed in distinguishing them at all – while at the same time confronting the rich tangle of social and cultural practices, including the problem of where to place the practical or mechanical arts, that complicated achieving any such independence. Just as critical was the problem of how both the knowledges and practices entailed in the "arts and sciences" enter such relationships of separation and convergence only in *time*, in comparative rates of motion, a mode of historicity or temporality that entered the early modern discourse on art and science as the question of "progress."

My title, *Transfiguring the Arts and Sciences*, speaks to the more contradictory dimensions of this modern discourse as it changed its shape and meaning over time, becoming somehow both clearer and yet more difficult in the Romantic age. At one level, I shall use *transfiguring* to mean the process in which, from the 1790s to about 1830, the fundamental categories "art" and "science" could be shifted, as it were, upward, as in the German expression *hinaufzubilden*, the word used by Friedrich Schelling in his later theological writings to designate the way in which the "excluded and dark" unconscious matter of the world was "progressively elevated ... to clarity." Schelling thus uses *transfiguring*, as Thomas Pfau helps us see, in the sense of "raising up to form" – to build up by making conscious, to educate (*bilden*) upward.[36] This sense of transfiguring the arts and sciences upward would correspond historically to the shift in emphasis from skills or "ingenuity" to "genius," in the language of sciences and arts alike, designating one's consummate mastery of an art or science as well as the implication that this very mastery confirms one's possession by a greater power – for some Romantics, possession by divinity itself, for others, possession by a driving West Wind. Humphry Davy at London's Royal Institution and Schelling in his lectures *On University Studies* at Jena could both, on such grounds, appeal to "the mind's arduous efforts to gain insight into the primordial nature and the eternal inner essence of its phenomena."[37] To the extent that *transfigure* suggests elevating, spiritualizing, or idealizing, moreover, I use the term in preference to more commonly used words like *transcend* or *transcendence*, terms which cultural criticism has perhaps used all too often and too vaguely, especially when what is at stake is a more precise historical measure of the increasing (or lessening) independence or authority of a discipline, field, or practice. At the pinnacle of this process of "raising upward" might be a scientific or artistic result, a knowledge or expressive outcome that appears unencumbered by the conditions that produced it. Our modern word for that condition is *autonomy*, perhaps the most vexed and contested term in the vocabulary of the arts and sciences as well as in the sociocultural inquiry into their production. This first form of "transfiguring" – the effort to realize literary, scientific, or artistic "autonomy" as an achieved state – has been, since the later twentieth century, the target of probing materialist, cultural, and historicist studies that have usefully aimed to deflate the claims of genius or mind as divinity's secular power on earth – but more important, to expose the blindnesses, illusions, or misrecognitions that claims to artistic, scientific, or literary autonomy inevitably entail. In a long series of debates on the problem of autonomy in arts, sciences, and "culture" more broadly, Marxism has forged various ways of grasping the notion of such autonomy as ideological but not entirely unreal. Most often, especially since the work of Althusser, the Marxist resolution of these debates has been to settle for the compromise expression "relative autonomy."[38] A more precise way of putting that status, inflected through the sociological theory of fields, would be to say that autonomy is not simply an illusion, though it can be profoundly illusory or misrecognized in both fields and modern disciplines. Neither an illusion nor an exalted state of self-determination, "autonomy" is historically, as John Guillory usefully puts it, "the object of struggle between fields, and as such can be won or lost, accumulated or spent, in relation to one field or another."[39]

Such "upward" transfiguring of arts and sciences was meanwhile complicated and contradicted by a lateral or *trans*-figuring – one that took place across the *and* of the expression "arts and sciences" – in which any art could potentially "figure" a science, any science might figure an art. Where the *hinaufzubilden* of "arts and sciences" would tend to aim toward the autonomy of each substantive term, the lateral movement figured the arts and sciences rather as entangled, intermediated, confusing, contingent, messy, disorderly – not upward from an unformed materiality, but cross-cutting among media and mediations that were inextricable from their very articulation. These lateral motions are most visible to us in the same semi-legible forms that were necessary to "advancing" the discourse on arts and sciences in the early nineteenth century – in print media, to be sure, but also in other key media, such as the *modeling* of art works or machines, or *lecturing*, an oral discourse conveyed within a world of print and most effectively modeled by the orientation of the lecturers toward their audiences. *Transfiguring* in this second sense designates the embedded entanglements of arts and sciences in the media that seemed to be clarifying, separating, and analogizing them in the early nineteenth century, which were no longer only print encyclopedias but also new quasi-mediatic forms like the arts-and-sciences Institutions, which one can surely read as "media" in their own right even as they claimed the meta-media forms of classic "institutions." But this sense of relational conflicts also entails the social embeddedness of practices that resist being "raised up" to a discourse – the kind of stubborn resistance that Robert Hooke of the early Royal Society had found when he tried to extract the various customary and skilled artisan knowledges that remained hidden away from the eyes of natural philosophers.

In this book, then, *transfiguring* in both senses I have been defining above will refer to what was in play within particular fields – artistic, scientific, literary – yet also to the relations or struggle *between* them. Although some of my Romantic-age authors in this book hoped to see the "arts and sciences" become the meta-disciplinary framework for *all* particular practices or disciplines of knowledge, I shall want to show how this transfiguring motion was complicated and frustrated by the practices, controversies, institutional contexts, and on-the-ground struggles that kept the discourse on "arts and sciences" a matter of continuing contention even after the significant transformations studied in this book.

Yet there is a third sense of *transfiguring* that has to do with the notion of "progress" in the "arts and sciences" as the Enlightenment understood that term. The verdict of the Quarrel of the Ancients and Moderns on this question had been easy enough to grasp in concept, more difficult in practice. By the early nineteenth century, Romantic writers like Hazlitt found it clarifying, in view of present political and institutional conditions, to reassert the argument that the sciences "progress" but the arts do not. That this was an ultimately disabling position to take for the arts may be clear to us now. Yet the choice between progressing or not progressing could well be complicated, in Romantic literary works, if one were to compare one's own personal history as a writer with public narratives of "progress" such as those to be found in essays like Hume's "Of the Rise and Progress of the Arts and Sciences" (1742) or in any number of eighteenth-century "progress poems" by Thomas Gray or James Thomson. In an essay on Wordsworth's "Intimations Ode," James Chandler has explored an especially clarifying case of a Romantic poet measuring his own fitful starts and stops, paths and dead ends, itineraries and reflexive reversals of those journeys toward maturation that, as a questioning parable of poetry's "progress," could find a very different means of progressing than Hazlitt's singular line of advancement.[40] The chapters to follow will trouble the notion of a "progress" in the "arts and sciences" in ways that are not all like Wordsworth's, yet will point to the complications that Romantic writing introduced with respect to time, change, progress, and other itineraries in the "arts and sciences."

Under the rubric "Questions of the Arts and Sciences," the first two chapters present a trajectory of cultural institution-building from early modern schemes or "projects" to the reshaping of those efforts as an ensemble of English arts-and-sciences Institutions (often called "useful projects") taking shape after 1800. Chapter 1 accentuates the Enlightenment tension between an emerging language and conceptuality of "institution," as mid-eighteenth-century philosophical historians (Giambattista Vico, Adam Ferguson, John Millar, Adam Smith) variously developed it, and the early modern practice and mapping of "projects" or speculative agendas that were often notorious for their reckless pursuits of profit or glory, but could also be serious attempts to envision social-welfare proposals to improve and protect human life in an often damaging market economy (as in Daniel Defoe's *Essay upon Projects*) – or to create new learned societies, academies, or publishing projects to organize the knowledges in an explosive book-printing age (as in Gottfried Leibniz's innumerable knowledge projects from 1675 to 1716). These welfare or knowledge-organizing projects would ultimately converge with the modern discourse on institutions, in the revolution-charged decade of the 1790s, to join Enlightenment tools with counterrevolutionary purposes in ways that would produce the several conflicting versions of a new learning organization in England, the Royal Institution. Even the process of *naming* this new entity sheds light on how different the arts-and-sciences Institutions to follow in its wake would be from the Societies and Academies built across Europe since 1660.

Romantic-age lecturing is often grasped as a speaker-to-audience relation of sometimes celebrity-frenzy proportions in London. Yet these lecturing agendas across many subjects were constructed and mediated by administrators like Thomas Bernard, whose career from welfare-reform to scientific and then fine-arts administrating at the Royal and British Institutions forms the framing narrative of Chapter 2. What's first essential to grasp is the strange history of the early Royal, which set out in the late 1790s to educate artisans and mechanics in the newest industrial technologies, yet reversed itself by 1802–4 to become the most "fashionable" new attraction for upper-crust and soon middle-class Londoners. Even while the modern social sciences had not yet developed far enough to wedge themselves into the category "arts and sciences" in this period – lectures on political economy, for instance, did not appear until the mid 1820s – we can detect a social-scientific approach to the very *organizing* of these public learning spheres, beginning with Bernard's own effort to use Scottish political economy to reshape British poor-rates and social-welfare programs in the 1790s. I briefly enter a historians' debate about the Royal Institution's important reversal of social aims, methods, and audience in order to lay out the wider picture of the arts-and-sciences Institution world in which the Surrey, London, Russell, and British Institutions extended their dominion across the metropolis between 1800 and 1823. With a focus on how to grasp the category of "administration" in this chapter, I situate Humphry Davy's, John Mason Good's, and other lecturing appearances within the multidisciplinary agenda of the Royal's and other Institutional lecturing series that attracted women, professionals, nobility, merchants, and intellectuals.

The next chapters then investigate three knowledge-producing fields of the early nineteenth century – the scientific, the artistic, and the bibliographical – in light of controversies over the nature of books, the rival claimants to expertise in the arts, and the historical as well as disciplinary questions posed by the idea that the Romantic period was beginning to produce something like a "second scientific revolution." In "Wild Bibliography," Chapter 3 explores the deep investments made by the London arts-and-sciences Institutions in building authoritative libraries, generating print journals, and promoting what was for Britain a new realm of specialist knowledge, bibliography, or rather the soon-controversial mode of "historical bibliography" that constituted the first version of what we now call the "history of books." Here Thomas Bernard's collaborator Thomas Frognall Dibdin played multiple roles as literary lecturer, bibliographical author, and main publicist as well as half-critic/half-advocate of that notorious episode in Romantic-age literary history called the Bibliomania. More broadly, I try to stage the competition between the *ordering* of knowledge by way of serious "arts and sciences" bibliographical efforts to organize and archive the emerging modern knowledges, on the one hand, and the *dis*ordering, Bibliomaniacal practice of uncovering and fetishizing Britain's oldest printed works through what were often disturbing "arts" of the book, from black-letter reading to the more biblioclastic performances of extra-illustrating and multi-mediation, on the other.

Chapter 4 turns to the British art field and its felt sense of "crisis" instigated in part by the founding of the British Institution for Promoting the Fine Arts in 1805. The best-known Romantic visual-arts journal, *Annals of the Fine Arts* (1816–20), arrived in Britain only after a new wave of art-critical writing that had been unfolding over the previous decade. In these journals and essays of 1806 to 1816, Royal Academy painters and British Institution art collectors and connoisseurs mounted an increasingly public struggle over expertise in the arts between "practice" and those who "look on." This chapter focuses on the problem of practice and knowledge, especially on the little-known art journal the *Artist*, launched by the painter Prince Hoare in 1807 against the connoisseurs and collectors who now had gained a formidable London art Institution to strengthen their claims to art expertise against the self-named "professional men" who, as practicing painters, sculptors, or architects, were now remediating themselves into print authors. These contentions would culminate in the great Elgin Marbles controversy settled (in favor of the artists) in 1816, for which this chapter tells a back-story of art controversies as what constitute a nineteenth-century field of art production mediated by print and institutions.

Chapter 5 investigates the historicizing of the sciences in relation to the new complexities of organization that put the arts-and-sciences Institutions in context of the specialist societies, discoveries, instruments, texts, and players emerging in the scientific field since the late eighteenth century. As Saree Makdisi has forcefully shown, the concept of "organization" long associated with medicine and physiology took on newly explicit political and economic meanings in the French Revolution controversy.[41] This chapter will argue that the radical critique of London's Romantic-age science by Richard Carlile and Thomas Hodgskin in the 1820s recognized the disciplinary transformations wrought by Humphry Davy and the specialist societies he could network with the new Institutions. Yet trenchant though it was, Carlile's *Address to Men of Science* (1821) also exposed the growing disproportion between a dominant scientific institutional apparatus for advanced research and the print media that radical science-critics were using to oppose it. This chapter follows the intricate relation between new scientific instruments and printed texts in such key controversies as the vitalist/materialist debate over the John Hunter legacy, one that especially registered in Romantic poetic and prose works by Coleridge, Keats, and others. More broadly, this chapter raises questions about the modes of scientific historiography in Romantic accounts of the scientific world. Long before modern science historians began recognizing a "second scientific revolution" in the early nineteenth century, an astute *Quarterly Review* writer of 1826 pictured it in absorbing detail as an institutional and disciplinary revolution in the British scientific field reaching from metropolitan to provincial and international impact.

In Part II, "Questions of the Literary," I ask how Romantic literary and political engagements with the discourse of "arts and sciences" produced some of the most ambitious arguments of Romantic critical writing. Chapter 6 focuses on the work of Coleridge and his complex effort to conceptually reorder the "arts and sciences" as a coherent world of knowledge that answers to literary, disciplinary, and religious demands. Coleridge's well-known appeal to seventeenth-century questions of knowledge and belief is a case of how Romantic writers, at a time when the authority of the Republic of Letters was failing and its legacies becoming more uncertain, would have to address the problem of *which* earlier version of the Republic of Letters they could use to stake their own claims in the literary field – the scholarly and religious, the commercial and skeptical, or the politically reformist. From his literary lecturing to the *Lay Sermons* (1816), *Biographia Literaria* (1817), and the 1818 version of *The Friend*, we shall see how Coleridge both repudiated commercial incarnations of the literary republic and resuscitated its seventeenth-century scholarly/religious precursor (the *respublica literaria*) in order to work out a coherent schemata for the sciences, fine arts, and that ultimate horizon of disciplinarity that he called "Method." My counterpoint for this Coleridgean mission will be Jeremy Bentham's arts-and-sciences projects, particularly *Chrestomathia* (1816), where we find an unmistakable trajectory in both writers from the political and institutional experiments of the 1790s to the mid-Regency efforts to theorize the passage from contingent conditions of practices to the assurance of knowledge. In this respect, Bentham's and Coleridge's cases for discovering the coherence or unity of the arts and sciences, which I explore by way of John Stuart Mill's influential pairing of these writers as philosophical contraries, prove to have considerably more in common even as their methods for making the "arts and sciences" a basis for social reconstruction again diverge. For his own part, by 1830, Coleridge could not think through a vision for reconstituting a National Church without refiguring it through the professors of modern arts and sciences, having himself played many roles in this matter since first appearing to lecture on poetics at the Royal Institution in 1808.

To ask further into the political question of the arts and sciences, Chapter 7 explores the multifaceted ways in which English Dissenters and other political reformers introduced critical dissension into the received and currently changing category of "arts and sciences," even while they forged memorable and often lasting ways of grappling with those practices and knowledges. From the works of William Godwin, Mary Robinson, Leigh and Robert Hunt to William Hazlitt, William Roscoe, and Percy Shelley, I shall show how Romantic-age reformers complicated the assumption that "arts" eventually or logically entailed "sciences" and I shall propose some origins of the division between humanist and scientific cultures that are quite different than those we suppose today. Among these will appear matters of historiography and fiction, commerce and knowledge, utility and vision, and the role of emerging knowledges in campaigns for Parliamentary reform. We may well not find our *own* understanding of what "literature" means yet emerging in the Romantic age, but Chapters 6 and 7 of *Transfiguring the Arts and Sciences* will suggest that a modern conception of what literature is, and how it became a "specialized" domain in its own right, as Raymond Williams put it, could only have come about through a long process, in the nineteenth and twentieth centuries, of simultaneously complicating, resisting, or internalizing the relations of "arts and sciences" as the latter took shapes from the early nineteenth century forward.[42]

PART I

*Questions of the arts and sciences*

CHAPTER 1

# *From the age of projects to the age of institutions*

> Man is the worst of all God's creatures to shift for himself.
> Daniel Defoe, *An Essay upon Projects* (1697)

> What constitutes this new and vast edifice, are libraries, museums, theaters of rarities, workshops of models, objects of art, chemical laboratories, and astronomical observatories ... a few projects.
> Gottfried Leibniz, "On an Academy of Arts and Sciences" (1716)

To imagine nineteenth-century London without the new Royal Institution founded in 1800, we should have to eliminate the following: British Romantic criticism, at least the literary lecturing of Coleridge and Hazlitt and the books that flowed from it; the scientific careers of Humphry Davy and Michael Faraday, instrumental in turning the older "natural philosophy" into new, discipline-organized and publicly acclaimed "sciences"; the education of women in the sciences, literary criticism, fine arts, and moral philosophy, since these institutions provided some of what was barred to women's learning at Cambridge and Oxford; popularizing books on the sciences (like Jane Marcet's *Conversations on Chemistry* and many others); a more wide-ranging redefinition of the discursive domain called "arts and sciences" itself that took hold after 1800; the modeling of such cross-disciplinary institutions (as we might now call them in an age still defining what disciplinary fields of knowledge are) for important successors like the London Institution (1806), the Surrey Institution (1808), the Russell Institution (1808), and others that constituted what social historians of British science have called the "London lecturing empire" of the early nineteenth century. More indirectly, we should then need to add the transatlantic impact of these institutions on the gestation of major American universities and research institutes – and on that professedly unique American institution called the popular lyceums, where British and American intellectuals, from Emerson and Douglass to Dickens and Twain, worked down to the turn of the twentieth century, and which eventually entailed all major currents of American political, ethnic, gendered, racial, and intellectual life.

We should also fail, at times, to grasp what Romantic writers meant when they used the term *institution*. Here is a passage from the 1798 version of Coleridge's "Fears in Solitude," a version that even well-informed readers may still confuse with the 1817 version appearing in most modern anthologies:

> We have offended, Oh! my countrymen!
> We have offended very grievously, and been most tyrannous.
>     . . . have we gone forth
> And borne to distant tribes slavery and pangs,
> And deadlier far, our vices, whose deep taint
> With slow perdition murders the whole man,
> His body and his soul!
>     Meanwhile, at home,
> We have drunk up, demure as at a grace,
> Pollutions from the brimming cup of wealth;
> Contemptuous of all honourable rule,
> Yet bartering freedom and the poor man's life,
> For gold, as at a market!            (lines 53–65 [1798])

These lines from 1798 tell us why the poem has become so interesting in the last decade or two: it speaks with unusual, disarming candor about the English poet's complicity with the imperial exploitation, slave-trading, and capital accumulation that became the great subject of British reform writing in these waning years of the eighteenth century. It is a poem about global power and home rule, of a vanquished periphery and a wealth-gorged center; it features the British radical's disgust with the slave trade and the conservative's horror of luxury. Like all of Coleridge's great poetry between 1795 and 1800, it pivots finely and provokingly between what the nineteenth century would come to differentiate more decisively as radical reformism and deep traditionalism. But in 1817 Coleridge interpolated five new lines:

>     Meanwhile, at home,
> *All individual dignity and power*
> *Engulfed in Courts, Committees, Institutions,*
> *Associations and Societies,*
> A vain, speech-mouthing, speech-reporting Guild,
> One Benefit-Club for mutual flattery.   ([1817] lines 60–66, my emphases)

The language Coleridge's new lines introduce has since puzzled even expert readers of the poem. These lines stand out from an otherwise classically phrased, poetically resonant depiction of London as both the national capital city and the metropole of the colonies abroad. For more traditional readers of Romantic poems, these lines may count as "the worst lines in the poem," worst because most unpoetical, and most unpoetical because – with its litany of "Institutions, Associations and Societies" – most sociological.[1] For Coleridge's more historically astute scholars, there has been disagreement about what precisely the new language refers to. Carl Woodring, writing in 1960, surmised that it referred to the institutions and societies of "organized utilitarian life after Waterloo." For William Keach, re-editing all Coleridge's poems for the Penguin anthology of 1997, this language more likely refers to radical plebeian organizations like the London Corresponding Society or Society for Constitutional Information of the 1790s.[2] Neither estimate seems full enough – though Keach's perhaps more so, since there was no dramatic emergence of such societies or associations between 1815 and 1817, but many of them in the 1790s. Still, Coleridge did not write the lines in 1798 when the radical associations remained a distinct and still-threatening presence in British political life. Why, then, in 1817? Rather than state or church, I would suggest "Institutions" refers here to the range of commercial, professional, protective, technological, as well as reformist and revolutionary corresponding societies sprouting everywhere in England since at least the 1760s. But it was in the breadth of Coleridge's and Hazlitt's own careers that the most performative of his words – the noun *institution* itself – had begun transforming the British cultural landscape by naming the new scientific, technological, philosophical, literary, and national institutions that all distinguished themselves from Burke's immemorial state and church institutions by operating in the commercial and metropolitan framework.

The present chapter pursues the cultural logic of this institutional emergence in the Romantic age by first returning to Defoe's "Age of Projects" in which even the wildest speculative schemes for profit or fame would call up a corollary response about the risk of such projects for the public weal and the vicissitudes of everyday life. Social safety nets were being imagined around 1700 well before the more sophisticated public-welfare experiments of the 1790s, out of which the Royal Institution for the sciences and arts would itself unexpectedly arise. Other European polities had their projectors as well. I take Gottfried Leibniz as a brief case of what producing "arts and sciences" schemes, print innovations, and knowledge institutions could look like in Defoe's age of projects. I then turn to the Scottish Enlightenment's elaborating of a modernity to be measured by the vectors of institutional change, a theory and conjectural history of institutions evolving *in* history that would necessarily seem to exclude the disruptive work of projecting. The rise of "arts-and-sciences" Institutions beginning about 1800 would improbably *join* these antithetical strains of early modern thinking by forging the institution *as* project and the project *as* an institution. The naming of the Royal Institution was also a moment in which to distinguish the early modern "academies" and "societies" devoted to advancing knowledge from a new kind of learning organization with unprecedented public impact and a restructuring of authority's relation to intellectual action and reception. The wider picture of London's changing topography of public knowledge practices will emerge in the following chapter, where the peculiar social genealogy of the Royal can help explain the lecturing, administrative, and print-culture makeup of the emerging "arts and sciences" Institutions spreading across the metropolis.

### The cultural work of projecting

I begin with two early modern projectors who had no relation to one another in fact, but who were rather linked by a sort of common ancestry to offspring they would never meet. Nearly contemporaries, Daniel Defoe (1660–1731) and Gottfried Leibniz (1646–1716) inhabited vastly different universes, one living perilously on the edge of the most raucous, unruly market economy yet to be seen in the modern age, the other entwining himself with institutional authority and security, forging intimate ties with the German absolutist state and the most conservative of Protestant churches. Yet both were projectors: Defoe's "economic man" Crusoe was one of modernity's most fantastic, metaphysically loaded imaginative creations, while in Germany Leibniz's whirling philosophical systems would run on the most practical rails laid down in scheme upon scheme. True, Leibniz would count as a very different sort of "projector" than Defoe, starting from the posture of institutional power rather than economic chance, more often calculating what Chartier calls the "order of books" than the perils of double-entry bookkeeping.[3] Yet to recall their projecting visions and texts from opposite ends of Europe and distant locations in the social order will also be to locate the common ground both kinds of projecting could produce: the public good as well as private advantage, learning, reading, and what the later eighteenth century titled "institutions" from economic to cultural and knowledge-producing kinds.

When Defoe published *An Essay upon Projects* in 1697, England had been plagued recently by notorious schemes or "projects" that swindled the gullible out of their money and reneged on greater promises of improving human life. Projectors made "Pretences of Fine Discoveries, New Inventions" while "People have been betrayed to part with their Money for Shares in a *New-Nothing*."[4] To their detractors, projects were the work of fevered imaginations, impractical, extravagant, unsocial, unpredictable, and often unlawful, without honor or sanction. As a mercantilist, Defoe shared an extended, more fundamentally critical suspicion of certain projects, and it's one chief aim of the *Essay upon Projects* to make ethical judgments on projects huge and small – thus Defoe's attack on stock-jobbing as illegitimate commerce. The East-India, African, and Hudson's Bay Companies have succeeded as projects only "with the greatest Intriegue, Artifice, and Trick."[5] The *Essay* set out to contrast those sorts of deceptive projects by beginning to write about a more undefined matter – social welfare in a new economic and political habitat unfolding since 1688. Long ignored as merely another project itself, the *Essay* has gained new interest today for the way it speaks to early modern hopes for improvement or, as Maximillian Novak puts it, the "belief that human thought and action could transform society," that ideas could become "a vital force for change."[6] Defoe's *Essay* articulates such beliefs by putting forward a surprising range of new, socially important projects: friendly societies, highway and infrastructure renovation, social-security or the "pension office," a "charity-lottery" to finance public projects, hospitals for the mentally ill to replace Bedlam, and, not least, colleges for women and academies for languages.

Along with new interest in the *Essay*'s social imagining is a certain suspicion of its motives. Projects as he envisions them unite private capital with public and national rewards: expanding the idea of what a projector is, Defoe ventures that "Every new Voyage the Merchant contrives is a Project"; this and other cases will show at length that the "good" project is one that has "*both* the *Essential Ends of a Project* in it, *Publick Good*, and *Private Advantage.*"[7] Thus it has become a key question for this text of whether to read Defoe as projecting a safety-netted promotion of the private gain or a more genuinely social program for human relations under a market system. For Mary Poovey, Defoe puts the merchant at the center of modern action and its social projects, thus forging an early articulation of "liberal governmentality" as well as anticipating by twenty years Bernard Mandeville's theme "private vices, public benefits."[8] Yet there are variously modulated versions of this attempt to balance private enterprise with public benefit or safety nets; it is rarely clear which of Defoe's two "essential ends" is to get greater weight. "I will allow the Author [of the project] to aim primarily at his own Advantage," he says elsewhere, "yet with circumstances of Public Benefit added."⁹ The "yet" in this sentence appears to be binding: public benefit is then the necessary, and not merely presumed, ethical and social condition of the private motive for profit.

In a nuanced consideration of these matters, Joanne Myers has argued in depth for grasping the aim of Defoe's *Essay* as promoting the connection and social tissue among British subjects in a market society. Defoe projects "a sociable subject," she proposes, for whom "one's own experiences and fortunes are inevitably bound to those of one's fellows."¹⁰ This is to see Defoe pushing for, if not quite modern welfare, then at least what he calls "Neighbours' Fare" as "acts of relationship in which individuals hold one another responsible for the good of the whole."¹¹ Rebuilding the national infrastructure, creating friendly societies, furnishing social-security pensions to workers, educating women to improve the social relations of marriage and public intercourse – all these would seem to entail a great social connectedness in the voraciously profit-seeking world of the late seventeenth century as well, even if such sociability hardly resolves the contradictions of a market society in itself.

I want to build further on Myers's insights by pointing as well to the collaboratively *productive* character of Defoe's "projects" – and in this they seem to me to anticipate a later kind of social or cultural institution-building in the following century that belies the notion of institutions as Burke's distant, "immemorial" centers of authority. If they encourage sociable subjects in their effect, the *Essay*'s projects also speak to the collaborative labor of constructing societies, pension-systems, reimagined commercial establishment, then colleges and academies. To get these projects realized, Defoe makes elaborately detailed, cost-by-cost calculations in the *Essay upon Projects* since they must be realizable, not chimerical – a rule not only for the merchant, Defoe proposes, but effectively for *all* moderns, since we all become projectors, Defoe suggests, whenever we "Contrive New Ways to live." But projects are often solutions to threats or circumstances of dire distress as well, as Defoe himself would know in having recently escaped imprisonment for bankruptcy. That we may even "project" as a means to survive threats of misery or extinction, Defoe underscores by calling Noah's ark "the first Project I read of," and then by taking up the collective project Defoe's age still believed had once occurred and still bewildered it:

> The Building of *Babel* was a Right Project; for indeed the true definition of a Project, according to Modern Acceptation, is, as is said before, a vast Undertaking, too big to be manag'd, and therefore likely enough to come to nothing; and yet as great as they are, 'tis certainly true of 'em all, even as the

Projectors propose; that according to the old tale, If so many Eggs are hatch'd, there will be so many Chickens, and those Chickens may lay so many Eggs more, and those Eggs produce so many Chickens more, and so on. Thus 'twas most certainly true, That if the People of the Old World cou'd have Built a House up to Heaven, they shou'd never be Drown'd again on Earth, and they only had forgot to Measure the Height, *that is,* as in other Projects, it only Miscarri'd, or else 'twou'd have Succeeded.[12]

If there is a joking allusion here to the popular image of the project as "laying an egg," or failing to hatch, there is also the conviction that "even as the Projectors propose," ideas can produce living results as well as epic unfinished ruins, while undertaking a project "too big to be manag'd" might only mean forgetting to do the math. (The *Essay* is filled with numbers, calculations, heights and weights to be measured.) One arresting version of this argument is, as Martin Gierl puts it, that "projects lie between utopia and realization," what we most hope for and how we can possibly manage to get there.[13]

Of the new projects proposed in the *Essay*, Defoe calls the Academy for language "the most noble and the most useful Proposal in this Book."[14] The "Babel" passage alludes both to an impossible project to reach the heavens and to the ensuing descent into multiple and scattered languages. Defoe's own version of alien languages is not foreign but domestic: those of the elite professions, for example, the languages of physicians, lawyers, and clergy educated at Oxford and Cambridge who speak or write – to the ear of a writer educated at a Dissenting academy – in a language "full of Stiffness and Affectation, hard Words ... harsh and untuneable to the Ear." As if to anticipate a coming age of new knowledge-organizing in conflict with the educated past, Defoe grants his imagined Academy judicial powers in the name of communicable and socially shared public English – "'Twou'd be as criminal then to Coin Words, as Money."[15] With a Dissenter's suspicion of the Royal Society that Joseph Priestley would come to share, Defoe's administrative plan replaces the unsociable pedants with twelve members of nobility, twelve gentlemen, and twelve commoners of merit who have mastered the King's English. They are to establish and enforce a communicable national language to encourage "polite learning" on a socially shared linguistic basis. As Novak remarks, Defoe treats the problem of projecting any of these schemes with a "mixture of hope and optimism with an expectation of failure."[16] Yet these cases in *An Essay upon Projects* may serve to intimate the long timeline Defoe's kind of projective thinking would come to have, by the end of the next century, on economic, social, and imaginational ways of organizing daily as well as specialized ways to live.

If Defoe's *Essay upon Projects* hardly managed its way out of the publisher's warehouse, Leibniz's German projecting schemes appeared prominently in all the leading European journals of the *respublica literaria* and tackled the problem increasingly posed by the Leipzig book fairs and German presses: "I even fear," he would say in 1780, that "people may be disgusted with the sciences, and that a fatal fear may cause them to fall back into barbarism. To which result that horrible mass of books which keeps on growing might contribute very much."[17] From "Precepts for Advancing the Sciences and Arts" (1680) to his last projects of 1716, Leibniz schemed to transform the produce of the presses into organized modes of modern knowledge. He offered impeccable credentials and intimate business relations to the secular powers, "a fact that gave some of his writings a decidedly more practical and conservative" turn than Defoe's.[18] Twenty years before co-founding the Berlin Academy of the Sciences in 1700, Leibniz projected a new means of turning Prussia's exploding book industry into a learnable and teachable order, seeming to grasp the new media of print so crucial to any advancement of knowledge as malleable in an unprecedented way. He proposed a kind of superbook encompassing all knowledges, though it would be nothing like the sort of encyclopedia to be widely produced in the coming century. In "Precepts for Advancing the Arts and Sciences," he projected a biannual *semestria* rather than the totalized book published all at once:

> only gradually by diverse attempts or by the work of several persons shall we come to those demonstrative elements of all human knowledge, and that will happen sooner or later depending on the disposition of those who have the authority and hence the power to advance good plans ... we must resort provisionally to a successive application of that great method. That is done by examining each science with the effort necessary to discover its principles of discovery.[19]

The difference between this printed succession and the all-at-once encyclopedia was not simply a change of medium: it had to do with what Leibniz called "a badly understood distinction between practice and theory." Some things require imagination and spontaneity rather than ratiocination: "in such things," he pressed the point, "we need to form a habit, as in bodily exercises and even in some mental exercises. That is where we need practice in order to succeed."[20] Habit, practice, only then "theory": or as Leibniz actually presented it, a theory *of* practice. He made an example of the artisan: "If a workman who may not know either Latin or Euclid is a man of ability and knows the reasons for what he does, he will possess a genuine theory of his art, and will be capable of discovering expediencies in any sort of situation." Leibniz spoke of an *"art* of discovery" which has little to do with the novelty of what is discovered. It was on this basis that in 1680 Leibniz could distinguish a bad projector from a good one. "A half-baked scientist puffed up by an imaginary science will project machines and constructions which cannot succeed because he does not possess all the theory required." He grasps only the "common rules" about the mechanics of moving forces: what he cannot grasp with his "imaginary science" is "[what] I call the science of resistance or rigidity which has not yet been put sufficiently into rules."[21]

I emphasize these last phrases because it is just the dimension of resistance or rigidity, what does not go according to plan, the way practice talks back to theory and puts it on the defensive, that Leibniz calls "a genuine theory of his art," that is, theory bespoke twice, once as rules, once as resistances. Grasping resistances, feeling one's way between the "rigid parts" and the "final action": this feel for the push and pull of the machine against the resistances to the machine is what no formal rule or what Leibniz calls no "half-baked" project or set of precepts can give to the art of discovery. On the plane of print culture, this is why the genre of encyclopedia could for Leibniz never adequately take the form of an English-style *Cyclopaedia* such as that invented by Ephraim Chambers in 1729 or revamped by Diderot in 1750. Though in many philosophical works Leibniz appeared to be the consummate philosophical idealist, this theory of practices undercut the well-hidden scholasticism of the new sciences that had been making their own way in the name of anti-scholastic claims.

So, three centuries before de Certeau, and twenty-five years before Robert Hooke tried to reform the Royal Society with a "scheme" to uproot hidden practices of knowledge from their lairs in the closets of artisans, Leibniz identified the crucial lag between customary and scientific knowledges: "Concerning unwritten knowledge scattered among men of different callings, I am convinced that it surpasses in quantity and in importance anything we find in books." For this unrealized expertise Leibniz looked to the practice of "hunters, fishermen, merchants, sea voyagers, or games of skill as well as of chance." He found a special case in the "games of children." Leibniz takes this last case to inflect what Francis Bacon and many others since were now calling modernity's great revolutionary devices, the compass, the gun, and the printing press.

> We owe the compass-needle to the amusement of children intent on looking to see how the needle turns. It is a fact that we owe to children the air-gun which they practically invented by stuffing the hollow tube of a feather at both ends with a slice of apple into which they had stuck each end

of the tube successively, forcing the stuff together toward the middle of the tube, and then expelling it by the force of the compressed air caught in the middle; this was long before a skillful Norman workingman took it into his head to imitate them on a large scale.[22]

And what of the print libraries?

> Imagine [Leibniz goes on] that an art is lost and that it must be rediscovered; all our libraries could not help supply the art, for though I do not disagree that there are a great many admirable things in books which men in the professions are still ignorant of and should take advantage of, it is nevertheless a fact that the most important observations and turns of skill in all sorts of trades and professions are as yet unwritten. This fact is proved by experience when passing from theory to practice we desire to accomplish something.[23]

This logic of discovery seems to underlie what Terry Cochran emphasizes as Leibniz's great and singular envisioning of what a print modernity will become. The special case was the Frankfurt book fair, upon which "Leibniz lays bare the conceptual scaffolding necessary to rethinking the world from the perspective of print."[24] Now he proposes a "commissariat" to supervise the coming-into-print of knowledge before the reading public and thereby to regulate the disruptive force of all those books pouring from the presses. Perhaps this was to propose a kind of licensing at Frankfurt apparently similar to the kind long controversial in Britain. But (as Cochran suggestively stresses) Leibniz's commissariat would be secular, unlike the largely theocratic licensing opposed by Milton and others, and far more interested in productivity than in censorship: "the realization," Leibniz calls it, "of all kinds of things, rules, and institutions that are useful and even necessary for the common good, concerning books, authors, booksellers, correctors, printers, and studies."[25] Moreover, print demands new kinds of institutions not because it has already become the mediatic foundation of all modern knowledges (as Elizabeth Eisenstein's thesis of an early modern "print revolution" would require us to think) but precisely because it has *not*.[26] Perhaps no philosopher of the early modern period registers its powers to destabilize and disrupt any coherent lines of modern knowledge more pointedly than Leibniz does in the late seventeenth century.

The Leibniz commissariat, then, proves less to be an adequate institution in itself than it promises to be an incubator of institutions for modernity's absorption of print culture into new and still unforeseeable kinds of knowledge production. An "institution for institutors," one might say, as well as an ingenious way to insert German scholars and other "inquisitive people throughout Germany" into the western European *respublica literaria* within which German actors had been lagging badly behind:

> To correspond and communicate among themselves and with neighboring and distant universities, to reach an understanding and thereby to preserve and multiply numerous new and useful thoughts, propositions, inventions, and observations that would otherwise disappear with their authors; this applies to the domains of natural science, mechanics, manufacturing, trade, and mathematics, as well as to those of history, politics, law, and others, opening the way for the youth in universities and elsewhere to become familiar with the occupations in a timely fashion, in a way more useful than when they unsoundly begin reasoning before steeping themselves in sufficiently rigorous studies.[27]

In fact – to anticipate later chapters in this book – Leibniz was himself moving from the Latin-writing early modern *respublica literaria* into the more distinctly modern, vernacular Republic of Letters just then being launched in print at Amsterdam by Pierre Bayle (with whom Leibniz was now corresponding). Many of his schemes or "projects" belong to this transformational moment – a question to which I'll return in the chapter on Coleridge. What is striking in these essays of Leibniz is not so much their emphasis on anything we should call canon-formation (there is, for example, only a moderate stress on transmission from a literary past) as the emphasis they put on *category*-formation. "It is no longer a question only of what is going to be passed on," as Cochran puts the point, "but of the criteria for determining which lines of thought are designated to carry the burden of history into the future."[28]

The future shape of that configuration of knowledges could not yet itself be projected as a completed diagram. Rather than projecting an encyclopedia (as Chambers, Diderot, or William Smellie would diagram the knowledge trees), Leibniz devised the notion of successively realized knowledge to be had in the semi-annual *semestria*, a kind of reference work Cochran brings to the fore of his work on modernity without quite seeing its radical difference from other plans for print knowledge. The *semestria* "condenses and represents new knowledge produced each year"; it includes all the apparatus of a complete or encyclopedic reference work (historical bibliographies, indexes, and so forth). But unlike ordinary encyclopedias to come, Leibniz's *semestrias* do not merely "update" the modes of knowledge. They also run a race with a new kind of time – the time of book publishing itself:

> The number of books increases to such an extent that if we delay too long the work would ultimately become so desperate as to be impossible. The result would be no less than total confusion, a scorn for all learning, and

finally the return of ancient barbarism; in such an indescribable mass of books it would no longer be possible to find and recognize the best in the midst of the bad and insignificant.[29]

This is *media time*, which we are only once again acutely conscious of today because of its extraordinary speed-up in present-day "new media." Thus the kind of hazard Leibniz foretells in the earlier essay: suppose that a particular art were lost to moderns, how could it be recovered? This question has an unsettling corollary: such an art would be lost, not because it doesn't reach print, but because it *is* published in books. Only by sequencing (in the form of semi-annual *semestria*) would a long process of building be able to take place. What would be teased out over time would be not so much the circle or the certainty of knowledge as the ongoing and practically derived probabilities of knowledge that come from reading and reflection over time; this sort of knowledge in and through (publishing and reading) practice is the scholar's equivalent of the workman's having a "theory" derived by "experience" from his own practices rather than from a scheme of rules applied in advance. It is a kind of projecting, but not the half-baked, rule-driven kind that makes the scientist for Leibniz (as later for Swift) a man to mock. "Projecting" becomes "instituting" through the same print media that threaten all knowledge and any future.

### The discourse of institution in the Enlightenment

Recalling these versions of early modern social and cultural projecting can only make more vivid the sweeping repudiation of this still-controversial topic in the Scottish Enlightenment, which built its stadial and conjectural histories in part against the projectors and their unpredictable visions. "Men in general," according to Adam Ferguson in 1767,

> are sufficiently disposed to occupy themselves in forming projects and schemes; but he who would scheme and project for others, will find an opponent in every person who is disposed to scheme for himself. Like the winds that come we know not whence, and blow whithersoever they list, the forms of society are derived from an obscure and distant origin; they arise, long before the date of philosophy, from the instincts, not from the speculations of men. The crowd of mankind are directed, in their establishments and measures, by the circumstances in which they are placed; and seldom are turned from their way, to follow the plan of any single projector.[30]

Ferguson's colleagues in Edinburgh and Glasgow would pursue further the question of "circumstances" or situations that human beings meet in unpredictable forms and at unforeseeable moments. But the projector remained a "prodigal" among Adam Smith's modern economic actors, and some of those writers most influenced by Smith would soon contend, like Defoe, for the "well-grounded projectors" whom, for instance, Jeremy Bentham defended against Smith in 1787. Here Bentham asked Smith to justify any theory of modernity without the "race of those with which the womb of futurity is still pregnant" and "whether whatever is now an establishment was not, at one time, an innovation?"[31] By the 1820s Hazlitt would be using the word again against Bentham himself.

To better grasp the force of the Scottish Enlightenment's place in the history of this discourse, I want to pause to recall the philological dimension, or what might be called the "transition" problem that inflected the difference between early modern and later usages of the terms *institute* and *institution*. In a brief, suggestive, but also somewhat problematic entry in *Keywords*, Raymond Williams distinguished between the early modern, active sense of *institution* as a noun or participle of action and process – to name powerful acts of founding, decreeing a law, educating, transmitting a legacy or inheritance, or consecrating a practice that had (or was expected to have) long-term authority and consequence – and the word's becoming "at a certain stage, a general and abstract noun describing something apparently objective and systematic; in fact, in the modern sense, an *institution.*"[32] Basing his conjecture on the *OED*, Williams located that fundamental transition at about the mid eighteenth century, and what's both useful, verifiable, and yet somewhat misleading about this brief account appears in writings throughout the later eighteenth century and Romantic age. In such writings (and here recent databases will confirm what the *OED* could not), there is a far more mixed picture where the nouns of *structure* intermingle with those of *action* (or agency). This dynamic instability in words like *institution* will become especially volatile where political and moral responsibility is at stake in Romantic writings, where the historicity of modern instituting is most self-consciously considered in relation to its present force and legitimacy. What results can be a complex, intense dance of agency and structure in key writings by Godwin, Coleridge, Shelley, Hazlitt, or Wordsworth – the claim for the poet as "institutor" belongs to this cluster of usages as well. But these are only the most widely read cases today of what will prove to be a culture-wide phenomenon in early nineteenth-century writings (and actions) across forgotten texts and situations as well. If the Scottish Enlightenment did much to give the conceptuality of institution a broadly *foundational* as well as historical force, then, the continued volatility of political, literary, philosophical, and "arts and sciences" contexts, from the 1780s to at least 1830, would complicate considerably their modernizing consensus in construing the shape and trajectory of modernity itself.

Williams's account can also be strengthened by noticing what kind of structural noun *institution* was becoming. The verbal force of *institute* and *institution* in the early modern age was not only active, it was also performative in a way that Bourdieu's concept of "rites of institution" partly captures – the power of naming that makes subjects *who* they are, and a power that must issue from a certain powerful social place, not just anywhere.[33] Another way to broaden out Williams's initial distinction would be to say that what had developed from the fifteenth through the eighteenth centuries was the capacity of the verbal form of *institution* (as the act of instituting) to cover so many concrete cases and make so many concretely foundational modern distinctions that it could become, in the new generality it achieves in the eighteenth century, a *general* category, or what Marx, in the methodological introduction to the *Grundrisse*, would call a "simple abstraction." As in the case of the term *production* that is Marx's focus in this early and somewhat more supple draft of *Capital*, a "simple abstraction" is one that can disclose (under considerable analytic pressure) a complex prehistory of concrete usages and situations.[34] This crucially transformative moment could not belong to a single decade or generation, though perhaps the span of a "century" might be long enough to encompass this work of social abstraction in the case of *institution*. The question is then, before the social sciences abstracted it further into the object of Durkheim's "science of society," what cultural work could the concept and language of *institution* do in the later eighteenth and early nineteenth centuries?

A related philological problem with the term *institution*, which also bears strongly on its conceptual force and meanings, appears in Giambattista Vico's second edition of *Nuovo Scienza* (1745). His first edition of that work in 1725 makes little or no use of the concept "institution" (nor does it emphasize another signature concept in the later version, the "imagination"), whereas the category of institutions appears forcefully in the title of 1745's Book 5, which gives us the Viconian notion that we can know the social world as well as we can know nature since we best grasp what we ourselves have made. Or so that memorable chapter reads when it is rendered into English as "The Recourse of Human Institutions Which the Nations Take When They Rise Again." According to Vico's translators Thomas Bergin and Max Fisch, however, the term *institution* "hardly occurs at all in Vico's Italian."[35] He used the Italian term *istituzione* a single time, the editors tell us, "and then in the technical legal sense" derived from the Latin expression for appointing an executor in a will (*institutio haeredis*), which would translate as one of Williams's "actional" or verbal senses of the terms. At all other times, Vico uses *ordinare, ordinamento, ordine,* or – most surprisingly and most frequently – *cosa* (meaning "thing"). To use the Italian terms for "order," "ordinance," and "ordain" would have been common in the eighteenth century – and those terms would correspond often to the English senses of *institute* or *institution* in the early modern period: to appoint an heir, to establish, to teach, to transmit, to educate. But Vico does not even seem to have followed common Italian usage when he deploys *cosa* (meaning "thing") in place of *istituzione*. His translators explain that here, Vico is "following a rare Latin usage in which *res* was used in the sense of institution" (such as in Varro's work *Antiquitates rerum humanarum et divinarum* or "Antiquities of Human and Divine Institutions"). It is here that translators Fisch and Bergin pause to ask a good question: why did Vico so evidently avoid the term for "institution" and use *cosa* instead? Their editorial answer to this question is worth quoting, I think, since it bears on subsequent English usage of the discourse on institutions.

> [It was] because the term "institution" was theoretically loaded: loaded, moreover, with the very theory he was most concerned to discredit; and because the term *cosa* was theoretically neutral or innocent. Why have we nevertheless rendered his *cosa* "institution"? Because in the course of the later eighteenth and the nineteenth century, and in part as a consequence of Vico's own work, the term "institution" was gradually unloaded; because it no longer carries, built in as it were, the rationalistic theory of the origin and nature of institutions, which in Vico's day was still the accepted theory.[36]

The term was indeed loaded in this way all across Europe, Bergin and Fisch might have added, and nowhere more so than in Britain.

This is why, in view of Vico's verbal and conceptual caution, it is important to see how frontally the Scottish Enlightenment confronted the problem of "institution" and its long early modern legacies and legends – by resolutely, if not always consensually, modernizing it as both a concept and an idiom. Perhaps no one did so more emphatically than the law professor at the University of Glasgow, John Millar. First published in 1771, *The Origin of the Distinction of Ranks* proposed a vastly ambitious account of historical institutions that, in seeking to refute the myth of nation makers and institution-founders, aimed to set aside in all its forms the rational-designer theory of the origin and nature of institutions. We might say, building on the work of James Chandler, that Millar made the term and concept *institutions* a truly comparative instrument both geographically and historically, a conceptual device to measure the "uneven development of nations and cultures," so that such fundamental questions as the origin and progress of social inequality could be measured and weighed across an unprecedentedly wide analytical field of time and geography.[37] Thus Millar could use an institution-based conceptuality to challenge long-embedded assumptions that "the institution of slavery is beneficial to a nation," or that the "institution of marriage" has always been the same everywhere, rather than specific to historical stages or cultural frameworks.[38] The word's new power as a comparative and classificatory device for an early critical social science would depend, in order to measure historical or socio-geographical difference, upon its being always used in the same way, as a noun of structure that puts slavery, marriage, and other "institutions" on the same plane of comparison precisely to show their rates of slower or faster change.

Thus for Millar, whether they celebrated Alfred in Britain or Brahma in South Asia, any accounts of charismatic nation- and institution-founding would now appear impossible to credit. "There is scarcely any people, ancient or modern," Millar began *The Origin of the Distinction of Ranks*, "who do not boast of some early monarch, or statesman, to whom it is pretended they owe whatever is remarkable in their form of government."[39] To discredit the intentionalist or voluntarist theory of institution embedded in the fable of the legendary founder, Millar presents the conjectural history of social institutions as a systematic critique of "fabulous history" and its magical attribution of originating powers. Inevitably, as it did for Ferguson and Adam Smith, making this argument about the origins of modernity has to entail the problem of the "projector" and why (as Ferguson put it) "the forms of society" can never really arise "from the speculations of men." "Instead of being actuated by a projecting spirit," Millar argues, "or attempting, from visionary speculations of remote utility, to produce any violent reformation," the so-called nation founders "confined themselves to such moderate improvements as, by deviating little from former usage, were in some measure supported by experience, and coincided with the prevailing opinions of the country."[40]

Yet this was not quite to say, as had Ferguson, that "nations *stumble* upon establishments ... the result of human action, but not the execution of any human design" (my emphasis).[41] Millar was thinking in a more complex way about how to explain the *kind* of historical and social contingency that his Scottish-Enlightenment collaborators were opposing to the "rationalist" theory of institution and the projecting spirit alike.

Thus he proceeds to explain the "founding" acts of nation- or institution-making as mediations of a habitus, dimly understood:

> Before an individual can be invested with so much authority, and possessed of such reflection and foresight as would induce him to act in the capacity of a legislator, he must, probably, have been educated and brought up in the knowledge of those natural manners and customs, which, for ages perhaps, have prevailed among his countrymen. Under the influence of all the prejudices derived from ancient usage, he will commonly be disposed to prefer the system already established to any other, of which the effects have not been ascertained by experience; or if in any case he should venture to entertain a different opinion, he must be sensible that, from a general prepossession in favour of the ancient establishment, an attempt to overturn it, or to vary it in any considerable degree, would be a dangerous measure, extremely unpopular in itself, and likely to be attended with troublesome consequences.[42]

This view is one that grasps the institutor as, not entirely mythic, but rather the one who most powerfully feels, articulates, and transmits the force of unarticulated practice and custom from "the system already established." No doubt Alfred had powers, but his power to say, in effect, "I hereby institute . . ." must ultimately have been a collective one, using a magical language and performing rites of institution he could not have invented, but which he used a certain powerful language to articulate: an act of wit, one might say in more literary terms, verbalizing what was so long felt and by so many, but ne'er so momentously expressed. I put it this way to help align Millar's posture, in poetic terms, more with Pope's than with Shelley's, for whom *instituting* would be a more radically creative moment and for whom the claim that the poet is an "institutor" was meant to inflame (especially in the context of rival, often utilitarian claims for the power to institute in the 1820s) rather than assure.

Thus in *The Origin of the Distinction of Ranks*, the great founder or apparently visionary projector credited with founding the (modern) nation reappears as the one who understood best the pre-established harmony, the orchestration without a conductor, of cultural dispositions and material situations. His act of institution brings to the language of institution or legislation the impact of the blindingly obvious, or rather the state of being blinded *to* the obvious by the instituting force of the originary. What I am also emphasizing here is that the power of the newly consistent noun-usage and foundational cultural history Millar sets in motion can likewise entail a constitutive loss of specificity about action in either past or present. It is a historical sociology, one might say, but one that will not preclude Millar's later stature as a proleptic ancestor to a modern, "structural-functional" sociology of institutions that by Talcott Parsons's time would appear resolutely anti-historical. It could already begin to appear that way in Francis Jeffrey's important *Edinburgh Review* summation of Millar's great work in 1803:

> It was the leading principle, indeed, of all his speculations on law, morality, government, language, the arts, sciences, and manners – that there was nothing produced by arbitrary and accidental causes; that no great change, institution, custom, or occurrence, could be ascribed to the character or exertions of an individual, to the temperament or disposition of a nation, to occasional policy, or peculiar wisdom or folly: every thing, on the contrary, he held, arose spontaneously from the situation of the society, and was suggested or imposed irresistibly by the opportunities or necessities of their conditions ... Millar taught his pupils to refer them ["human manners and institutions"] all to one simple principle, and to consider them as necessary links in the great chain which connects civilized with barbarous society.[43]

One of the other important "conjectural" histories produced by Jeffrey's precursors was, of course, Hume's "Of the Rise and Progress of the Arts and Sciences" (1742), to which I shall return in Chapter 7. For the moment, it is enough to remind us that the Scots' confidence in the overall stability of that category owed in part to its stadial histories and in part to its own powerful network of sustaining institutions: universities, societies, and academies. At the end of the eighteenth century, this network still belonged to the wider European Republic of Letters, a half-real, half-imaginary configuration (according to its recent historians) that would already be, at least in Britain, entering a moment of crisis, self-doubt, and eventual collapse. One dimension of that change would be an altered geography of knowledge production taking form between 1795 and 1830, one in which the great academies and societies, even the universities of England and Scotland, would have to be realigned in light of a new entrant into their sphere, the arts-and-sciences Institutions originating in London.

## Institutions, academies, societies

When the Royal Institution opened in 1800, it marked its unique ambitions by making an issue of names. Neither word in its title may sound counterintuitive today, yet it was far from an obvious choice then. Why not another Society or Academy? Since its choice of terms was to become so widely adopted in the nineteenth century – carried out further by the London, Surrey, Russell, British, Metropolitan, Southwark, Philomathic, and other Institutions in London and then a widening provincial adoption in Liverpool, Manchester, Cornwall, Birmingham, Leeds, and other cities through the 1820s – its distinction from what *society* or *academy* had meant becomes all the more important. Before 1800, European and British knowledge organizations had generally divided between academies and societies, terms that James McClellan has traced to the founding of England's Royal Society and the Paris Academy in the 1660s. Such forms could often be hard to tell apart on the ground, and their titles could oscillate back and forth in cases like the Berlin Academy, which had been first titled *Societas Scientiarum* when Leibniz founded it in 1700.[44] It's hard, then, to draw fast and sure distinctions between these changing organizational forms as they produced some seventy new academies and societies through the eighteenth century. But McClellan proposes a broad and, for Britain, a quite critical distinction between the two types.

Societies tended to be larger in membership and more diffuse in structure than academies.[45] The Royal Society of Great Britain founded in 1660 retained an average membership of about 300 or more fellows, many of them non-active "members" rather than active organizers, only 21 of whom formed a governing core that conducted the Society's regular business and published its *Philosophical Transactions*. The highly focused scientific societies that burgeoned in England from 1788 (with the founding of the Linnean Society) tended to repeat this pattern on a much smaller scale. As loosely organized networks of specialists and amateurs, Societies were nodes in the early modern network that called itself the Republic of Letters, but they also tended to replicate its loose-jointed forms of connection that composed, in Bourdieu's phrase, the Republic's wider "intellectual field."

Academies were often more exclusive entities, most often (as in Paris or Berlin, but importantly not in England) funded and run by the state. They tended to be composed of activist and equally credentialed men (gender being a fundamental qualification) like the forty painters, sculptors, and architects who self-organized to create the Royal Academy of Arts in 1768. Whereas the Royal Society published its members' research collectively in the widely accessible *Philosophical Transactions*, the Royal Academy spurned periodical publication and issued for print publication mainly Joshua Reynolds' *Discourses* – public lectures, by "invitation only," that would be published as a book only after Reynolds' death in 1790. As we shall see, one cannot speak of such cultural institutions as organizational structures alone; *how* they mediated their knowledge production (whether as "natural philosophy" or as "aesthetics") to wider publics – as periodicals, books, lectures, models, or in other media – was always critical to their modes of functioning. So too, especially when we come to the far more public and elaborate apparatuses of the "arts-and-sciences" Institutions beginning in 1800, were their administrative operations.

The "society form," McClellan conjectures, tended to flourish in Protestant, maritime, and relatively more democratic nations in Europe, while the "academy form" answered more often to Catholic and more authoritarian governments (pre-revolutionary France, absolutist Prussia). What is important to know about these mainly Continental cases for England is that, having produced both a Royal Society and a Royal Academy in the seventeenth and eighteenth centuries, the religious and political bearings of their Continental counterparts would not appear to obtain here. But McClellan's distinction does prove useful in the longer term. By the late eighteenth century, the Royal Society for natural philosophy may have appeared bogged down in minutiae, uncreative and uncompetitive by Continental standards (a key reason offered for innovating the new organizational type pioneered by the Royal Institution in 1800) – but it was rarely called tyrannical or authoritarian. The Royal Academy for art, on the other hand, was challenged from its inception as exclusivist and dictatorial – from 1768 through the early 1800s, its elite professorial membership (about 5 percent of Britain's practicing artists) provoked constant challenge and dissents, of which Blake's "Annotations to Reynolds" (1808) is still among the most pungent.

Thus there were few precedents to what the Royal Institution declared in 1800 by an extraordinary act of self-naming, and its founders were well aware of requiring justification – even in these years after Burke had sanctified the idea of institutions itself – for the bold departure:

> After mature deliberation upon all the terms in the European languages, which have been used to distinguish public bodies; such as schools, academies, colleges, universities, societies, corporations, &c. it was found, that every one is either appropriated to well known establishments, or less adapted to the views of the present society than the word Institution, already well known for near a century in the famous "Instituto" of Bologna.[46]

As I shall show in a moment, there were important omissions here – the Royal Institution founders Joseph Banks, Count Benjamin Rumford, and Thomas Bernard were quietly avoiding such recent usages as the post-revolutionary and state-run French *Institut National* or, closer to home, England's left-wing and rapidly discredited Pneumatic Institute conducted by Thomas Beddoes in 1797–98, which first employed Humphry Davy to experiment with nitrous oxide. Instead, Bologna's *Accademia delle Scienze dell'Istituto di Bologna*, founded in 1714, seemed fittingly distant, aristocratic, and Italian enough to serve as a learned precedent. But there is an especially interesting dimension of the Royal Institution's choice of precursor, given its long-term reputation as a scientific institution above all else. Briefly, the 1714 Institute at Bologna had been formed out of two smaller academies organized by Luigi Ferdinando Marsigli – one for the sciences, and one for painting and related fine arts. Marsigli's proposal was to join them in a single Institute, as reflected in the title of their first periodical publication in 1731, *De Bononiensi Scientiarum et Artium Istituto atque Academia Commentarii*. A group of forty painters had organized the Accademia Clementina di Bologna, funded by the great arts patron Pope Clement XI, who defined their bylaws. According to the Scholarly Societies Project,

> although this institution was founded in 1714 as an Institute with two constituent Academies, one for the sciences and one for the fine arts, after 1802 or 1803, the Academy devoted to the fine arts ceased to exist, leaving only one constituent Academy, that devoted to the sciences ... It seems reasonable to assume that the Latin name of the organization, at least for the period of its *Commentarii* (1731 to 1791), was something like: Bononiense Scientiarum et Artium Institutum atque Academia ... the name of the overall Institute (in 1739) was probably Istituto delle Scienze e delle Arti di Bologna.[47]

Marsigli's aim, McClellan suggests, was to "reform" the still-medieval conditions of the sciences at the oldest University in Europe – professorships in chemistry, architecture, natural history, and other fields were established to rival the University of Bologna's departments. "In a pedagogical breakthrough, institute professors were expected to teach in new modes, using demonstration, experiment, and practical work as aids" – including the provision of laboratories and observatories.[48] The University of Bologna itself would then belatedly introject these new methods and restructure into its own scientific and arts education curricula in response to the *Istituto*'s bold innovation. This was just the kind of institutional fission that would happen more conspicuously in England between 1800 and 1830, where the new sciences-and-arts Institutions in London would accomplish a comparable effect on Britain's oldest universities, societies, and academies. That was before they would have similar, though much harder to follow, transatlantic effects in the United States.

The most significant precursor to go *un*mentioned in the Royal Institution's 1800 *Prospectus*, however, was the today still-obscure Anderson's

Institution, founded in Glasgow in May 1796 by John Anderson, a professor of natural philosophy at the University of Glasgow. This institutional experiment would be closely studied by Count Benjamin Rumford as he and his collaborators were organizing a new institution for metropolitan London. As we shall see further in Chapter 2, Rumford raided the Anderson Institution for both faculty and organizational innovations. But it would prove of great importance for the Scottish Enlightenment as well. I refer to the fact that John Anderson was making his own institutional break from the University of Glasgow, performing what Richard Sher calls a "bifurcation of the Glasgow Enlightenment."[49] Anderson's new Institution opened scientific lectures to women as well as men, furnished a mixed curriculum of instruction in both high sciences and mechanical arts (although no "fine arts"), and generally modeled a mode of what would later be called "adult education" to the middle classes of Glasgow.[50] Thus, four years before the Royal Institution would claim originality in these matters, Anderson's project performed a largely unheralded but profoundly consequential act of breaking with both the University of Glasgow and what Sher calls its "Hutchesonian vision of the University and the Enlightenment as largely classical, moral, moderate, aesthetic, and character-building." What was Anderson's motive? As we shall again find in the London lecturing world, it would have to do with a set of beliefs and projects usually thought to be very far from the secular and sophisticated world of "arts and sciences" in Britain. Sher calls it "a popular and evangelical Presbyterian Enlightenment of 'useful knowledge,'"[51] one that used the term *Institution* to set it apart from the academic Enlightenment of Hutcheson, Adam Smith, and John Millar. This institutional chemistry would be remixed, so to speak, when Count Rumford and Thomas Bernard, first in unity and then in unexpected antagonism, would put their own agendas to work in London. There, with the more powerful patronage of Joseph Banks and the King of England, the Royal Institution would be constituted as the outcome of a struggle between Rumford's vision of using science and technology for the "common purposes of life," and the Anglican evangelical Thomas Bernard's drive to make a public profession of sciences *and* fine arts a major public and moral force in Romantic-age London.

## Words and institutions in Romantic writing

As Coleridge knew when revising "Fears in Solitude" for republication in 1817, the "Institutions, Associations, and Societies" formed in the later eighteenth century and early nineteenth were precipitates of a greater emergence of what some analysts of his age had begun to call "civil society." This is why his list does not refer to the ancient, long-founded institutions of the state, church, family, and so forth, but rather to the dislocation of those traditional structures by the newer, economically organized and politically defined groups who had been naming themselves "Institutions" or "Institutes" in the past half-century, but with especially intensive activity since 1800. As a noun, *institution* distinctly connoted the forces of self-organizing modernity, as for instance in the French Directorate's renaming and regrouping of the older French academies as the *Institut National*. "Fears in Solitude" does not refer to Godwin's "positive institutions" of *Political Justice*, the institutions of governance, but rather to the force with which Coleridge explicitly links it here – the force of the market, "pollutions from the brimming cup of wealth." The analogy is precise – the new collective formations were not specifically *in* the market, but instead forged a kind of parallel presence, formations which had sprung up between the traditional order and the aggressive, unbounded commercial markets of the past century. Hence they defined themselves as both economic agents – directing and at the same time protecting themselves from market energy and anarchy – and political agents outside and beyond the traditional apparatus of the state.[52] At the same time, Coleridge's own acquaintances, friends, or patrons figured among the new institutional agents who also helped Coleridge manage his own lecturing career – the Wedgewoods, the Wilberforces, George Beaumont, Richard Saumarez, and Thomas Bernard. An unholy alliance emerged here: between all previous forms of "honorable rule," on the one hand, and the commodity-driven "brimming cup of wealth," on the other. This polluting bargain between capitalist ambition and political discourse, made concrete in any number of the institutions and associations to which Coleridge alludes, defined a third sector, neither precisely the market nor precisely the state, of social and cultural power. Science, religion, literature, and the fine arts would become entailed in the emerging institutional ensemble being built. For the moment, Coleridge registers this widening circle in terms of language. The following verse he had first written in 1798, but in the poem's revised form published in the Regency, the poem's language and preoccupation *with* language takes on a rather different meaning:

> The sweet words
> Of Christian promise, words that even yet
> Might stem destruction, were they wisely preached,

> Are muttered o'er by men, whose tones proclaim
> How flat and wearisome they feel their trade ...
> Oh! blasphemous! the Book of Life is made
> A superstitious instrument, on which
> We gabble o'er the oaths we mean to break,
> For all must swear—all and in every place,
> College and wharf, council and just-court;
> All, all must swear, the briber and the bribed,
> Merchant and lawyer, senator and priest,
> The rich, the poor, the old man and the young;
> All, all make up one scheme of perjury,
> That faith doth reel; the very name of God
> Sounds like a juggler's charm. (lines 63–80 [1817])

Language – here the act of enunciating, its tone and intonation – becomes a touchstone for the historical process in question, a court of appeal to distinguish perjuries, truth-telling, and shadowy realms between them. We recall how, in Shelley's writings on poetry, powers of language (especially metaphor) will distinguish between the fully institutionalized genres, especially verse, and the instituting or world-founding power of "Poetry." In Romantic projects of poetic genre-reform, the languages of poetry are often opposed as the institutionalized and the instituting; as poetic diction and lyrical-balladeering in Wordsworth's and Coleridge's joint preface, or as "verse" and "Poetry" in Shelley's rethinking of the older categories of poetic genres. It is one remarkable feature of Romantic writing on modern institutions that the concepts of language or rhetoric, and genre or discursive convention, become means of divining or interpreting the greater processes at work in the institutionalizing activity of modernity as a whole. There was in the Romantic age, and we have now learned to see again, a quite real, historically produced tension between these modalities of the modern discourse on institutions.

CHAPTER 2

# *The administrator as cultural producer: restructuring the arts and sciences*

> Whoever speaks of *culture* speaks of *administration* as well, whether this is his intention or not. The combination of so many things lacking a common denominator – such as philosophy and religion, science and art, forms of conduct and mores, and finally the inclusion of the objective spirit of an age in the single word "culture" – betrays from the outset the administrative view, the task of which, looking down from on high, is to assemble, distribute, evaluate, and organize.
> Theodor Adorno, "Culture and Administration" (1961)

Today we have learned to recognize a great many kinds of Romantic-age cultural producer – from poets, novelists, and playwrights to actors, painters, scientists, editors, journalists, even professors – but we have not found it easy to identify those who organized, mediated, or otherwise worked secretly or openly to "administrate" culture in this or other periods. Administrators are often difficult to track along the familiar pathways of print culture; they deliberately leave few paper trails, even in the age of the memo. A larger reason we know so little historically about administration is related to our strong disinclination to consider administrators as cultural "producers" at all, preferring to think of them instead as bureaucrats, functionaries, or apparatchiks, a picture of the administrator that has an especially strong Romantic provenance.[1]

According to the philological record, the word's relatively rare appearances before 1800 in English refer to political governance or ecclesiastical authority; as the Calvinists liked to put it, Jesus Christ was "God's Administrator General of the Humane World."[2] Then the word *administration* began to appear gradually in reference to the arts, sciences, education, or other kinds of cultural production after 1800. The term *manager* was a word early moderns often used to designate the governors of playhouses or, at a somewhat higher level, the managers of corporate bodies for producing knowledge like the Royal Society. Meanwhile, the term *director* took on great commercial significance in the seventeenth and eighteenth centuries, beginning in the Netherlands and then becoming the nomenclature of authority for the British East India Company. For the new British arts-and-sciences institutions of 1800–25, *directors*, *managers*, *proprietors*, and other administrative terms became far more than titles or posts – they became a key part of deciding how public culture was then being widely organized.

Few users of this language may have been more sensitive to their nuances than now little-known figures like Thomas Bernard (1750–1818). To social and economic historians of the eighteenth century, Bernard is best known as the Anglican-evangelical founder of over twenty charitable, welfare, or philanthropic institutions between the mid 1790s and his death in 1818.[3] His founding of the Society for Bettering the Condition of the Poor in 1796 produced a milestone in the history of British social economics and welfare provision. Yet Bernard lived other and curiously intersecting lives as well. Historians of science are aware of him as a somewhat shadowy manager and co-founder of the Royal Institution promoting the sciences; art historians have recently focused on one of Bernard's most important and nationally consequent creations, the British Institution for Promoting the Fine Arts in 1805. His curious career, in light of this trajectory, raises the question of how one of the Romantic period's most effective, innovative, yet conservative welfare-reformers could also become one of its leading administrators of the "arts and sciences" – and why?

I shall use Bernard's little-recognized but far-reaching impact on his moment as a keynote in this chapter, since he was the rare figure who was able to traverse both modern fields of artistic and scientific production in a singular but strange career that has usually earned the misleading vocational title of "philanthropist." By framing his career as an *administrator* instead, I mean to catch an early modern moment of cultural administration in the making – one in which the governmentality of the arts and sciences can be glimpsed in a wider framework of economic, communicational, and political transformation in Britain. I also hope this early case of cultural administration will reflect back to us something of the genealogy of today's visible tensions between a corporatizing university, under the steering power of administrators who can be far removed from the specializations they manage, and the academics, intellectuals, specialists, or other producers of culture and knowledge who alternately criticize and collaborate with a process that few can claim yet to fully understand.

The administrator's tale will also open the lens more widely to grasp the ensemble of arts-and-sciences Institutions that networked with other specializing societies or academies, yet accomplished the one breakthrough to a wider public sphere those societies and academies could not – by constructing a viable audience for the refiguring domain of "arts and sciences" in London and then across England. These publics for scholarship and popular learning would not look, nor often feel, the same as the reading public framed by the eighteenth century's Republic of Letters.[4] The English were not only now reading or discussing, one might say they were also in some important new sense *living* the arts and sciences as they entered its three-dimensioned institutional spaces, whether it was to hop from lecture to lecture at different London locations, or, as Gillian Russell has vividly described the face-to-face experience of lecture-going, to engage in new forms of sociability.[5] Londoners could also feel a somewhat fetishized sense of personal contact with authors, scientists, and poets whom, in an earlier day, they could only have read about: "Our Roscoes, our Davys, our Coleridges, our Campbells, and our Hazlitts, have personally appeared among us, at these institutions, vivifying our minds, and shedding light on our paths."[6] This star-system of celebrity lecturers helped lend to the Institutions a larger national importance as well: "No country but England," Peter George Patmore could write by 1823, "possesses any thing of the kind. It is only here that extensive and really important institutions like these can be conducted with the spirit and effect that they are." What effect in particular? Patmore cites the Surrey Institution to show that what distinguishes the English case from the Continental is

> that permanent rank which they hold, entirely by the exertions and the property of private individuals strictly in the middle classes of life. Here is an institution (and there are four such in London, of which this is on the smallest scale) diffusing more taste for literary and scientific pursuits, and causing more books to be purchased and to be read, than half the institutes and academies of France put together.[7]

This combination of private ownership and public impact had been distinguishing England from France, Germany, and even Russia in the early nineteenth century as the ensemble of arts-and-sciences Institutions across England formed a striking exception to the state-run universities and knowledge institutes formed most recently in Paris and Berlin since the 1790s. If London stood apart from all other European capitals in not having its own university, the arts-and-sciences Institutions had begun, with their combination of public outreach and claims to original or disciplinary knowledge, at least to feel as though they could almost incarnate what London lacked. Yet the sense that one was achieving *real* knowledge in this cascade of hundreds of lectures on so many topics was always elusive. For all his admiration of the new phenomenon,

Patmore also noted that their "mixed and popular character" stimulated a certain "anxious craving" and "diligent search after knowledge" – an insecurity that grasping so avidly at the arts and sciences in these visibly public institutions could also betray their getting but a "superficial semblance of knowledge, which only serves to shew the real absence of it."[8]

The first part of this chapter will show a most unlikely origin for the fashionable Romantic-age arts-and-sciences Institutions that dazzled Patmore and others. This was the problem of the poor and the old English welfare system that, by the 1790s, could no longer cope with emerging conditions in either the British economy or the nation's volatile political situation in the wake of the French Revolution. Born out of this maelstrom – by means of a remarkable and still partly obscure reversal of its original purposes – the Royal Institution would set in motion a new sphere of London and eventually England-wide public learning for a cross-class and cross-gender public, both fashion-conscious and intellectually alert, who seemed very far from the social origins and intended audience of what Thomas Bernard and his collaborators first projected in the 1790s. Yet this genealogy is important in revealing why there would be so extraordinary an emphasis put upon the *administration* of London arts and sciences, one that originated in the project of managing education for the artisans and mechanics in a counterrevolutionary way. I shall then turn to what distinguished these early nineteenth-century Institutions through their lecturing and other media across a wide range of knowledge topics and expressive practices, from chemistry to painting and poetry to moral philosophy, some of these soon destined to achieve modern disciplinary authority by the end of the Romantic age.

### Centers of action: knowledge and social welfare

What became the Royal Institution of Great Britain in 1800 could be said to have begun in the American colonies, where both Thomas Bernard and his future 1790s collaborator Benjamin Thompson (1753–1816, known after 1791 as Count Benjamin Rumford) were born in Massachusetts, educated at Harvard University, and grew up in Tory-sympathizing families who took the British side when the colonies rebelled in the 1770s. Both left North America, at different times, in flight from the colonists' impending victory, and both could be said to have carried some part of this early life-stage into what they later built in Britain. Bernard may have gained a taste for both power and social management from his father, Sir Francis Bernard, first baronet and colonial governor of Massachusetts Bay Colony, whose harsh administrative policies were partly responsible for stimulating the Boston-area colonists to stage mass protests in the decade before 1775. For his part, Rumford stayed in America long enough to spy on colonial armies for the British, and he would later provoke suspicions even in Britain that he was always scheming at something, the implications of which were never fully revealed. When the two men met (probably for the first time) in England in 1796, finding they had common interests and enemies, Bernard was already something of an administrator in the making, and Rumford had been proving with widely noticed inventions, scientific credentials, and sometimes outlandish social visions that he was a classic projector.

Since "innovation" was a term often reserved for Enlightenment social theorists or Jacobin revolutionaries in 1790s England, Thomas Bernard's own innovating actions would most often be portrayed as "philanthropy." By the time he founded the Society for Bettering the Condition of the Poor in 1796, he was combining his own Anglican evangelicalism and a growing appreciation of Adam Smith's political economy. Something of his longer-term impact on British intellectual and political culture appeared in the late nineteenth-century claim by the reformer George Holyoake that it was Thomas Bernard who, in his many *Reports* for the Bettering Society, "first used the term 'science' in connection with social arrangements."[9] Holyoake's remark is worth keeping in mind as we also observe in the chapters below that while "social sciences" were not yet part of the array of knowledges called "arts and sciences" in the early nineteenth century, some of their key elements can already be seen at work in Bernard's use of Smith's economics in poor-relief programs, in Benjamin Rumford's penchant for applying the heat sciences to methods of managing restive populations of the poor in Bavaria and England, and not least in the social-statistics-gathering of Patrick Colquhoun (1745–1820), a key member of Bernard's Bettering Society.

But it was Bernard who largely powered the Bettering Society by writing at least one-third of its 184 *Reports* that would be published over a twenty-year span and that may have circulated as many as 24,000 copies each year (or roughly twice the circulation of the *Edinburgh Review* or *Blackwood's Magazine*).[10] These reports had accumulating impact. By 1816 Robert Southey, as Kevin Gilmartin points out, was taking Bernard to be England's foremost authority on counterrevolutionary reforms of the older welfare system in Southey's widely read *Quarterly Review* article, "The Poor" (1816), pronouncing the verdict on Bernard's methods, "This is true radical reform."[11] What Southey undoubtedly recognized also was that, in the

1790s, the new approach being outlined by Bernard and others represented a broader sea-change in British welfare thinking. Since 1601 the English Poor Law had dispensed money to the poor by taxing each parish in the land; by the 1770s, a parish like St. Martin-in-the-Fields in London was taxed at £10,000 yearly.[12] Late eighteenth-century demands by wealthy landowners for what might now be called "cutting taxes" invited new thinking about shifting the financial load off the wealthy. But what set Bernard apart from other conservative critics of the old welfare system was in part his readiness to hold the wealthy responsible for its failings:

> If the poor are *idle* and *vicious*, they are reduced to subsist on the benevolence of the rich: if the rich (I except those to whom health and ability, and not will, is wanting) are *selfish, indolent, and* NEGLECTFUL OF THE CONDITIONS ON WHICH THEY HOLD SUPERIORITY OF RANK AND FORTUNE, they sink into a situation worse than that of being *gratuitously maintained by the poor*. They become PAUPERS of an *elevated and distinguished class*; in no way personally contributing to the general stock. (emphasis in original)[13]

The Society's *Reports* often urged landholders to invest in a new agenda for what today is called, as a means to abolish an older economic safety-net, "welfare reform," an educational and economic agenda strongly inflected by the evangelical mission Bernard shared with his collaborator, William Wilberforce. Here, expensive and ideologically unpredictable kinds of economic welfare in England would be replaced by new modes and media of pedagogy summoned under a unique heading – scientific knowledge.[14]

This is why Bernard urged "the inquiry into all that concerns the POOR, and the promotion of their happiness, a SCIENCE," especially the science of Political Economy. Adjusting Scottish commercial doctrine to Anglican evangelical mission, he argued why "the Division of Labour, applied to *intellectual purposes*, leaves the master the easy task of directing the movements of the whole machine" (emphasis in original).[15] What he seems most to have gathered from Bell and Smith was the notion of differentiated *system* – that is, the "whole machine" which would afford a clear path for the directing powers of the welfare planner. This kind of ambitiously systemic viewpoint allowed Bernard and his evangelical collaborators to distinguish these new welfare provisions from mere obedience to the older paternalistic charity of the Church of England. We also read of some oddly familiar innovations for social mobility in Bernard's *Reports*, such as a twelve-step program to personal success for managing time, saving money to make a bargain, changing personal behavior – "sinning is an expensive occupation," said the eleventh rule – and other ways for the poor to think of themselves as preparing for the rewards of the market as much as for a lifetime of labor.[16]

As the Bettering Society combined moral mission with a growing laboratory for educational experiments, Bernard represented a leading edge of what Boyd Hilton has called the rational wing of late eighteenth-century evangelicalism, prepared to use any scientific or rational means to achieve atonement or redemption. If it seems counterintuitive that evangelicals would take so keen an interest in both the sciences on the one hand, and the English economy and commercial exchange on the other, Hilton makes an illuminating case that Evangelicalism of this sort – rather than the kind whose advocates babbled in tongues – was "a *contractual* religion ... Sin constituted a *debt* owed by humans to their divine banker. Individuals stood in a *commercial* relationship with God, whose ultimate *merchandise* was Heaven" (emphasis in original).[17] Operating in the volatile British economy, rather than the prayerful meeting house, could become for moderate evangelicals like Bernard "an arena of great spiritual trial and suspense."[18] If they were economically keen, Hilton adds, the rational evangelicals were also largely "indifferent to aesthetic matters."[19] Yet Bernard himself would prove an exception to this rule after 1800, when he began programming art and poetry lectures into the Royal Institution lecturing agendas and then, in 1805, established another powerful London base of influence, the British Institution for Promoting the Fine Arts in the United Kingdom.

Bernard's agenda for educating the poor would play out in an unpredictable way over the next ten years. One of his most vigorous arguments in the Bettering Society *Reports* was that the eighteenth-century charity school had shown too much the synoptic picture and too little the division of modern knowledges or the student's own learning process:

> it *teaches* everything, but does not allow the pupil to acquire anything of himself ... general and vague ideas are infused into the mind on all subjects, without anything precise or permanent being obtained on any; and it is thus that a kind of *bird's-eye view* of the arts and sciences is offered to the intellect, without any fixed or distinct knowledge of any of them. (emphasis in original)[20]

This encyclopedic "*bird's-eye view*" seems to have been a target of Bernard's well before he became institutionally prominent at the significantly higher-level "arts and sciences" of either the Royal or British Institutions. Thinking with Adam Smith did not lead Bernard to be more receptive to larger-scale social theorizing. It rather led to a fairly cautious experimental approach based on observation and on what Colquhoun would soon be producing as detailed, statistical information about the poor and how they coped.

As Bernard applied the methods of political economy to poor-relief and therefore to reshaping its fundamental rationale, it is also ironic to read him redefining the old Tudor poor-relief system as nothing better than a project foisted on a gullible public:

> Let us therefore make the inquiry into all that concerns the poor, and the promotion of their happiness, a Science ... For a period of more than two centuries, the attention of the nation has been engaged by a succession of projects, for the management of the poor; – almost all of them originating in benevolence; and every one of them received in a manner, and with an interest, that distinctly marked the public anxiety upon the subject. The good effects however, as to the poor, have been limited and uncertain; the project having originated not in them, but in the projector; – not in fact, but in speculation ... Let us then give effect to that master-spring of action, on which equally depends the prosperity of individuals and of empires – THE DESIRE IMPLANTED IN THE HUMAN BREAST OF BETTERING ITS CONDITION.[21]

Among present-day "projectors" Bernard may also have been thinking of revolutionary antagonists, Paine, Godwin, or even Jeremy Bentham, who had recently defended the role of the "projector" in letters to Adam Smith.[22] The irony of this posture was that Bernard was also joining forces with a volatile projector, Benjamin Thompson, recently granted the title Count Rumford for his work containing the restive political energies of the poor in Bavaria by building workhouses and other containment devices to manage social change. In Rumford's extravagant plans to build the scientific management of social formations at ever higher levels, Bernard was soon finding that this was a moment – a time when Bentham's speculative social designs were also beginning to circulate – when the whole matter of the "project" was ripe for a major refiguring in its own right.

Rumford returned to England in 1796 as the now-prominent author of scientific articles, inventor of thermodynamic devices (including the expensive Rumford Stove soon installed in many English mansions), essayist, and social speculator, but he has been no less controversial to later cultural historians than he was for the English progressives who read his new book of 1796, *Essays, Political, Economical, and Philosophical.* Jeremy Bentham paid close attention to Rumford's projects; it was while shaping his own plans for a comprehensive institutional design for poor relief that Bentham contacted Rumford in 1796. The two found common cause in "their mutual desire to apply technological innovation to social problems," with Bentham asking Rumford to give a critical reading to his "Essays on the Poor Laws."[23] At a further remove, the Unitarian radical Samuel Coleridge thought he saw in Rumford's writings a worthy successor to Joseph Priestley, using science to improve the lot of the miserable: "born / For loftiest action," he wrote of Rumford in *The Watchman*, "on life's varied views to look around / And raise expiring sorrow from the ground."[24] Others, like Charles Lamb, would give Rumford a sinister voice in unpublished verse: "I deal in Aliments fictitious / And teaze the Poor with soups nutritious; / Of bones and flint I make dilution, / And belong to the National Institution."[25]

Coleridge's and Lamb's contrasting views of Rumford were to reappear in two important histories of the Royal Institution. Henry Bence Jones revived Coleridge's benevolent reformer in his important 1871 history, *The Royal Institution: Its Founder and Its First Professors*, the first history of a modern scientific institution since Thomas Sprat's *History of the Royal Society* in 1667. Depicting Rumford as the "founder" of the Royal, Bence Jones would depict Thomas Bernard as the betrayer of Rumford's noble scientific project to "fashion" and (though the historian of science did not say so) to the arts and literature as well. A century later, Morris Berman mobilized the tools of social history, in the still-influential study *Social Change and Scientific Organization* (1978), in order to dispense with Bence Jones's account as largely mythical, reviving Lamb's Rumford as an irresponsible adventurer, "professional courtier," and exploiter of the poor. Unlike Bence Jones, he paid little attention to Thomas Bernard, accentuating instead the control exerted by the aristocratic Board of Agriculture.[26] Following Berman, cultural historians have pointed out how Rumford's "self-fulfilling, dehumanizing equivalents (food as fuel, work as heat) cast the poor in utilitarian terms," as Sandra Sherman puts it, thereby "conflating physics and poor relief."[27] Yet it is also worth recalling what excited Coleridge and Bentham, and why joining "physics and poor relief" was just the sort of imaginative leap Bernard and, among others, Joseph Banks as President of the Royal Society, had been looking for in England, effectively seeking out a scientific projector to solve economic and now political pressures too intense for familiar solutions. Rumford concocted ambitious blueprints for huge "useful projects," a potent term soon enlarged to the more historically long-lived notion of politically and economically urgent "useful information." Such projects could well seem exotic – "like the Laputans, Rumford wants to project virtuosity and intends to dazzle"[28] – but Bernard and Banks would grasp them as powerful historical innovations promising to wrestle the control of English poverty from a welfare legacy now faltering and to improve the capitalizing of British agriculture into the bargain.

By the 1790s – as British encyclopedias were already giving up the galvanizing metaphor of the "tree of knowledge," and thus its visualizable unity – Rumford's writing also registered the tension between the linear print medium of his own *Essays* and what he now called the "symphonic" or multi-dimensional shape that emerging knowledges should take as "sciences" increasingly promised to close the gap with "practical arts." In one passage, for instance, he would try to define the new kind of social institution he had in mind by comparing it to a symphony:

> Though all the different parts of a well-arranged establishment go on together, and harmonize like parts of a piece of music in full score, yet in describing such an establishment it is impossible to write like the musician *in score*, and to make all the parts of the narrative advance together. Various movements, which exist together, and which have the most intimate connection and dependence upon each other, must nevertheless be described separately; and the greatest care and attention, and frequently no small share of address, are necessary in the management of such descriptions, to render the details intelligible, and to give the whole its full effect of order, dependence, connection, and harmony. And in no case can these difficulties be greater than in the descriptions like those in which I am now engaged, where the number of the objects and details is so great that it is difficult to determine which should be attended to first, and how far it may safely be pursued, without danger of the others being too far removed from their proper places, or excluded, or forgotten.[29]

In 1796 Rumford was already noting the difficulty of translating or remediating the polyphonal character of an "institution" into the linear medium of print, yet pointing his readers toward the necessity now of making that leap. This sort of institutional imagination attracted attention at the highest levels of contemporary knowledge-work. In 1799 Banks formed an alliance with Rumford and Bernard that proved economically and politically promising enough to raise one of Rumford's most ambitious ideas, a new "institution" to accomplish the physics of poor relief in London by way of a major metropolitan project. Known informally as the Rumford Institute, what later became the Royal Institution of Great Britain took its formal shape when fifty-eight landed aristocrats joined with Banks to launch a new project which would bring the latest scientific and technological know-how to London's most educable workers, mechanics, and artisans by building a metropolitan institution for advanced technical education on a scale never seen in England.

By appealing to the rural gentry to launch this social experiment in the upscale West End of London, Bernard and Rumford urged Banks to create "*a centre of action* . . . to which persons may apply for examples, for models, and for engravings accompanied by printed instructions."[30] Had it been opened in London in 1799 as originally planned, this would have been the first Mechanics' Institute in England, a quarter-century before the one actually formed in 1824. Its original architecture, mapped out and partly built by James Webster, would house and teach working men how to run, and even sometimes to make, the newest machines, including (it was proposed) James Watt's and Matthew Boulton's extraordinary steam engine. There would be lectures to both mechanics and their wealthy employers, but most important to Rumford was to forge a largely visual and tactile education to *model* the knowledge rather than only verbalize it: "Workmen must *see* the thing they are to imitate; bare descriptions of it will not answer to give them such precise ideas of what is to be done . . . Something *visible and tangible* is necessary to fix the attention and determine the choice."[31]

Visibility and modeling were key to "improvement": the resulting action would stimulate the poor to achievement and prepare them to join, as skilled workers, England's technology revolution during its ongoing war with France. Moreover, by combining visual modeling, oral instruction, lecturing, and print media, Rumford's Royal Institution – as approved along these lines by George III in May 1799 – would teach London's workers how to raise productivity without needing to be trained by tradesmen, manufacturers, or other middlemen. With Banks's backing, aristocratic donors poured thousands of pounds into constructing stairways, lecture rooms and seating, kitchens, and living quarters for the mechanics – all carefully built to remain out of the view of their employers who would be seated separately. Meanwhile, costs soared as these elaborate fittings were constructed from mid 1799 forward. Personal suspicions and ideological questions, such as Banks's growing doubt that the politically restive artisans and mechanics should receive a potentially dangerous scientific or technological education, also began to be raised.

How exactly this Rumford-inspired project failed is still a matter of dispute among historians of the Royal Institution. What is certain is that all these plans and half-built structures were dismantled with remarkable speed when the strongest resistance to Rumford's agenda was mounted from two quarters – the steam engine's inventors James Watt and Matthew Boulton, who decided to refuse the Institution the right to model their machines, and the Tory landholders who feared communicating such information to the readers of Tom Paine. It's doubtful the Lunar Society to which Watt and Boulton had belonged would have had any interest in Rumford's imperious and counterrevolutionary programs of social control by way of amazing new inventions. But Boulton's case for withholding the steam engine from Rumford's modeling plans was grounded elsewhere, in perhaps a more aggressive defense of the intellectual-property principle than any of the better-known copyright debates of the later eighteenth century.[32] Boulton's son put the point clearly to his father:

> [The Rumford plan] will not in all probability be much relished by the British Manufacturer ... An Institution for diffusing general knowledge & science may be useful, but if the manufacturers find that it is intended to be made a vehicle for disclosing the particular arts & machinery employed by them, their opposition to it will be found equally powerful as the support of the patrons, tho' composed of such exalted personages.[33]

The result of Watt's and Boulton's decision to withhold their steam engine from Rumford's social design would be far-reaching. Without actual, complex, and up-to-date technology to display and teach, the Rumford vision was effectively crippled at the outset. It could only be a matter of time before its other components – model kitchens, model heating devices, and similar incarnations of scientific practice – would be cast aside in the glaring absence of the driving invention of the age. For years afterward, Humphry Davy would tell his audiences of the transforming effect of the Watt/Boulton decision on popular knowledge of the sciences as applied to human work.

The rapid conversion of the Rumford project into the fashionable Royal Institution Londoners came to know in the early 1800s amounted to a major dislocation or time warp in the trajectory of British urban culture – instead of workers training at the machines, London greeted the Humphry Davy phenomenon, the celebrity lecturer in chemistry who could draw huge crowds of the eminent and fashionable to hear the latest thinking on the sciences. Meanwhile, Rumford bitterly complained against the abandonment of his visionary programs for "the common purposes of life," and his pleas would be heard again in Bence Jones's Victorian narrative of these events in 1871, where he mournfully notes this moment as a turning point in the making and using of knowledge in English everyday life:

> Gradually the "usefulness of science to the poorer classes and to the common purposes of life" ceased to be the prime object of the Institution. The school for mechanics, the workshops, and the models, the kitchens and

the Journals, died away; and the laboratory, the lectures, and the library became the life of the new Institution, and its object became "the diffusion of knowledge and the application of science to the improvement of arts and manufactures."[34]

As Rumford's erstwhile co-founder, Bernard moved quickly to reformulate the Institution's mission. No longer calling the Institution a "centre of action," he shifted rhetorical gears to operate a new project of "giving fashion to science and forming a centre of philosophical and literary *attraction*."[35] This announcement to the funders of the Institution in May 1803 was the public signal that the post-Rumford years had begun; it was to open the extravaganza of the "arts and sciences" lecturing and publishing empire which dominated London (and soon provincial) life over the next twenty-five years. Bernard's frank pursuit of "fashion" and an upper middle-class audience did not prevent others, though, from seeing the Institution in more academically grand terms. The Tory-edited *Critical Review* would opine that the great universities at Oxford, Cambridge, and Edinburgh were prestigious and important enough, yet distant, few, and "far too scanty to fertilize the immense tract of civilized society." The new London phenomenon promised to change that: "The foundation of the Royal Institution we regard as an epoch which marks the progress of civilization in this great metropolis."[36]

But Joseph Banks and the Royal Society were not amused. While Banks had hoped for Rumford's plan to join a series of metropolitan projects springing into action under the broad canopy of the Society, the RI's takeover by Bernard and his new collaborator, Sir John Hippisley, portended the opposite: publicity-driven scientific displays for an unruly, alarmingly miscellaneous, all too fashionable urban audience far beyond the power of the Royal Society to oversee. Rumford found himself an outcast from his own project. His bitter letter to a Paris professor of chemistry complained that Bernard and his new allies were "not only totally unknown in the Scientific world, but they have not the smallest knowledge in any one branch of Science!"[37] Once Rumford left London permanently for Paris, Banks slowly gave up. "It is now entirely in the hands of the profane," he wrote to Rumford in 1804. "The Institution has irrevocably fallen into the hands of the enemy, and is now perverted to a hundred uses for which you and I never intended it."[38] These letters reveal how closely Banks had integrated Rumford's original project into his conception of British sciences as led and expanded by the Royal Society – to promote scientific knowledge "among the poor and the rich," but never to address the sphere of commercial life or, as we shall see, the visual arts or the literary – the domain Banks was calling "fashion." It also shows how sharply Banks distinguished scientific work from the topics of belles-lettres, moral philosophy, fine arts, and "history of commerce" that Bernard was now in the process of programming into the Royal Institution. To Banks, Rumford was not the charlatan depicted by his enemies, but an important and now long-gone collaborator for its regeneration in an industrial and politically volatile age. Clearly the reach Banks had hoped for was not into the sphere of fashion, commerce, and arts from which he recoiled in 1804.

### Centers of attraction: a theater of arts and sciences

Thomas Bernard seems to have become a true administrator in this conversion from centers of "action" to "attraction" by cutting his ties to Rumford and quietly moving behind the scenes to manage what some called the "noonday opera-house" of the Royal Institution and its fabulous public displays of entertaining knowledge on Albemarle Street.[39] By 1809, the two arts-and-sciences Institutions he had founded or co-founded since 1800 – the Royal and the British Institutions – would figure prominently in Rudolph Ackermann's expensive urban atlas, *The Microcosm of London*, which portrayed a metropolis combining "social and cultural institutions," as Ann Bermingham points out, with "the theatres, the shops, and the markets; the things that made the city an exciting and interesting place."[40] Ackermann's capital city was not Hogarth's – there were no Gin Alleys, Tyburn, or Bedlam in his pages – but rather a London featuring bright new cultural institutions along with their seeming opposite, "institutions for the care and instruction of the poor such as Newgate Women's Chapel, Christ's Church Hospital School ... and St. Luke's Hospital." This was, in other words, much more Thomas Bernard's kind of London than anything the aristocratic improving landlords or Joseph Banks had imagined when they first financed the Royal Institution.

Nonetheless, in virtually all accounts of the Royal – from its internal records and its active publicity machine to its various scientific or cultural histories – Bernard himself is rarely onstage, but moves quietly, almost invisibly in the deep shadows of the proscenium. It is still difficult to be certain of his role beyond his official titles of treasurer and lecture manager, but one can feel his magnetic pull almost everywhere a decision is being made or an institutional-history page is being turned. Honing his skills as administrator, one associate later said, Bernard became "the great stirring and influential member of the *committees* ... no important measure was thought of being carried into effect without his concurrence and guidance," and he was reputed to show "the happiest *tact* in the management of bodies corporate – divested of the mace and the fur gown."[41] Even his only known portrait, bland as it is, foretells the characteristic ability to exercise power with self-effacing calm.[42] While setting aside displays of imperious authority, Bernard also essayed the role of the modern administrator who may be first the beneficiary, but soon the antagonist, of the more flamboyant "projector" whose latest London incarnation had been Count Rumford. Inheriting the projector's visions, he disavows their methods and eliminates risk while pursuing cautious innovation. Bernard "put other persons forward as the nominal promoter of his schemes," recalled a family memoirist, "while he was furnishing them in most cases with ideas."[43] Yet his decisions shepherded or launched some important public careers: Davy's as lecturing scientist, Coleridge's as literary critic, Sydney Smith's as moral philosopher, Thomas Frognall Dibdin's as a British bibliographer. What makes Bernard an administrator of the greatest interest is not that he sustained continuing influence in either the scientific field for long or the artistic field after his death in 1818, but rather that he achieved what was for this time a uniquely higher level – professing to direct "taste" in both fields, a taste we might now call middlebrow, making it the administrator's task to produce an arts and sciences agenda aimed to both instruct and please "the moderately well-informed."[44]

The wide public enthusiasm for lecture-going in the Romantic age is usually attributed to the power of the lecturers. But one measure of the administrator's capacity to shape both the taste and the composition of the Royal and other Institutions' audiences can be taken by the surprise that Londoners professed when they saw spectators they had least anticipated in the heretofore masculine world of scientific knowledge. Women filled the lecture halls. Robert Southey found them "all upon the watch ... with their tablets and pencils, busily noting down what they heard."[45] The RI would long claim it invented the mixed-gender public for nineteenth-century sciences and arts – "a sight not to be paralleled in the civilized world," its own journal would later say, as "our countrywomen flock to give their all-powerful countenance to pursuits which ennoble the mind. While beauty and fashion continue to patronize mental improvement, it will ever be unfashionable to be uninformed."[46] Humphry Davy's impact as a magnetic, sensual, and flirtatious lecturer may help explain the strong female response to scientific matters at the Royal Institution, though as Jan Golinski has pointed out, his perceived "sexual chemistry" could make him more controversial in other ways.[47] But neither Davy nor Bernard could really claim originality for the idea of radiating Enlightenment to women in public lectures. The Royal's model in this respect had surely been the Anderson Institution, which had been inviting women to its Glasgow lecture halls since 1796, something Bernard and Rumford had studied before the physics professor Thomas Young opened his first London lecture in 1802 by inviting women to make the Royal Institution "a kind of subordinate university to those whose sex or situation in life has denied them the advantage of an academic education in the national seminars of learning."[48] When Southey, Francis Horner, and others took note of the new female audience for learning, they often tried to trivialize or politicize it. Learning chemical or literary knowledge could very well "make the real blue-stockings a little more disagreeable than ever and sensible women a little more sensible," Horner wrote to John Murray in 1804. "Your chemists and metaphysicians in petticoats are altogether out of nature – that is, when they make a trade or distinction of such pursuits – but when they take a little general learning as an accomplishment they keep it in very tolerable order."[49] Horner and others soon proved short-sighted about what the Institutions' public effect could be on women like Jane Marcet, who produced widely sold books including *Conversations on Chemistry* (1806) after hearing several years of Davy's chemical lecturing, or Eleanor Porden, whose *The Veils, or the Triumph of Constancy. A Poem in Six Books* (1815) earned accolades from even the customarily hostile Tory *British Critic* for revealing "very intimate acquaintance" with chemistry and natural history she learned at the Institutions.[50] Women, Dissenters, and others denied British university educations would indeed find the London arts-and-sciences Institutions, as they multiplied through the Romantic age, an alternative intellectual world. They could also find it a sociable one of a quite different kind than had often prevailed in the eighteenth-century Republic of Letters.[51]

From 1805 onward, arts-and-sciences Institutions began appearing all over London, generally on the model of the Royal. Yet each new version of such an Institution marked an extension of audience, and often, in its own mode of administration, a kind of embedded dispute or controversy driving a distinctive agenda. Unlike the genteel Royal, the London Institution exuded the smell of new money. It was constructed in 1806 in the City by a breakaway faction of bankers, merchants, and colonialist interests, led by Sir Francis Baring, a Royal Institution proprietor and a director of the East India Company who was hoping to set up intellectual shop in the financial heart of London.[52] The mission was to break with the landed capital that dominated governance of the early Royal Institution and begin making a stronger case in London for the affinity of science and commerce. "What a start or pulsation was there at the projecting of this establishment!" wrote one observer. "The *City* character was stamped on every stage of the proceedings – and premium and per centage seemed to be engrained in its very nature."[53]

Historians of these Institutions have given the impression of a spontaneous welcome by eager audiences, but the London Institution had to work unusually hard to win over its own projected public, a business world hardly ready to embrace the arts and sciences. "It has been said that literary and scientific attainments are incompatible with that attention to business, with that activity to mind, which is essential to those who would flourish in mercantile and commercial occupations," argued William Brande in a widely printed inaugural address; a half-century later, Thomas Huxley would still have to rehearse this argument to resist the common London businessman's recalcitrance to scientific theory and experiment.[54] The London Institution adopted the Royal's organizational model – library and reading rooms, lecturing, and soon publications (though no laboratory) – and its private-funding structure administered by a range of "managers," "visitors," or "proprietors." Fascination with *how* the new Institutions were being administered, and by whom, preoccupied all interested parties in this moment. Thus the Unitarian *Monthly Magazine* was also revealing the rational Dissenters' interest in these questions when it introduced readers to the London Institution by devoting five of its six pages to detailing "The Direction and Administration of the Institution."[55] Publishers and readers alike were trying to comprehend the new Institution model for arts and sciences that, unlike the print media they had long known, now offered a reconfigured relation of cultural producers to potential new audiences, linking investors to the kinds of culture they could promote and landed or merchant capital to a direct means of hands-on control over the place, the time, the audience, the lecturers, and the curricular agendas of "arts and sciences" in the metropolis.

Something more than a commercializing purpose seemed to drive the Surrey Institution, founded in 1808 on Blackfriars Road. Appearing colorfully in Thomas Rowlandson's aquatint picture of the Institution's imposing auditorium, the Rotunda, the Surrey gave the age its most striking image of a Romantic-age lecture in *The Microcosm of London*.[56] Unlike the Royal, the Surrey drew its audience from its local middle-class and Quaker neighborhoods, but it matched the Royal and London Institutions with spacious library, notable scientists, and research laboratory. It *more* than matched the Royal in literary critics: Coleridge and Hazlitt launched some of their most ambitious literary lecture series there in 1812–13 and 1818–19. Frederick Accum lectured on chemistry and combined it with commerce in the book *Chemical Amusements* (1817), while provoking the more high-minded Davy to mutter that he was little better than a "cheat and a Quack."[57] Ackermann's widely cited description of the Surrey as a commerce-oriented venue of public culture appeared too early in the Surrey's tenure from 1808 to 1823, however, to register the political and religious notoriety that would also soon attach to it. The *Anti-Jacobin Review* and similar journals sometimes portrayed it as a hotbed of Dissenters and radical fire-breathers.[58] We have other indicators of an administrative struggle for control of the Surrey in its early years, one registered by admirers of the Methodist scholar and bibliographer Adam Clarke as taking place between New and Old Dissenters (specifically Wesleyan Arminians and Unitarians), who may have been carrying their profound disputes of doctrine about the Trinity, the rites of baptism, and the agency of God on earth to the inside of an Institution that Ackermann was depicting as a commercial gem.[59] This doctrinal fight for control of the Surrey Institution (and, equally important, of its library, as we shall see in the next chapter) remained largely invisible to the public. But the episode shows again how volatile the whole trajectory of British arts and sciences could become, not only for secular knowledge production, but likewise for a British religious field that was now becoming so fractious that even its best-educated participants – Coleridge will be the key case in Chapter 6 – could not agree on what the long-touted claim of the modern arts' and sciences' superiority to the ages of barbarism still really meant.

As a case of how intertwined these matters could be, consider the Surrey's natural-philosophy lecturer John Mason Good, a Unitarian doctor and polymath who lectured to overflow audiences on "The Philosophy of Physics" at the Surrey Institution beginning in 1811 and continuing for four years. Good has perplexed subsequent educational historians who have called his work either "popular science flavored with piety" or – I think more accurately – an ambitiously cross-disciplinary effort to connect researches in physics, biology, psychology, and philosophy.[60] Unlike the majority of London lecturers, Good produced a curious and still compelling book from his talks in 1826, *The Book of Nature*.[61] He had unusual humanist credentials for a lecturer on physics. A skilled translator of Latin and other classical languages, Good had published in 1805 the first full English version of Lucretius' *De Rerum Natura* since Thomas Creech's translation of 1682, one that Good based on the notorious "Jacobin" edition of Lucretius' Latin issued by Gilbert Wakefield in 1797.[62] Good's thick two-quarto volumes of his English-language Lucretius found their way into Percy Shelley's library and may well, as Michael Vicario has argued, have shaped his notions of a material universe in some unusual ways.[63] This earlier classicist career may help explain why, six years later at the Surrey Institution, an audience expecting to hear an update on the newest English sciences would instead receive a rarely discussed case of Romantic-age philosophical materialism that introduced the rain and swerves of Lucretian atoms to a public who still, by and large, believed the nature of physics was Newtonian mechanics. According to Colin Kidd, one of J. M. Good's few recent readers, these lectures also gave a "compelling defense of monogenesis" forty years before Darwin and thereby "a scientific account of racial diversity."[64] But readers of Lucretius and his commentators today might also be struck by John Mason Good's strenuous attempt to make a Dissenter's effort, rather than a Deist's, to reconcile atomist materialism with Christianity.[65] A Unitarian when he began translating *On the Nature of Things* in 1797, Good was beginning to embrace a Trinitarian, essentially Methodist mode of Dissent by 1810, the time when the Surrey Institution's archivist Adam Clarke – himself a learned Methodist intellectual and bibliographer – invited Good to talk on the sciences. The normally invisible, behind-the-scenes dispute between administrative factions, in this case concerning matters of religion, would thus have come to the Surrey's audience in the form of a "physics" mediated by a great Latin poem and the lecturer's own internal struggle to reconcile Lucretian atoms with mysteries of the holy triad. Good's lectures would not make a contribution to modern disciplinary physics. But they are a good case of the ways in which relations between knowledges and beliefs become far more *internally* complicated in this Romantic-age institutional context than we usually understand by the notably public resonance of the expression "arts and sciences."

Few of the Surrey's religious or political complexities seem to have appeared at the Russell Literary and Scientific Institution in Bloomsbury (also begun in 1808), a seemingly cooler-headed and more professional Institution founded by Whig lawyers and MPs. Among the institutors were Francis Horner, a co-founder of the *Edinburgh Review*, the English constitutional historian Henry Hallam (father of Arthur Henry Hallam), and Samuel Romilly, the Whig lawyer advancing bills in Parliament to abolish capital punishment.[66] The Russell Institution has come to be seen as more historically minded and "literary" than the others, though it has left the sketchiest paper trail of London's five major arts-and-sciences institutions. Its administrative core – linking the Russell Institution to the agenda of the *Edinburgh Review* as well as to Whig political programs under the reign of Pitt and Castlereagh – attracted Dissenters like William Hazlitt to deliver ten lectures at the Russell on "The Rise and Progress of Modern Philosophy" in 1812. Those lectures, unpublished in Hazlitt's lifetime, may well have been an extension of the arguments he had begun advancing in *Essay on the Principles of Human Action* in 1805, which Uttara Natarajan has read provocatively as advancing a new synthesis of a progressive "British idealism" that bears on Hazlitt's later idealizing postures on the fine arts during the Regency.[67] The Russell Institution would also seem more literary than its counterparts insofar as Francis Horner's decision to invest his *Edinburgh Review* capital in the new Russell Institution formed an important link between London "arts and sciences" and the Scottish literary world.

As we shall see shortly, the lecturing programs of these four major London institutions alone would justify calling them "arts and sciences" institutions, despite their reputation among historians as primarily scientific. But it will be particularly important for this book's argument that while all nineteenth-century London guidebooks grouped the Royal, Surrey, London, and Russell Institutions in one category of urban attractions, associated with the sciences, they put an important fifth – the British Institution for Promoting the Fine Arts in the United Kingdom (1805) – in a different, "fine arts" category alongside the Royal Academy. There were obvious reasons for this. The British Institution promoted the visual arts, especially painting, and over the next decade it would conduct a subterranean, rarely public warfare with the Royal Academy over the relation of contemporary British painters to the European Old Masters. This was fundamentally a struggle for dominance in the belatedly emerging British art field, as I shall investigate further in Chapter 4, and thus my including it among the London "lecturing" institutions mainly known for their scientific projects will require a further justification. Such a rationale will depend partly on the meanings of "institution" I have elaborated in Chapter 1, and partly on the pivotal place that administration was now coming to possess for altering the modern relation and meaning of "arts and sciences" as such.

The British Institution has been strategically important for social historians trying to explain the great "patrician renaissance" that Linda Colley has argued dominated British culture in the late eighteenth and early nineteenth centuries. She cites the way Viscounts, Marquesses, and other aristocratic notables controlled the show at the British Institution by lending priceless Old Masters – Flemish, Italian, and French oil paintings in the main – for public display. Such actions by wealthy collectors would, Colley argues, serve to make the implicit but unmistakable point that "aristocratic property was in some magical and strictly intangible way *the people's property also*" (her emphasis).[68] The British Institution fits this profile in several ways, yet what I have been calling the Institution phenomenon in Romantic-age London makes this case less straightforward. Among major lenders of Old Masters to the British Institution, and one of its key administrators, was John Julius Angerstein (1732–1823), a leading City merchant, colonialist, underwriter of Lloyd's Insurance, and likewise an earlier co-founder of the merchant-based London Institution in the City.[69] Angerstein had expertise in art history and possessed thirty-eight invaluable Old Masters paintings; as a connoisseur he joined Richard Payne Knight, a Whig MP, the most notorious of England's libertine connoisseurs, as one of nine directors of the British Institution. Unlike the "English School" ambitions of the Royal Academy to promote contemporary national painting, the British Institution aimed more in the long term to integrate English art production with the leading Continental art since the Renaissance. This meant, as John Brewer has shown more broadly, that collectors and connoisseurs would enter into increasingly tense struggles with painters to dominate the British art field.[70] There were no lectures at the British Institution – instead there were *models*, not Rumford's new technologies, but the art collectors' Old Master paintings displayed for any would-be artist to contemplate or copy. By 1809 the British Institution was prominent enough in London to appear vividly this way – a scene of painters imitating art – in Ackermann's *Microcosm* as the art careers of Benjamin Haydon and many others began depending on the British Institution's provenance of European art history.

It is at the administrative level that the British Institution can best be seen as belonging to the new cultural order. For art producers, the Institution's ambition to join English to European visual arts, though valuable to them as painters, came at a steep cost. However else it differed from the Royal, the Surrey, or the London, the British Institution departed *more* decisively from the artist-organized Royal Academy by its key administrative ruling: no artist could play any role in its management whatever. That prohibition effectively turned student-painters into an audience for the British painters or Old Masters they came to glimpse or copy. There were publicly announced rules to govern how much of a given painting a student could copy, limiting the size as well as representation of the priceless paintings the collectors did not want simply duplicated or, worse, forged for the market.[71] As I shall show further in Chapter 4, the

British Institution extended and complicated the British art field by establishing new positions and position-takings that the artist, the public critic, or the connoisseurial art-expert could adopt in the years leading up to the great Elgin Marbles controversy settled by Parliament in 1816. For my purposes now, it's enough to note that as founded by Thomas Bernard as an "Institution," the BI entered a process of reconfiguring the discourse on arts and sciences in a most concrete way, especially by generating increasingly public debates over art-expertise and what kind of knowledge the visual arts might themselves represent.

### Lecturing the "arts and sciences"

I have so far postponed addressing the new Institutions' most famous and public kind of cultural production – the lectures – since I've wanted first to establish their complex social genealogy and to underscore those highly self-conscious modes of organizing, administrating, and audience-seeking that shaped the *way* such lectures would articulate or sometimes confuse the rapidly changing category of "arts and sciences." Lecturing itself had a long, often distinguished, yet extremely variable history across early modern Europe and Britain. But the institutional reconfiguration of public lecturing in Romantic-age England owed more initially to Thomas Bernard than perhaps to any other cultural organizer. He managed the Royal's lecturing programs from 1802 to 1811, often generated their topics, appointed and sometimes fired the lecturers, and modeled what we'd now call in hindsight their multidisciplinary array of knowledges. As Joseph Banks turned away in disgust at the Royal Institution's seeming betrayal of serious scientific knowledge in the direction of arts and "fashionable popularity," the lecturing curriculum framed by Thomas Bernard – a rough prospectus for all other Institutions to follow – could look as shown in Table 1.[72]

It is striking that, for an Institution studied only by historians of science, these early seasons at the Royal Institution offered audiences 159 lectures in the sciences but 182 in what we should now call the fine arts and humanities.[73] We might also be tempted to see certain key affiliations in this list. On the non-scientific side, we should feel inclined to put together English Literature with Poetry and Dramatic Poetry and the lectures on Belles Lettres in a literary category; to put Painting, Engraving, Drawing, Perspective, and Music in another, fine-arts group; and to see Moral Philosophy and History as broadening out the "humanities." But we should then need to see how differently London audiences must have

Table 1 *Royal Institution lecture series in seasons 1805–7*

| Lecturers | Subjects | Number of lectures | |
|---|---|---|---|
| | | 1805–6 | 1806–7 |
| Mr. Davy | Geology and Chemistry | 22 | 28 |
| Mr. Allen | Natural Philosophy | 25 | 32 |
| Rev. W. Crowe | Poetry and Dramatic Poetry | 21 | 24 |
| Rev. T. F. Dibdin | English Literature | 10 | 12 |
| Rev. J. Hewlett | Belles Lettres | 8 | 8 |
| Dr. Crotch | Music | 13 | 25 |
| Rev. E. Foster | History of Commerce | – | 8 |
| Mr. Douglas Guest | State of the Fine Arts in Spain | – | 4 |
| Mr. Wood | Perspective | – | 9 |
| Dr. Shaw | Zoology | 12 | 12 |
| Dr. Smith | Botany | 14 | 14 |
| Mr. Craig | Drawing in Water Colours | 8 | 8 |
| Rev. Sydney Smith | Moral Philosophy | 14 | – |
| Mr. Opie | Painting | 6 | – |
| Mr. Landseer | Engraving | 4 | – |

heard the component parts of such categories. For instance, listening to these "English Literature" lectures at the Royal would have meant, from 1805 to 1807, learning about neither imaginative "literature" as we now conceive of it, nor about the more spacious Enlightenment category of all educated discourse published in print, as it had essentially meant for the past two centuries. Instead these lectures by Thomas Frognall Dibdin gave a far more peculiar history of "literature" that was even quite foreign to the Enlightenment Republic of Letters. His "English Literature" lectures concerned the *books* themselves, not their verbal contents, as objects of knowledge – as historical bibliography and book history, the history of printing and publishing, libraries, and the antiquarian book trade. Thus this lecture series would come far closer in topic and focus to the "mechanical arts" of printing and publishing, as well as to a very bookish, antiquarian's version of the "history of commerce." Nor could his audience yet tell how closely this particular lecturer was already on the way to bringing the subject of English Literature to what would soon emerge, with near-scandalous notoriety, as the Romantic-age Bibliomania.[74]

Meanwhile, "Poetry and Dramatic Poetry" would have still belonged, in Bernard's mind and probably Rev. Hewlett's, more to the category "fine arts" than anything Dibdin could be picturing in the long history and fascinating vicissitudes of the codex. In the lecturing world as elsewhere, the scope of the word *literature* and its relation to poetry, fine arts, and the sciences was becoming increasingly unstable in this moment. Samuel Taylor Coleridge, meanwhile, should have appeared on the lecture list above. In Fall 1806 Bernard tried to persuade him, through entreaties from Humphry Davy, to lecture on "Principles Common to the Fine Arts." This topic would have explicitly joined poetry to painting, sculpture, and music, and would have fulfilled, in Bernard's scale of imagining, a symmetrical pairing of Davy on fundamental questions in sciences and Coleridge on such questions in the arts. Why Coleridge turned this offer down, and then reappeared a year later with a new lecture-series title "Lectures on the Principles of Poetry" to give in the winter of 1808, has been partly explained elsewhere; it's clear that Coleridge himself felt insecure with his possession of the European visual arts and had taken a crash-course in Continental painting and sculpture during his recent travels to Malta and Italy.[75]

Yet there was, I think, a larger issue. Both Coleridge topics would have entailed some form of aesthetics, but it was the meaning of "fine arts" and its relation to "poetry," a relation Coleridge was starting to see more acutely after his philosophical studies in Germany, that would come to matter, as I shall show further in Chapter 6, for what he thought over the next two decades should finally count as "literary" in the Romantic age. It would also be misguided to expect to find in the arts-and-sciences Institutions of this period any final answer to the question many Romanticists now pursue – just when and how did the modern "specialized" category of literature as fictional and imaginative category most clearly emerge in the nineteenth century? But it is important that these Institutions nonetheless were stimulating both administrators and lectures alike to find what was "common" to one domain of knowledge practice and what most differentiated it from others.

The strangeness of Bernard's program was partly that it put seemingly similar topics side by side that hardly seemed compatible outside the Royal Institution. The Royal Academy artist John Opie's lectures on painting would have been grasped in 1806 as verging far closer to poetry, as a fine art, than it would to the topic of John Landseer's lectures on the commercial engraving of painted works. As a newly appointed Professor of Painting at the Academy and ready to prove his expertise across London, Opie gave at the Royal Institution in 1806 what a painter-colleague who heard the lectures grimly called "a spirited attempt to display the depths of his professional knowledge, amidst a circle assembled for entertainment and fashionable delight. His lectures impressed respect on his audience."

Or, to put it less delicately, Opie made a bad show at his lecture series. Discouraged that his non-professional audience had needed to strain so hard to show "respect," he resigned his post after six lectures. The overall verdict was that Opie "was abrupt, crowded, and frequently unmethodical; rather rushing forward himself, than leading his auditors, to the subject."[76] His overweening Academy methods of public argument seemed to prove no match for the London audiences at the new Institutions, who may have been "moderately well-informed," but who also showed they could be demanding, taking no expertise for granted, wanting to be taught but prepared to hiss their dissent (as Hazlitt would learn from his own early rough going when first lecturing at the Surrey).

In the engraving lectures, John Landseer's case was more volatile and complex. London lecturers had become semi-independent contractors: they designed a lecture series in response to an administrator's invitation, yet from that point forward their fate lay in the hands of the Institution, as both Coleridge and Landseer would find to their dismay at the Royal Institution from 1806 to 1808. Subject to rules that no independent print author could have abided, Institution lecturers were forbidden to engage in political debate, make judgments of living persons, or articulate any explicit religious view. Coleridge ran afoul of these rules by showcasing educational controversy in his "supernumerary" lecture of May 3, 1808 – interrupting his poetry-lecture plan to take Andrew Bell's side against Joseph Lancaster's in a current, heated debate about educational methods and monitorial schools, thus committing both a political and a "living person" violation at the same time.[77] Coleridge was censured but not expelled.

The art engraver Landseer would be dealt with more severely, fired by Thomas Bernard in 1806 for an offense that lay deeper in the prehistory of the new Institutions themselves. While a Royal Academy painter was both authoritative, and – within the norms of Reynolds's neoclassicism – creative, engravers like Landseer, who had worked mainly in London's commercial "literary" galleries, were imitators of paintings that in their turn imitated (or represented) literary works. The Shakespeare and Milton galleries of 1790–1805 had been the leading commercial London galleries for promoting both the "sister arts" philosophy of closely related expressive forms and the commercial relation between art and its public that John Boydell had done most to advance until the catastrophic collapse of the literary galleries by 1804–5.[78] At the Royal Institution, Bernard expected Landseer to give the audience an inside, appreciative glimpse of the commercial art-engraving world in which he had toiled for the past twelve years. Thus RI managers were taken aback when Landseer – still hoping like his fellow engraver William Blake for entry to a Royal Academy that excluded him – used his lecture series of 1805 to launch an attack on Boydell's reputation and with it the whole sphere of commercial art production in England. He also used this lecture to claim for engraving, as Thora Brylowe has astutely shown, the status of a "fine art" instead of a commercial or artisan product.[79] This case suggests a pattern at the Royal Institution that there may be little evidence for generalizing across the lecturing-Institution world, but it is noteworthy in itself. For Bernard the arranging of lectures was not a casual matter, but rather put together practices and knowledges that could seem to be equalized – or, to put it in our own terms, could seem to be "multidisciplinary" – as they appeared on the program, yet were expected to be quite the opposite in lecturing practice. At least we cannot say that the Royal Institution was, as the lecturing agenda might first appear, actually leveling hierarchies of expertise and craft, fine art and practical arts in the London public world. The 1805 episodes instead suggest it was often putting such topics together precisely to widen the conceptual distance between them. This was the line over which Landseer had so egregiously stepped.

After this fourth, obstreperous lecture performance, Landseer was fired, and he soon made no one doubt that it was Thomas Bernard who held the hammer at the Royal Institution. In his published *Lectures on the Art of Engraving* (1807), Landseer told the bitter story, combining his rejection of John Boydell's commercial ethos of art with his fury at Bernard. "With the mistakes or malignity of such a man, whether he be the conductor of a publication of Engravings, or *the director* of a public institution, may no artist or man of science in the conscientious pursuit of his duty come into collision" (emphasis in original).[80] Landseer's scathing criticism of Institution administrators went further than most – going in fact to the heart of the matter:

> if a man knowing nothing, or knowing little, of Science or Art, were to undertake to engage or manage Lecturers on the Arts and Sciences – unable to exercise any judgment of his own, he must depend on the opinions of others (the value of whose opinions he could not estimate); and the same personal recommendation which *might* introduce a man of science to his notice, would be much more likely to introduce a pliant parasite, or a blockhead of bold pretensions ... Not being able to measure the value of a discourse by any better, or by any other, test, than the *number* of auditors it may obtain, he will assuredly, and for very obvious reasons, fail *as far as depends on him*, to "convert the frivolous part of the metropolis" into any thing better; and – but there is no end to the mischiefs of ignorant superintendence [emphases in original].[81]

As we know from the history of Renaissance patronage, the problem of arts administration did not begin in the nineteenth century, but it was surely now beginning to be experienced in a new way.[82] The "ignorant superintendence" Landseer cites at the Royal Institution would develop over the next two centuries as a recurring, widely felt, and seemingly intractable contradiction in the cultural shaping of the arts and sciences themselves. "No half-way sensitive person," Adorno remarked, "can overcome the discomfort conditioned by his consciousness of a culture which is indeed administrated."[83] Landseer was unforgiving as well as sensitive. Lecturers in London found themselves subject to an administrative stratum with no visible controls except the larger cultural market itself. Landseer used the principles of the Republic of Letters – everyone, as Pierre Bayle once put it, must be subject to criticism from everyone else – to make his point: "Are not poets, painters, statuaries, architects, musicians, managers of theatres, players – in short, authors and artists of every description, subject to perpetual comment – in conversation, in newspapers, in reviews, and various other ways? Are managers of institutions, or even the highest servants of the crown, exempt from critical animadversion?"[84] That sort of question was already on the minds of many British artists who were confronting another administrative policy enforced by Bernard at the British Institution for Promoting the Fine Arts.

The case of Sydney Smith's "moral philosophy" lectures has a special role in this history. In 1804 Smith was the first invited lecturer to take the Royal Institution decisively beyond its original focus on chemistry and physics into realms we should now call "humanities" as well as "arts." Those lectures unexpectedly became an overnight sensation on a scale that could only compare to Humphry Davy's acclaim: "Galleries had to be erected for the accommodation of the crowd of fashion and talent which thronged to hear him," the *Quarterly Review* later reported, estimating his audience at 600 to 800 listeners each night.[85] Smith's embarrassed reaction at his sudden London fame had something to do with his intellectual standing among the Edinburgh lawyers and professionals with whom Smith had co-founded, three years earlier, the *Edinburgh Review*. "My lectures are just now at such an absurd pitch of celebrity," Smith confided to Francis Jeffrey in April 1805, "that I must lose a good deal of reputation before the public settles into a just equilibrium respecting them. I am most heartily ashamed of my own fame."[86]

There was more than candor entailed here. The Romantic period's most familiar media landmark, the founding of the *Edinburgh Review* in 1802, happened to coincide with the public emergence of Humphry Davy as the Royal Institution's rising-star chemist and lecturer; in January of that year Davy delivered his stunning inaugural address to introduce lectures on chemistry, but also to place his ambitions within the wider framework of the "arts and sciences" as a whole. This was the lecture Wordsworth heard or read about, we now recognize, just before he wrote a crucial new addendum to "Preface to *Lyrical Ballads*" concerning the deeply uneasy relationship between the poet and the "man of science." (Had he waited longer to see Davy thronged by huge audiences and media acclaim, Wordsworth might have been less able to write about the "isolated" work of the scientific investigator in his comparison.) The *Edinburgh Review* founders, meanwhile, may have seen a rival in – and certainly could glimpse the emerging powers of – the new institutional lecturing scene blossoming in London. This is partly why the *Review*, though supremely confident of what Henry Cockburn would call its own "electrical" impact on the British Republic of Letters, would become first repelled, then deeply involved in the London arts-and-sciences lecturing phenomenon.[87] Of its four co-founders (Henry Brougham, Francis Jeffrey, Francis Horner, and Sydney Smith), only Francis Jeffrey abstained. On reflection it is not hard to see why the *Edinburgh Review* would be unable to stay distant from the London events, since its emerging critical authority was based on assessing nearly all the knowledge fields that were now finding a new public means of communication in London: geology, botany, physics, chemistry, moral philosophy, economics, and poetry.

The *Edinburgh Review*'s approach began with aggression and ended with absorption. In 1803 Henry Brougham first turned critical fire on the Royal's physics professor Thomas Young, who had just published in *Philosophical Transactions* a theory of "light waves" disputing Newton's conception of light as corpuscular particles. Brougham's review accused Young of denaturing Newton's physics and the Royal Institution of using Young's supposed faulty physics to cheapen the name of natural philosophy that the Royal Society had long dignified (a review which does not explain why the Royal Society would have chosen to publish it).[88] Yet only four years later, when Davy had become an international scientific success, Brougham wrote again, this time to exempt England's most authoritative new man of science from his aristocratic (as Brougham thought) institutional context. Davy's "political sentiments are as free and manly," Brougham now maintained, "as if he had never inhaled the atmosphere of the Royal Institution."[89] Clearly Brougham was not remembering Davy's sensational introductory lecture of January 1802 when Davy vigorously endorsed his Institution's premise of social inequality as the necessary foundation of knowledge. "The unequal division of property and of labour," Davy told his applauding audience, and "the difference of rank and condition among mankind, are the sources of power in civilized life."[90] In 1804 Sydney Smith contradicted Brougham's own posture by going to Albemarle Street to deliver his moral philosophy lectures to unforeseen levels of popular success. But the most telling sign of the *Edinburgh Review*'s sustained preoccupation with the new London scene was Francis Horner's decision to co-found the Russell Literary and Scientific Institution at Great Coram Street in 1808. By this time the *Edinburgh Review* had to recognize that the new London arts-and-sciences Institution world was enacting a much-changed form of public Enlightenment, and the avatars of the Scottish Enlightenment could not afford to remain, as Francis Bacon liked to say, "lookers-on."

## Transmuting enlightenment

At the center of excitement stood the Royal Institution's most charismatic figure. Humphry Davy had been hired by Count Rumford in 1801 from Thomas Beddoes's now disreputable provincial Pneumatic Institute. Once Rumford had left the Royal Institution (in 1802), it was Bernard who chiefly used the bright and malleable Davy to begin refashioning the Institution's public outreach by recognizing the potential of Davy's remarkable rhetorical powers and personal attractions. His sensual appeal to the women in his audience could, as Jan Golinski shows, cut both ways; his flashy green velvet coat and extravagant rhetorical manner helped conservative detractors brand him as an effeminate dandy, while his masculinity seemed compromised in another sense to the radical reformers who remembered he had once been of their party before turning to London for aggressive social climbing among the elite.[91] His lower-class Cornish origins made him unacceptable to the intimate society of his own aristocratic backers as well. But the dissonance between Davy's social habitus of origin and his high-flying professional role in a new metropolitan world of ambition and distinction may have helped stimulate him to produce that soaring rhetoric of science that singled him out among virtually all London lecturers.[92]

What Davy all too willingly relinquished – Golinski calls it Joseph Priestley's "democratic epistemology" and his "vision of the moral order of public science" – allowed him to align his researches with aristocratic sponsors and to make their social view of the world part of his own scientific vision.[93] It was also Priestley's late eighteenth-century way of mediating his ideas to others, across networks of sociable acquaintances and through wide-scale publication quite apart from the organs of the Royal Society, that most separated such "natural philosophy" from what Davy would now frequently call "science" in the newer sense of the experimental study of nature. This all-too-public profession of class privilege as a basis for modern knowledge production can make Davy appear to be, for historians like Morris Berman, virtually dangling by his aristocratic handlers' puppet-strings, thus making his own developing claims to scientific accomplishment seem suspect if not somewhat fraudulent.[94] Yet this was not the picture of Davy that even his sternest radical critics of the Romantic age, such as Richard Carlile in the polemical *Address to Men of Science* (1821) or Thomas Hodgskin's blasts at Davy in the *Chemist* (1824), would see by the height of his fame and scientific reputation. On the contrary, radical critics of the 1820s took Davy to be a scientific "revolutionary" who had eclipsed the age of Joseph Priestley by the very force and persuasiveness of his chemical authority. To Carlile it was only *because* Davy had won legitimate scientific authority in England that his perfidious "royal science" and dedication to landed property or priestcraft were all the more to be publicly criticized as a betrayal of scientific truth's universalizing claims.[95]

Golinski's landmark study of scientific chemistry's disciplinary formation at the turn of the nineteenth century offers the most incisive picture to date of what it meant for Davy and the Royal Institution to mobilize their non-specialist and mixed-gender audience as a new ally and mediator of knowledge production and of Davy's own growing disciplinary command from 1802 to 1820, when he succeeded Joseph Banks as President of the Royal Society. Golinski shows persuasively why, as Davy adapted opportunely to the new hierarchical conditions of London's "public science," he would find at the Royal Institution two crucial allies for gaining disciplinary authority across not only Britain but the Continent as well. If one was the new public audience he often wooed and impressed, the other, likewise critical ally was the great instrument that could combine Volta's superb instrument, the battery or Voltaic pile.[96] Such resources – the audience, the instrument, and the gentlemanly network, all mediated by the administrative prowess of Thomas Bernard – had been unknown to Priestley, who often pleaded for the wealthy to support scientific experiment and rarely got an answer.

These discipline-shaping powers also made Davy's lectern an instrument with which he could address the wider modern discourse on the "arts and sciences." The January 21, 1802 lecture was eye-popping in its sheer scope of reference. It would argue for the dependence of all other sciences and technical or mechanical arts upon either the theory chemistry provided or the tools and skills it made possible. Davy would also make a move of uncommon boldness. Though many have written about the way he achieved "sublime" effects in the lecture room, stunning his audience into assent, it would be more clarifying to see not only the deliberateness of his rhetoric, but also the *kind* of rhetoric he used to draw together such a willing public. That rhetoric remains visible on the printed pages from his lectures; it is, I think, what rhetoricians would call "epideictic" rather than deliberative rhetoric that evoked a sense of high purpose and shared national spirit as much as any particular chemical argument. It was especially in the inaugural speech to a lecture series when Davy seized the moment to deploy an epideictic rhetoric of ceremony, the language for occasions of great praise or blame (for Davy, celebrations of scientific modern knowledge). Above all it was an opportunity to call forth what unites the community of listeners in a greater whole, even to reveal to the audience those "otherwise unexpressed virtues" they might now feel they recognize themselves *always* to have had. If epideictic rhetoric classically entails occasions for blame or praise, it could be especially powerful for enunciating "a *mutual* sense of the praiseworthy."[97] This mode of rhetorical address is difficult to imagine Joseph Priestley having often used, since epideictic rhetoric presumes an audience of spectators rather than a group of participants. This community-constructing dimension of Davy's lectures would prove a signal contribution to how Romantic-age listeners and readers would increasingly think about not only "science," always Davy's first professed objective, but also about the "arts and sciences" as a whole. If Wordsworth's 1802 additions to the "Preface" on poetry and science were indeed a response to this first lecture, it may help explain why Wordsworth went to such lengths to depict the man of science as a lonely, unsociable investigator tilling slow fields of inquiry with only a chance of discovery – and no chance of summoning "the finer breath and spirit of all knowledge."[98] At the Royal Institution Davy was actively summoning some sort of collective spirit, though perhaps hardly "fine" in the way a poet like Wordsworth could hope to excel.

The greater whole of "arts and sciences" seemed to demand of Davy, or so he decided, a constant epideictic, ceremonial, galvanizing restatement of how his own science fitted that whole of knowledge at the start of a lecture series, no matter how detailed or empirical the ensuing ten or twenty lectures could become. Since confidence for this vision was grounded for Davy in landed and mercantile property, it was not a huge further leap to say that "we can only expect that *the great whole of society* should *ultimately* be connected together by means of knowledge and the useful arts."[99] This vision of a whole also summons a potential future arising out of the unexpected and immanent, not the immediately visible or the science experiment of the evening, but what the present scientific matter portends once it is framed in this epideictic way: the ultimate *coherence* of arts and sciences that could be figured forth even in the present uncertain moment. In this calculus, the "fine arts," including poetry, are politely left to the side, yet Wordsworth was not wrong to detect a distinct aggression in this vision of an immanent whole, particularly when Davy invited to his table the poet and the humanist – "persons of powerful minds, who are connected with society by literary, political, or moral arrangements" – only to demand they use a "language representing simple facts," the better to "destroy the influence of terms connected only with feeling."[100] The aggression Wordsworth must have perceived in this lecture was not only that Davy was using his wealthy public audience to turn "science" on a path that could only leave "poetry," in Davy's "ultimate" future, fairly speechless. It may also have been the realization that Davy could now use a powerfully articulated arts-and-sciences Institution platform to tilt and wield the *whole* modern discourse of "arts and sciences" further away from poetry as a mode of human knowledge. Davy had sounded the classic Enlightenment themes of this discourse – civilization v. barbarism, mental v. manual labor, and the rest – but, more important, he now stood in a place fitted to authorize a dramatic public impact by wielding that discourse in this particular way. It may only be surprising that Wordsworth's reply in the "man of science" section of the "Preface" was so relatively muted in responding to Davy's assertions that many readers still now read Wordsworth as largely celebrating their walking hand in hand.

Had Wordsworth or other readers missed the point, they would find it more distilled in Davy's 1807 short essay "Parallels between Science and Art," written for Bernard's new journal of arts and sciences, the *Director*. Here Davy mounts a more direct if less rhetorically astute case that no matter how we rank the fine arts – painting by its immediacy of sensation and emotion, poetry by its combined visual and intellectual powers – the "system of the arts" can be both compared to the sciences and found coming up crucially short. Readers of this brief essay may feel it does little more than rehearse the old "system of the arts" argument in which poetry, painting, sculpture, and music are weighed for their merits and faults – and that is indeed key to the new point Davy makes in 1807. Poetry can be more verbal and philosophical, painting more visually and affectively powerful, music more ethereal, sculpture more tangible, yet in the calculus of "fine arts" it is impossible to rank them with certainty. But while science can be likened to the fine arts in a rough way – science also draws on imagination, "rapidity of combination, a power of perceiving analogies" in its process of "discovery" – there is one crucial superiority. "The pleasure derived from great philosophical discoveries ... is more durable and less connected with fashion or caprice. Canvass and wood, and even stone, will decay. The work of a great artist loses all its spirit in the copy. Words are mutable and fleeting; and the genius of poetry is often dissipated in translation." Nearly all such fears about the material mediation required for the fine arts had been voiced before in poetic tradition and aesthetic reflection – but not in the new "arts and sciences" Institutions by a now-powerful chemical speaker. "Nature cannot decay: the language of her interpreters will be the same in all times. It will be a universal tongue, speaking to all countries, and all ages."[101] As published by the *Director* in 1807, this version of Davy's case for the sciences could unite a firm grip on his London audience and the power of his Voltaic battery with the force of Bernard's arts-and-sciences administration now appearing assertively in the medium of print.

I want to conclude by pointing to where the "mechanical arts" were now fitting into Davy's picture, since much of his reputation would depend on being seen as a genius of "applied science." The 1807 essay provides an almost startling refutation of this way of seeing him. We should recall that, widely credited for inventing the miner's safety lamp in 1816, Davy refused to patent it in the name of a scientific dedication free of commerce. "Parallels between Science and Art" shows him having much larger missions on his mind, and here the "mechanical arts" themselves have a much-altered relationship to the "arts and sciences" as a whole than anything we should guess from reading an eighteenth-century encyclopedia. Using the steam engine, and doubtless thinking of its past role in changing the direction of the Royal Institution itself, Davy redefined the place of the "mechanical arts" and the technology that the Royal would never be showing its public:

> The mechanical arts delight us only indirectly, and by indistinct associations; the fine arts either directly, or by immediate associations. The steam engine may be an object of wonder, as connected with the power by which it was produced, and the power which it exerts; but to understand its beneficial effects requires extensive knowledge, or a long detail of facts. Mechanism in general is too complicated to produce any general effect of pleasure. Inventions are admired by the multitude, more on account of

their novelty or strangeness, than on account of their use or ingenuity. The watch which is the guide of our time, is employed and considered with indifference: but we pay half a crown to see a self-moving spider of steel.[102]

Appearing in the middle of the essay, this passage shows why "science" can now be better grasped in terms of the fine arts – even if they gain a signal advantage over them – than it can be understood, in the encyclopedic tradition, as intimate with the mechanical arts. It was the publicly inexplicable steam engine that helped Davy mark the new "parallel between science and art" as a relation between relatively accessible knowledges ranging from chemistry and electricity to poetry and painting, a world from which the newest mechanical technology was now seceding from public apprehension. Coming from Humphry Davy, it was also a theoretic principle: even if the sciences can be usefully applied, a realm of mystery had entered the equation formerly understood as "arts and sciences." The Watt/Boulton defense of intellectual property rights, one might say, would eventually figure into new definitions for what the "arts and sciences" were coming to mean as articulated in the English metropolitan world.

CHAPTER 3

# *Wild bibliography: the rise and fall of book history in the nineteenth century*

> I meant to have written you an Essay on the Metaphysics of Typography.
> 
> Samuel Taylor Coleridge to Joseph Cottle (1798)

One of the least expected fields of inquiry to emerge among the London arts-and-sciences Institutions began calling itself the "history of books." Such bibliographical book history was not the same history of print that we associate today with the work of Robert Darnton, Elizabeth Eisenstein, or Roger Chartier, which is of much more recent origin and which remains, to judge by a special issue of *PMLA*, not fully at ease with what its editors call "the idea of literature" or literary history.[1] Advocates of a new bibliographical field in the early nineteenth century believed book history *was* literary history, and they construed that history as a wide array of codex histories – those of writing, printing, typography, bookmaking and binding, the formation of private libraries and public archives, as well as nearly all categories of modern knowledges and imaginative works. From 1797, when the word *bibliographia* first appeared in a British encyclopedia of arts and sciences, to 1814, when Thomas Hartwell Horne published the two-volume *Introduction to the Study of Bibliography*, such efforts amounted to a then-unprecedented effort to reveal to British readers what Jerome McGann, with reference to the digital, has called the "bibliographical codes" of the printed word.[2] Thomas Frognall Dibdin, who would become the most publicly visible (and then notorious) among the new bibliographers, was so confident of this kind of bibliographical history-writing that he told his readers, "The History of Books is the history of human knowledge."[3] Despite their familiar sound now, those were new words for British readers to contemplate in the first decade of the nineteenth century.

Few would doubt that the practices of bibliography have been somehow critical to establishing the modern domain and authority of the category "arts and sciences" – but just *how* and *when* is less easy to say. The Romantic age "dreamed in books," in Andrew Piper's suggestive phrase, yet for Britain the bibliographical moment arrived much later than on the Continent, where bibliographical writers had been compiling and even theorizing about organizing and grasping the modernity of books since at least Gabriel Naude's mapping of a book collector's library in *Bibliographica Politica* in 1633.[4] "One would go much further in the arts and sciences," the French bibliographer Adrien Baillet said forty years later, "if one had sure knowledge of the books which must be read and of those which should be omitted."[5] On the whole Europe's early modern book collectors had an incalculable impact on the long-term formation of the very archives upon which we now so heavily depend to reconstruct and grasp "modernity" itself; between 1600 and 1800, "the private collector," David McKitterick remarks, "was supporting scholarship at its very foundations."[6] Yet the earliest bibliographies on the Continent had been faltering, discontinuous efforts to account for these private collections, and there would be no clarifying coordination between the various national centers of bibliographic labor. Eighteenth-century encyclopedias using the phrase "arts and sciences" remained oblivious to such projects, and from what we know of the antiquarian rare book auctions in London beginning in 1677, the bookish collectors kept aloof from an emerging commercial Republic of Letters that valued urbanity and sociability over pedantic obsessions.

So I want to make sense of the fact that after 1800, the London arts-and-sciences Institutions would work hard to stimulate bibliographical writing, build large urban libraries with special provision for rare early modern books, proliferate "reading rooms" across the metropolis, and put a high premium on hiring the most knowledgeable bibliographers and librarians to steer their investments in the book and the archive. It was in the early stages of England's "second scientific revolution" that the new field of bibliography found itself increasingly in demand, and I shall argue in this chapter that the *ordering* of the modern print archive accumulating since the sixteenth century had something important to do with a long-standing but unfulfilled hope to construct a scientific print culture in England, more than a century after the Royal Society itself had repeatedly tried and failed to attain one.

I also want to show how this emerging bibliographical or bookish field of knowledge was soon to become entwined with, and sometimes indistinguishable from, bibliography's garish twin, the notorious and volatile Bibliomania of the Romantic age. Bibliography's offer of new material and intellectual knowledge became so hotly contested, in fact, that its leading advocate Dibdin would have to reassure his readers there was nothing in the new bibliographical field that would "offend the grave, disgust the wise, or shock the good."[7] There were, in fact, some bibliographical shockers in store for those who picked up the latest news about the new attention to books as material forms, and there was enough offense or disgust – along with more calculated efforts to diminish its impact – to eventually ruin Dibdin's own reputation by the mid 1820s, and to discredit the book-history enterprise itself by the end of the nineteenth century. Recollection of this episode had so largely disappeared from literary and cultural history by the 1950s that today's historiography of print, books, and reading would essentially have to be built all over again.

Long considered a somewhat clownish sideshow to British literary history, the early nineteenth-century Bibliomania had its memorable landmark at the raucous 1812 Roxburghe antiquarian book auction where swaggering aristocratic book-warriors outbid each other in a rising crescendo of bibliographic violence until, at last, one bidder topped all others by paying £2,260 sterling for the 1471 Valdarfar edition of Boccaccio's *Tales*. This speculative bubble in the antiquarian book trade eventually subsided by the 1820s, and by 1832 Dibdin would be writing the sequel to his famous books on *Bibliomania* that now had to be titled *The Bibliophobia*. Recent critical attention to this moment has helped put it back on an intelligible map for cultural history. Following Linda Colley's account of the "patrician renaissance," Philip Connell grasps the Bibliomania phenomenon in the context of an aristocracy that displays its own property in costly rare books as if they could represent the national wealth. Deidre Lynch finds late-Romantic essayists, particularly Leigh Hunt and Charles Lamb, both mocking and imitating the book fetishists in their intimate essays of personal, bookish *amours* with their own private libraries. Of special relevance to this chapter, Ina Ferris has shown how the Bibliomania enhanced a widening genre of "bibliographical writing" and authorship, from Dibdin to Egerton Brydges and the late nineteenth-century Bibliophile Society, as passion for the old materiality of fine books became a peculiar but persistent way of resisting the trend to an increasingly streamlined and homogenized commercial book production.[8]

My own purpose in this chapter will be rather different. While the new Romantic-age bibliographers were starting to amass a huge if discontinuous database of early modern book knowledge, in service to a wider project of reconfiguring the "arts and sciences," the more extreme and disorderly practices of the bibliomaniacs were effectively raising the larger question of what a "book" really is. Hence I shall want to read them as perhaps the nineteenth century's most unwanted specialists in the instability of the book itself, pursuing insights into codex culture (in their own significantly crazed ways) that today's more disciplined book history has only recently begun to recuperate.[9] Thus, to begin understanding what was at stake in the simultaneous rise of biblio-history and Bibliomania in Britain, I shall raise two kinds of question. Why would an explosion of interest in antiquarian, early modern printed books create such a violent commotion for those living in a modernizing print culture around 1800 that was becoming – to adopt the terms and argument used by Adrian Johns in his important debate with Elizabeth Eisenstein – increasingly stabilized, credible to its public, and trusted as the essential medium of the modern discourses of knowledge?[10] I shall want to keep in mind in what follows that around 1800, at least five key features of the modern book's growing stability or "fixity" had recently come into place: the principle of copyright or intellectual property; the growing authority and professionalizing of authorship; the rise of a lucrative book-trade industry in anthologies and reprints that owed its existence to the 1774 copyright decision; the power of reviewing journals; and the modernizing of the printed page. By these measures, we should expect that the stability or fixity being gradually achieved by print around 1800, a view of book history argued most influentially by Johns, should have been making the bibliographical codes of the book *less* visible then, not more so. That the opposite happened – the simultaneous ordering and disordering of the printed basis of modern knowledges that I shall call "wild bibliography" in the Romantic age – will raise a second, more sociological kind of question. To whom, exactly, did the "biblio" in the broadest sense become a "mania" in the first decades of the nineteenth century? Whose interests were most at stake in the modern history of print, not only commercially but also institutionally? Whose cultural visions were being advanced, and whose put at risk?

### Civilizing, or bibliography and the "arts and sciences"

As a first approach to public controversies about bibliography and the Bibliomania in early nineteenth-century Britain, we should see what it meant for an enormous number of long-sequestered early modern printed books, confined since the fifteenth, sixteenth, and seventeenth centuries to private libraries, to suddenly go public when the French Revolution confiscated the nation's aristocratic and clerical estates. An estimated 12 million volumes of early modern print – confined since the fifteenth, sixteenth, and seventeenth centuries to private libraries – cascaded into a public realm hardly prepared to receive them (for late eighteenth-century France, a staggering number: the contents of four Widener libraries). Throughout the 1790s, the new republican state faced this deluge of print by instituting, all across Paris, government warehouses to domicile the books and courses of public instruction to teach rudimentary and unfamiliar bibliographical methods. Librarians were rapidly professionalized, men of letters were expected to catch up on their knowledge of the material history of printing, and what before had been the specialized province and knowledge of only the keenest booksellers or collectors was being reshaped as a subject any educated print citizen could be expected to know at least something about. By 1802, the French bibliographer Gustave Peignot coined an ambitious word, *bibliologie*, to embrace the scope of this project. For him *bibliologie* meant not merely the listing and classifying of books but also what he called "the *theory* of bibliography, including the totality of human knowledge."[11]

As Peignot's then-unfamiliar expression "theory of bibliography" may suggest, however, a key emphasis on words like *study*, *philosophy*, *theory*, or *science* would differentiate the newer bibliographical attention from the older book catalogues or bibliographical compilations going back to the mid seventeenth century. It also helps distinguish the rare enough English bibliographer before 1800, such as Samuel Paterson, whom the *Monthly Magazine* memorialized as one of those scholars who gave England irreplaceable antiquarian lore, but who wanted (properly, in the *Monthly*'s judgment) nothing to do with the new and obscure-sounding bibliographical theories issuing from Paris. As Paul Keen shows in his study of late eighteenth-century commercial modernity in England, this assessment did little justice to the scope of Paterson's ambition to construct a vast library that would contain a single "system of universal bibliography and literary history,"[12] reminiscent in its own way of Leibniz's most extravagant projects.

Peignot's ambition would be of a quite different order, and it is what stimulated Dibdin and Adam Clarke (1760–1832) to think more speculatively about the problem of "the order of books." Peignot's *bibliologie* projected a second-order level of observing the older first-order practices of bibliographic listing, classifying, or describing. As British readers began hearing much more, in their very different and counterrevolutionary context of 1800, about title pages, editions, publication dates, or lurid tales of violent Bibliomaniacal collecting passions in weekly or monthly magazines,[13] they were also being encouraged to study the bibliographical realm as a mode of public and, despite the old age of the books, of *modern* knowledge. If they opened one of the earliest British bibliographical research studies, such as Adam Clarke's eight-part *Bibliographical Dictionary* (1802–6), they would discover a wide-ranging, cosmopolitan account of over 25,000 books in a reference work of global reach – citing Arabic, Persian, Armenian, and Syrian publications as well as those of European nations and even China.[14] If they reached volumes 7 and 8 of that sprawling work, readers would find more – theories and mappings of modern knowledge that Clarke had mostly translated from French works, but that were decidedly of a bibliographical rather than an encyclopedic type.

Here there was no single Tree of Knowledge, as in the encyclopedic projects from Chambers to Diderot, but a forest of "grand trunks" (knowledge less as a tree than as a stand of Sequoias) that were irreducibly multiple and, in their tangled branchings, strikingly complex. Adam Clarke compared four of these "systems" in 1806, finally preferring the one elaborated in the later eighteenth century by Guillaume de Bure, which largely owed less to Enlightenment encyclopedism than to the researches of the Jesuit-trained Jean Marnier, a scholar, bookseller, and library-maker of the mid seventeenth century. As Clarke updated Marnier's and de Bure's schema, "typography" moved from a mechanical art to one of the "liberal arts," while "literary and bibliographical history" now became a prominent category of historiography and included branches called the "history of the sciences" and the "history of arts" in its wake.[15] My point – to leave out many fascinating details in Clarke's rendering of these earlier bibliographical systems – is that the new bibliographical book history in Britain was proposing a decidedly theoretical turn on the older descriptive or enumerative bibliographies, a turn that was hardly predictable from earlier Enlightenment dictionaries of the arts and sciences.

This new level of bibliographical attention in Britain also explains why it became deeply caught up in the ongoing effort to forge a scientific print culture in Britain. Adam Clarke and William Beloe (author of *Anecdotes of Literature and Scarce Books*) were hired as chief librarians at the Surrey and Russell Institutions, Richard Porson became archivist of the London Institution, and Thomas Dibdin was called upon to play a rather different bibliographical role at the Royal Institution. A "scientific print culture" in Romantic-age Britain would have little to do with the late nineteenth-century rise of specialist scientific journals, which equated disciplinary authority with that particular form of (now inordinately expensive) print publication.[16] Since the new bibliographies in Britain, like older ones on the Continent, assumed "literature" to mean the whole of published knowledge, the libraries and bibliographical projects launched after 1800 in London had quite a different objective than deepening specialization in this or that disciplinary domain. Nonetheless, they were hoping to give Britain an "*order* of books," in Chartier's resonant phrase, that England had rarely been able to contemplate in the past.

To understand why such English bibliographical writers or experts would be sought out by the new arts-and-sciences Institutions after 1800, which built libraries as conspicuous and well publicized as their lecture halls, we need to recall the state of English natural philosophy's relation to the history of print since the 1660s. The Royal Society had repeatedly tried and failed to build an internationally recognized library to demonstrate England's scientific leadership by showing natural philosophy's place in the entire printed archive of modernity. This long-sought aim would be partially answered by the founding collections of the British Museum in 1753, seeded by the natural history collections of Sir Hans Sloane and then impressively upgraded by the King's contribution of his own private library.[17] Yet as its critics were still complaining nearly a century later, the British Library remained chaotic, a jumble of book and natural-history collections jostling for space, nowhere near as demarcated as in the great Continental libraries and museums, according to Charles Lyell in his wide-ranging essay on "Scientific Institutions" in the *Quarterly Review* for 1826.[18]

This history of uncertainty and frustration about the relation of early modern sciences to archives of printed books helps explain why, when the Royal Institution turned from the Rumford plan to educate London artisans and mechanics toward the very different agenda of lecturing to an educated, upper-middle-class public audience, the Royal Society's President Joseph Banks worked (however uneasily) with Thomas Bernard and other Institution managers to establish a commanding library. That library would soon materialize at the death of Thomas Astle, England's most recent and influential historian of writing and print, whose 1783 book *The Origins and Progress of Writing* had included a narrative of the printing revolution and its apparent foundation for the rise of the sciences and the dissemination of modern knowledges. Unlike the Royal Society, the Royal Institution would start out with a firm archival grounding in print culture by incorporating Astle's 30,000-volume library; meanwhile, Astle's *Origins* was enlarged and republished in 1803 partly to dramatize the power of the new library and the vision of printing and knowledge that its author had bequeathed to the Royal Institution. Hence three of the Royal's most important public productions over the next two decades would be the print catalogues of its library featuring the 30, then 40, then 50,000 volumes as its original Astle collection expanded. It is important to note in these catalogues that the number of its "scientific" books was not noticeably larger than the categories of history, classics, moral philosophy, or fine arts. Moreover, these catalogues depict the newly reshaped category of bibliography standing prominently among the major forms of emerging knowledge.[19] The aim of such a library was not specialist, that is, but a comprehensive library demonstrating the Royal's interest in *all* domains of knowledge, including poetry, mythology, and philosophy, yet also demonstrating the decisive place of the sciences at the center of the knowledge-reading world.

There was another, more social aim of such libraries. Since the arts-and-sciences Institutions were attracting notably large numbers of women to lectures in the early 1800s, the libraries began to be conceived as ingenious correctives to what Thomas Dibdin called "the irremediable mischief" of the circulating libraries and their well-publicized, notorious temptations for young women readers.[20] The Royal's largest of all Institution libraries appears resplendently in Ackermann's *Microcosm of London*, the only surviving image of these Institution libraries to my knowledge, but there is no evidence here that London women were switching from the excitement of novels from circulating libraries to the higher pleasure and instruction of the arts-and-sciences libraries. In Thomas Rowlandson's color plate, twenty-one men browse, read, or converse without a woman in sight.

This much-publicized library gave so strong a lift to the Royal Institution's profile as an intellectual center that Bernard began searching for a lecturer who might best capitalize on the display of a printing historian's richly stocked archive. The choice was Thomas Frognall Dibdin (1776–1847), who had just published a well-received book on Greek and Roman antiquities, and who lectured at the Royal to explain to London audiences "The Art of Printing," a ten-lecture series, and then, more ambitiously and bibliographically driven, the 22-lecture series from 1805–7 Dibdin called "English Literature." Set alongside star performers like Davy and Sydney Smith, the Dibdin lectures aimed to link the early modern nation's production of books and the impressive powers of the new London scientific world now reaching out to public acclaim. Nevertheless, his lectures had to be strange. To judge by what little survives of them, these antiquarian public performances must have been the most non-narrative talks about literary history ever given. With little attention to authors, periods, or phases of national development, Dibdin focused his roughly

500 listeners every week on a lengthy chronology of rare or unique editions, publication dates, hot-blooded book auctions, or reasons why they should not fear the book collector's mania for the "black-letter."[21] Just before beginning his own lectures at the Royal Institution in early 1808, Samuel Taylor Coleridge attended the last of Dibdin's. No two versions of English literary history could have been less alike. Coleridge would fashion his own lectures, sometimes reportedly with sublime effect, on the power and originality of the poets who gave English literature the voice of a dawning national spirit.[22] There could have been little feeling of transport in Dibdin's antiquarian literary history, which depicted modern authors as indentured to previous books and writers, collectors as the shapers of a national literary heritage, and English books as rarities in the vast universe of time, as densely material as planets in a Copernican sky.

Hence did the arrival of bibliographical self-consciousness on British shores contribute to shaping what the arts-and-sciences Institutions meant to a burgeoning scientific print culture, and, considering the sciences' own powers to redefine the scope of the "arts" in these decades, to the way in which a wider transformation of the "arts and sciences" in modernity were to be grasped as well. The unlikely courtship of the modernizing sciences with antiquarian biblio-history was to prove volatile in the long run, but in the short term it could be immensely productive. Besides lecturing and teaching, the new scientific and arts institutions generated their own formats of print to herald the changes underway. To link the scientifically focused Royal Institution with the British Institution for Promoting the Fine Arts, for a key instance, Dibdin and his patron Thomas Bernard launched the journal the *Director* in 1807, where Dibdin made his first and possibly most ambitious case for the new field of bibliographical history. Dibdin's weekly articles titled "Bibliographiana" made his arguments for bibliography's promise while pushing against the more extreme practices of the British antiquarian book collectors, urging them to transform their private pursuit of book wealth into a national public good – and thus drafting much of what would appear in 1809 as the first and briefest edition of *The Bibliomania; or Book-Madness*. That early version of his argument was straightforward, even earnest, by contrast to the fanciful, baroque dialogues among aristocratic collectors featured in the enlarged 1811 rewriting of the book (with the subtitle "A Bibliographical Romance") that would bewilder, amuse, or irritate countless readers in five different editions through 1903.

Later on, after Dibdin had became famous, notorious, and then dead broke from his involvement in the Bibliomania controversy, he would credit this moment in 1807 for germinating a career that would turn out to be as contradictory a vocation as any in the Romantic age: the bibliographical author. Dibdin was not the first bibliographer in England, coming as he did after Joseph Ames and Samuel Paterson. But as Ina Ferris has written about these bibliographers as authors, Dibdin did the most to make bibliographical *writing* a rising print genre in the early 1800s.[23] Though Egerton Brydges, Clarke, Beloe, and others wrote in this new genre, Dibdin became the most flamboyant, and, as anyone who reads his bookish counterpart to *Biographia Literaria* in 1817 – Dibdin's massively expensive and intricate *Bibliographical Decameron* (1817) – can tell, the most baroque of these authors. As with the floridly styled "Romance" version of the 1811 edition of *The Bibliomania*, Dibdin's increasingly self-referential prose would also become a tempting target for the English and especially the Tory reviewing establishment.

The disappearance of collector culture from twentieth-century bibliography has obscured the tensions in Dibdin's *Bibliomania* writings between the collector's private acquisitive obsessions and the effort to make book history a pivotal field among the "arts and sciences." "It is much to be wished," he wrote in the 1811 edition of *The Bibliomania*, that

> whatever may be the whims of desperate book-collectors ... we had a more clear and satisfactory account of the rise and progress of the arts and sciences ... Over what a dark and troublesome ocean must we sail, before we get even a glimpse at the progressive improvement of our ancestors in civilized life. Oh, that some judicious and faithful reporter had lived three hundred and odd years ago! – we might then have had a more satisfactory account of the *origin of printing with metal types*. (emphasis in original)[24]

This is a rather different Dibdin than the public figure splashed with glitter from the gaudy Roxburghe sale of 1812. It helps explain why he could think his bibliographical book history was on the way to becoming a pivotal field of study within the broader restructuring of scientific, literary, and fine-arts knowledges being accomplished by these new cultural Institutions.[25]

Dibdin's other serious project, from 1807 to 1810, was to re-edit the only undisputed classic of British bibliographical scrutiny before this time, Joseph Ames's four-volume *Typographical Antiquities* (first published in 1749). It was with regard to this large undertaking that Dibdin would claim in the *Director* that

> Typography has given keys to science; and by pointing out where these keys are lodged, we shall be enabled to unlock those treasures of genius and instruction, which for ages have been accumulating, and of which a considerable part has yet escaped the researches of man.[26]

How, any modern reader would be entitled to ask, could typography give "keys to science"? As Adam Clarke had pointed out in 1806, the history and intelligibility of typography were still "amazingly obscure."[27] Dibdin's high-flown promise that it would offer "keys to science" may have signaled an effort to put his own bookish activity into roughly the same discursive and experimental space as Humphry Davy's chemical and electrical breakthroughs at the Royal Institution. But he was not alone in using the term *typography* in a strangely exalted sense around 1800. Several years earlier, Coleridge had used it in an analogous way while writing to urge his publisher, Joseph Cottle, to think more innovatively about the design, format, and typeface of Wordsworth's and Coleridge's forthcoming book, *Lyrical Ballads*. Finding it difficult to persuade Cottle to adopt a very black ink, a streamlined title page, or expensively wide margins, Coleridge remarked, "I meant to have written you an Essay on the Metaphysics of Typography."[28] We still can't tell what Coleridge's never-written essay on typographical metaphysics might have looked like, and the problem partly lies in the way we today define that term. A recent, credible study on typography and interpretation defines it, as almost everyone now does, as "the selection and arrangement of type, and other visual elements on a page."[29] Yet in the late eighteenth and early nineteenth century, it entailed significantly more – beyond the visual look of the page, "typography" extended to the physical form of the book, the history of printing, the accrediting of its invention, its development and dispersion. If type*faces* had some privileged place among those bibliographical codes and histories, it had partly to do with a sensitive reception of printed words and visible letters that modern readers, according to the antiquarian bibliographers, were in danger of losing.

### Barbarism, or the bibliographical shockers

Thus far, I have been pointing to how the various proponents of book history in Britain shortly after 1800 hoped their work would become a new force for the stabilization of British print culture – and the domain of "arts and sciences" it appeared to support – by providing it with a history and a method of organized study. Instead, and it is this turn of events I want now to explore, it provoked a range of controversies that would eventually bring the whole bibliographical field into discredit. To begin with the more bookish side of these struggles over the nature of the book, the riotous Bibliomania, I shall turn to the well-nigh Gothic, visually provocative, and biblioclastic practices of rare-book collectors that both supported and threatened the project of gaining modern knowledge by way of bibliographical book history. There was another side to this controversy as well, less visible to the public eye at most times, yet it would be in some ways more critical to Britain's own history as a Protestant nation whose state religion was a "religion of the book," the same phrase sometimes mockingly pointed at the Bibliomaniacs who could worship at a shelf of fine-leather codices.

### Black-letter reading

According to Thomas Dibdin, the "violent desire for the black-letter" (or Gothic type) elicited more aggression and expense than any other bibliographical feature of the Bibliomania.[30] By far the most highly valued black-letter texts were the incunabula that mimicked the manuscript book in the last half of the fifteenth century. But they had also appeared in popular street literature, the black-letter ballads, and, of course, the 1611 King James Bible. In that Bible's pages, the Holy Spirit spoke in black-letter type, while the Roman typeface of commentaries, cross-referencing, and chapter summaries designated human invention.[31] By 1800, use of Gothic type in Britain had dwindled to decorative status in commercial printing, but the bibliomaniacs were now promoting the hyper-expensive black-letter books and ballads as the *ne plus ultra* of aristocratic print possession. Tory classicists like Thomas James Mathias professed to be repelled by the ugly, repulsive, broken-faced type that now brought back to the public eye some of Britain's most plebeian media of reading (the typeface of balladry and bawdry). Black-letter mania, that is, would confuse what the mainstream commercial print world had been increasingly successful at sorting out, as if the pedants and the peasants, the monks and the pagans, the haunted castle and the popish plot, were animated all at once, now in quantities and at levels of prestige that seemed to mock the achieved hierarchies of the streamlined modern printed page.

There seemed to be a special shudder when the "black-letter mania" at rare-book auctions was put alongside a rather different practice called "black-letter *reading*." To read any black-letter printed work in the early nineteenth century already entailed the sheer difficulty of making legible the crabbed letters of this now alien family of types. But the expression "black-letter reading" referred less to that problem of legibility than to a *method* of reading that was also proving to be a viable method of writing literary and cultural history. Put simply, "black-letter reading" referred to searching for an author's distant textual sources, or to what Dibdin called reading deeply into the "slender and subtle materials of others, on which later poets and writers have built up a precarious reputation."[32] As a practice of interpretation, it was a method of plunging the reputedly original modern author back into the dense thicket of print and production from which he had drawn his own materials. In this proto-historicist mode, John Ferriar's *Illustrations of Sterne* (1798) and Francis Douce's *Illustrations of Shakespeare* (1807) took pains to embed the works for which the most radically original claims of authorship were currently being made in the historical matrix – often reaching into literally "black-letter" print in the process – of their textual materials and sources. High-Church Tories, in their wider attack on bibliographic inquiries, lumped this practice with virtually all historical scholarship, from source-criticism to the scholarly editing of nationally important poets. When the *Anti-Jacobin Review* condemned "black-letter reading" in a review of Henry John Todd's new edition of Edmund Spenser, the term would refer to editorial annotation: "to load the pages of our early poets with the various opinion of different critics and commentators, that the original meaning of the author is often buried under the strange, and sometimes absurd conjectures of tasteless, or fanciful annotators." This "pedantry ... tries to discover mystery when none is meant, and to draw personal or political allusions from plain narrative and description."[33] In such works "illustration" is not visual but contextualist, as we should call it now. While Dibdin cautioned his *Bibliomania* readers against the fantastic price-gouging entailed in the "black-letter mania" at the rare-book auctions, it's also clear he admired (as an antiquarian scholar himself) the depth of historicist inquiry entailed by "black-letter reading" while the anti-Jacobin denunciation of bibliography coming from Mathias and William Gifford intensified in the period 1800–25. There was no unified Tory approach to matters of the book.

Though sometimes professing "disgust" at the new bibliographical obsessions, the bibliophile Egerton Brydges enthused over black-letter reading's power to give us "a new delight in the contrast with modern modes of communicating our thoughts" where "forms of phrase which have lost all force from their triteness are relieved by new combinations, and the operations of the mind seem to derive an infusion of vigour from the new light in which they are clothed." Pulling aside the familiar veil of the modern printed page, Brydges adds, the black-letter also affords us an unexpected way to converse with the dead, "opening the grave, and bidding the dead to speak" by "creeping back to converse with our ancestors, in their own idiom."[34] I would accentuate that last phrase. Defamiliarizing the modern book – by way of historicizing its idioms of production, practices, and provenance – Brydges's version of "black-letter reading" perplexed the choice between old and new media that the contemporary print industry was anxious to assert by spurning the new appetite for the "black letter" in any form. Thus it would be tempting to argue that in its black-letter mode, the early nineteenth century's wild bibliography could stimulate some of the most vigorously "close" readings to be seen anywhere in the age.

### Extra-illustration

The other outlandish Bibliomaniac practice was related to the black-letter mania in one key way: it combined collecting with reconstruction, this time not in the mode of deep-historical black-letter reading, but in the workshop of creative destruction that was the collector's own private library. This longest-lasting of all Bibliomaniacal outrages against the modern book – lasting well into the twentieth century, in fact – was a practice of *biblioclasty* that has been known more widely as "extra-illustration." It would take place when a collector tore old books down to their foundations in order to produce a single, one-of-a-kind, massively larger and expensively recomposed extra-illustrated book of grandiose proportions.[35] Practices of extra-illustration have somewhat confusingly been called "Grangerizing," a reference to James Granger's *Biographical History of England* (1769), a work of history that adopted a strikingly bibliographical way of assembling visual images of English history. Granger made, in Luisa Calé's clarifying summation, "a catalogue and taxonomy of all the known English Heads arranged into subject headings under the name of the sitter, class, and period."[36] The practice quickly enlarged beyond head-collecting and came to refer to any enlargement and reassembly of a book by intercalating *visual* materials (most often engravings) whether they were heads, full bodies, buildings, landscapes, or war scenes. Most extra-illustrated editions one can find today were done at the relatively polite scale of adding tens or hundreds of engravings to the original book. But the more extreme cases – with insertions numbering in the tens of thousands – appeared in the nineteenth century to be literally dismantling the codex form itself, hopelessly damaging a great many valuable antiquarian books along the way, when collectors performed extraordinary acts of authorship in their own right. They pillaged thousands of early modern books, tearing them apart to collect visual plates or author's heads, in order to recreate a sometimes gargantuan book of their own making. What resulted were effectively multi-authored, multimedia concoctions, as when a three-volume folio of Lord Clarendon's *History of the Rebellion and Civil Wars in England* (written 1641–60, published 1707), the most authoritative account to date of the English Revolution, could be transformed by extra-illustration into 61 volumes of elephant folio. The new production cost some £10,000 to produce and had uploaded some 19,000 engravings, portraits, or author heads.[37] Posing as a traveler to London, Robert Southey commented in 1807 that "you rarely or never meet an old book here with the author's head in it; all are mutilated by the collectors."[38] The ritual beheading of authors by collectors may have belonged to one of the stranger cults of authorship – no collector snipped off the heads of authors in less valued books without reinstalling them in large numbers to adorn the new one. The migration of authors' heads from codex to codex – like some great guillotine in the library, rolling heads from one pile of old books only to reanimate them in some fantastic new one – also tore loose perhaps the most fundamental mooring of the nineteenth-century book, the principle of authorship itself.

It was Dibdin's *Bibliomania* that first warned in 1809 against the biblioclasts' apparent disregard for any and all orders of knowledge that could be constructed out of a study of old books by recklessly chewing or cutting them up in the manic collector's form of authorship in the private library. We need again to distinguish between the bibliographical project and the instructively, if also destructively, different practices of the Bibliomania in order to see their intimacy and to understand why Dibdin's career was poised so intriguingly and (to his cost) so unstably across the divide between them. Take it one way, and we have new orders of book knowledge which carve out histories and futures for the humanities that situate themselves between the "arts and sciences"; take it another way, and we have the cut-ups of the crazed bibliophiles, who tell a truth unintelligible to the same orders of emerging knowledge.

John Hill Burton, a polite bibliophile unusually sensitive to these possibilities, would call extreme extra-illustrators the "Ishmaelites of collectors" whose bloody work eats away at the codex foundations of civilized history.[39] No version of this practice might impress students of the Romantic period more than the five-volume, large-folio, extra-illustrated edition of Thomas Mathias's *The Pursuits of Literature* (1798) held at the Houghton Library. Page after page of this vitriolic work are here faced with stunningly detailed, full-body engravings of his victims – in one chapter, photograph-quality sitting portraits of Godwin, Paine, Horne Tooke, Mary Robinson, Inchbald, Hannah More, Joanna Baillie, Wollstonecraft, and hundreds of less-known cultural producers who had faced the scorpion's tail of Mathias's discursive rage. The collector-producer of this edition ("W. B." from Bath) may have meant to celebrate Mathias's famous work, but it is hard to read today without the opposite effect – the startling detail and clarity of their engraved expressions staring back, as if in embodied form, to reply to the shrill assassin of their public figures. It was also a perhaps unintentionally brilliant means of refuting Mathias's tireless prosecution of anyone who was putting undue emphasis on the material construction of the modern book.

At a time when the overall stabilization of the printed book had reached its definitive plateau in the century of the steam press and the stereotype plate, the extreme extra-illustrators were running the history of print in reverse. Rather than thousands or millions of identical printed copies issuing from a single plate of type, they ran the tape backward by disrupting many books to fashion one scarcely plausible, unsellable, unportable, certainly unduplicable, but unfailingly spectacular printed book. And they might have met their Ishmaelite deaths by the early twentieth century had not a significant new context given them further power to disturb. Even while deploring their literary mayhem, Holbrook Jackson, writing *The Anatomy of Bibliomania* in 1930, could appreciate what to make of these bibliographical shockers in the age of visual mass culture:

> The extra-illustrator viewed the printed word solely as the raw material for his graphic interpretation ... In this way madness lies, not alone in hectic research and *wild* pursuit of materials, but in the character of the passion which seeks to substitute pictures for thoughts and the written word, in itself a notable relapse into barbarism ... as they who promote picture-theatres and picture-papers well know.[40]

Threats to civilization? This is a rather different role for the nineteenth-century Bibliomaniacs than their better-known reputation as gluttonous aristocrats hoarding costly Moroccan-leather-bound books usually suggests. We might say that the black-letter-readers and the manically productive extra-illustrators reached alternately far behind and far ahead of their own modernizing moment, gleefully exposing the contingent makeup and built-in hierarchies constituting the modern codex form.

### Wild bibliography and the "religion of the book"

In the Romantic age there was no popular opposition to the bibliographer's work, nor did William Cobbett take a rural ride through the antiquarian library. On the contrary, the radical publisher William Hone, following a religious conversion, joined the bibliographical defense of "black-letter reading" in 1823 with his book *Ancient Mysteries Described*.[41] Like Hone's *Mysteries*, black-letter-readers turned their intensive attention not to the old Quarrel between Ancients and Moderns, but rather, in an often emotional way, to the *early* modern and its still-obscure relation to the appearances of modernity at the start of the nineteenth century. This is why it would be inadequate to identify the wild bibliography of the Romantic age with an aristocratic or Burkean conservatism alone.[42] The new battle over books was more often occurring intramurally among Tory conservatives, particularly among Anglican, Methodist, and evangelical versions of what to make of print and print-history in the modern age. In this sense, the bibliographical controversies of the Romantic age may help us grasp some of the deeper divisions within what Colley has termed, perhaps too homogenously, the "patrician renaissance."[43]

One of those divisions requires special emphasis. Bibliographical study in Britain seems to have been intensifying a dispute over what it might mean for Protestantism to be a "religion of the book." Though well regarded for his *Bibliographical Dictionary*, Adam Clarke was far more famous in his time as a "raving Methodist preacher," the controversial author of the imposing eight-volume *Commentary on the Bible*. That lifelong project, Clarke wrote to a friend, "contains a history of the world, and of the church, for upwards of two thousand four hundred years," using its scope and bibliographic detail to criticize orthodox Methodism for sustaining the dogma of the Eternal Sonship of Christ, while deploying considerable knowledge of natural philosophy and book history to press its case.[44] The ensuing theological debate pivoted on the question of whether the Son of God issued from the same substance as God himself or was produced, as it were, from earthly materials ready to the divine Hand. It could also be read in bibliographical terms as an allegory for the problem of authorship. Clarke's *Commentary* gained a small army of subscribing Dissenters even as he denied his writings supported any "sects or parties." Only his considerable scholarly and bibliographical reputation kept Clarke himself from being expelled by Calvinist critics from the Wesleyan Methodist Conference during this heated pamphlet war of the 1810s. Bibliographical history-writing seemed to be pressing too hard on legacies of the old Calvinist and Arminian struggles that helped fuel civil war in seventeenth-century England.

To be sure, Dissenters came in all political stripes, including Tory, and it still remains difficult to situate the finer strands of Dissent among the era's complex political alignments.[45] Bookishness made for some strange affinities: among the many ordained ministers who pursued some form of bibliographical research or compilation in the nineteenth century, Clarke and Dibdin had far more in common than their Dissenting and Anglican commitments might first suggest. Both were animated by evangelical visions of what an emerging modernity should begin to look like. One strong sign of Dibdin's otherwise rarely visible affiliation with Thomas Bernard's evangelical projects is the peculiar "dream vision" that interrupts every version of his Bibliomania books and first appeared while he was collaborating on Bernard's *Director* in 1807. Here is the focal point of that dream:

> [In] all the metropolitan cities of Europe – London, Paris, Vienna, Berlin, and Petersburg ... I seemed to be perfect master of every event going on in them – but particularly of the transactions of *Bodies Corporate*. I saw Presidents in their Chairs, with Secretaries and Treasurers by their sides ... Here, an eloquent Lecturer was declaiming upon the beauty of morality ... there, a scientific Professor was unlocking the hidden treasures of nature ... Again I turned my eyes, and ... viewed the proceedings of two learned sister Societies, distinguished for their labours in *Philosophy* and *Antiquities* ... "These institutions," observed my guide, "form the basis of rational knowledge and are the cause of innumerable comforts; for the *many* are benefited by the researches and experiments of the *few*." (italics in original)[46]

This dream vision of a coming order of the "Arts and Sciences," governed by modern professions and bodies of learning, is remarkable for the way it projects a fundamentally *administrative* view of that world ("perfect master of every event going on in them"), one Dibdin was undoubtedly learning from Bernard as they collaborated in producing the arts-and-sciences journal in which this lengthy text first appeared. The dream-passage goes on to promote an Anglican evangelical program of social reform in the early 1800s – welfare provision, including "Asylums and Institutions for the ignorant and helpless"; the abolition of slavery, long an evangelical project; religious toleration for all sects of Christianity, along with a more frightened vision of the "*eastern* empires" that are "yet ignorant and unsettled." While his later, on-and-off-again ecclesiastical career seems to have moved him much closer to High-Church Anglicans in their dispute with evangelicals by the 1830s, this earlier posture strongly suggests that Dibdin's campaign for a public historical bibliography was grounded in the same religious but essentially modernizing vision of knowledge-diffusion, welfare-provision, anti-slavery campaign, and evangelical politics that descended, in this case, from the Clapham Sect and the labors of Hannah More.[47]

Why did British evangelicalism, in either its Dissenting or Anglican modes, become so deeply invested in the new British concern with book history? The paradox is telling. Anti-institutional in one important sense (by rejecting the absolute authority of the Church in any of its Protestant or Catholic modes), evangelicals were – whether Tory or Dissenting, Anglican or Methodist – powerful and effective institution-builders in another way. By the mid Victorian age it could be hard to tell one kind of Dissenting lineage or evangelical commitment from another as they had smoothly meshed into a wider institutional order, as for instance the Royal Institution and the British Institution for the Promotion of the Fine Arts would meld almost seamlessly into the Royal Society and the National Gallery before 1850.

Meanwhile, what partly separated Adam Clarke from his orthodox Methodist opponent Richard Watson, and Dibdin from the fierce High-Anglican T. J. Mathias, were bibliographical convictions about the complexity and instability of printed texts and lineages of cultural transmission.[48] Watson and Mathias demanded the firm outlines and readerly accessibility of modern print media as means to sustain their doctrinal orthodoxy. The *Anti-Jacobin Review* went further, linking Clarke's public posture as bibliographer at the Dissenting Surrey Institution with notorious Methodist rituals called "love feasts," "band meetings," where "three or four persons, always of the same sex, confess their faults to one another"; or "watch-nights," which produced "at least three acts of adultery on the eve of every new-year's day." By all other reports a mild-mannered bibliographer and cautious scholar, Clarke appears in the *Anti-Jacobin Review* to be "a fiery specimen of true *covenanting piety*" who mounted the stage of the Surrey Institution to steep the brains of a "heathenish assembly of philosophers" in a bewitching brew of old revolutionary poisons.[49] Such attacks were hardly indiscriminate: the *Quarterly Review, Anti-Jacobin Review,* William Gifford (who edited both), Mathias, and others made varied but sustained attacks against the bibliographical as well as bibliomaniacal way with a book throughout the Romantic age. More than accounts of modern nationalism like Colley's would suggest, Britain's counterrevolutionary establishment after 1800 was far from united on matters concerning the nature of the book in relation to haunting legacies from the political, religious, and (English) revolutionary past.

## Undoing Romantic-age book history

In one sense, the part Thomas Frognall Dibdin played in disturbing the nineteenth century's sense of security about the modern printed book cast its shadow over the whole Victorian age. *The Bibliomania, or Book-Madness* was republished four more times after 1811 (in 1842, 1856, 1876, and 1903, each edition more elaborate than the one before it). But as we also know, nineteenth-century British culture would come to normalize Dibdin's 1807 dream vision with its proliferation of societies, institutions, and other organizations devoted to differentiating and specializing the fine arts, humanities, and sciences (including bibliophile societies), even as Dibdin himself became a figure of ridicule, the fool of literary history, after his final drubbing by the *Quarterly Review* in 1825.[50] Early British book history would become a vanishing mediator of modernity's histories of knowledge. Adam Clarke's progressive Methodism would similarly blend into a more orthodox Nonconformist Protestant majority by the High Victorian age, while his volatile bibliographical role in the period disappeared from the maps of intellectual history.[51]

As for the Bibliomaniacs' role in the age of wild bibliography, the blackletter mania subsided after 1825 while furnishing the materials for the more scholarly systematic study of incunabula by Henry Bradshaw, William Blades, and others, an accomplishment that would require a simultaneous forgetting of the "pre-scientific" era of wild bibliography (in the fullest sense, a "historical bibliography" of an especially volatile kind).[52] Disavowing Romantic bibliography's multiplicity of codex histories, the New Bibliographers of the early twentieth century peeled off the histories of the library, printing, book production, and any intelligible relation to cultural history by refocusing the bibliographical project on author, meaning, and stable text. When today's book history polemically accentuates the difference between editing "books" and editing "texts," particularly in the work of Donald McKenzie and Jerome McGann, their argument for editing a "social text" effectively makes a more disciplined return to the Bibliomaniacs' long-misunderstood insights into the nature and historical mutability of the book.[53]

We might also contrast the ways collector culture had exploited ownership of the book with these later nineteenth-century and early twentieth-century attempts to exploit authorial ownership of the text on the conviction that "textual integrity and regulated intellectual property are somehow mutually entailed."[54] The property-secured stature of authorship left bibliographical labor without legitimate intellectual property and feminized it at the same time. The bibliographer is "a handmaiden to literature," as *The Cambridge History of English Literature* put it in 1915; her work "cannot be identified with literature any more than the bibliographer (as such) can be regarded as an author."[55] On the whole, the New Bibliographers of the twentieth century professionalized earlier British bibliographical study by expunging both the memory of its origins and the historical fascinations or ethical visions that often animated it. They often did so in the name of science, making analogies between their new methods and natural history, botany, entomology, or Mendelian genetic evolution.[56] Portraying Romantic-age bibliographical book history as prescientific, as I hope to have suggested, has a rich irony. Today's book history, although in many ways it has advanced well beyond its precursor, is in other ways still trying to catch up with it. Such matters as the meaning of "literary history," or genealogies of the library and of discipline-organizing, are currently among its most urgent topics. In trajectory, book history could become the new matrix of the humanities, as Leah Price speculates, the larger field of which "literary history" becomes only a subset, or the archeology of the new communicative media and systems that still require its knowledge to make their own way – just as early modern printing required the look and feel of the manuscript book to launch its own more definitive futures.[57] Current print history has many forms – from the most focused and matter-of-fact, to the most ambitious ways of rethinking the book's place in modernity – but it is not yet fully clear what visions or ambitions drive it. What, to put one contemporary book-history scholar's rhetorical question more pointedly, is book history really *for*?[58]

This chapter has been giving a history of "historical bibliography," the mode of the book-collecting culture and the eighteenth- and nineteenth-century bibliographical writers who moved closer, after 1800, to making that many-faceted mode of bibliography a serious, organized, and even theorizable mode of knowledge. That it was so deliberately dismantled in the later nineteenth century in the name of a more disciplined "science" than anything Dibdin or his Institution collaborators had accomplished in the early nineteenth century also points to a different meaning of "predisciplinarity" than as simply a mode of unorganized knowledge that anticipates a later disciplinary centering. This meaning would refer to some unopened box in an already-constituted discipline – a black box of the kind Bruno Latour describes that, once closed, functions more or less silently as a current and essential part of what makes a particular discipline tick. Re-open that box, we might say, and the disciplinary clock will no longer be the same; it will have to start recursively accounting for what it could previously merely presume in its own constitution. Defining predisciplinarity in this way might explain what happened when the discipline of analytical or critical bibliography dominant through most of the twentieth century came to be questioned about the black-boxed category it called "historical bibliography," especially by Donald McKenzie in his Panizzi

Lectures *Bibliography and the Sociology of Texts*. By re-opening that box, McKenzie could well claim that, far from being a negligible or even extra-disciplinary part of modern bibliography, "all bibliography is historical bibliography."[59] This justification for the history of the book that we now associate with the work of Darnton, Eisenstein, Chartier, McGann, or Johns has stood up and worn well since McKenzie's lectures of 1985. But three decades later we still have a rather murky sense of where historical bibliography itself had come from, and thus, I think, a radically incomplete picture of what it was the New Bibliographers of the early twentieth century had stuffed into that darkened cube.[60] That a serious bibliographical enterprise to give print foundations to the rapidly proliferating "arts and sciences" and a maddening bibliomaniacal disordering of books were so deeply entwined in the early nineteenth century's "wild bibliography" also suggests to me that what we are speaking of as "predisciplinarity" today is not only a matter of before-and-after discipline, but also a recursive dimension of disciplinarity itself.

CHAPTER 4

# *Print and institution in the making of art controversy*

> For who can take upon him to write of the proper duty, virtue, challenge, and right of every several vocation, profession and place?
> Francis Bacon, *The Advancement of Learning* (1605)
>
> The marring of Art is the making of the Academy.
> William Hazlitt, "On the Catalogue Raisonné of the British Institution" (1816)

In early 1806, the painter Prince Hoare published a trenchant, dire assessment of Britain's contemporary art world: "The present moment is considered by artists as teeming with the crisis ... of the Destiny of their Art in England."[1] In that year there was still no art-critical press in England to report what might be taking place in the visual art field; the only significant event of the past year had been the opening in London of the British Institution for the Promotion of the Fine Arts in Great Britain. But both the print media and the English art institutions would soon take note of the emergency Hoare outlined in his first book, *An Inquiry into the Requisite Cultivation and Present State of the Arts of Design in England*. The crisis was simultaneously economic, professional, and aesthetic. The visual arts seemed to have lost their intellectual bearings, their chance of being taken seriously on the Continent, and even perhaps their own audience and market in Britain. Hoare's response in the *Inquiry* was to make an energetically renewed case for state or public patronage of the arts that had first been put forward, with little public support, by the painter James Barry in 1775. On the media side of the question, Hoare pointed to the absence in Britain of any print publication offering sustained attention to the visual arts. By the following year, Hoare himself began to produce one. This new weekly journal, the *Artist*, vowed to do something transformative for the state of the arts in Britain by conducting a remarkable experiment in print – putting visual artists collectively on the "public stage" as print authors writing polemically on behalf of their own arts.

As I shall try to show, this translation of art-practices into print authorship would have its own complexities – and its unanticipated outcomes – in changing the British art field and its relation to the public world. Hoare's journal entered its artist-contributors into direct, open public contest with a range of antagonists, new and old – eventually putting the *Artist* into the midst of a new kind of discussion for Britain, the public arts controversy.

Most students of the Romantic period would count *Annals of the Fine Arts*, published between 1816 and 1820 by the architect James Elmes, as the first, the best-known, or the most important arts journal of the age – among many other reasons, for publishing Keats's, Haydon's, and Hazlitt's writings on art. It has been called "the first of the 'quality' art magazines in England," a handsomely published and richly elaborated quarterly journal spanning some 225-plus pages in each issue during its five-year tenure.[2] Born in the great Elgin Marbles controversy, it first appeared just *after* Parliament voted to keep the Marbles for Britain in June 1816, and so the *Annals* was more the beneficiary of that stormy debate than its mediator. Without denying the *Annals*' importance or its qualities – and I'll come back to these in my conclusion – it was quite arguably less original than it claimed when describing itself, in its opening issue of July 1816, as the "first attempt at a Journal of the Fine Arts" in England.[3] Rather, the *Annals* looks to have been the beneficiary of an intensive, decade-long period, which I would want to date from about 1806 to 1816, when Britain saw a newly focused, extraordinary and persistent interest in the visual arts taken by print media of all sorts, one that had little or no real counterpart in earlier decades of journalistic attention to the visual arts or their most visible public form, the Royal Academy exhibitions[4] – a short list of which would have to include the *Artist* (1807), the *Director* (1807), *La Belle Assemblée* (1808), the *Examiner* (1808), Ackermann's *Repository of the Arts* (1809), the *Champion* (1813), the *New Monthly Magazine* (1814), the *Quarterly Journal of Science and Art* (1816), the *Edinburgh Review* recurringly throughout the period, the *London Magazine* in the 1820s, not to mention the ongoing attention of four or five London newspapers. Art historians have devoted little or no attention to the print media that reshaped the public's knowledge of the visual arts or the public debates that might flourish around them.[5] One question to ask of this newly focused media attention to the arts from 1806 forward is: why so much – and why then?

The larger question posed by these new art journals is how they mediated "controversy" between the public sphere, where today such controversies can be more intense and sensational than ever, and the world or field of art production. Students of art controversy can disagree widely about where such disputes begin or play out. Michael Kammen's cultural-history picture of American art controversies, for instance, depicts them as typically emanating "at first from within the art world itself because of vested interests and resistance to innovation; then from public figures and religious groups who carry weight with officeholders; more recently, and powerfully, from the media." He is a careful enough historian to weight these three "flashpoints" of art controversy differently according to the local moment, but most of his examples accentuate the artists' effort to provoke the public, or emphasize the way media and the politicians react to the provocation.[6] That essentially modernist view of art controversies sharply contrasts with a media-centered perspective, such as Richard Howells's, which argues that the arts themselves have little or nothing to do with the public controversies brewing around them. Political, religious, and media actors, in Howells's view, use the arts to advance their own agendas of power with little interest in aesthetic matters and without regard to the "intrinsic value" of the art works themselves.[7] Yet if the first picture treats nearly all art controversies as modernist provocation by the art world, the second oddly exempts artists and the art field from any significant place in the public and political storms that have sometimes raged around their productions, effectively leaving art *out* of the politics of arts controversy.

In this chapter I ask how print media have figured into art controversies, which is also to ask how the arts and that kind of argumentative or intellectual exchange we call a "controversy" materializes for a particular public. The expression "art controversy" itself seems to have first appeared in the 1850s and 1860s, when British and American magazines or books used it to mean disputes between insiders of the art world (painters, sculptors, critics, and others). Not a surprise – the term *controversy* had been used in similar ways since the 1600s to describe religious quarrels or legal debates among knowledgeable insiders to modern ecclesiastic or juridical fields.[8] This link between art controversy and the specialists may now seem at odds, however, with the way "controversy" is commonly used today to designate a broad dispute or struggle in the realm of public opinion, as articulated or exacerbated by major media and key political actors. I am pointing to a historical arc within the very notion of the art controversy, one that begins by recognizing that there is an "art world" distinct from, yet having an impact upon, everyday life. That relationship – the perception that art is both specialized and of public importance (national, political, international, social, global) – would get only more complicated from the nineteenth to the twenty-first centuries.

Great art controversies have their distinctive public faces of antipodal dispute, but they also have crucial backstories and substructures. These entail the less publicly visible level of long-gestating antagonisms that were or are deeply grounded in social definition and cultural practice. One might say, following Bourdieu, that a specific modern "world" or cultural field, such as an art world, can already be called a sphere of *embedded controversy* – that is, they are structured by arguments on what the field means, what its stakes are, and why it matters to play the particular game that defines the action of the field.[9] An art world, on this view, is more rhetorically elaborated (and surely conflicted) than the one we usually think of when, following the classic definition of an art world offered by Howard Becker – a useful one but only a start – we call it simply a "network of people whose cooperative activity, organized via their joint knowledge of conventional means of doing things, produces the kind of art works that the art world is noted for."[10]

Since the early nineteenth century, controversies about the arts have correspondingly changed their shape; political nations and religious groups were usually less legibly involved in art controversies than they seem to be today. The great exception to this rule was most concisely signaled by an American handbook of cultural literacy published in the 1880s. "What violent art controversy took part early in the present century?" was the question put by *Queries: Devoted to Literature, Art, Science, Education* (1885) – and no one could doubt the answer, "That concerning the Elgin Marbles."[11] The Elgin Marbles affair of 1801–16 could be recalled as so culturally and emotionally "violent" – even today, few public controversies over the arts can be said to match its scope and heat – because it raised great public questions about cultural imperialism, the spoliation of cultural treasures, national identities, and international relations. When England's political ambassador to the Ottoman empire engineered the transfer (or theft) of Athens's decaying Parthenon ruins to London from 1801 to 1812 in the age of Europe's war with Napoleon, he was claiming a right to cultural spoils by international warring nations that would be contested most famously by Lord Byron's remarkable denouncing of Elgin's actions in *Childe Harold* (1812), helping set off what has been called "the most famous and longest-running debate over cultural property in the world."[12] It would take an 1816 act of Parliament to resolve the decade-long controversy (in favor of the British artists and the British Museum) after a battle joined by leading politicians and the print media, William Hazlitt and the painters, Byron and the art critics. Manifestos denouncing or defending the seizure of the Marbles have reappeared continuously since then, as late as the 1990s.[13]

Yet the public reputation of the Marbles debate has obscured what nineteenth-century observers knew very well – that if the great controversy was clearly about international cultural property, it was also crucially about the specialists, about power and authority inside the British art world, and the way its outcome would have serious effects on how the visual arts would be grasped by a wider British (and soon American) public in the nineteenth and twentieth centuries. By returning to the scene of the oldest art controversy in modernity, I hope to suggest that there are local, contingent, or conjunctural dimensions to a given art controversy, on the one hand, yet also a long-term framework for grasping how modernity's emerging fields align toward or away from one another, thus defining the potential scope of such controversies, on the other.

## Artists into print: expertise and authorship

The *Artist* marks a turning point in British art writing partly because, like other efforts after 1807, it was responding to a much-altered institutional art field. Except for the Royal Academy (founded in 1768), the British art field was the least highly and most belatedly institutionalized of any in Europe – before 1800 there were no art institutions in Britain outside London or Dublin, but by 1830 art institutions were springing up all over England and Scotland.[14] "Between 1790 and the 1840s," Holger Hoock observes, "the arts emerged as a new policy field ... British artists, writers on art, and politicians for the first time engaged in coherent debates about the role of the state in relation to the social and educational functions of the arts and their organizational structures."[15] Organized by forty leading painters and sculptors in 1768, the Academy dominated the art scene through the early 1800s, mounting impressive and prestigious public exhibitions or the presidential lectures – the masterly aesthetic theory – of Joshua Reynolds. Just as often the Royal Academy evoked resentment, and sometimes eloquent opposition. As early as 1775 the painter James Barry called attention to aristocratic influence by means of great-man patronage at the Royal, and demanded public or state patronage to replace it (an argument renewed by the *Artist*). Journalists stopped by the annual exhibitions to mock the spectators as well as the Academy painters. William Hazlitt later attacked the British art institutions as a whole, ostensibly for intimidating the public: "the rank and station of the painter throw a lustre round his pictures, which imposes completely on the herd of spectators, and makes it a kind of treason against the art, for anyone to speak his mind freely, or detect the imposture."[16] Even painters inside the Royal Academy, like Henry Fuseli, viewed the rise of academies and other art institutions as "symptoms of Art in distress."[17] Establishing Britain's first art academy in 1768, in fact, would do as much to crystallize the "crisis" Prince Hoare diagnosed in the early 1800s as it did to formulate an English aesthetic and thus to put Britain on the European art map.

Hoare's new approach to an arts journal raised pointedly the question of what an artist is and why that question entails *expertise*, both in senses of expertise *in* the arts, and of arts *as* expertise. There is no question, as John Brewer has pointed out, that the British painters' ongoing struggle with the connoisseurs and collectors for the right to speak on behalf of the arts formed one of the deepest fault lines within Britain's eighteenth-century art world. The latter had dominated eighteenth-century art criticism and thus its canons of taste.[18] Though some collectors were content to cultivate their art-object gardens, many had been aggressive taste-makers in print, especially Richard Payne Knight in a wide range of publications, most recently *An Analytical Inquiry into the Principles of Taste* (1805).

The *Artist* set out to challenge the expertise of the connoisseurs in 1807 with what was then a novel, even audacious strategy: it promised to grant painters, sculptors, architects, and other visual artists the power of authorship by having them publicly sign their articles – this was an age of anonymous, unsigned periodical writing – in order to win recognition as authentically "professional men" of the liberal arts. It was a claim for expertise, the author's name standing for a known body of visual work and standing also as a rebuke to the authorship of critics and connoisseurs who had not produced the arts they were judging. The *Artist*'s forthright attacks on antiquarians, collectors, and connoisseurs – indeed the whole of what Jonathan Richardson had once called the "science" of "connoissance" – depicted the connoisseurs and collectors as Norman invaders of the British art world, while arts-practitioners figured as "the native Professors of this island."[19]

We speak today of "remediation" when a given medium is translated or otherwise sublated into another medium (manuscript into print, painting into photography, visual art into literary words).[20] In the *Artist*, early nineteenth-century painters, sculptors, and architects would be effectively remediating *themselves* by becoming print authors in what Hoare certainly recognized was a most precarious emergence on the public scene. Risking embarrassment and fearful of exposure, "the English Artist, while he approaches the presence of his countrymen in a garb and character to which he is unaccustomed ... dares not expand his thoughts in the freedom of utterance, without some such previous explanation of his designs as may gain him the confidence of the reader."[21] To win that credibility, British art producers must depend on their own art-practices as "authentic sources" for their discourse since they have no other credentials. This is why Hoare and his contributors consistently adopted the title of "professional men" who possess an expertise capable of rivaling the aesthetic learnedness of the antiquarian collectors and the connoisseurs. Thus Hoare's artists appeal not to the authority of eighteenth-century aesthetics but rather to Lord Bacon's *New Organon* and to the kind of knowledge grounded in *methods*, that is, "science," for authority as against the "unprofessional guides" who have dominated British art writing for nearly a century. "It is the design of *The Artist*," Hoare says, "to seek professional information on the subject of the liberal Arts" and connect this knowledge to "modern improvements in science."[22] Such rhetoric marked a noticeable shift of emphasis from the earlier Royal Academy discourse of Reynolds toward the language of professionalism, scientific validity, and public impact. Compared to the first seven Discourses given by Reynolds from 1769 to 1776, for instance, Hoare's *Artist* uses an aesthetic vocabulary – the words *taste*, *genius*, *art*, or even *artist* – roughly an equal number of times over a comparable span of pages. ("*Genius*" in Reynolds gets eighty-four usages, in Hoare seventy-four usages.) But they enlist the words *science* or *scientific* about four times as often as Reynolds; the word *professional* more than three times as often; the words *public* and *publication* about ten times as often as did Reynolds. Overall, Hoare's contributors engage the terms *professional*, *scientific*, and *public* or *publication* anywhere from five to ten times as often as Reynolds had done in his own seven lectures a short generation earlier.[23] That is only a quantitative indicator, but a telling one, of the British art field's tilt toward the language of professionalism, scientific comparison or rivalry, and ambition to win public validation.

In the twenty-one weekly issues it published in 1807, the *Artist* put this language to work aggressively. For contributors, Prince Hoare recruited the painters James Northcote, John Opie, and John Hoppner, the architect John Soane, the sculptor John Flaxman, and others from the Royal Academy who supported the campaign for state patronage of the arts. These art academicians dashed through the open door the *Artist* provided to proclaim the power, legitimacy, or autonomy of their art by acting as public authors. For the ninth issue James Northcote submitted a paper on "genius" to argue against the "sister arts" relationship of poetry and painting. As if he were writing an English addendum to Lessing's *Laocoön* (1784), Northcote claimed that English painting had been far too dependent on poems, metaphors, and stagecraft for its models or execution. Hence the painter demonstrates that his capacity does not enable him to judge or choose for himself, but that, instead of applying to nature directly, he receives his ideas through the medium of another's mind, whom, like a weak bigot, he has made, of his equal, his protector and saint ... To paint, therefore, the passions from the exhibitions of them on the stage, or from any intended descriptions of nature by the poets, is to remove yourself one degree farther from truth.[24]

Meanwhile, asking why British sculpture had not yet prospered, John Flaxman blamed the works of Gianlorenzo Bernini, and the Italian Baroque mode in general, for producing fantastic mixtures of genre and "such aerial effects" (as he said of Bernini's most famous productions) as would result in "breaking down the boundaries of painting and sculpture, and confound[ing] the two arts" altogether.[25] John Soane, recently appointed Professor of Architecture at the Royal Academy and the future antagonist of John Ruskin, mounted an aggressive attack on the "builders" and other artisans who had shown architectural ambitions and seemed to threaten his own hard-won stature now as an academic architect trying to enjoy the autonomy of his profession but still shackled by the material conditions of building in Britain. The tone is often angry and frustrated, as in Soane's startlingly ferocious complaint against the supposed pretensions of artisans to be architects or have anything to do with the creative act. And to sound the keynote theme for the *Artist* as a whole, the portrait painter John Hoppner used his entry to attack the recently published book on aesthetics and taste by Payne Knight, the most articulate and disliked of the connoisseurs.[26] In these and other articles by the artists-turned-authors, the professional autonomy of each of the arts, with their increasing separation between the art media, became the most insistent theme of the *Artist*.

Thus did practitioners of what had long been devalued as a "mechanic" art or craft try to win their way into the ranks of a public sphere where they had learned to think and write (as the Enlightenment phrase went) "for themselves."[27] Securing professional credibility for painters who picked up the pen was no small aim or accomplishment for the *Artist*, as we shall see in its later, unexpected impact on a public controversy like the Elgin Marbles debate that had not yet crystallized during Hoare's print experiment in 1807.

Yet why did Northcote, Soane, and Flaxman tilt so far and, by earlier standards of what the eighteenth century often called the "sister arts," so aggressively toward the language of painterly or architectural autonomy and the separation of arts according to their medium? Such claims would not seem to be as strongly voiced again in Anglo-American art commentary until, perhaps, the moment of Clement Greenberg's "ideology of modernism" in the 1940s and 1950s.[28] This is a more complex question to answer than the present chapter can fully pursue. But I would make two brief suggestions. First, the *Artist*'s case for public patronage was being argued, not on the formalist autonomy of individual art works (such as Greenberg and the American New Critics would argue in the next century), but for the art *producer*'s autonomy as a "professional" who should be subject to neither institutional control (as we shall see below the painters especially had reason to fear in 1807), nor to the architect's client's wish to treat him as a mere employee or "builder" (the anxiety of John Soane in particular). Second, this cluster of arguments by Royal Academy artists is overtly anti-commercial in a far stronger sense than it would have been a mere twenty years earlier. For the period 1804–7, as the work of Morris Eaves, Thora Brylowe, and Luisa Calé has taught us, was also a watershed moment for the British art field – I refer to the failure of the great commercial art-literary galleries of John Boydell, James Macklin, and Henry Fuseli (around 1804) after exciting audiences in the 1790s with their rich interplay of literary, narrative, and epic verbal genres with painting, sculpture, and other visual arts.[29] The Boydell Gallery's collapse ended hopes that British artists could win support from a commercial public for more than a generation: Northcote and Soane were among the first to shift the case for painting and architecture sharply toward the anti-commercial rhetoric of the artist's autonomy.

What would the artist's "autonomy" mean for the relation of arts and sciences I have been exploring in this book? We need to recall that the question of autonomy first concerns the interior space of struggle and collaboration among many agents for what Bourdieu calls the monopoly on the definition of the field – in the present case, the right to declare and the ability to persuade others what art *means*.[30] For Northcote, Soane, and others now publishing in the *Artist*, autonomy first of all would mean the "artist's" superiority to the mechanics, the artisans, the engravers, or in Soane's architectural case the "builders" who have claimed credit for their own labors in the collective making of Britain's visual field. Thus it was not a question of gaining autonomy from a degrading commercial field, as Bourdieu's later and more literary model of nineteenth-century French modernism would suggest. It was the loss of commercial viability, for British painters in particular, and the collapse of previously vital commercial art markets like Boydell's Shakespeare Gallery, that seemed to dictate making virtue of necessity by seeking the distinction of becoming a "writer," an intellectual in the Republic of Letters speaking authoritatively on the basis of one's expertise. And it is the literary dimension of this claim to autonomy – that it entails raising one's stature in the art field by gaining stature in the wider discursive field of letters – that could alter the balance of the "arts and sciences" in England, where all fields, including the scientific, need to make their claims to importance legible and discursive. It could well have been John Opie's embarrassment at the Royal Institution in 1806 – the Professor of Painting as failed public lecturer – that led Academy artists to try using print, with Hoare's new project, in early 1807. As we shall see below, even that project would come out of a dispute about how to construe the relation of arts and sciences.

Yet there was another side to the *Artist*, quite unlike the essays I have cited, and it belongs to Prince Hoare's own conception of trying to broaden and remediate the very idea of "artist" as understood in the early nineteenth century. He knew that a journal devoted only to painting, sculpture, or architecture would reach too small a circle of specialists. The *Artist* was addressing multiple readerships – first, to be sure, the community of art producers (especially the leading artists at the Royal Academy), whose sympathy and support for public or state patronage Hoare would unquestionably need. But Hoare was also seeking a wider public who might be persuaded to see the interests of "artists" as broadly shared and nationally important. Thus the *Artist* reached out well beyond the scope of the "fine arts" as then understood to embrace the theater and the novel. Hoare invited James Cumberland and Thomas Holcroft to write on London's drama scene, and to defend the "art" of the novel he recruited the Jacobin novelist Elizabeth Inchbald. Hoare had been close to the Godwin circle since the mid 1790s and had met Inchbald in the year she published *Nature and Art* (1796). Now for the *Artist* he urged her to submit an essay on "the *art* of novel-writing – the *art* of dramatic composition – the *art* of conversation" (emphases in original): above all, to write on why and how the novelist will count as an "artist" as such.[31] In one of the stranger and most interesting alliances formed in early 1800s London, Hoare was mingling Royal Academy painters and sculptors with Jacobin novelists and playwrights, and if it's a good question why the likes of Holcroft and Inchbald were being invited to publish alongside distinguished Royal Academy painters and architects on the subject of "art," it is also worth asking how the low-status genres of the novel and theater could possibly qualify for the status of "liberal arts" and its expertise that Hoare was aiming to justify and explicate in the *Artist*. The incongruity of coupling the novel and theater with sculpture, painting, and architecture may seem less noticeable today since both the British novel and the drama would rise markedly in stature, from subliterary to distinguished, in the twenty- to thirty-year period after this moment. But unlike his own Royal Academy contributors who write so aggressively for the separation of arts, Hoare seems to have embraced a far wider conception of the "liberal arts" as reaching a wide public audience by inter-mediating the arts (theater was said, of all media, to most constitutively combine and rearticulate the relation of verbal and visual arts) – and not by narrowing their specialties by dividing and purifying media. Yet if Hoare's own editorial approach was to encourage collaborative crossings among the arts by making the category "liberal arts" now open to theatrical life, novel-writing, and art-magazine reading, he seems to have achieved little editorial authority to unify such a project or the very different publics it was reaching toward. Hence the *Artist* comes across as a self-divided project, half dedicated to purifying and separating the individual arts so as to achieve the professional autonomy of the painter, architect, or sculptor – and half devoted to widening the category of "liberal arts" by embracing the novel and theatrical genres as "arts" rather than mere urban entertainments.

This may explain why, according to its key peer audience, the Royal Academy painters and sculptors who had first encouraged Hoare's venture the *Artist* "failed." Henry Fuseli expressed early support, but he was soon telling dinner parties of his "great contempt" for the *Artist*, a publication he had "never heard mentioned by anyone." Hoare, he added, brings the editorial perspective of "watergruel w.out salt." The architect-turned-painter George Dance found "much sound and little sense" in the *Artist*. Every writer was taking aggressive positions, but the pages of the *Artist* lacked the grit of detail or the instructive curves of historical narrative – in short, the artists themselves were finding little or nothing to learn.[32] Worse, from a professional standpoint, the *Artist* encouraged reckless claims that could unwittingly reveal that practicing British artists, claiming to speak on the basis of their practice, could be especially unfit to make larger judgments on the European arts. Northcote was said to have "exposed himself" by thoughtlessly writing off the work of Nicolas Poussin, the most philosophical painter of the French school, as "the pedant of painters ... the learned painter in distinction from the natural painter."[33] The *Artist*'s case for the authority of artistic practice over the discourse *about* the arts was turning out to be anti-intellectual in a disturbing sense. By its thirteenth issue in June 1807, the *Artist* already seemed to be undermining its own case. Being grounded in one's own practice did not necessarily mean knowing how to think about or argue it effectively in print. Northcote "had undertaken to write upon His art before He understood it ... those who knew most of their art were least disposed to talk much of it."³⁴ Writing for print on the basis of one's "practice" – Prince Hoare's main criterion for managing a print journal as the forum of "professionals" in the field – revealed the risk that failure in the realm of making agreeable judgments of taste might discredit the practice of artists writing publicly altogether. By the internal evidence of the art world itself – especially that most internal of all British art world documents, Joseph Farington's gossipy and revealing diaries – the *Artist* was a failure, and with it the experiment to translate expertise in art-practice into authority in print. Meanwhile, the effort to bring theatrical and novelistic writers into the arts discussion seemed to go unnoticed.

Failure, then, in 1807 – but that would not be the whole story.

**Institution and contradiction in the art world**

To see why a print intervention like the *Artist* could fail among its peer-reviewers, yet ultimately achieve a long-term impact on shaping arts controversies in Britain, I want to shift the focus now to the institutional side of the relationships we have been tracking. We normally think of print media since the eighteenth century as occupying a commercial place in civil society – supported by subscription or bookstall sales, periodicals and newspapers, as well as books, thus having a largely marketplace existence (hence the importance of book-trade studies in the field of print history). Yet some kinds of print, especially those connected to the rapidly shifting category of the "arts and sciences" in Europe and the US, would also have an important institutional basis or connection: the *Philosophical Transactions* (1665), which established legitimate scientific-experiment reporting and sharing across Europe, affiliated with London's Royal Society, is one clear case. The authority and prestige of Joshua Reynolds's *Discourses on Art* (1792) as representing the Royal Academy is another. These cases stand out, but many ventures in print, especially after 1800, would have far more tangled relations with modern institutions on the one hand, the marketplace of reading on the other.

In light of Adrian Johns's powerful rethinking of the history of print as the problem of establishing credibility for books and quasi-books (like the *Artist*), we need to ask how Hoare really expected practicing art producers to win the credibility normally lent to learned writers, scholars, or established critics.³⁵ Most painters could not begin to match the connoisseur's learning or his access to museums or private collections; worse, they had no practiced skills in the arts of polite discourse required for recognition in the Republic of Learning. Hoare's way of confronting that knotty problem bears close attention:

> Although his title thus embrace every branch of refined learning ... [the artist] shall be found destitute of many acquirements which combine to form the *writer*, and his Essays in these departments will therefore be regarded by the candid reader as the *sentiments* rather than the *writings* of their respective authors. In his *graphic* part, if he is less able to polish his sentences than the Greek Painters and Sculptors are believed to have been, who composed treatises on their art, he contemplates with pleasing hope, *under the auspices of modern Institutions* [my italics], the prospect of his country extending to him those resources of instruction, which she affords to the student of many an Art and Science; and he feels a confidence, that as her name inspires him with the ambition, her acknowledged power will furnish him with the means, of rivaling the proudest models of Grecian art.[36]

Artists, Hoare suspected, could not compete undefended in the marketplace of arguments that had been long celebrated as the Republic of Letters. He thus points in particular to the new arts-and-sciences Institutions in London which equip painters with the symbolic capital – and thereby the credibility – expected of "writers." Hoare was attempting to convert the recognition of painterly practice into the credentials of public writer who in the process becomes credible to speak for the arts *and* (this is where the wider sphere of the new institutions will come in) within the greater category of the Arts and Sciences. He doesn't say the painters become *good* writers in the sense normally understood by that expression, but *credible* writers thanks to their institutional mediation.

Today all art historians agree on the central role of the Royal Academy in Britain's burgeoning art world, but the status of the new player in the field – the British Institution for Promoting the Fine Arts in the United Kingdom founded largely by Thomas Bernard in 1805 – still remains uncertain. Some cultural historians, like Peter Fullerton or Linda Colley, make it central to the unfolding role of the arts in British national life; others, like Holger Hoock, have made the British Institution relatively marginal.[37] Yet it was clearly critical to Prince Hoare and the *Artist*, for it was the British Institution and its publishing ambitions that provoked Hoare to invent the *Artist* in the first place. His polemic against the prevailing taste-makers (the connoisseurs and collectors) owes to the fact that the new British art institution was not only organized by those taste-experts and wealthy patrons, it was also uniquely censorious of practicing artists. The British Institution enforced a new administrative rule: unlike the peer-organized and peer-reviewing Academy, no artist would be allowed to have any hand in the governance of the British Institution, whose Directors were all collectors, patrons, and connoisseurs. Therefore there would be no "professors" of art either. All artists, regardless of stature, would become students at the British Institution, copying the Old Master paintings lent by collectors under strict rules governing the size, scope, and style of their copying. Thus the old antipathy between the connoisseurs/collectors and the practicing British artists should have become a public feud between the Royal Academy and the new British Institution, yet all parties publicly insisted there was no struggle underway at any level of national and institutional importance. Denial of the serious rivalry between these institutions only exacerbated the division – it would come out instead in the form of print media, especially the *Artist* and its now-little-known opposite, the *Director*.

It was Bernard who first invited the painter Prince Hoare to become a periodical-publisher and editor of his proposed project the *Director*. But Hoare turned down Bernard's offer when he refused to concede Hoare's demand that if he were to edit, only "professional" men should be asked to write essays on the arts and sciences. *How* the two men argued this point is most interesting. According to Joseph Farington, the increasingly heated exchange went like this:

> [Bernard] applied to Him to take the management of [the *Director*], which Hoare was inclined to do, and said He could be well assisted on the subject of art by *Professional Men*; to which Bernard immediately objected, and said they were not to be admitted to be contributors to it by their writings. – Hoare observed that He thought otherways, – & that on the *subject of Chemistry & natural Philosophy* he should be glad to have the assistance of *Davy*, & on *Poetry* that of *Coleridge*, to which Bernard replied that Coleridge would write of the *Arts*, & Davy on (blank in diary) but not on the subjects mentioned by Hoare ... saying that what should be written ought to be by those who *looked on* rather than by those who *practice*. [my italics][38]

When Hoare rejected Bernard's terms, he lost the editorship of the *Director* and decided, in a combative mood, to start up the *Artist* on his own terms instead. That so privately argued a dispute, so far inside the specialist realm of the British art world, could have later consequences for a Europe-wide debate about the Elgin Marbles and cultural imperialism seems hard to fathom. Yet there was a large and historically consequential question being argued here: what is more culturally authoritative, the views of "those who practice" or those of "those who look on"? By "looking on," Bernard seemed to mean those who see and speak for a larger whole – the sciences as such, rather than chemistry or geology; the "arts" as such, rather than poetry or painting. Indeed the whole category of "Arts and Sciences" is being disputed here, and though it is easy today to fill in the "blank in diary" – surely Bernard meant to say, "Coleridge on the Arts, Davy on the Sciences" – it was just that relationship that was so uncertain and arguable in the early nineteenth century.

My point is that it was within the kind of new cultural Institution Thomas Bernard had been founding or administering – especially the Royal in 1800 and the British in 1805 – that the coherence of matching the fine arts to the natural sciences was rapidly taking shape, by shifting the key categories upward from specialized disciplines (Chemistry, Poetry) to what were now beginning to become the meta-disciplinary categories of the "arts and sciences." It was from this higher administrative, organizing, or conceptual level of the "arts and sciences," thus redefined, that Bernard could so emphatically reject Hoare's plea for what otherwise could seem self-evidently sensible – the "professional" standard of writing on the basis of one's expertise or practice. And as lecture-manager of the Royal Institution, Bernard himself had the power to carry out this administrative, meta-disciplinary program. It was also in 1806 that Bernard invited Samuel Coleridge to lecture on "Principles of the Fine Arts," while Humphry Davy wrote and spoke with an increasingly general sense of Science rather than chemistry, geology, or "natural philosophy."[39]

In resisting Bernard's higher administrative logic and recalibration of "Arts and Sciences" as a meta-disciplinary rubric, Hoare's *Artist* was also waging a campaign to differentiate the knowledge produced by art-practices (as "professional," even quasi-scientific) from the knowledge produced by those who "looked on," whether on the basis of the eighteenth century's aesthetic discourse on taste, or the modern institutional restructuring of a ranked hierarchy of knowledge-positions from administrative to practical. Today the question of whether art-practice in the university counts as "research," and how it could be thought to do so in relation to the more recognized research-producing disciplines that *we* have come to call Arts and Sciences in the university, is genealogically descendant from this early nineteenth-century reshaping of the category "arts and sciences" itself.

## Conjunctures: mediating the public art controversy

Do print media start art controversies? Mediate or amplify them? Serve as a forum for the sides of a controversy to argue it out? Become controversial in their own right? One can doubtless find a historical case to verify any of these guesses, but in the early nineteenth century, England's most famous art journal, *Annals of the Fine Arts*, basked in the glow of the artists' victory over their long-time antagonists, the connoisseurs, while having had little to do with waging the battle itself. On June 7, 1816, a Parliamentary Select Committee ruled that Britain should keep the Elgin Marbles in the British Museum (and pay Elgin £35,000 for his trouble – or labor of cultural theft, as many would call it long afterward), a decision ratified the next day (June 8) by both the Tory London *Times* and the Whig *Morning Chronicle*. By the 1880s European art historians were calling this moment "a complete revolution in taste."[40]

The *Annals* mediated the ensuing aesthetic and ideological lessons of the great debate rather than the Elgin Marbles controversy itself. It promoted what some cultural historians have called "Romantic classicism," a posture with lasting effect on British and American art worlds and public discussion in the nineteenth century.[41] The *Annals* thus came to represent not only all things Grecian, but also the renewed genre of poetic *ekphrasis*, "literary representations of visual representations," when it published John Keats's *Ode on a Grecian Urn* and similar poems.[42] *Annals* deserves a full study of its influential mediation of the arts to nineteenth-century readers in its own right, but it probably doesn't deserve its prominence by association with the Elgin Marbles debate itself, which it had little materially to do with.

Instead, I have been arguing in this chapter, print journals like the earlier *Artist* mediated the embedded controversies that had formed the substructure of the Elgin Marbles affair long before the latter burst into public view from 1812 onward. My case for the long reach of the *Artist*, a journal that seemed to fail among its own peer-reviewers in 1807, will then rest on three final propositions. First, a kind of "remediation" occurred in the early nineteenth century when visual-arts producers were turned into print authors, but it was not the remediation of a visual work by a verbal work (which would be a case of *ekphrasis*) – it was rather the remediation of artists as writers, with all the risks of exposure and failure this move between fields (essentially the artistic and the journalistic) entailed. This was the effort of the *Artist* in 1807 and again briefly in 1809. It was not a case of *ekphrasis* (individual works were rarely mentioned in these journals), but rather what I might call an event of *ekmediaphrasis*, the attempt to remediate a whole field of visual-arts producers into the intelligible range of a print sphere, which would ultimately have to be called the journalistic field. Though it "failed" by the peer-review judgments of the Royal Academy in 1807, the *Artist* succeeded in generating waves of consequences for British arts journalism, commentary, and ultimately legal testimony to the British state.

That impact on the flourishing of arts journalism between 1807 and 1816 appears often indirect, yet widespread. New weekly journals of political opinion, such as Leigh and Robert Hunt's weekly *Examiner*, took up the campaign for state patronage that Prince Hoare and his "artists" had renewed from its older eighteenth-century articulations by James Barry.[43] Robert Hunt's weekly column "Fine Arts" cast the arts into the Hunt brothers' broader, hugely influential case for a truly progressive "liberality" based on both radical Parliamentary reform and the nation's interest in seeing the arts flourish. Students of the Romantic age know this journal as the veritable print center of second-generation Romantic writing, and of the "Cockney School" of poets, critics, and painters (particularly Benjamin Haydon). What might be called the left-wing arts classicism of Byron, Shelley, Keats, and Hazlitt (who found themselves on opposite sides of the Elgin controversy itself) owes not only to the *Examiner*'s campaign for arts reform; it also has roots in Prince Hoare's linking of the case for public patronage of the arts with 1790s political Dissent. Meanwhile, the upscale fashion magazine *La Belle Assemblée* extended its mediation of the "Elegant and visual arts" from painting and sculpture to novel and theater, citing the *Artist* as a precursor.[44] More broadly, the *Artist* became almost routinely cited as a source of knowledge about the art world and its producers in the nineteenth century, though its twentieth-century notice has become sparse.

The strongest evidence of its reach may have come in mid 1816, as Parliament was taking its final testimony from painters and sculptors urging it to purchase Elgin's Marbles for the British Museum. When the painter Benjamin Haydon delivered decisive testimony against the opinion of connoisseurs, the terms of his pamphlet, *The Judgment of Connoisseurs upon Works of Art Compared with That of Professional Men* (1816), reiterated the rhetoric of the *Artist*. And while other observers of the time associated *Annals of the Fine Arts* with the painters' victory in the Elgin Marbles controversy's outcome, the *New Monthly Magazine*'s report on Parliament's decision remembered Hoare's the *Artist* for "putting the pen into the hands of many excellent artists, convincing them that they could write and judge the better for their knowledge in art, and that literature is not a species of freemasonry kept from the uninitiated."[45] The prestige of connoisseurial opinion in Britain would not be recovered for decades, until it became broadly incorporated with the later rise of the discipline called "art history." That discipline, of course, would be founded entirely within the newly authoritative university structure of disciplines called "art and sciences," of which the visual arts themselves, as practices, remained outside.

The case of the *Artist* in the early nineteenth century answers to neither current model, modernist or media-centered, of how a controversy is mediated between an art world and a public. Rather I have been putting the emphasis on the *conjuncture of disputes* that give rise to a great public art controversy. The *Artist* had its greatest impact not on its peer-reviewers in the art world (where it was much maligned) nor on the wide public who eventually read passionate arguments for or against keeping the Elgin Marbles for England, nor even those who have since replayed the controversy as a long-standing case of either cultural spoliation or universal rights to art. Rather it provoked further mediation – through the *Examiner*, *La Belle Assemblée*, the *New Monthly Magazine*, *Annals of the Fine Arts*, and further publication on art down through the nineteenth century (as well as some scholarship today). It also helped alter the relation of "fields" – artistic, journalistic, eventually academic – each of which had its own projected or actual audiences, publics, or clients. On this view, the so-called "public" of the art controversy is the one projected variously and compositely by the fields in question – the art world, the journalistic or mediatic field, the political system, and not least (especially today) the religious field. Each of these worlds, systems, or "fields" has its own dynamic and trajectory, to be sure, yet they are constantly in motion toward and away from one another. In the age of "new media," as we currently call it, the task is thus to think harder about what we mean by the contested relation of arts, institutions, media, and publics we call an "art controversy."

CHAPTER 5

# History and organization in the Romantic-age sciences

> To study the history of the arts and sciences has become a kind of religion. In it, philosophers discern ... the intentions of the world spirit.
> Friedrich Schelling, *On University Studies* (1803)
>
> The history of science is science itself.
> Wolfgang Goethe, *Theory of Colours* [*Farbenlehre*] (1810)
>
> There is no such thing as science, and this is a history of it.
> Steven Shapin, *Never Pure* (2010)

From Joseph Priestley's *The History and Present State of Electricity* (1767) to William Whewell's *History of the Inductive Sciences* (1837), the history of sciences may have informed Romantic-age readers about past events or discoveries, but it played nowhere near the role then that it plays today – one anticipated by Goethe – when everyone from the leading proponents of evolutionary theory (Stephen Jay Gould, Richard Dawkins, Daniel Dennett) to the most cross-disciplinary of cultural historians of science (Steven Shapin, James Secord, Simon Schaffer) possesses roughly the same knowledge base and rhetorical skill to make the "history of the sciences" a bestselling and a critically admired genre.[1] Yet the apparent directness of this new accessibility to the sciences can misleadingly make us forget how thickly any humanist's ability to speak of such sciences today must be mediated – by histories and historians, to be sure, but also by sociological and anthropological studies, or even (this is truly a circuitous route) by sailing down the canals and up the streams of the arts, the artisan crafts, the media of communication, among them, lecturing and printing.

In her history of discipline formation from 1680 to 1820, Robin Valenza singles out physics (Newton) as the paradigm of scientific disciplines; as we know, most other "scientific" inquiries remained far less organized until after 1800, while some, natural history in particular, resisted the disciplining process altogether.[2] A rich outpouring of new scholarship on the Romantic sciences in the past twenty years is in part thanks to the persuasiveness of the "second scientific revolution" said to have taken place in these decades. Yet that paradigm also carries the risk, Simon Schaffer has argued, of a certain amnesia. "Interdisciplinarity acquires its own disciplinary history ... by tak[ing] as accurate the stories disciplines have told about themselves."[3]

We have a strong example of this in the recent history of the concept "Romantic science." Half a century ago, the question of Romanticism and science was so vexed a subject that few risked approaching it. In the year of C. P. Snow's *The Two Cultures* (1960), the science historian Charles Gillispie described the "counter-offensive of Romantic biology against the doom of physics," as well as Lamarck's and Goethe's "resentment of mathematics." For twelve pages Gillispie interrupted his main narrative of a modernity unfolding by way of scientific objectivity to watch Goethe struggling with the *Farbenlehre*, "the great author making a fool of himself."[4] Gillispie ascribed Germany's *Naturphilosophie* to "cultural nationalism," making it "profoundly hostile to science," just as Nature in Goethe's sense (as Gillispie argued suggestively) was "not objectively analyzed" but "subjectively penetrated." Sexualized and feminized, Romantic science opened intellectual action to a certain vagueness and disorder, "flux and process," so as to confuse "proper science."

In the 1980s, Romanticists did not so much probe the disciplinary history of science presumed by Gillispie as they neatly reversed it: the new advocacy for Romantic science took the form of a dramatic narrative staging a domineering Newtonian mechanics (or Baconian empiricism) against Romantic rebellion, following the plotline of Frye's and Bloom's reading of Blake against celestial mechanics.[5] "The leading figures of romanticism," Joel Black argues, citing Wordsworth and the Schlegels, "were transgressing visionaries who aspired to achieve a grand synthesis of poetry and science ... the forerunners of today's Poppers, Kuhns, Feyerabends, Goulds, Hackings, and the present breed of historians/philosophers" who have criticized the "progressivist, gradualist, functionalist, and positivist biases of modern science."[6] This case could be a most attractive opening to learning the genuine intimacy of Romantic-age writers with the sciences of their times and helped produce a crop of important case studies of Wordsworth, Coleridge, the Shelleys, Byron, *Naturphilosophie*, and so forth.

Yet the "grand synthesis" imagined by Romanticists has not answered the difficult questions of how knowledges differentiate or how cultural and knowledge fields mutually constitute one another – less as some "grand synthesis" or interdisciplinary machine than as a sometimes crazy-quilt assemblage of unevenly developed crystallizations. In this chapter I take up questions of "organization" that ranged from the scientific to the institutional in the early nineteenth-century formation of knowledge fields. For this strategy, I shall come at the problem of Romantic-age scientific texts and knowledges in three parts. In the first, I set Richard Carlile, the prolific radical publisher, in dialogue with Humphry Davy, who had ascended from his tumultuous lecturing career at the Royal Institution to become President of the Royal Society by the time Carlile was writing *An Address to Men of Science* (1821). By this time, Davy had surged to the forefront of British scientific disciplinary power as the most widely accredited chemist of the times. To his past and present stature, Carlile would pose questions to a man of science in particular: what is a critical intellectual, whose interests does he serve, and on what basis can the expert in one field speak clearly and politically to the interests of the participants and beneficiaries of all fields? In the next part of the chapter, I extend this question – which ultimately depends on comparing the power of Carlile's iron publishing press to the new power of Davy's scientific lecturing institution – to the broader issue of literary and scientific "instruments" in the early nineteenth century. Here it becomes a matter of various sorts of "mediation," from publishing venues to laboratory instruments, and the interplay of such media that allow us to test recent theories of authority and knowledge.

The chapter then shifts to a late-Romantic assessment of the sciences that should be far more prominent than it has been, given what it suggests to us about the differentiation of knowledges in the new geopolitical situation emerging after the Napoleonic wars. If the sciences now proliferate by way of a differentiating process accomplished by learned societies, academies, or other institutions in London and the provinces, how do we then explain the greater effect accomplished on the level of nations, which themselves have their centers, peripheries, and colonies? In the *Quarterly Review*, Charles Lyell devoted special attention to the John Hunter Collection, whose complexities of structure suggested a prototype for the emerging disciplinary complexity of the sciences as they had been subdividing and reclassifying themselves since 1788. His reading of the Hunter Collection as a veritable national institution was also a means of replying to the new plebeian science of London, whose popularizers, like Richard Carlile at the Rotunda, would demonstrate for large popular audiences the unsuspected powers of "matter." Thus Lyell's alternative, institution-based vision of scientific emergence was aimed to redirect the evolution of

British science from that urban plebeian sphere to the provinces and the aristocrats' landed estates. Ultimately it would point to the emergent world system of the new scientific age.

The intellectual and political legacies of Hunter's physiology also help focus a view of the Romantic "co-production" of the second scientific revolution (1800–40) by literary and scientific writers alike. To be sure, I am not alone in arguing this case – it has been more broadly the basis for a veritable explosion of research into the relations of literary and scientific production in the Romantic age during the past twenty years. Noah Heringman puts it eloquently in his recent collection on Romantic science when he speaks of "the mutually constitutive nature of literary and scientific discourse in Britain during the later eighteenth and early nineteenth centuries."[7] This kind of mutual co-production, it must be added, was in no sense an easy or amicable one, and it would be a mistake to take the intimate familiarity of literary writers with contemporary sciences (and the reverse), or famous collaborations of the poetic and the scientific like the one between Davy and Coleridge, as evidence of a harmony that was to be lost in the disciplinary evolution of what Snow would notoriously call two irreconcilable worlds of scientific and humanistic discourse.

## The politics of scientific revolution: an encounter

In 1821, from a jail cell in provincial Dorchester, the radical publisher Richard Carlile produced a pamphlet, *An Address to Men of Science*, in which he positioned himself as an ideological and materialist critic of early nineteenth-century science, both an advocate of science and something of a precursor for what, nearly two centuries later, would be called the "science wars." The 1821 pamphlet makes it clear that Carlile was fascinated and persuaded by the new sciences – Davy's electrochemistry, William Herschel's astronomy, William Lawrence's physiology – that had emerged only in the previous thirty years. Making little reference to the late eighteenth-century world of Joseph Priestley, Carlile registered instead what social historians of science have called the "end of natural philosophy" and the rise of the modern, far more autonomous scientific disciplines, of which Davy's chemistry was the most recent to achieve disciplinary authority in Britain.[8]

Carlile's 1821 polemic underscored the ideological bearings of the new sciences – which have "crouch[ed] to the established tyrannies of Kingcraft and Priestcraft" – but it also testifies to the extraordinary force with which they captured the imaginations even of their most radical critics.[9] Carlile made the striking and, for his time, original case that what the post-1800 sciences purvey is not the Newtonian world picture, but a new "materialism," a picture of the universe dissolving and recreating in a ceaseless flow of material processes. Britain's contemporary chemists and astronomers, Carlile proposes, appear to be the "greatest of all revolutionists" insofar as their findings have "silently and scientifically undermined all the dogmas of the priest," and they are "materialists" since they impress the proof that "matter is imperishable and indestructible" upon our awareness. We have today become more fully material beings than we were before, as Carlile puts it in a reflexive turn of the argument, because we are now prepared to grasp our *own* materiality, and to comprehend more precisely how we ourselves will "fertilize the earth for a fresh production."[10] At a considerable distance from Newton's clockwork universe, the cosmos of Humphry Davy becomes for Carlile "a great chemical apparatus," explosive and generative, dissolvent and regenerative. It is only because of the power this scientific revolution has been having that Carlile, having registered its impact and complexity – and its potential opening onto future comprehension and action in the world – regarded it as so critical in the 1820s as to open a combative political campaign, joined by many others through this decade, against Davy's new and sophisticated means of controlling the knowledge production he now so conspicuously authorizes.

The scientific revolution of 1790–1820 has created a new type of scientific intellectual, Carlile implies, a figure unlike the natural philosopher who, like Joseph Priestley, extends the methods and materials of his experimental work to non-specialists who may replicate and grasp for themselves what the natural philosopher has begun. "The directions I have given are sufficient," Priestley had typically told one correspondent, "to allow any person to do everything after me."[11] Radical publishers like Joseph Johnson had been intimate with chemists and inventors in the 1780s and 1790s as experimentalists like Priestley had labored to organize small, sociable, and readily duplicable scenes of experimentation. Recalling the realm of later eighteenth-century natural philosophy, and how Humphry Davy had built his own disciplinary authority – now widely felt in the 1820s – can help situate Carlile's vivid perception of what made the Romantic-age sciences "revolutionary" in a decidedly counterrevolutionary time.

It will help to recall how Priestley had worked in the eighteenth-century "commonwealth of learning" and what transformation the Romantic-age Institutions could bring to natural philosophy. Priestley's works "mostly succeeded in reaching a broad readership among the enlightened public," as Jan Golinski writes, a heterogeneous readership among the professional commercial, gentry, and aristocratic classes, but Davy's highly targeted lectures at the Royal Institution had a built-in audience weighted initially toward the wealthy, though it soon enough broadened into the middle classes.[12] Where Priestley published voluminously across scientific and other genres, Davy would publish rarely, except papers in *Philosophical Transactions*, winning him European readers and scientific acclaim, while lecturing for a decade at the Royal to audiences of 500 to 1,000 listeners each night. Priestley's experimental scenarios were wide open for interested participants to inspect; Davy's own laboratory, unlike his lecture hall, was closed to all but gentlemen or scientific peers. Priestley's Dissenting connections could sustain him both personally and through encouraging a wider forging of networks among friends, discussants, and colleagues, even "self-organizing philosophical societies." Davy's new context was the heavily administered Institution that separated the lecture stage from the seated audience. From the 1760s to the 1790s, Priestley formed allies of personal connection and communal influence, but Davy was a far more embattled scientific being, fearful of rejection by the social elite he courted and above all driven by a competitive hankering for peer recognition rather than the collaborative ethos that Priestley always seemed able to assume.

In such ways, Davy's chemical revolution at the Royal Institution had been uncoupled from a rational progressivist politics. By exposing the contradiction between Davy's practical materialism and his proclaimed neo-aristocratic idealism at the Royal Institution (and now the Royal Society), Carlile located the distance between the professionalizing of science and the public political positions it might be expected to support. Since one can no longer assume the progressive or liberating tendencies of scientific production, one must now *demand* of the new scientists that they employ their expertise and their powerful discoveries to "speak out," "stand forward and support me, sound a loud blast in the cause of Truth, of Reason, of Nature and her laws." Carlile effectively defined the scientific intellectual not simply as one who should have the courage to speak and write candidly in the public sphere (certainly little in this essay resembles Kant's point or philosophical tone in "What is Enlightenment?"). Rather the scientific intellectual must speak to universal justice on the basis of his disciplinary and authoritative command of a crucial domain of knowledge. What Carlile was calling for Davy and other scientists to do suggests he had something like Michel Foucault's "specific intellectual" in mind, who speaks out politically from within his real sphere of expertise. Foucault, we recall, opposed this specific intellectual to Sartre's philosophical "universal" intellectual who would speak out on anything in the public sphere regardless of his expertise. But since Carlile was calling for Davy's scientific expertise to be the basis for his joining Carlile's campaign against kingship and priestcraft – a significantly larger domain of critique than Foucault allowed the "specific intellectual" – it may be more accurate to see Carlile singling out the scientific authority figure to adopt a kind of half-way posture between these specific and universal models for an intellectual role.[13]

In any case, Carlile's pamphlet signaled a recognition that a scientific "field" had now emerged in a more decisively disciplinary form than anything known to Priestley's Republic of Letters. In this process, the sciences had developed a distinction between a large-scale scientific sector – explicitly linked to economic resources, political alliances, and above all widespread public reception – and a more restricted field in which "knowledge" was produced with sophisticated instruments for other scientists. Between the lecture hall open to the public and the laboratory attended only by specialists at the Royal Institution, this separation had since 1802 been made most explicit in Humphry Davy's own career. That career also featured the two-handed performance, Carlile understood, of "true science" on the one hand and the social-economic exploitation of science for political ends on the other. This is partly why the *Address to Men of Science* seems more to forget than to sustain the older, publicly responsive natural philosopher Priestley had stood for. The knowledge game has fundamentally changed, in short, and the 1821 *Address* speaks to this turning point in the historical relations between scientific knowledge and public politics in Britain.

Equally striking in the *Address* is Carlile's self-positioning toward the new mode of scientific authority. He admits that he has never actually attended a scientific lecture nor a scientific society meeting in these busy science-cultivating years of the early nineteenth century. What Carlile might have witnessed, had he attended scientific lectures at the Royal Institution, was the process by which Davy had transformed the clumsy and widely questioned apparatus invented by Volta into the now "black-boxed" scientific apparatus of Davy's most impressive chemical discoveries. Turning the new Voltaic pile – a sophisticated electrical battery – into a proven scientific instrument at the Royal Institution was to dazzle not only the fashionable lay audiences who attended Davy's lectures and lionized him in society circles, but also the Continental chemists who were impressed by nothing greater than turning a doubtful assembly of barrels and copper wire into a productive, hard-to-duplicate electrochemical apparatus on the stage of the British scientific institutions.

Carlile's own black-box was the radical publisher's hand press, and it is telling when he insists in the *Address* that "the printing press has come like a true Messiah to emancipate the great family of mankind." This is the print-culture equivalent of a scientist like Davy claiming that the new sciences are revealing how "The whole universe might be aptly termed a great chemical apparatus."[14] The effort to harness one to the other revealed the depth of Carlile's hopes and doubtless also his illusions. Davy's Voltaic apparatus (and other instruments becoming ever more complex) was now accredited to publish "truth" in ways that were no longer commensurable with the truth-telling instruments of print culture, radical or otherwise, and the difference accounted in part for the perceptible gap between Davy's privately achieved professional authority and the public commitments that might arise from it. Later Carlile compares his own persecutors who jailed him for publishing seditious reading matter to "The Judges who condemned Galileo ... [who were] quite mild and humane when compared with mine."[15] Enlisting himself in the rolls of Galileo's defiant-heroic science could not change the mismatch of strength between Davy's Voltaic pile and the Regency radical's hand-operated publishing press. The chain and relative position of such instruments was already, along with the forms of audience they were used to reach, being altered.

### Disciplinarity and "organization"

Thirty years before *An Address to Men of Science*, Edmund Burke had argued in *Reflections on the Revolution in France* that "The objects of society are of the greatest possible complexity."[16] There was nothing complex about a church-and-king mob burning Joseph Priestley's house and laboratory on the historically resonant night of July 14, 1791. But it was with Burke's help that anti-revolutionary writers at the turn of the nineteenth century developed a rhetoric of complexity aimed to refute the seemingly simple atoms and social diagrams sketched by natural philosophers and political reformers alike, thereby, as Burke held, seeking to damage a delicate social order arising out of innumerable acts, decisions, prejudices, local customs, and accidents from the past. Burke himself linked such complexity to historically evolved forms of "organization," and indeed the *OED* registers the following passage from 1790 as the first use of the term *organization*, long associated with medicine or physiology, to mean "social organization." Unlike the French Revolutionaries, Burke urged, the English Revolutionists of 1688 had "acted by the ancient organized states in the shape of their old organization, and not by the organic *moleculae* of a disbanded people." His foundational term for organized complexity was "institutions," the uncharted outcome of all the organizational moments of the past "moulding together the great mysterious incorporation of the human race."[17]

To be sure, Burke's language of complexity was an ultimately successful tactic for oversimplifying all that was reasonably complex in progressive social theory of the later eighteenth century, using a classic weapon in the arsenal of those "political men of letters" he appeared to renounce. Where Burke had pitted historical complexity against the seemingly reductive designs of Enlightenment, Thomas Malthus would incorporate scientific rhetoric into the argument for complexity toward similarly conservative ends. To such apparent radical simplifications as Godwin's *Enquiry concerning Political Justice* (1793), Malthus responded in 1798, "I see great and, to my understanding, unconquerable difficulties."[18] By this time, of course, Godwin himself had been revising the original text of *Political Justice* in order to account for the consequences of complexity in human motives, affects, and actions. The 1796 and 1798 revisions of *Political Justice* sharply qualified the Enlightenment confidence of 1793 by invoking the innumerable and frustratingly counterintuitive contingencies that had come to shape the real outcomes of historical intentions and political acts.

Meanwhile "mechanism" was becoming one of the key conservative code-words for simplicity, even before Thomas Carlyle mobilized the metaphor of mechanism to encompass all modern British fields of knowledge and cultural production in 1829. In the great John Hunter debate of 1811–19, for instance, "organicists" or "vitalists" struggled with "mechanists" or "materialists" in what actually became an elaborate dialogue about rival meanings of "complexity" and especially – the more focused term in the Hunter debates – "organization." Such arguments were nearly always a means of situating oneself with respect to the last hegemonic religious system in Europe.[19] "Christendom," wrote Coleridge in Chapter 15 of the *Biographia Literaria*, "has been so far one great body, however imperfectly organized, that a similar spirit will be found in each period to have been acting in all its members."[20] Certainly Coleridge knew what an idealization this was – Christendom had *become* so "imperfectly organized" in the recent centuries of its post-Reformation crisis, and what was surely now at issue was how far it remained, in any real sense, "one great body" at all. To grasp Christendom as an *organized* body was already, in 1817, to deploy the language of "body" in contemporary, and just then highly politicized, scientific terms.

According to the debate that had been taking shape around John Hunter's physiological collections at the Royal College of Surgeons, bodies that organized themselves into life were coming to be defined as "materialist" bodies; bodies generated into life by some prior force or principle were "vital" or "idealist" bodies. As a surgeon in the eighteenth century, Hunter had assiduously collected skeletons, heads, and organ specimens from animal and human bodies, partly from surgical practice and partly from voyages to the South Seas in the 1770s. By the time of his death in 1793, the size of Hunter's collection – some 14,000 specimens – had outgrown the square footage of his own house. Only after arranging these alcohol-preserved body parts in a certain order, as later displayed at the Royal College of Surgeons, was Hunter granted credit for transforming the period's natural-history collections from curious "cabinets of rarities" to "a systematic and illuminated record of the operations and products of life."[21]

But Hunter's collection remained enigmatic. His own writings seemed to straddle both sides of the relation between vital life principles and a materialist grasp of physiological organization. When John Thelwall tried to clarify this question by writing the "Essay on Animal Vitality" in 1793, Coleridge replied by citing the ambivalence of his own recent poem the "Aeolian Harp." There Coleridge had pictured his own physiological organization trembling into vitality as vast, plastic breezes played the features of his body into erotic music, only to censure himself, by poem's end, for his all-too-material flight of pleasure. To Thelwall he confided that, try as he might to find some principle of the "whole," Coleridge could "contemplate nothing but parts, and the parts are all little!"[22]

For the concept of "organization" somehow referred to both organ stucture and living process together in an unfathomable configuration. Yet it was a far more specific term than it is today because it was only beginning to do its exceptional historical work. Saree Makdisi places William Blake's work in this moment of the 1790s when political and economic meanings of "organization" emerged to articulate the controversy over "the best way to organize society," while the identical language of organization could be articulated for opposing purposes – organizing into "various classes of labour and opulence," for instance, or into political tendencies marked anti-Jacobin or radical.[23] The importance of this point for the work of knowledge-organizing in Britain would arise especially, if I may build on Makdisi's clarifying point, out of one version of the complex 1790s proliferation of meanings about what it meant to "organize" or "be organized." This was a debate over the meaning of Hunter's physiological work that involved John Abernethy, William Lawrence, Samuel Coleridge, T. C. Morgan, and John Barclay, who took turns interpreting Hunter's weird collection of specimen jars and line drawings in order to grasp the "fitness and orderliness of things that seemed to defy explanation."[24]

In 1816 the physiologist Lawrence stood before the Royal College of Surgeons to interpret Hunter's great collection as a materialist legacy. "Life," Lawrence lectured, "is merely the active state of the animal structure ... Every action of a living being must have its organic apparatus. There is no digestion without an alimentary cavity; no biliary secretion without some kind of liver; no thought without a brain." Then he added pointedly, "An immaterial and spiritual being could not have been discovered amid the blood and filth of the dissecting room."[25] Lawrence tried to locate the secret of living systems in the cellular action of tissue, although, as one historian of physiology comments, "in what way a particular organization *causes* a particular property [of life action]" seemed a lot less clear.

Coleridge believed Lawrence had failed to account for Hunter's most striking idea, that of a "life or vital principle, *'independent of the organization.'*"[26] The laborious result of his intervention, *The Theory of Life*, now runs to seventy pages in the *Collected Coleridge*, and it is based on a striking innovation of method. Lawrence and Abernethy, in their respectively materialist and vitalist interpretations of Hunter's collection, focused on surviving and ambiguously written texts. Rather than Hunter's writing, Coleridge made a critical decision to interpret his physical collection, that is, Hunter's technical apparatus as itself a kind of text, preparing this weird collection of specimen jars to be interpreted as Hunter's greatest text by calling it the "unspoken alphabet of nature."[27] Coleridge thereby sought to transform the debate on the organization of human and animal bodies into an explication of the "method" by which Hunter had intellectually organized his sprawling collection. In this way, Coleridge tried to make the undecidable complexity of Hunter's own materials the key to the clarity of his ultimate interpretive meanings. In *Theory of Life*, Coleridge seems to have thought he had found a way to trump Lawrence's arguments. We need to recall here that despite the widening meanings of *organization* in the early nineteenth century, there was no such corresponding term as *self-organization* in this period, although it has since been an important idea for historians of the period like E. P. Thompson, for whom it was crucial to show that in the Romantic age, the English working class was culturally organized *itself* in ways, and especially cultural ways, that an earlier materialist tradition had failed to explain. In the Regency quarrel between self-professed idealists and materialists, a notion of self-organization entered the John Hunter debate. Coleridge called it an absurdity and accused the physiologist Lawrence of self-contradiction. "I repel," Coleridge wrote,

> the assertion and even the supposition that the functions are the offspring of the structure, and "Life the result of organization," connected with it as effect with cause. Nay, the position seems to me little less strange, than as if a man should say, that building – with all the included handicraft, of plastering, sawing, planing, etc. – were the offspring of the house; and that the mason and carpenter were the result of a suite of chambers, with passages and staircases that led to them. To make A the offspring of B, when the very existence of B *as* B presupposes the existence of A, is preposterous in the *literal* sense of the word, and a consummate instance of the *hysteron proteron* in logic [emphases in original].[28]

The notion that the organizational entity called a "house" should be thought of as generating the acts of plastering, sawing, and planing that would seem to have produced it in the first place – or that the mason and carpenter are somehow *results* of its rooms and stairwells – might have struck Lawrence as preposterous as well. At least no self-producing houses appear anywhere in his texts. Yet Coleridge's leap to single out this particular *hysteron proteron* was not as arbitrary a move as it first appears. In fact, it would be possible to say now that Lawrence's arguments as a whole were driving toward precisely that conclusion. To suggest that the architect or mason would be a house's way of producing another house – or that Coleridge himself might be a library's way of making another library – would be to follow the logic of the process first called, in late twentieth-century theoretical biology, *autopoiesis*, a "self-production" that is neither "mechanical" nor wholly illogical, but reflexive and self-referring, since organisms or systems would tend to "produce and eventually change their own structures." To think in this way – a way that has seemed increasingly plausible since the concept of *autopoiesis* has been adapted into the sociology of Niklas Luhmann and has been adopted into literary and media theory – is to think in terms of a system or network that generates its own components, while in turn those components reflexively generate the boundary of the system.[29] As Coleridge suspected, such self-producing organisms or systems (even if they were plausible to the religious mind) would require no motivating spark of vitality or divine prime mover at all. Everything would take place in the complex interactivity of organisms with their environments. Thinking about this problem eventually led Coleridge to abandon Abernethy's vitalism and pursue instead, as he would in the "Essays on Method" in the 1818 *Friend*, the language of "evolution."

There were also compelling literary consequences for this organizational discourse. Coleridge's architectural analogy in *Theory of Life* seems to have been reformulated in the *Biographia Literaria* (a text composed within the same year), when Coleridge insists that the structural style of Westminster Abbey "is *essentially* different from that of Saint Paul, even though both had been built with blocks cut into the same form and from the same quarry."[30] That distinction helps Coleridge decide what is essential and what is merely material in the language and organization of Wordsworth's *Lyrical Ballads*. And both the *Biographia Literaria* and the *Theory of Life* would likewise propose the principle of "individuation" – as "the inmost principle of the *possibility*, of any thing *as* that particular thing" – that helps us distinguish works of imaginative "genius" from merely mechanical works of "talent" that earn their plaudits in the literary marketplace. This principle was indeed the "vital" one that Coleridge was using to refute Wordsworth's all-too-mechanical and inadvertently materialist theory of poetic language in "Preface to *Lyrical Ballads*" (a theory of poetic language as rooted in daily and bodily practices). He had tested this kind of argument in his unpublished engagement with Lawrence's more willfully materialist theory of physiology in the John Hunter debate and *Theory of Life*.

## Texts and instruments

Yet it was his reading of Homer that allowed Coleridge to situate himself most firmly between the emerging sciences and a properly "literary" domain. In the midst of a religious polemic against modern materialists, Coleridge argued to readers of *Aids to Reflection* (1824) that philosophical and political materialism had "received a mortal blow" from "the increasingly *dynamic* spirit of the physical Sciences now highest in public estimation":

> It is not in Chemistry alone that we will be indebted to the Genius of Davy, Oersted, and their compeers; and not as the Founder of Physiology and philosophic Anatomy alone, will Mankind love and revere the name of John Hunter. These men have not only *taught*, they have compelled us to admit, that the immediate objects of our *senses*, or rather the grounds of the visibility and tangibility of all Objects of Sense, bear the same *relation* and similar proportion to the *intelligible* object – i.e. to the Object, which we actually *mean* when we way, *"It is such or such a thing,"* or *"I have seen this or that,"* – as the paper, ink, and differently combined straight and curved lines of an Edition of Homer bear to what we understand by the words, Iliad and Odyssey.[31]

We can grasp the power and meaning of the sciences because we know an analogous power and intelligibility through literature, and particularly through the material or bibliographical basis of literary transmission, the paper, ink, and typographical codes of the "edition." This distinction between the book's material form and verbal structure – which taken together would constitute what Chartier calls the "form" of the book – did not mean Coleridge was especially impressed with the new British bibliography, but it does suggest that he would develop his own literary notion of textual "form" in response to the problem of deciding what the intellectual and material dimensions of literary works actually are.[32] And certainly Coleridge was not claiming mere convergence of either science and literature or poems and bibliographical supports – the rigor of his analogy kept those two domains firmly distinct. He does seem to claim, though, that the literary *and* the scientific could both be grasped in the relation they instituted between materialities and the ideal. Just as he embraced Hunter's technical apparatus of specimens rather than his posthumous writings, Coleridge invoked here a peculiar and telling instrument. The modern print edition of Homer, a material vehicle of an immaterial *Iliad* and *Odyssey*, helps him to make the distinction between the *sensible* objects and experimental devices of Davy's galvanic-pile electrochemistry or Hunter's specimen-jar physiology and their intelligible scientific truths. Such a distinction also gave Davy and Hunter philosophical stature; it separated them from mere purveyors of "experiment" who crowded the scientific lecturing institutions and private societies of the day.

Consider how much more complicated Coleridge's analogy might have been had he put, in place of the Homer edition, say, the King James edition of the Protestant Bible. Here the relation between sensible (or literal) scripts and intelligible (symbolic) truths had become, in the age of the Higher Criticism in which bibliographers like Adam Clarke were working, unstably suspended. We get a fair sense here of how the analogy between scientific and literary instruments worked to stabilize the emerging domains of the properly fictional or symbolic and the properly referential or scientific. Coleridge's careful calibration of such instruments – both as a producer of literary texts and as a close reader of current scientific devices – entailed no "visionary synthesis" but rather something more like a Romantic *co-production* of the modern scientific revolution.

For contrast, there is Keats. In 1816 he proclaimed his own belated "discovery" of Homer's epics by comparing it to modern discoveries in astronomy and in exploration of the globe. In the sonnet "On First Looking Into Chapman's Homer" (1816) – which concerns the same Elizabethan edition of Homer that Coleridge possessed in his library – Keats equated the experience of Chapman's "loud and bold" translation to feeling "like some watcher of the skies, When a new planet swims into his ken" – that is, like William Herschel must have felt in March 1781 when he seized upon the point of light in the night sky that would come to be known in astronomy as the "discovery" of the planet Uranus. This is the center of a poem that compares discoverers in their great domains – poetic, scientific, and geopolitical – and likewise their instruments: editions, telescopes, expeditionary forces. Recent commentaries on this poem have revealed the complexity and ambivalence of Keats's own claim to "discover" Homer's *Odyssey* by way of a modern translation, and how this episode of literary discovery is further complicated by Keats's analogy to the New World imperialism of the Spanish conquistadores.[33] The Herschel analogy has escaped similar scrutiny because it so effectively overdetermines the trope of "discovery." And it does so by marvelously economic poetical means. The Anglo-Saxon word "ken" in the sonnet's tenth line usually means "range of vision," but it can also mean "range of knowledge." The word silently encloses the fifteen years after 1781 during which Herschel's telescopic "range of vision" was disputed by rival researchers and denied the status of authentic discovery. Not until the late 1790s was Herschel's claim finally certified as belonging to the "range of knowledge," or effectively authorized as a "discovery" rather than an extravagant claim.[34] By 1816 its discovery status had become so assured that Keats could generalize all the specificities of the case in a single phrase "some watcher of the skies." This passage appears widely in modern histories and textbooks of astronomy, and there is no doubt about why. For literary purposes, to use the language of the sociology of science, Keats had effectively "black-boxed" the protracted process of "discovering" Uranus in order to secure more visibly complicated discoveries – one literary (of Homer), the other colonial (South America).

Keats's poem suggests precisely the reversibility of Coleridge's Homeric example. There Chapman's Homer would secure the meaning of the new sciences, but here it is secured *by* them. In both cases, the relationship between the emerging literary and scientific domains of the nineteenth century suggests a process of unintended co-production, if we can use that term to describe what we might now call a multidisciplinary process of calibrating instruments – from poetical editions to galvanic batteries, telescopes, and specimen collections, or we might say from bookish and literary organization to scientific – as a principal means of producing the analogous disciplinary formation of literary and scientific spheres.

## Institutions and the differentiating of knowledges

Near the end of the Romantic age in Britain appeared two very different histories of the modern sciences: best known is the three-volume *History of the Inductive Sciences* (1837) by William Whewell, a Cambridge don and in some sense the originator of a modern historiography of science in both narrative style and historical method. Whewell dated the origins of modern science to antiquity and marked its decisive modern seventeenth-century revolution in ways that would become, until recently, typical of the way subsequent historians were to chart the history of modern science. The shorter history is far less known and now seldom read – a historical sketch in the *Quarterly Review* (1826) by a little-known lawyer whose impact had not yet been felt in the contemporary sciences. When Charles Lyell published "Scientific Institutions" shortly after John Gibson Lockhart assumed editorship of the *Quarterly Review*, he was not yet the author of *Principles of Geology* (1830), nor did he offer, exactly, a "geological" reading of recent British scientific history in his essay (but, as a sign of the times, it was now worth reviewing "institutions, societies, and associations" as fully as reviewing books). Lyell narrated a very different story than Whewell's concept-based history of science by mapping an institutional revolution of modern sciences over the previous forty years, one that seemed decisively to distinguish the earlier period of "natural philosophy," from the middle of the seventeenth century to the end of the eighteenth, from what now emerged at the turn of the nineteenth century as an irreversible disciplinary and institutional transformation. Thus, long before Thomas Kuhn coined the expression "second scientific revolution" in 1977 – a thesis with enormous consequences for the subsequent cultural history of the sciences – Lyell framed precisely such a picture in 1826.[35] His fascination with scientific disciplinary emergence and institutionalization suggests a cultural stratigraphy of the new formations of British knowledge in the early nineteenth century that more famous landmarks, like Whewell's "internalist" science history, would subsequently screen out of view.

Charles Lyell entered the venerable Tory publication as something of an undercover agent. As Michael Rectenwald shows in a compelling study of his career in the context of England's nineteenth-century "public science," Lyell had been raised by a Tory family and educated at Oxford, yet while in London in the 1820s he studied for the bar, and became a liberal Whig and likely a reformist advocate for disestablishing the national (Anglican) church. Choosing not to advocate for reform publicly because of his family connections, Lyell found "science and educational reform ... a 'safe' means by which he might enter into the spirit of the age" now leaning more intensively toward Parliamentary reform. To become a *Quarterly Review* contributor in 1826 he thus covered his tracks: "I must not sport radical," he confided to one friend, "since I am become a Quarterly Reviewer." His ensuing essays on scientific institutions and the major British universities thus show him walking a fine line between reform and orthodoxy.[36]

Rather than Whewell's synthetic "logic of scientific discovery," Lyell pointed to the infrastructure and local conditions that have made British science a revolutionary force in senses quite different from the heyday of "natural philosophy." Three new kinds of complexity emerge in his evolutionary argument about the changing landscape of science – first, the complexity of what is being learned or proposed about nature itself, especially in biology and physiology; second, the complexity of the new scientific differentiations and subdivisions of knowledge emerging at the same time; and third, the analogous complexity of both national and international redefinition and self-division in Britain and Europe.

In "Scientific Revolutions" he dates the end of the old world of "natural philosophy" to the founding of the Linnean Society (1788), the Geological Society (1807), the Astronomical Society (1821), and many others, those little, differentiated worlds in which the assembled specialists would work together on the model articulated half a century earlier in another world, by Hume in the world of natural philosophy, when he described the work of the Edinburgh Philosophical Society: "the united judgments of men ... correct and confirm each other by communication, their frequent intercourse excites emulation from the comparison of different phenomena remarked by different persons."[37] Each of the new specialist societies, Lyell implies, achieved its distinction by recapitulating the older ethos of the Republic of Letters, a sphere of actual competition but ideal consensualism in the progress of educated knowledge. Yet, it could still be asked, why was the founding of the Linnean Society – hardly the first scientific society to be founded since the Royal Society in 1662 – so revolutionary an event? Perhaps because it was itself devoted to matters of classification, Lyell makes it the most significant "subdivision of scientific labour" attempted since 1662, mainly in its differentiating of zoology and botany from other kinds of natural history under the larger tent of the Royal Society. Apparently unaware that Joseph Priestley had argued something like this for the distinction of electricity in his history of that emerging discipline published in 1767, Lyell called 1788 the advent of the first *divisions* within the main division called "natural philosophy," and therefore the beginning of a process which itself will come to define the distinctiveness of the sciences in the period 1788–1825: the power to *generate* modern divisions, subdivisions, and distinctions, and therefore the classificatory agency par excellence.

At least this is the impression given by the *Quarterly*'s attention to another historic landmark in Britain's newly revolutionary sciences, the founding of the College of Surgeons (1800) and particularly the incorporation into the College of the collections of "the celebrated John Hunter." We now have ample evidence that Hunter's museum collections were already becoming legendary by 1800, the legacy that connected the new College to the older natural history while also rendering the latter, apparently, a thing of the past. Note, for example, how the *Quarterly* describes the outstanding feature of John Hunter's enormous collection:

> Besides the numerous specimens now exhibited, he left behind him nearly one thousand drawings, with a view either of illustrating the preparations now in the collection, or of supplying deficiencies. In these the external forms of many animals, as well as their anatomical structure, are delineated, and particularly those delicate and evanescent peculiarities in the organization of some plants and animals which are discernible only in living subjects ... illustrating the internal organization both of animals and plants, and the manner in which, under different circumstances, the same functions are carried on in different genera and species.[38]

The new scientific knowledges and forms of publication seemed to accentuate, among other things, previously undisclosed kinds of "organization" – both internal and external, as found in plants and as found in animals. In fact, the *Quarterly*'s science writer would develop an unusual analogy, one that he works out (though he does not make explicit) only when he has finished his catalogue of institutional landmarks in Britain between 1788 and 1825. The sciences are becoming complexified, both internally and externally – and subdividing from one another ("botany" is no longer the same pursuit as "zoology"); they likewise subdivide internally. What has happened in the sciences, he makes clear, is a simultaneous external and internal process of complexifying by way of differentiation, division, and demonstration of complicated internal and external patterns of organization. Also revealing is that the more modern science seems to differentiate itself *according to* its newly discovered scientific objects or methods – its new institutions, laboratories, museums, nomenclatures – the more it also finds out how "under different circumstances, the same functions are carried on in different genera and species." The same process of differentiating also performed the labor that it took to produce a higher abstraction called "science." Science, that is, becomes "science," in a wholly unprecedented sense, only by means of such self-differentiating. Hence Lyell proposes that the era from 1660 to 1788 can be periodized as the pre-revolutionary epoch of modern science (or, we might now say, its predisciplinary age), the single-celled progenitor of what was to become the multicellular sciences born of the spectacular differentiating and thereby self-defining process the *Quarterly* describes so intensely in 1826.

Still, despite these new and complex advances, Britain seemed to waver on the very pinnacle of its new scientific successes. Unlike France, which had long-since committed itself to the separation of scientific labor and display from other essential discourses and knowledges, Britain could not seem to decide for sure what knowledge should be connected to, or housed alongside, what. In 1826 the local case-in-point was the controversy over whether the National Gallery of Pictures should be housed inside the British Museum, or remain at its current quarters in Julius Angerstein's home at 100 Pall Mall. One has to imagine fine oil paintings hung disconcertingly side by side with utilitarian, line-drawn animal portraits produced by salaried employees. Among many other liabilities, the *Quarterly* reviewer cites this one: "To retain a gallery of the fine arts and cabinets of natural history even as distinct departments in the same building is objectionable, as there is the highest probability of the mutual interference of such unconnected repositories of national treasures in the event of future enlargements of the original design."[39] Though it was, after all, a *British* museum, considerations of national unity were now outweighed by the prospect that had to be built in to any conception of a "discipline" – namely its "future" expansion, self-division, complexification, and more or less autonomous expansion. But since the National Gallery was a *collection* that might expand willy-nilly, according to whatever new Old Masters it acquired or whatever new British painters came into its holdings, and by no means part of an advancing progressive "knowledge," the plan even to mix them in the same building suggested the British, unlike the French or Germans, did not yet fully grasp what a "discipline" of knowledge really was.

Thus come into play, at this point in Lyell's argument, the lecturing and research, "arts and sciences" Institutions building audiences for science in London since 1800. Lyell accentuates the difference between specialist societies and these far wider, more spectacular, and more multidisciplinary public displays for a huge audience of middle-class and aristocratic "fashionables" who also heard other disciplines lectured about as well as moral philosophy, the fine arts, and, with Samuel Coleridge, literary history and theory. Here was being tacitly articulated the relation between various sciences and between what were becoming now differentiated as the "human sciences" descending from natural philosophy and political economy, on the one hand, and moral philosophy on the other. The two new forms of institutionalizing, the scientific societies on the one hand, and far-flung English arts-and-sciences lecturing institutions on the other, together articulated to Lyell a new scientific field composed of distinct institutional sectors: one for the scientists who produced knowledge *for* other scientists, and one for the lay public who were learning the broader mission of science by way of spectacular public demonstration. Bourdieu's sociology of the modern fields suggests that once the line between these two sectors was so firmly drawn – in this case, between science-for-other-scientists, now increasingly commanded by the specialist societies, and "public science" for the lay audience – the scientific field itself was reaching a stage of *relative* autonomy far beyond what in the older sphere of the Republic of Letters had functioned as "natural philosophy." Though Charles Lyell had little sociological perspective on the new institutions, he recognized the complementary yet quite distinct functions now being performed by specialist and public sectors in constituting the new coherence of science as a whole.

Here was a process for which, to appreciate its magnitude, Lyell felt he had to invoke even the name of Milton and that poet's own important political moment at the dawn of modern science. Yet it was a risky comparison, as this passage on the political controversies after 1789 will show:

> When we remember that, at no distant period, rival theories of a purely philosophical nature, and as unconnected with the affairs of human life as the elements which strove for mastery in Milton's chaos, "around the flag, of each his faction," derived, nevertheless, exclusively from the ranks of his opponent political parties, their zealous champions, we are at a loss to conceive by what happy accident the Institutions in question have so long escaped this prevailing contagion; and the addition of a few similar instances would persuade us that "Chance" here also, as in the poet's allegory, "is high arbiter, and governs all."[40]

As I have been arguing in earlier chapters, the new scientific Institutions and societies, in fact, did not escape the political "contagion" by chance, but by means of elaborate effort, inventive projecting, and administrative strategizing aimed to achieve the careful insulation of Britain's scientific

Societies, Institutions, and Academies from political debate in the past thirty years. Assigning political struggle to Milton's "Chaos," Lyell renders the new scientific institutions as a great bridge over the troubled waters of French revolutionary and British popular politics that has roiled the early nineteenth century. Evoking Milton so opportunely also makes little sense of Milton's own misgivings about the scientific revolutions Lyell is now extending far beyond Milton's time. Almost any account of *Paradise Lost*'s "bridge over chaos" (Book 10) would suggest that if "chance" governs the realm of Chaos (Milton calls it the "umpire" mediating between the "factions" of heat, moisture, light, and air), the bridge or any other construct achieved by the "arts and sciences" is a massive effort to overcome the contingency and chance that roils beneath its constructions. Some scholars have seen in Milton's epic a demonic anticipation of just what Lyell has been celebrating. "The fallen angels are masters of organization," writes Jonathan Sawday in a fascinating book on early modern machines in cultural discourse, "Milton's hell is a technocracy."[41] Lyell, as Blake might say, wanted to be of Milton's party without actually reading him.

By portraying what was (according to Richard Carlile) the deeply political emergence of scientific institutions since 1788 as serendipitous, the *Quarterly* focuses attention on a different social process that was surely no less political, that is, the way in which a modern self-organizing process of scientific emergence can now be understood as a *national* force. The awakening to sciences that had begun in London, Lyell reminds his reader, has now increasingly galvanized the provinces by 1826.[42] It is here in the "native districts," Lyell thinks, that the real social power of the new scientific revolution can be unexpectedly discerned. Britain proves to resemble ancient Greece and early modern Italy more than it does ancient Rome in one essential way – like Greece and Italy, Britain is "subdivided into numerous independent states" (or provinces) "each impressed with a sense of national dignity."[43] Composed of rivalrous, relatively independent cities or republics, early Greece or early modern Italy knew a world of emulation and competition for rewards. This is why the intellectuals of Greece – a more compact and therefore more minutely subdivided world even than sixteenth-century Italy – were understood as representing their *local* attachment in their public, intellectual or philosophical struggle for recognition and dominance. "To this day every lover of classic lore remembers well that Sappho was a Lesbian, Leonidas a Spartan, Thucydides and Plato Athenians"; by contrast, modern admirers of Milton, Newton, or Marlborough scarcely know what towns or provinces bred them.[44] The modern scientific complexifying of the "Republic of Learning" must therefore be understood as rousing to "philosophical" awareness the still-inarticulate subdivisions of the British nation. So Lyell could contrast Grecian complexity with a totalizing and totalitarian Roman model, where the centralization of power simplified intellectual life so that Romans became "mere scholars of Greece." He also contrasted the potential of Britain with modern France, which had "drained the deserted provinces of native talent" – and which was now giving current plebeian science in London its Lamarckian evolutionary designs.[45]

Nowhere could it be clearer how the once internationalist character of the "Republic of Letters" was being reversed by the scientific and literary revolutions of 1780–1820. For nearly two centuries the Republic of Letters had formed an organized system of informational networking and scholarly exchange across the cities of Europe. Now the "Republic of Learning" (in the *Quarterly Review*'s account) must be understood, against the canons of progressive Enlightenment, as making "philosophical," and explicit, the field already organized within the inarticulate subdivisions of a nation. That the most advanced agents of the nation's thinking (its leading intellectuals and scientists) should thereby rouse to explicit form the nation's least advanced entity (its underdeveloped provinces or local spaces) also confers greater value and power on the intellectual fields themselves. "Thus in Greece and Italy the value of the illustrious deeds of individuals was doubly enhanced to each separate portion of the people, while the united communities in each, still laid claim, *as one nation separated from the rest of the world*, to the glories of their common citizens" (emphasis in the original).[46]

In 1826 Lyell tied the institutional self-differentiation of new scientific objects and disciplines to the internal complexities of living beings on the one hand, and the emergent complexity of a nation-organized world system on the other. Hence did these three levels of organization – the institutional or disciplinary, the biological, and the geopolitical – furnish the *Quarterly* reviewer with homologies of complexity that suggested, in its own right, an irreversible process of evolution. We know that in this period there were prominent metaphors available to describe the relations of small parts and large wholes, particularly the metaphor of the *organism* transported into England from sources in German idealism and biology. But what I have described above does not accentuate the *finished* complex whole that is claimed by organicist thought. Rather it emphasizes an ongoing process of complexifying even while it articulates shifting, unstable relations between parts and wholes. No attempt is made to tidy up the comparison of three quite separate levels of differentiation into one complete or totalized process – the institutional level (emergence of new sciences and forms of knowledge), the biological level (emergence of complexly organized beings), or the historical level (emergence of great internally complex nations). Obviously, though, the *Quarterly* reviewer intends *homologies* between these structurally similar or even identical processes. Natural, historical, and institutional modes of "organization" are meant to converge into one irreversible process of modernity's unfolding in time.

## What counts as knowledge

Lyell's history of "Scientific Institutions" – the kind of narrative that an increasingly disciplined domain of knowledge begins to tell about itself – closes Part I of this book by confirming what my earlier chapters have tried to show: the convergence of the discourse on "arts and sciences" that is so pervasive in the Romantic age with the newly recognized powers of "institution" that by now appeared as a means to expand the international reach of British culture and knowledge production. Two important observations should be made about this moment. First, to recall my discussion of "transfiguring" at the beginning of this book, Lyell was able to narrate a contemporary scientific revolution this way only by being able to transfigure the sciences "upward" in such a way that all the mechanical practices or "arts" evident earlier in this period will have vanished into his scientific-institutional world. There is nothing utilitarian in his picture, for instance, indeed no mention of the other important mode of instituting in the mid 1820s, the Mechanics Institutes in London and across England or the instituting in 1826 of the University of London. His *Quarterly Review* picture, on this score, is a polite one indeed, presuming a social constituency for scientific knowledge that has far more in common with what will develop in the early 1830s, the administrative restructuring of British sciences by the "gentlemen of science" or the British Association for the Advancement of the Sciences. I would argue that his parallel portrayal of a self-sufficient sphere of "fine arts" – which he says ought to have its own buildings, not share the British Museum with scientific collections – likewise assumed a sublation of a vast range of visual and literary practices into the world now signified by the "Grecian marbles" and the National Gallery of Pictures. The historical logic of Lyell's account is to narrate a "progress of the arts and sciences" that ceaselessly differentiates sciences from fine arts, libraries from museums, chemistry and geology from the old natural philosophy in a widening gyre of "minute subdivisions" that drive the differentiating process to ever-further degrees of separation of one domain from another. That logic would reappear variously in Herbert Spencer's biology (as well as his sociology) at the mid nineteenth century, or in Talcott Parsons's theory of institutions as enacting "functional differentiation" in the mid twentieth, or as it does today in the form of differentiating, autopoietic "systems" in the influential work of Niklas Luhmann.

Second, and like these later, more social-scientific versions of modernity-as-differentiation, Lyell offered an evolutionary narrative of "arts and sciences" almost magically free of social contradiction, public controversy, political struggle, or the complex and contingent relationship between "knowledge" and "practices" of many kinds. By contrast, the foregoing chapters have argued a very different picture of the Romantic-age convergence between the cultural work of new institutions and the social reshaping of "arts and sciences." The conjuncture of political controversy and economic competition that generated the Royal Institution known to the nineteenth century has played a paradigmatic but far from isolated role in these various cases of fields in which practices and knowledges were transfigured in their relations both to one another and to those who worked within these fields.

To point these cases toward the next part of this book, I want to make more explicit an ongoing pattern in these earlier cases of administration and lecturing, bibliographical knowledge and book practices, the struggle over art producers and curators or connoisseurs, mechanical knowledges and "scientific." In every field I have considered thus far, the expression "arts and sciences" can be roughly and unevenly mapped onto a relationship between "practices and knowledges" that has become a new point of focus today in the midst of disciplinary questions and interdisciplinary experiments across the lines of separation of knowledge domains so confidently asserted by Lyell at the end of the Romantic period. Where and how do "practices" become "knowledges," one might ask, and what then counts as "knowledge"? Radical critics of Romantic science like Richard Carlile and admirers like Lyell both perceived it as a firmly bounded domain commanded by disciplinary expertise – highly organized in new institutional frameworks, "advancing" in either alarming or admirable ways, and capable of being criticized or celebrated without reference to the "arts" in either their practico-mechanical or fine-arts modes.

Why, from the late 1790s to the late 1820s, did the "arts" in all senses of the term recede decisively further from what was now counting as knowledge in the scheme "arts and sciences"? Three years before "Scientific

Institutions," Thomas De Quincey had advised in the *London Magazine* to think about "literature" in what was still a new way: "All that is literature seeks to communicate power; all that is not literature, to communicate knowledge."[47] We now know what a disabling distinction that could be for the humanities as a whole. The "arts and sciences" Institutions formed in the early 1800s, as the lecture-series example in Chapter 2 suggested, staged a far more mixed array of knowledge-directions than Lyell's late 1820s mapping of disciplines would imply. Neither the art field nor the abortive field of bibliographical book history would be counted as making credible "knowledge" claims by the mid 1820s in the way now widely being accredited to the sciences. To show this mixed picture of Romantic-age "arts and sciences," I have been using the sociological term "fields," adapted in a revisionist spirit from Bourdieu's sociology of cultural fields, understanding these emerging fields as engaging in controversies over the authority of practices and knowledge claims that were themselves changing the meaning of "arts and sciences" in the early nineteenth century. In Part II of this book, the present disciplinary position from which I have been writing – that of literary and cultural studies – will permit special, more focused attention on what was at issue in the "arts and sciences" for the emerging "literary" field, one that would not in this period be able to settle the changing meanings of the word *literature* itself.

PART II

*Questions of the literary*

CHAPTER 6

# The Coleridge Institution

Liberty prevails in the Common-Wealth of Learning. This Common-Wealth is a State extremely free. The Empire of Truth and Reason is only acknowledged in it; and under their Protection an innocent War is Waged against any one whatever. Friends ought to be on their Guard, there, against their Friends, Fathers against their Children, Fathers-in-law against their Sons-in-law, as in the Iron Age. Every body, there, is both Sovereign and under every-body's Jurisdiction.
[Pierre Bayle] *Dictionary Historical and Critical*
(English translation, 1735)

Look back on the history of the Sciences. Review the Method in which Providence has brought the more favored portion of mankind to the present state of Arts and Sciences.
Samuel Taylor Coleridge, *The Friend* (1818)

A cloud of perplexity ... seems to have been, at all times, hanging over the import of the terms *art* and *science*.
Jeremy Bentham, *Chrestomathia* (1816)

In earlier chapters I have taken the "arts and sciences" into Romantic-age knowledge projects, institutions, and cultural fields: in particular the scientific sphere, the art world, and that strangely conflicted field of study called the bibliographical. This aim has meant following the densely intercut domains of print, lectures, exhibits, and institutions as both separate modes of mediation in their own right, while also becoming *inter*mediated in cultural practice. Part II of this book will raise "Questions of the Literary" and thus move these matters more pointedly into the literary field. Yet I have also been suggesting the degree to which the "literary" was already at work in all these arts-and-sciences domains of the early nineteenth century – in questions of authorship and expertise, printed texts and scientific instruments, or efforts to order the arts and sciences bibliographically as an emerging "history of books." Perhaps even the expression *arts and sciences* should itself be called in part a "literary" one in the Romantic age, as its language both figured and transfigured the terms of this dialectic across the pivot of the conjunction *and*, mediating their divisions and their contingent modes of convergence.

If today we take the expression "Arts and Sciences" to designate a disciplinary system in the university, writers of the Romantic age – especially *as* writers – still believed the arts and sciences to belong largely to what early moderns called the Republic of Letters (also called the Commonwealth of Learning, or in Germany the *Gelehrtenrepublik*). In recent years the "lost continent" of this Republic has begun to be recovered for the history of knowledges, often as a contrary to modern disciplinarity and specialization.[1] From roughly 1500 to about 1800, the early modern Republic of Letters developed through Latin-writing epistolary networks of scholars to formal organizations like the Royal Society or academies of art, to vernacular commercial print cultures, and to the discourse of Enlightenment. The Republic of Letters offered in all these practices and institutional nodes a social and economic self-conception of the world of producers and users of knowledge, a normative guide to conduct and cognition alike. That it also was a kind of collective fiction did not keep its imagined geography from exercising real effects and providing cultural producers of all kinds, from antiquarians to polite essayists and from philosophers to journalists, with shifting standards and rules of operation. Measuring "the ideal and the reality" of the Republic, Lorraine Daston and others have found it fraught with contradictions familiar to any student of the seventeenth and eighteenth centuries: order and anarchy, commercialism and philosophical ideals, cosmopolitanism and an increasingly nationalist division of language-based learning spheres.[2]

Recent historiography of print cultures has also made it possible to periodize the early modern Republic of Letters in a way that registers its internal tensions as well as its broader transformations – from the scholarly, Latin-writing *respublica literaria* of the early modern era, to the vernacular and commercial republic emerging in the late seventeenth and early eighteenth century, and then to the politically focused, reformist literary republic crystallized in the later eighteenth century. For students of the early nineteenth century, such periodizing helps us see why, in retrospect, there would be such conflicting notions in the Romantic age as to what the Republic of Letters had been – and to what claiming ownership of any particular version or conception of it (the scholarly, the commercial, or the political) might and should portend in their new historical moment. The work of Ian Duncan and Paul Keen has helped us grasp what it meant for the conceptuality of the literary republic to begin failing in the 1790s and to create a "crisis of literature" in the last conflicted decade of the eighteenth century – a crisis in the very category that had embraced so wide a range of educated knowledges in the literary republic.³ Duncan calls this moment the "disaggregation" of the Republic of Letters around 1800, one that compelled its various elements – writing, audience, literary authority, the system of genres, and not least the relation of specializing and broader knowledges – to undergo new modes of redefinition and reorganization over the next thirty years. Few of these modes had as much public impact as the new arts-and-sciences Institutions and their widening reach across England, and then more indirectly, across the Atlantic.

Yet no institutional or imaginary context for knowledges as long lasting as the early modern Republic of Letters simply disappears. When the *Analytical Review* vowed in 1788 to become "Historians of the Republic of Letters," their plans testified to an already palpable sense of this historicity of early modern learning and publication, and it was no small part of the Romantic writers' own innovative acts to rethink (and sometimes reenact) that history of letters by way of extraordinary imagination and invention.⁴ In the next two chapters I want to make more explicit the *literariness* of the discursive domain called "arts and sciences" by turning to the kinds of Romantic writing – poetry, the novel, literary and cultural criticism – that would, by the twentieth century, become the formal subject of literary study, now itself located in a disciplinary system named "Arts and Sciences."

In Chapter 6 I shall take Coleridge to be the literary republic's most provocative and perhaps perversely illuminating Romantic historian. He grasped its evolution as a complex process of differentiating spheres, citing from the vantage point of 1832 "three silent revolutions in England: 1. when the Professions fell off from the Church, 2. when Literature fell off from the Professions, 3. when the Press fell off from Literature."⁵ Coleridge's long-noted fascination with seventeenth-century precursors was relevant to the titling of his most important work in literary theory, *Biographia Literaria*, which alludes both to the *respublica literaria* and to its modern commercial counterpart he so often renounces in this work. As Coleridge pulled fitfully away from a contemporary Republic of Letters he had never fully embraced, the *Biographia* began working to restore the "ex-dignitaries of the *Book-republic*" who had belonged to an older cultural formation than the Addisonian or Scottish commercial republic still authoritative in the reviewing establishment the *Biographia* struggled to repudiate.⁶ I then turn to his wider project to rethink the "arts and sciences" in Coleridge's writings on "method," and for this purpose I recall John Stuart Mill's classic comparison of Coleridge to Jeremy Bentham as the great philosophical contraries of their time. What complicates Mill's (or any later) version of this contrast is the way both Coleridge (in "Treatise on Method" and the 1818 *Friend*) and Bentham (in *Chrestomathia*) make new efforts to rethink the Enlightenment pairing of "arts and sciences" as a question of the coherence between cultural practices and disciplinary knowledges. From the *Friend* to his last work on national institutions in *Church and State*, the "arts and sciences" would become to Coleridge a guiding if troubled problematic or heuristic for a body of political and metaphysical philosophy that would otherwise seem to speak well beyond them.

Coleridge's and Bentham's attempts to theorize the coherence of the arts and sciences will both frame and contrast with Chapter 7's account of how the Dissenting writers and reformers of the Romantic age pushed back against such systems as they dealt with more intractable contradictions when confronting the political or economic conditions struggles that mediated the arts and sciences to public life. Unlike Coleridge, who tended to be strategically vague about real histories of knowledge and its material circumstances, Dissenters and reformers accentuated the historicity of sciences and arts and their relation to past and present acts of institution. These acts would crucially include the institutions of writing-genres: the authority of Enlightenment historiography, for instance, and the critical powers the novel or "romance" might have to dislocate its authority to tell why "things as they are" now prevail. This chapter will also show how the reformers and Dissenters could rethink the way poetics and the fine arts could be ambitiously hopeful means of social transformation, even while the "useful arts" and the proliferating sciences could create difficult obstacles to finding common ground among the political reform projects themselves.

## Writing and lecturing in the Coleridge Institution

To avoid being a "mere literary man" plying a trade in a market, Coleridge became, as Byron wryly remarked, "the man of lectures," establishing a career as literary critic and theorist in the newest cultural institutions on the London scene.[7] In a somewhat extraordinary gesture, Coleridge insisted his most important "publicity" was occurring beyond the print-based literary republic altogether: "Are books the only channel through which the stream of intellectual usefulness can flow?" he asked readers of the *Biographia*. "Is the diffusion of truth to be estimated by publications; or publications by the truth, which they diffuse or at least contain?"

The place and power of "my opinions" were affirmed, not in print, but rather among the "numerous and respectable audiences, which at different times and in different places honoured my lecture rooms with their attendance."[8] For a London lecturer whose public speaking would eventually feel "too much like a retail dealer in instruction and pastime," as he told one correspondent in late 1818, it was still true that "lecturing is the only means by which I can enable myself to go on at all with the great philosophical work to which the best and most genial hours of the last twenty years of my life have been devoted."[9] Having lectured at the Royal in 1808 and the Surrey in 1812, Coleridge also learned how to step out and begin forging something of a Coleridge Institution unto himself, setting up lecture series at Willis's Rooms, Fleur-de-Lis Court, Scots' Corporation Hall, or the Crown and Anchor Tavern and learning rudiments of the local administrative procedures and advertising campaigns needed to make his own portable arts-and-sciences Institution work as well as it did. For help he used the network of allies he had begun acquiring through Humphry Davy at the Royal Institution, while Thomas Bernard appears in his letters through 1812 as a personal lecture-manager, setting up engagements at the London Philosophical Society or Willis's Rooms for what later became the most widely published Coleridge lectures – those on Shakespeare and poetics delivered in 1811 and 1812.[10]

Questions of language, disciplinary specialization, and broader public access to knowledge have been well raised for this period's problem of defining poetry itself by Robin Valenza.[11] I want to take them further in this chapter by noting, first, that such issues bear on the conceptual collapse of the Republic of Letters as a normative framework for educated communication around 1800. We can recall that in the literary republic, the array of educated discourses called "literature" had been so spacious a term that it could embrace both emerging knowledges and specializing languages on the one hand, and publicly accessible discourse on the other. Or, to use a scientific term of that age, literature in the early modern sense acted as the "ether" in and through which the arts and sciences breathed, connected, differentiated, or "advanced." With the disarray of the literary republic in the 1790s and beyond, pressure on the scope and meanings of the term *literature* intensified, while the London arts-and-sciences Institutions were playing no small part in firming up the distinction between literature, for example, and science, without yet giving the term the more "specialized" mission of fictiveness and imaginative writing it would eventually have.

In critical works of argument and speculation like the *Biographia Literaria*, one language belonging to any workable definition of "literature" – that of poetry – could be used to engage both what was pertinent to the "arts and sciences" and to the institutional conditions of what was still in 1817 being called the Republic of Letters. Coleridge's polemics against that republic are explicit enough, but his allusions to its most animating expression, "arts and sciences," can seem odd and somewhat cryptic. In Chapter 20 of the *Biographia* Coleridge quotes generously from Wordsworth's *Poems* of 1815 to make his ongoing case against the theory of the "Preface to *Lyrical Ballads*" that while the words of poetry themselves are "sufficiently common," their poetical ordering is surely not. Here he asks, if Wordsworth's and other poets' *words* are common enough, "in what poem are they not so? If we except a few misadventurous attempts to translate the arts and sciences into verse?"[12] Given the crucial role Coleridge would now begin giving poetry in assuring the coherence of "arts and sciences" from 1815 onward, this claim of untranslatability is an interesting, if offhanded, indicator of larger questions. The poetic misadventures he refers to must have included Erasmus Darwin's *Zoonomia* (1794) and similar poems lacing botanical language with poetic verse, or even Coleridge's own "Religious Musings" (1795), which in its "organizing surge" of enthusiasm for late eighteenth-century natural philosophers had used words like *sentient* in much the sense Joseph Priestley had given them in *Disquisitions Relating to Matter and Spirit* (1777).[13] Meanwhile, Coleridge was revising "Fears in Solitude" to include a language of "Institutions, Associations, and Societies" that was now inextricable from the British arts-and-sciences world he had been lecturing in himself. But apart from poetic language as such, his curious phrasing in works like *On the Constitution of Church and State* concerning "all the so called liberal arts and sciences," in one of that work's crucial passages defining the nature of the "clerisy," would also invite disparate readings and misreadings.

As rough drafts for what Coleridge would theorize as the "clerisy" in *Church and State*, Coleridge used his literary lectures – which became all the more useful to his philosophy-in-progress because, as Peter Manning remarks, they *remained* unpublished – to adapt August Schlegel's untranslated formulations about how poetry performs its intellectual work.[14] No longer rule-structured from without, he argued in an 1812 lecture on *Romeo and Juliet*, the poetic text was now said to be "organized" from within: "It must embody order to reveal itself; but a living body is of necessity an organized one."[15] It is quite possible to read this substituting of "organization" for the older concept of poetic "rules" as a certain displacement, not a rejection, of the early *respublica literaria*'s analogy between rules of state and rules of literary production.[16] Meanwhile, the category of "organization" reflected the influence of the new sciences, especially Hunter's physiology in England and Schelling's *Naturphilosophie* in Germany, where the "organizing" of bodies became the focus of debates about divine or material sources of life's origin. As I have suggested in Chapter 5, the term *organization* had been a heatedly polemical one in what were often called the "vitalist/materialist" debates around 1816, and Coleridge's involvement in that controversy was also moving him toward conceptions of "organization" that would refer socially to the "organizing" of the emerging institutional order, as it were, from "within" – guided by a "clerisy," a learned class of those who thought, read, and wrote among themselves but no longer directly to or for the public.[17]

In both lecturing halls and the *Biographia*, Coleridge took up the effort to preserve poetry's place among the emerging disciplines. Valenza makes a cogent case for why Wordsworth's and Coleridge's critique of poetic diction belonged to a "culture-wide debate about the connections among disciplinarity, language, class, and audience."[18] She shows in her Wordsworth chapter how imaginative genres could acquire disciplinary force by becoming a "poetry" that specializes by speaking to a general humanity in an accessible idiom resistant to the closed languages of adjacent "disciplines." This new defense of poetry, elaborated in a "Preface to *Lyrical Ballads*" that Valenza attributes to a collaboration between Wordsworth and Coleridge, worked to situate it among the specialized disciplines by "using a common language in a specialized way" and thus by paradoxically taking "ownership of the national language" as its unique claim to a role in the division of intellectual labor.[19] Valenza traces this defense from the earliest "Preface" of 1800 to pages of the *Biographia Literaria*, at least those in which Coleridge still seems in accord with his former collaborator.

While maintaining a place among the disciplines, however, poetry for Coleridge would also become the beginning of a more extensive problem and theoretical search. Poetry cannot only *remain* among the emerging disciplinary knowledges – and this is where he goes well beyond Wordsworth's effort to keep poetry viable among knowledge fields – it must somehow also become *essential* to their comprehensibility. In that case, what we should call "theory" can go well beyond making the case that "the language of poetic *belles letters*" should be strategically distinct from those of "other arts and sciences," and Coleridge's version of theory will freely invent a nomenclature of its own (*esemplastic* and other coinages in the lectures and *Biographia*). Poetry cannot henceforth occupy a place between the emerging specializing languages without its own philosophically inflected language to so position it. Coleridge's key criticism of the Preface that he may once have co-authored focuses on the question of where and how it grounds its own knowledge – in the empirical sphere of Wordsworth's "experience" of the most common everyday acts, de-sophisticated from urban culture, or in "the best part of human language, properly so-called, [which] is derived from reflection on the acts of the mind itself"?[20] This now well-known distinction is worth recalling in the context of what makes a "discipline" in the early nineteenth century, since Coleridge will extend it beyond the *Biographia* to the legacy of modern sciences themselves. In the 1818 *Friend*, it will help distinguish, for instance, Francis Bacon's philosophical ground from the Royal Society's practices of contingent experiment.

The implication of poetry as an imaginative genre in the problem of "arts and sciences" likewise concerns its generic antagonist in Wordsworth's *Preface*, namely the *novel* and that genre's increasing pressure against poetry's appeal among the reading public. Though the novel as such rarely appears in Coleridge's own arguments, it is clear that his conceptual problem of what counts as "real" in the language of poetry goes beyond Wordsworth's seemingly naïve appeal to everyday experience and refers also (if less explicitly) to the novel's own kind of "realism." In recent scholarship on this question, John Bender takes a close measure of the way "experiment" and "experience" approach a common horizon in eighteenth-century scientific discourse and novels alike. The eighteenth-century novel "contrives situations – often extreme and counterintuitive – that transform fictional experience into decisive experiments in the course of their action."[21] Bender points to the degree to which this fictional experimentalism can resemble the situational approach of moral philosophy, as when Hume comments, "When I am at a loss to know the effects of one body upon another in any situation, I need only put them in that situation, and observe what results from it." Thus novel readers can themselves effectively act like moral philosophers as they "constantly judge evidence, probability, and the chain of cause and effect" in a Fielding or Richardson novel.[22] In a shift of emphasis between fictional genres, Michael McKeon suggests that Restoration and eighteenth-century "drama was the first of the genres to pursue the aim to elevate the arts to the status of quasi-scientific knowledge," insofar as it based the credibility of stage presentation on empirical criteria of cause and effect, experiment and result.[23] One might similarly grasp the famous collaborative "experiment" in *Lyrical Ballads*, without too much distortion, as having been undertaken along the same lines. Where one poet tries the hypothesis of placing his workaday characters in highly unusual and intense circumstances ("treat the natural as supernatural") in order to see how they respond and reveal their true nature, the other reverses the hypothesis by treating a supernatural situation by the norms of empirical and experiential validity.

In the 1811 and 1812 lectures, Coleridge's argument for treating Shakespearean drama, however, *as poetry*, and thereby making him far more "philosophical" than theatrical, is also a measure of how far Coleridge believed he now had to distance poetry from these fictional genres that narratively or dramatically mimicked the natural sciences' appeal to experiential context or credibility. This is partly why Coleridge increasingly positioned poetry in the philosophical role of representing the "system of the fine arts" – not only implicitly in the literary theory of the *Biographia Literaria*, but more insistently in the new work he was now pursuing on the complex question of unifying the "arts and sciences." To take up this emerging work of 1816–18, it will be useful to remind us why Coleridge cannot be aligned with one of the most influential formulations of Romantic writing on poetry, literature, and the sciences, De Quincey's opposition of the "literature of power" to the "literature of knowledge." Undoubtedly De Quincey drew in part for that eventual formulation upon the *Biographia*'s argument in Chapter 14 that "a poem is that species of composition, which is opposed to works of science, by proposing for its immediate object pleasure, not truth."[24] But the crucial difference to be explored in the 1818 *Friend* and related texts will be to conceive poetry and knowledge not antithetically, but as a larger system of mediation between truth and those experimental sciences of the day that were still in search of a "method." Far from opposing literatures of power and knowledge as poetry and science, Coleridge would devise a singular way of dividing knowledge itself – philosophic "Method" as against experimental sciences or "Theory" in *The Friend* – so that poetry as the most philosophical of the "fine arts" would fit between the two sides of knowledge production as a fundamental mediator or "Middle Method." I shall explore further this solution to the problem of rethinking the coherence of the "arts and sciences" in the pages below, but it is worth remarking here that Coleridge anticipated and put into question by 1818 the mapping De Quincey was to impose, first in 1823, on the relation of "arts and sciences" as an opposition between literatures of "power" and "knowledge." The latter was a bad map of the complexity entailed by arts and sciences, we might say, and Coleridge required a more complicated and tendentious one. In 1816–18 that effort also brought Coleridge instructively closer to another emerging philosophical system for rethinking the "arts and sciences," the one being mapped out just then by his unexpected rival, Jeremy Bentham.

## Learning curves: Bentham and Coleridge revisited

Was there a "theory" of the relation between arts and sciences starting to emerge in the Romantic age? The long-gestating discourse about them had played many rhetorical roles in British discourse, from measuring civilization against barbarism, moderns against ancients, or early moderns against contemporaries, to the innumerable mapping schemes projected by the encyclopedists. Yet in the years 1816–18 a theory of some new kind did seem to emerge – depending on the scope and meaning of what we call "theory" – in several unexpected and, for many readers, indigestible forms. Coleridge composed two of these, a preface to the new *Encyclopaedia Metropolitana* (1817) titled "Treatise on Method," and then an ambitious revision of the "Treatise" in the "Essays on Method" that formed the *summa* of his new book version of *The Friend* (1818). The aim of both would be "to exhibit the Arts and Sciences in their philosophical harmony." It has become common to think of Coleridge's works on "method" as unique to Romanticism in this respect, as Richard Holmes thinks when he contrasts Coleridge's effort in "Treatise on Method" to "encompass both arts and sciences in a single exemplary schema" with its opposite, "the Benthamite or utilitarian concept of knowledge as an empirical gathering of value-free data."[25] But Coleridge was hardly alone in trying to rethink the problem of "arts and sciences" at a more philosophical level. Bentham himself was mounting such a project in his 1816 *Chrestomathia*. Nineteenth-century readers looking for guidance to the wider trajectories of modern knowledge often paired or compared Coleridge's "Treatise on Method" with *Chrestomathia*, treating them as if both writers had climbed into the same rarified, perhaps clarifying conceptual atmosphere.[26]

"It would be difficult to find two persons of philosophic eminence more exactly the contrary of one another," John Stuart Mill told British readers in two lengthy essays of 1838 and 1841, than Bentham and Coleridge, "the two great seminal minds of England in their age."[27] Mill's way of setting up these contrary figures was subtle and dialectical enough to grasp certain commonalities. Both were "teachers of teachers," little read by the multitude; up to a point, each could well be read as achieving the same scope, "not a piece of party advocacy, but a philosophy of society," as Mill remarked of Coleridge, "a philosophy of history," moving then "towards the philosophy of human culture."[28] These shared grounds put into greater relief the Progressive and Conservative political tendencies, the Lockean and Kantian epistemologies, and the Utilitarian and Romantic cultural visions

Mill saw Bentham and Coleridge as representing. Though widely noted in the nineteenth century, Mill's essays had become obscure enough in the twentieth that F. R. Leavis at Cambridge University had to republish them in 1950 for an English-studies curriculum that had long forgotten them. In this landmark edition, Leavis spoke cogently to the question of what a "liberal education" should be and why it "cannot confine itself to the critical study of literature" alone.[29] By 1950 such confinement, as conducted by "practical criticism" in Britain and "new criticism" in the United States, had effectively sidelined not only Mill, Bentham, and other social writers of the nineteenth century, it had diminished as well the study of the Romantic age as a time of wide intellectual and social as well as literary transformation. What Mill's "Bentham and Coleridge" essays had to offer Leavis and others in this situation was "key and complementary powers by reference to which we can organize into significance so much of the field to be charted."[30] By 1958 Raymond Williams was beginning to chart that wider field of cultural history by putting Mill's essays into a rich but problematic line of moral and literary criticism he called the "culture and society" tradition, drawing Mill himself partly into that tradition to examine why he found so much to admire in Coleridge and (in much less detail) how Bentham articulated an "*alternative* conception of man and society" to the Coleridge–Mill–Arnold genealogy he was reconstructing.[31]

On the whole, literary and cultural studies have largely inherited the picture John Stuart Mill drew of "Bentham and Coleridge" as formative yet antithetical forces in British intellectual history since the Romantic age, but we need to see why the problem of "arts and sciences" in the Romantic age complicates Mill's verdict that Bentham and Coleridge "seem to have scarcely a principle or a premise in common."[32] What they surely had in common was the premise that the "arts and sciences" would require rethinking as a coherent whole in view of the extraordinary new and various kinds of knowledge production in the early nineteenth century and the failing authority of the encyclopedic tradition. Both put particular emphasis on a single term – "among the objects of invention or discovery," Bentham argued in *Chrestomathia*, "is *method*"[33] – while construing the role and meaning of "method" in virtually irreconcilable ways. So this was the timely moment, Coleridge proposed in his Prospectus to the *Encylopaedia Metropolitana* about 1816, to make a fundamental modern turn in the long unharmonized category of "arts and sciences":

> The new discoveries in all the different branches of Experimental Philosophy which every year has brought with it, for the last twenty years, are unparalleled in the history of human knowledge, and the accessions have been of

such a nature as no mere supplementary Postscript to former works can possibly embrace. For in many instances they affect the whole theory and consequent arrangement of the Art or Science to which they belong. Our project is in this respect therefore singularly fortunate in point of time. It will have to collect and combine the rich but scattered elements of *future* Science; while a still more important argument for our plan and for the period of its execution, will be found in the manifest tendencies of all the Arts and Sciences at present, from the most purely intellectual even to the labours of the common mechanic, to lose their formerly insulated character, and organize themselves into one harmonious body of knowledge [emphasis in original].[34]

I want to take this telling passage in two parts. First, with regard to recent events in "experimental philosophy," we can observe that Bentham likewise took careful note in *Chrestomathia* of "an immense mass of art and science, all *new* within these few years," that compelled one to rethink the whole map of knowledges that had now been undergoing some new transfiguring in time and shape.[35] Nor is it incidental to their separate projects of 1816, which would soon enough diverge into Mill's contrary political, social, and philosophical programs, that both recurred to the turning point crystallized in Humphry Davy's chemistry and electricity at the Royal and other "arts and sciences" Institutions that had raised important new questions about the relation of fine arts to scientific knowledges, and likewise of the "fine" to the useful or mechanical arts as well.

But where Coleridge's passage above turns to "*future* Science," we begin to see how this point of convergence opens onto conflicting accounts of what the present "tendencies" of "all the Arts and Sciences" were revealing themselves to be. To Bentham "method" became an invaluable tool for expediting and disciplining further knowledge production in a Chrestomathic learning project that aimed ultimately to educate the many.[36] Yet it would famously achieve systematic coherence at the cost of one category of "arts" that its effective powers could not accommodate: the "fine arts." To Coleridge "Method" conceived quite differently had to become the ultimate intellectual horizon of "*all* the Arts and Sciences" – with a pivotal, mediating function to be enacted by poetry and the fine arts. We might now call his conception of Method an absolute horizon of disciplinarity, the horizon toward which he could see "the manifest tendencies of all the Arts and Sciences at present ... organize themselves into one harmonious body of knowledge." But there will be no place in his schema for the "useful" or mechanical arts, let alone the "labours of the common mechanic." In 1816 Bentham and Coleridge both acted on the perception that, since the 1790s, the key questions of the modern "arts and sciences" had been fundamentally shifting from *classifying* to a more complex sense of *organizing*. But then arose the key questions: organizing in what direction, for what social aim, by whom and for whom?

Readers of Coleridge are familiar with his complaint that the "Presbyterian book makers" of the *Encyclopaedia Britannica* had concocted an arbitrary, "immethodical" alphabetical or topical means of organizing knowledge where, to take one of his more striking formulations, "the desired information is divided into innumerable fragments scattered over many volumes, like a mirror broken on the ground, presenting, instead of one, a thousand images, but none entire."[37] What Bentham saw was less a shattered mirror of nature than the Encyclopedic mind imposing its own willful categories on the material world, as if it were substituting the things of logic for the logic of things. The "cloud of perplexity" that still hung over the *Encyclopedie* and similar projects had to do with the way it ordered the elements of "science" and "art," not too arbitrarily, but rather too resolutely, as if the two categories were impermeable to one another, or as if

> a determinate number of existing compartments are assignable – marked out all around and distinguished from one another, by so many sets of natural and determinate boundary lines, whereof some are filled, each of them by an *art*, without any mixture of science; others, by a *science*, without any mixture of *art*: others, again so constituted that, as it has not ever happened to them hitherto, so neither can it ever happen to them in future, to contain in them anything *either* of art *or* of science. On some such supposition, accordingly, appear to be grounded questions such as the following: – *how many arts* are there? How many *sciences?* – such a thing, (naming it), is it an *art* or is it a *science*? – i.e. such a word, (mentioning it) is it the name of an art, or is it the name of a science? [italics in original][38]

To see neither art nor science walled off in separate categories, Bentham argues that "in the broad field of *thought* and *action*, no one spot will be found belonging to either, to the exclusion of the other"; far from remaining natural or stable, "art" and "science" were constantly occupying one another's place over time, inevitably overflowing one another, mutating as they multiplied. He defined this fluidity of the "arts and sciences" by the principle of "joint-tenancy": "In whatsoever spot a portion of either is found, a portion of the other may be seen likewise. Whatsoever spot is occupied by either, is occupied by both."[39] This joint-tenancy principle meant the "arts and sciences" themselves were effectively resisting classification as they transformed themselves, and one another, over time – perhaps a surprising thesis for a thinker often regarded as schematic and ahistorical. Temporality, as Frances Ferguson has emphasized, equally became critical for Bentham's larger designs for education which filled out the second half of *Chrestomathia*.⁴⁰ The temporality of "arts and sciences" disarranges the clear categories imposed by the encyclopedists and it is also why the terms *practice* and *knowledge* in Bentham can be no more decisively set apart than their correlates *art* and *science*. In effect, he was asking, where did a whole range of practices and learning curves really resolve into the clarity of a definite realm of "art" or of "science"? This question of practices led Bentham to try reshaping the "arts and sciences" from earlier spatializing encyclopedic classification schemes by stipulating that, over time, art *becomes* science, science *reveals* its internal art; "correspondent therefore to every *art*, there is at least one branch of *science*; correspondent to every branch of science, there is at least one branch of art."⁴¹ In view of the way Coleridge will detach "Method" from *all* material practices in *The Friend*, it will be worth accentuating how tightly Bentham tried to fit the art/science and practice/knowledge relationships to the process of *change* as they become more active and focused:

> *Practice*, in proportion as *attention* and *exertion* are regarded as necessary to due *performance*, is termed *art*: *knowledge*, in proportion as attention and exertion are regarded as necessary to *attainment*, is termed *science*. In the Latin language, *both* are with great advantage comprehended under one common appellation, viz. *disciplinae*, from *disco* to learn: *disciplines*, with which our English word *discipline* agrees in sound as well as in derivation [emphases in original].⁴²

As used here, the term *discipline* acquires the temporal dimension of a learning curve, or a practice/knowledge continuum that is mediated by "method." "Man cannot *do* any thing well," he goes on, "but in proportion as he *knows* how to *do* it; he cannot in consequence of *attention and exertion*, *know* any thing, but in proportion as he has practiced the *art of learning* it [emphases in original]."⁴³ Put another way, Bentham's practices mutate into theory and are then regenerated by theory; while theory turns reflectively on its awareness of the practices enough that it is able to further generate the learning curves that went into making it. Up to a point, the dialectical relation of "doing" and "knowing" in this passage could work to offset the many other ways in which Bentham's thinking could very well force the process into a more mechanical efficiency. It opens the category "arts and sciences" to a relation between "practices" and "knowledges" in ways that Coleridge's absolutizing of Method in *The Friend* will do everything to forestall. Moreover, this part of *Chrestomathia* might serve to signal that when we now attempt to think through the relation of "practices" to "knowledges" within the system of "disciplines" housed in the contemporary university, we are also, perhaps less explicitly than Bentham did in 1816, engaging with what is at stake in the institutional framework we still call "arts and sciences" as well.[44]

If *Chrestomathia* can be understood, for all its often unwieldy apparatus of conceptual divisions and proliferating neologisms, as effectively an *action* theory of the "arts and sciences," Bentham's broader ambitions to change the social order by rethinking the relation of practices and knowledges might be better grasped in this light. Apart from the Lancaster-school monitorial education plans that have been well detailed by Alan Richardson, *Chrestomathia* recognizes emerging knowledges and practices that will have a more pervasive effect on everyday life.[45] What the joint-tenancy principle of "arts and sciences" accomplishes for Bentham is a way to conceive knowledges and practices as forming a kind of dynamic, if distinctly aggressive, system. Beyond the boundary of this disciplined system, Bentham proposes provocatively, is "waste," or the *outside* of the system, where everyday practices swarm in a disorganized and "inartificial" whirl – something perhaps comparable to William James's "blooming buzzing confusion" of everyday life, or to Niklas Luhmann's incomprehensibly complex "environment" that remains swarming beyond, and inaccessible to, any more highly organized but less complex space (such as a "science") that has been demarcated as a "system."[46] Unlike Luhmann's closed systems, however, it is important to note that Bentham saw the realm of "waste" as *immanent* to organization: "Whatsoever spot is thus occupied, so is much taken out of *the waste*; but neither is there any determinate part of the whole waste, that is not liable to be thus occupied." Where Luhmann's systems remain closed to their environments except as "irritation," Bentham's unorganized spaces, practices, and knowledges of everyday life can all potentially become a new sphere of art/science "joint-tenancy." "Day by day," Bentham says in one of his more aggressive passages, "acting in conjunction, *art* and *science* are gaining upon the above-mentioned waste – the field of *inartificial practice* and *unscientific knowledge*" (emphases in original).[47]

While it is clear Bentham still believed "science" was gaining knowledge of Nature, it is striking how the *Chrestomathia* accentuates the system of science/knowledge and art/practice as especially gaining on the everyday life practices and knowledges he calls "waste." Though Mill does not speak to this particular work, Mill believed Bentham meant his analytical procedures to put under critical pressure the wasteland of "ordinary modes of moral and political reasoning ... not reasons, but allusions to reasons," and above all "sacramental expressions."[48] But *Chrestomathia*'s more explicit aim is often to gain a knowledge of the *social*, as Bentham roughly indicates by the place he gives the new practice of "*Statistics*: a newly cultivated branch of *Geography*, having for its subject the quantities and qualities of the matter of *population*, of the matter of *wealth*, and of the matter of *political strength*, – existing or supposed to exist, on the *territory*, or in the *political state*, to which it applies."[49] Taken in that direction, the *Chrestomathia* can be read as refiguring the "arts and sciences" in such a way as to make feasible the emergence of a disciplined science of society, for which statistics was an emerging art of counting and predicting. But taken more broadly, Bentham's might be grasped as reviving the old problem put by Robert Hooke for the Royal Society: "the Arts of Life have been too long imprison'd in the dark shops of Mechanics themselves, & there hindered from growth, either by ignorance, or self-interest."[50] Hooke's frustration that the artisans and craftsmen could or would not speak their knowledges to the Royal Society led him to a program of historical investigation of skilled craft knowledges that we shall find Coleridge anxious to nullify in *The Friend* as a caricature of Bacon's "method." Hooke's and now Bentham's urgency about bringing practices and knowledges that have been inaccessible to enlightened knowledge into the modern light of day drives the argument of *Chrestomathia* to theorize a systematic sphere of practice and knowledge in which "no parts . . . are not radiated to the surveying eye."[51]

While the educational program Bentham developed out of these arguments is beyond the scope of this chapter, Frances Ferguson's illuminating studies of his arguments for institutionalizing the approach of *Chrestomathia* help make clearer how the rethinking of "arts and sciences" in this work belongs to a wider "effort to minimize metaphysical claims in an effort to make social value visible." To turn next to *The Friend*'s discourse on method, from Bentham's "surveying eye" to Coleridge's more theologically inflected "singleness of eye," will be also to see how Coleridge uses the "arts and sciences" to make the providential claim, as Ferguson puts it, "that there is a design that is only intermittently available to persons."[52]

Treated as a schema, Coleridge's 1816 "Treatise on Method" offered a seemingly clarifying triangular figure. On the ideal or philosophical side, there is "Method," or something like pure science that has been transfigured beyond mere experiment into a lasting law of nature and mind; on the practical side, there is "Theory," which comprises the experimental, observation-based sciences that depend erratically on hypothesis and contingent material conditions. If electricity belongs to Method as a case of pure science, chemistry and botany remain on the experimental side of this division as erratic, unmethodized, or mixed sciences, and for this Coleridge sometimes calls them "scientific arts." Between these two poles, as a mediating "Middle Method," Coleridge placed the "fine arts," with poetry at the head, both as ideal and as grounded in worldly experience. The two versions of this argument – in "Treatise on Method" and its more elaborated form in the 1818 *Friend* – took ample time to narrate this model as a story. For many years the experimental science of electricity had wandered among "insecure hypotheses" (regarding fluids, light, or gases), contingent conditions, and unstable conclusions, until the year 1798, when Volta's experimental imaginings produced his invention of the electrical battery and thus his discovery of "the law of Polarity, or the manifestation of one power by opposing forces."[53] This, Coleridge believed, was the real (and ideal) basis for Humphry Davy's extraordinary success in revolutionizing chemistry at the Royal Institution. Coleridge told a second story to give the full meaning of this transfiguration of experiment-based "useful" science into a truly lawful knowledge (or "Theory" into "Method," to maintain Coleridge's terms). This was the tale of the magnetists, who made plenty of their own discoveries and inventions, particularly the compass, and yet kept finding that their best efforts "led to no idea, to no law, and consequently to no Method." Where Bentham's sciences all appear in *Chrestomathia* in various, unevenly developed states of learning formation – new ones emerge from matrices of practice and knowledge, others drop out as unscientific – Coleridge saw no learning curve, or lack of one, that could explain why electricity found the Law and magnetism did not, or why the "theories and fictions of the electricians contained an *idea*" while the magnetists whirled fruitlessly in their speculations ("the *reiteration* of the problem, not its solution").[54] The same two stories could clarify the fate of zoology (wandering in error until it realized the law of Method through the work of John Hunter) and botany (ceaselessly rearranging its classifications and getting no further than any other such Theory).

But if they were to form a "system," such arts-and-sciences knowledge could not depend on these pure and mixed sciences alone. The great role of the "Fine Arts" was to mediate these sides of science, idea-based and practice-based, by acting as both ideal and experiential at once. This "Middle Method" of fine arts often appears incarnated in these writings on method as the philosophical Shakespeare drawn from Coleridge's literary lectures, and it is nowhere so influential on modern Romantic scholarship as in the form of a trope – the thesis that chemistry is "poetry realized into nature" and Shakespeare's plays are "nature idealized in poetry" – that figures the relationship between literature and science in the Romantic age.[55] Yet the elegant tripartite schema of Method, Theory, and Fine Arts that Coleridge tried to work out in the "Treatise on Method" was, as he would bitterly report in a letter to C. A. Tulk, mangled by his unphilosophical and unaesthetic collaborators on the *Encyclopaedia Metropolitana*: "The Prospectus was altered in two essential points – first, the Fine Arts were removed from their place in the system, as the *intermediate* Link between the *pure* Sciences, in which both the matter and the form are wholly from, in and for the mind – and the *applied* Sciences &c – This with other senseless changes of less importance deformed the rationality and beauty of the arrangement."[56]

By deforming the "rationality" of the plan, Coleridge may have meant that even he knew the division between "pure" and mixed or "applied" sciences would be impossible to understand (electricity and physiology would prove more useful and applicable, if anything, than botany or magnetism) without a mediating figure to help distinguish them. By "beauty of the arrangement" Coleridge was surely referring to the crucial, harmonizing part of the plan to be played by the fine arts. "The manifest tendencies of all the Arts and Sciences at present, from the most purely intellectual even to the labours of the common mechanic," that is to say, would not be able to "lose their formerly insulated character, and organize themselves into one harmonious body of knowledge" since there would be no "harmony" without the Fine Arts. The "pure" and the practice-based sciences would remain insular in that case, and perhaps more crucial from Coleridge's point of view, there would likewise be no social harmonizing either that "*all* of the Arts and Sciences" had been envisioned to provide between the most purely intellectual work of the professions or clergy and those of the common mechanic. This was as important a reason as any why there would be no further encyclopedias to recommend in the new 1818 version of *The Friend*, where the harmonizing of the "arts and sciences" provides the key mission of its new and finalizing "Essays on Method."

But Coleridge is doubtless also drawing on an older argument, descending from Adam Smith, that associates harmony in the fine arts with soothing the pains and dissonance of social inequality. The special case for Smith (as for Rousseau), as James Chandler argues in a penetrating analysis of Smith's work on moral sympathy, was instrumental music, and how its aesthetic issues of harmony work in tandem with the discourse on sympathy to do the work of social harmonizing where inequality is most otherwise unbridgeable.[57] We usually expect Coleridge to deploy poetry as the most philosophical and representative of the "fine arts" in these works, and in *The Friend* he elaborates Shakespeare's case even more fully than in "Treatise on Method." But Coleridge's musical references are relatively rare, and so the prominence of music for his reshaped concept of the fine arts as mediation of the knowledges and practices is particularly telling in the sixth of the "Essays on the Principle of Method." In a devious play on the "harmonizing" of arts and sciences, Coleridge takes note of the glass-and-steel *harmonica* invented in 1763 by Ben Franklin. Harmonicas play intriguing sounds, but "a true musical taste is soon dissatisfied with the Harmonica, or any similar instrument of glass and steel," and this is because the concretely mediated *sound* of the harmonica becomes dissonant with the "proportion" or relationality of the mind's musical sense: as if every instrument were to be measured against the ideal Music that precedes it.[58] Inventions like the harmonica may remind us also of the more famous allusion to music in the *Biographia*, where Coleridge complains that in modern print culture, language itself is now "mechanized as it were into a barrel-organ" and so "supplies at once both instrument and tune."[59] The Fine Arts mediate between true ideational Method and observation-based Theory because they have a built-in means of recognizing that any mediated sound, picture, or word is subject to the judgment of the Idea, a delicate arrangement that will fail if the jangling medium overpowers the soft speaking of the Idea. Harmonizing the "arts and sciences," this is to say, is Coleridge's ideological measure of why "*all* the Arts and Sciences" have important social work to perform in the early nineteenth century.

Thus *The Friend* restores the "fine arts" to their harmonizing place in the system. But conceptually the real difficulties would lie in the question of Method. The constant supposition of *The Friend* is that Method means "the material world is found to obey the same laws as had been deduced independently from the reason."[60] The philosophical itinerary of Method would entail three parts: first, that a true science be regarded as *relational* rather than substantive. Hence the "law of polarity" discovered by Volta has its philosophical power in arising from the specific science of electricity, yet reaching across many other domains in the power of its antithetical truth. Method also "implies a *progressive transition*" as its Greek etymological root indicates (*methodos*, or "path of *Transit*"), a path one could never find in the arbitrary classifying of the encyclopedists. Yet even this notion of a kind of progressive movement forward cannot fully be understood without the third condition of Method: "as, without continuous transition, there can be no Method, so without a pre-conception there can be no transition with continuity."⁶¹ This third condition of Method – its "Starting-post," its "leading Thought," or what Coleridge attributed to Francis Bacon, the crucial importance of "the Initiative"⁶² – has been understood differently by critical readers of the 1818 *Friend*. In a secular idiom, J. R. de J. Jackson translates this "Initiative" as a "hunch," a sort of inspired intuition; Jerome Christensen calls this concept of intention "the projective logic that relates an original purpose to its ultimate end."⁶³ The initiative, the hunch, indeed what could even be called, in a most inchoate state, the *project* will seem to come out of nowhere, yet it grasps the *end* before it knows the middle. In that sense, "Method" is virtually a system unto itself. This notion of originality cannot easily be set aside even when some imputed divine spark is cast away. Coleridge's scientific contemporaries had begun calling it "discovery" and began rewriting the history of knowledges, especially scientific, according to its irruptive appearance.

One reason to think of the "Initiative" as far more politically sensitive a matter than the problem of "relational" or "progressive" knowledge – both also key attributes of Method – is that the same force of Initiative that generates method can also generate the ambition to dominate: "the mind is stretched into despotism, the discourse may degenerate into the grotesque or the fantastical."⁶⁴ Like *schwarmerei* in *Biographia Literaria*, the kind of enthusiasm that leads not to imagination but to its politically infected opposite, "Initiative" in *The Friend* has a hazardous counterpart in that conviction which may just as well drive the mind to conceive political system – say Jacobinism – as to philosophical truth. For Coleridge's poetic control sample, Hamlet plays the role of the mind infected by method as the fantastical, while Shakespeare's design works through that madness to achieve philosophic knowledge Hamlet himself cannot have. In a sense, Shakespeare, poetry, and the fine arts as such save "Method" from itself, from its own instability as an "Idea" that may otherwise become so unmoored from the world as to make it a fantastic plaything or an object to dominate by sheer force of political will.

Coleridge's "Treatise on Method" could assert the primacy of Method without being able to offer a philosophical accounting for it; in *The Friend*, the genealogical basis of reaching Method in the modern knowledges can appear to be prefigured, as it were, by the "British Plato," or Francis Bacon, as Coleridge wrestles him away from the long shadow of the Royal Society. In Bacon, Coleridge finds "intellectual or mental initiative, as the motive and guide of every philosophical experiment." To the extent this notion means more than asking the right question, it must suppose that nature will answer the mind that understands it in advance. What "gives birth to the question"? It is not Bentham's learning curve, in which an "art" is acquiring the power of a "science" that extends itself again to inform an art. It is rather, Bacon would say in *Novum Organum*, "*Lux intellectus, lumen siccum,*" Idol-free reason, "the pure and impersonal reason."[65]

In so constructing a line of authority from Bacon's *Novum Organum* to Volta's law-discovering invention of the Voltaic battery in 1798 – a battery first "proven" publicly in Humphry Davy's Royal Institution experiments of the early 1800s – Coleridge found a way to bypass the "mechanical corpuscular" ideology of the Royal Society. If the Royal *Institution* instead was thus England's public birthplace of electricity's law – the "principle of polarity, the manifestation of one power by opposed forces" – Coleridge could also call upon Davy's resulting disciplinary powers as a key precursor for his own philosophical method. Before becoming a "law" in Volta's discovery and Davy's science, research on electricity had been observational, contingent, mere "Theory" in Coleridge's schema. It is not so much that Method makes the only measure of a discipline of knowledge – geology, chemistry, and physics, indeed all sciences of "Theory" and experiment, will still count in some sense as disciplines. It's rather that the criterion of Method provides an *ultimate* horizon of disciplinarity against which all less-realized knowledges can be measured.

In making Bacon the "English Plato," the obstacle to Coleridge's theory who was the great Newton could be politely set aside rather than renounced. But the Royal Society itself gets its polemical due in an unexpectedly scorching moment of the Bacon chapter in *The Friend*, when Coleridge cites Robert Hooke as crafting a "comical caricature" of Bacon's methods in a posthumously published text less known than Hooke's *Micrographia*, but perfect for the purpose at hand, "A General Scheme, or Idea of the Present State of Natural Philosophy and How Its Defects May be Remedied." With a main section called "Method of Improving Natural Philosophy," Hooke's *Scheme* makes a telling foil for the transfiguring arguments of "Essays on Method" in *The Friend*. The science in question here is natural history, which clearly had not yet become a true science for the Royal Society – and was even less so in Coleridge's own moment. Hooke's role as curator of the Royal Society made him a target of criticism in his lifetime. "I could easily believe Hooke was not Idle," Robert Moray had written in 1665, "but I could wish hee had finished the taskes lying upon him, rather than learn a dozen trades."[66] Rather than the Baconian "initiative" or Platonic hunch Coleridge has been at pains to theorize, Hooke's text cited kinds of preliminary knowledges that would be required for establishing, in his words, "even a foundation upon which any thing like a sound and stable *Theory* can be constituted" for the naturalist.[67] Thus, in Coleridge's much-modified quotation, Hooke's "appalling catalogue":

> The history of potters, tobacco-pipe-makers, glaziers, glass-grinders, looking-glass-makers or foilers, spectacle-makers and optic-glass-makers, makers of counterfeit pearl and precious stones, bugle-makers, lamp-blowers, color-makers, color-grinders, glass-painters, enamellers, varnishers, color-sellers, painters, limners, picture-drawers, makers of baby-heads, of little bowling-stones or marbles, fustian-makers (*query* whether poets are included in this trade?), music-masters, tinsey-makers, and taggers; – the history of school-masters, writing-masters, printers, book-binders, stage-players, dancing-masters, and vaulters, apothecaries, surgeons, seamsters, butchers, barbers, laundresses, and cosmetics! *&c.* (the true nature of which being actually determined) will hugely facilitate our inquiries in philosophy!!![68]

Those last inserted exclamation points try to ridicule Hooke, but few passages from the early Royal Society years could better point to the mediations really at stake in its project to study and master nature. To push the Royal Society forward with his "Scheme" of reform meant going backward, deep into the past of the practical "arts." For the Royal Society's "nature," like Columbus's in the "new world," someone had been there before (many someones). Hooke's vast catalogue of preceding knowledges that would need to be mastered before any genuine "Theory" could be advanced by natural philosophy appalled Coleridge, and not, I think, as Trevor Levere argues, because it "furnished Coleridge with a fair instance of the Baconian natural historian confronting separate things and single problems."[69] Instead, Coleridge leverages Hooke away from Bacon since the deeper problem is that Hooke's catalogue required *histories*, precedents, and always-already constituted knowledges before modern science could fully know what it was doing. Hooke's catalogue, meant to reform the Royal Society's presumption of gentlemanly rights to knowledge production, required taking seriously the "knowledge" of those who had spent artisan lives in skilled practices. To make the arts and sciences cohere into a greater whole, Coleridge advised, "look back at the history of Science," but not *these* histories. We have already met these practices of everyday life in Coleridge's critique of the "Preface to *Lyrical Ballads*," where practices could be either Wordsworth's source of authenticity or Coleridge's evidence of "disconnected" experience never adding up to a coherent, educated whole.[70] If Hooke here becomes a figure for the deluded Wordsworth, the Royal Society becomes a theater of contested legacies: that of Bacon's

"English Plato" and that of Hooke's searcher for lost knowledges, receding now into incommunicable time.

Coleridge had a precedent for this vigilant watch against Hooke's kind of scientific historicism, and it had come in the early lectures of Humphry Davy. To briefly recur to the 1802 Royal Institution lecture: there Davy had claimed that chemistry is not only connected *to* the technical, practical, and mechanical arts, but that it *precedes* them. He cited bleaching, dyeing, tanning, metallurgy, methods of working soil, porcelain and glass making, and in all such cases, "the artist who merely labours with his hands, is obliged to theory for his discovery of the most useful of his practices."[71] The manual and artisan arts, Davy agrees with Diderot, require the discoveries of "science" to advance beyond the primitive state of "mere labours." But Davy raises the condition "obligated to theory" to an even larger cultural principle. There cannot be anything to learn *from* practices, since scientific thought is always far ahead of them. A later version of this point came in the 1805 inaugural talk for Davy's "Lectures on Geology": "the greatest and most important inventions which have arisen from scientific principles have never been ascertained till long after the principles themselves were developed."[72] The stance Davy developed in these lectures was calculated to develop a sense that *all* knowledge and all useful practices are connected into an ultimate whole. And this whole – this immanence of connection in the apparently disconnected knowledges and practices of the present moment – is also what makes it essential that, as he put it in 1802, "we do not look to distant ages, or amuse ourselves with brilliant, though delusive dreams concerning the infinite improveability of man, the annihilation of labour, disease, and even death."[73] Historical and perfectibilist visions alike go out of play – whether as Robert Hooke's late seventeenth-century historicist scheme to "reform" the Royal Society, or as William Godwin's more systematic effort to reform Davy's own social order.

In an argument that has run through this book, I have been accentuating the double-sidedness of these early nineteenth-century efforts to transfigure the "arts and sciences." To do what Coleridge attempted in *The Friend* of 1818 or the "Treatise on Method" would *require* a moment like this brief, close, yet literally marginalizing encounter with Robert Hooke. Philosophy would have to settle accounts with history, theory with an array of practices. The attempt to make the "arts and sciences" cohere in something like Coleridge's triadic schema of Method/Theory/Fine Arts would have to exclude a wide range of practices and histories that might well have been important (as they are now for us) to make sense of the history and future of knowledges.[74] Conversely, Bentham required, as a way to make "knowledge" and "practice" a coherent system of "arts and sciences," displacing from his system the "fine arts," which would ten years later appear in his 1825 book *The Rationale of Reward* as mere "arts and sciences of amusement."[75] We shall see in the next chapter why England's reformers and Dissenters of many kinds could be attracted to aspects of each modeling of the "arts and sciences," yet finally be repelled by both.

To refer one last time to Mill's pairing of Coleridge and Bentham as philosophical contraries, let me put the comparison on a more institutional level. We know about Coleridge's way of associating his career and his literary and philosophical theorizing with Davy and the Royal Institution, but it is not so well recognized that Bentham had his own, more combative stake in the history of London's "arts and sciences" Institution world. Bentham's *Chrestomathia* was conceived as a critical reply to the Royal Institution's social construction of "arts and sciences," as we read in a passage intended for the 1816 edition but left out and only published posthumously. It reveals a polemical motive behind the otherwise dry, often technical language of the published book, and it shows why he meant to transform what was first begun at the "dignified institution distinguished by the appellation of the Royal" in 1800:

> Whatsoever degree of usefulness may belong to that institution, an indefinitely greater degree of usefulness must belong to the one here proposed: There, it was all amusement and decoration; here, to amusement, will be added solid and substantial use; there, it was confined to adults; here, it will be imparted, and indeed confined, to children, who, by it, will be raised to the level of men; there, it was, and is, confined to a few – even of the ruling and influential few; here, it will be communicated to a large, and, it is hoped, to a continually increasing portion of the subject many.[76]

Both Bentham and Coleridge worked to translate the arts-and-sciences problematic from print forms into new institutional projects, while it would be difficult to think of any two Romantic-age institutional designs as dissimilar as theirs – Bentham's practical day-school, or for that matter the University of London, so often credited to *Chrestomathia's* vision and method of knowledge in the nineteenth century, and Coleridge's National Church, a speculative institution no less ambitious to transfigure the "arts and sciences," and to which I now turn.

### Church and state, arts and sciences

Well before theorizing Method, the 1818 *Friend* had ranged widely through matters of state, politics, international law, ethics, religion, communication, and shreds of philosophy: in fact the whole range of "human institutions." For this framework Coleridge gave a special place to

Robert South, the seventeenth-century divine who gave the sermon "All Contingencies under the Direction of God's Providence" in 1684. The topic of this chapter is government:

> Human institutions cannot be wholly constructed on principles of Science, which is proper to immutable objects. In the government of the visible world the supreme Wisdom itself submits to be the Author of the Better: not of the Best, of the Best possible in the subsisting Relations. Much more must all human Legislators give way to many Evils rather than encourage the Discontent that would lead to worse Remedies. If it is not in the power of man to construct even the arch of a Bridge that shall exactly correspond in its strength to the calculations of Geometry, how much less can human Science construct a Constitution except by rendering itself flexible to Experience and Expediency: *where so many things must fall out accidentally, and come not into any compliance with the preconceived ends; but men are forced to comply subsequently, and to strike in with things as they fall out, by after applications of them to their purposes, or by framing their purposes to them.* (my emphasis)[77]

Most of this epigram to *The Friend*'s chapter on the state is a literary invention. Only the last (italicized) lines were actually quoted from South's 1684 sermon; the rest are ventriloquized in terminology South could not historically have used (such as "human institutions cannot be wholly constructed on principles of science"). This post-1750 language is a good example of the way Coleridge constantly blended early modern texts with the contemporary language of "institutions" and political questions, as well as making the more cogent point, attributed to an old *respublica literaria* scholar, that in the nineteenth century the idea of providence itself could now *only* be inflected through the problem of modern institutions.

The Anglican Church, Coleridge's 1830 work will argue, has since South's century become only one sect in a modern religious field: now by "*all* the intellect of the kingdom, determined to be one of the many theological sects, churches or communities, established in the realm ... The Church being thus reduced to *a* religion, Religion *in genere* is consequently separated from the church, and made a subject of parliamentary determination, independent of this church."[78] This is also where "the professions fell off from the Church" and the beginning of that devolution of the learned *respublica literaria* into its vernacular, commercial form best known to the eighteenth century. So it will be important in the rest of this chapter to attend to Coleridge's effort somehow to align the *modern* sphere of cultural production (from the literary reviews to the "arts and sciences") with the now-broken world of the "Christendom" that he was still hoping to make coherent with modernity in the sixteenth chapter of *Biographia Literaria*: "Christendom, from its first settlement on feudal rights, has been *so far* one great body, *however imperfectly organized*, that a similar spirit *will be found* in each period *to have been acting in all* its members."[79] This passage, like many others in Coleridge, reminds us not to treat the discourse of "arts and sciences" as an unblinkingly secular one. It does not take the current challenge by proponents of "intelligent design" against evolutionary science to remind us that, far from a modern compromise with the pagan ancients, the modern category of "arts and sciences" ultimately descended from modernity's tortuous conversation with itself over the legacies of Christendom, religion as such, and secularity as a most precarious successor to both.

As Kevin Gilmartin points out in *Writing against Revolution*, *On the Constitution of Church and State* might be the Coleridge text that is the most deliberately unclear about its historical referents in a body of work filled with vague conjectures concerning the past. What finally does become clear is that the notional, projected National Church of this work will not be the state-established Church of England, but the institution to be located alongside the state and independent of it. That means it would be an institution within civil society – where the public sphere is, and where Coleridge calculates it to do the most to reach into every village, classroom, and research chamber. That sociopolitical location also gives the National Church a far stronger recursive relationship to the old *respublica literaria* upon which Coleridge had been drawing intellectually (if often fictionalizing in his quotations) for the work of the past twenty years. This has importance since, though it is well known that Coleridge envisioned an order of the learned, a "clerisy," to become the "third estate" after the landholders and commercial classes that "constitute" the nation, it has been much less clear *who* precisely Coleridge meant to fulfill that clerical role and leadership. At issue as well is the distinction between "cultivation" and "civilization" about which so much since has been written or criticized.

Chapter 5 of *On the Constitution of Church and State* makes the crucial distinction between "civilization" and "cultivation" that Raymond Williams put into genealogical line with Arnold's later argument for "culture." But the same distinction is not a sure guide to what sorts of knowledge or moral vision the agents of "cultivation" would bring to the national table. Philip Connell's searching chapter on Coleridge's educational thought puts the matter this way: "the important distinction was now that between 'cultivation and civilization,' the former drawing together

Christian education and social discipline into a seamless unity and counterposing them to 'all the so called liberal arts and sciences, the possession and application of which constitute the civilization of a country.'"[80]

Yet it is difficult to imagine the kind of "clerisy" Connell interprets from Coleridge's passage, for this body would need to have, in what was to Coleridge a perilous moment by his own account, considerable national, cosmopolitan, intellectual, and hegemonic *force*. Coleridge's own phrasing invites ambiguity:

> The Clerisy of the nation, or national church, in its primary acceptation and original intention comprehended the learned of all denominations; – the sages and professors of the law and jurisprudence; of medicine and physiology; of music; of military and civil architecture; of the physical sciences; with the mathematical as the common *organ* of the preceding; in short, all the so called liberal arts and sciences, the possession and application of which constitute the civilization of a country, as well as the Theological.[81]

Since we cannot tell when and where this "original intention" or "primary acceptation" might have first existed (as Coleridge insists it *did* once exist), we have to accept the premise that the National Church embraced all the traditional professions (law, medicine, clergy) as well as those incipient "professions" that could not yet have won such high standing when the Church embraced them and before the professions "fell off from the Church." Assuming that the moment of this fall was the major crisis of the National Church, either in the later sixteenth century or sometime in the seventeenth up to the English Revolution, it would be anachronistic at the least to say it embraced the "physical sciences" as well; at least nowhere else does Coleridge present the Royal Society as a holy body. As for the mathematical being the "common *organ*" of those sciences, it would be premature by over a century to make that argument, since it was the "mathematization" of the sciences that would lead Thomas Kuhn to first use the expression "second scientific revolution" to characterize the events occurring within Coleridge's own moment.[82]

Thus the passage is slippery at the least. But the crux of this much-quoted description of the clerisy comes next: "in short, all the so called liberal arts and sciences, the possession and application of which constitute the civilization of a country, as well as the Theological." Why "so called"? Does this phrase show doubt about the modifier "liberal" (still an explosive word in 1829, designating both secularity and progressivism if not radicalism)? Yet "liberal arts" had been in common use for two centuries without a political rider attached. Does it put in doubt the now ubiquitous language of "arts and sciences" that has been circulated endlessly by the "Presbyterian book-makers" as well as those arts-and-sciences lecturing institutions in the Romantic age that Coleridge is now calling, on another page of *Church and State*, "lecture-bazaars"? This is somewhat more likely; Coleridge had referred to the overblown character of the expression as a promotional public phrase, as when he demurs in *Lay Sermons* about "the extreme over-rating of the knowledge and power given by the improvements of the arts and sciences, especially those of astronomy, mechanics, and a wonder-working chemistry."[83] Or it could be that the "so called" is quite neutral, merely registering that this is what advanced knowledges are now called, that they belong to "civilization," and that the point of the clerisy more importantly is not to separate itself from those arts and sciences, and thereby "civilization," as might some old-fashioned clergy, but rather to integrate it with cultivation and to lead, as it were, "from within." In short, however clearly conservative and religious it is, it is also a modernizing vision and not a culture-v.-society vision. The force of Raymond Williams's division between those entities in nineteenth-century discourse has led a generation of readers to see the antithesis even in texts where, as in *Church and State* I think, the intention is plainly the reverse. Otherwise we should be confronted with the spectacle of a group of pious churchmen guiding the national mission despite whatever the merely civilized professors of the "so called liberal arts and sciences" think or say. That would hardly amount to a fully hegemonic program in which the English National Church could stand polity-to-polity with the great Continental nations. The point is rather that civilization cannot make its own way, no matter how powerful and necessary, without being "grounded in *cultivation*, in the harmonious development of those qualities and faculties that characterize our *humanity* [emphases in original]."[84]

What is more crucial for Coleridge is that theology be placed at (or restored to) the head of this "*learned* of all denominations" for, among other purposes, securing "the ground-knowledge, the prima scientia as it was named – PHILOSOPHY, or the doctrine and discipline of *ideas*." In the original National Church, the theologians "took the lead, because the SCIENCE of Theology was the root and trunk of the knowledges that civilized man, because it gave unity and the circulating sap of life to all other sciences, by virtue of which alone they could be contemplated as forming, collectively, the living tree [not the Encylopedist's tree] of knowledge."[85] The point of reestablishing the National Church sundered by the English Revolution is not to relegate the modern arts and sciences to some pre-1640 condition – there would then have been little point in such texts as *The Friend* or *Aids to Reflection* in strenuously trying to put in order the explosion of knowledges Coleridge frequently attributes to the decades since 1790.

The last point to be made is that, however the National Church is to be construed, it is above all *to be instituted* and the conspicuous language of *institution* in *Church and State* follows the pattern I have discerned earlier: an almost even balance and interplay between what Williams had called the active noun of process and action on the one hand, and the structural noun denoting the durable and established on the other. We have seen a range of evangelical, Anglican, Presbyterian, Dissenting, Deist, and other religious tendencies at work in Romantic-age London, all finding a stake – as I shall show in the next chapter, for Dissenters an especially strong if conflicted stake – in the "arts and sciences" as a question of institution. This entwinement belongs partly to the history I have referred to before. According to Max Weber's sociology of religion,

> The concept of the *institution (Anstalt)* was not fully developed in the purely legal sense until the period of modern theory ... In substance it, too, is of ecclesiastical origin, derived from late Roman ecclesiastical law. The concept of institution was bound to arise there in some manner as soon as both the charismatic conception of the bearer of religious authority and the purely voluntary organization of the congregation had finally yielded to the official bureaucracy of the bishops and the latter had begun to seek for a legal-technical legitimation for the exercise of the ecclesiastical rights of property.[86]

As Coleridge might have surmised himself, Weber locates the descent of the whole early modern vocabulary of "institutes, institution," and so forth from the legal apparatus of Christendom. It is often the breakup of Christendom – the moment of 1453 or later versions of that break, such as the "fall" of the National Church – to which institution-inquirers like Coleridge almost obsessively recur in works like *On the Constitution of Church and State* (1829). By locating not only the concept of institution but the modern *problem* of institution(s) in the struggle between the prophetic/charismatic claim to religious authority and the bishops, Weber's sociology of religion and law would give one powerful version of the concept of a dynamic "field" of practice and contest in which institutions are both stakes and pivots for wider practices and ways of thinking.[87]

CHAPTER 7

# Dissenting from the "arts and sciences"

> We are so far advanced in the Arts and Sciences that we live in retrospect, and doat on past achievements. The accumulation of knowledge has been so great, that we are lost in wonder at the height it has reached, instead of attempting to climb or add to it; while the variety of objects distracts and dazzles the looker-on.
> William Hazlitt, *The Spirit of the Age* (1825)

> The arts and sciences, which should have been primary planets and fixed stars in the parliamentary system, are become mere satellites of property, and hence the vortices in which we are whirling to destruction.
> Leigh Hunt, *The Reflector* (1810)

From Chambers's *Cyclopaedia* to Coleridge's "Essays on Method," writers, philosophers, and encyclopedia-makers often tried to picture or theorize the stability and coherence of the relation between "arts and sciences," producing a wide range of maps, trees, and mental graphs. This chapter will follow a new dissension within the category that opened after 1800, especially among progressives and reformers who, battered by the anti-Jacobin ascendancy that followed 1789, would tend to complicate and divide, rather than try to unify, the category "arts and sciences" in ways that could hardly have been anticipated in the era of rational Dissent's vigorous exercise of natural philosophy, poetry, mechanical invention, and decorative and useful arts from the 1760s to the 1790s. By 1825, having lectured at the Surrey and Russell Institutions, Hazlitt knew very well the phenomenon of dazzlement and profusion that had been circulating outward from the London art and science Institutions and the promotional zeal professed by the Bernards, Dibdins, Rumfords, and Davys as well as by the English press. Thus he would write of the *burden* of the arts and sciences, or rather the ubiquitous public discourse about them with its always renewable, relentlessly similar historical tales, beginning with the distinction between past and present itself: ancients v. moderns, barbarism v. civilization, or (in the Rousseauist mode), the claims of nature against those of arts and artifice. But Hazlitt also raised the question of coherence, if now in a far more skeptical way than had Coleridge or Bentham. While Thomas Bernard's "looker-on" in 1806 had turned the mere observer that Francis Bacon once meant by that expression into an all-seeing, meta-disciplinary spokesman for the whole category of arts and sciences, Hazlitt's distracted and bedazzled observer of 1825 has little plausible vantage point left for making sense of them.

While Coleridge took up yet another, more philosophically justified scheme in *The Friend*, Bentham in *Chrestomathia*, the Dissenters, and their reformist allies in the early nineteenth century often accentuated the explanatory power of *narrative*, whether as histories or as novels. Godwin's critical reflection on historical and novelistic genres would grapple with the Scottish legacy of philosophical history. It would not primarily focus on the "arts and sciences" as such, yet Godwin's political and narrative writing would point a strong eye toward the implications of that discourse in a larger assessment of justice and ethics, the revolutionary past, and the precarious moment of possible revolution at hand in the 1790s. Shelley's *A Philosophical View of Reform* (1819) and *A Defence of Poetry* (1820) advanced something far more like a powerful and polemical revision of the conjectural histories set in motion by David Hume on arts and sciences and John Millar on institutions. Though wary of its widespread public idioms, Hazlitt made his own vigorous interventions in the "arts and sciences" discourse during the previous decade, though they were also ones we may today find distinctly problematic. Far from trying to reconcile the category as a whole, Hazlitt took up strong, even extreme positions on the "arts" side of this dialectic, in particular as regards the "fine arts," and to the detriment, John Barrell has influentially argued, of a British public art.[1]

Hazlitt's 1825 picture marks the long and circuitous travels taken by English rational Dissenters since the burning of Joseph Priestley's home and laboratory on the night of July 14, 1791. The crisis and decline of rational Dissent in the 1790s would leave its survivors to take increasingly varied and contradictory postures toward the "arts and sciences" as a schism opened within the English Enlightenment on questions of politics and economics, visions and institutions, aesthetics and statistics. By the late years of that decade, some writers drew a more sociologically explicit picture of the 1790s crisis in the Republic of Letters, the repression of the public sphere, and the ensuing consequences for the "cosmopolitanism" that had been taken in the eighteenth century as axiomatic for the growth of arts and sciences. Mary Robinson's 1800 *Monthly Magazine* articles on London portray an especially dark vision of the metropolis at just the moment, as we have learned from Ian Duncan and others, Edinburgh's star was about to rise as the "Athens of the North."[2] Despite that dire picture, the Dissenters' conversation circles rebounded and flourished into the early 1800s, not least in debating what they found most stimulating and most troublesome in the combination of print production and lecturing output from the metropolitan learning Institutions. We need to recall that despite the Royal Institution's aristocratic beginnings, the London, Surrey, Russell, and other Institutions turned pointedly, from 1806 to the 1820s, toward embracing the traffic of knowledge and commerce, inviting all sorts of Dissenters, "new" and "old." These would include Hazlitt, Richard "Conversation" Sharp, John Mason Good, and Adam Clarke among the lecturers, administrators, or archivists, and Quakers, Socinians and Unitarians, Arminians and Methodists figuring prominently in the Institutions' audiences from 1808 to the 1820s.

After 1800, one might say, the Dissenting intellectuals went all over the map when it came to the discourse of "arts and sciences," from the rare celebration to the frequently arched eyebrow in Godwin's and Hazlitt's decidedly skeptical, searching examinations across a range of genres and situations. Unlike Coleridge or his German interlocutors, they made little effort to transfigure the arts and sciences into an emblem of "mind" and its illimitable powers (Hazlitt's idealizing posture toward the fine arts has to be the limit case in this respect). Far more often they addressed the tangle of practices that underlay this discourse, the situations or "vicissitudes," as William Roscoe called them, that made a historical understanding of them essential – an inquiry that would weigh in against the misleading appearance of some internal dynamic thought to drive the forms of knowledge to "rise and fall" on their own, regardless of historical moment or social circumstance.

The same debate could also bear on the analogous question of *genres* and whether their historical vicissitudes were caused by some internal evolutionary dynamic or by contextual pressures and contingencies. Paying historical attention was not new to the British reformers – Priestley showed a strong historical sense in both political and scientific realms, while the *Analytical Reviewers* group had set out to be "historians of the Republic of Letters" in 1788. But this historical attention took a darker swerve in the 1790s to register the present English and European political crisis in the light of a longer history of modernity itself. In a turn against Scottish encyclopedism and the wider "philosophical history" of modernity to which it lent substance, Dissenters like Godwin began searching for alternative histories and reshaped narrative genres in which to reconstruct them. From *An Enquiry concerning Political Justice* to *The Enquirer* and the later historical fictions, he asked more pointedly how institutions bear on knowledge and self-knowledge, sociability and conversation, study and reading, autodidacticism and long-term, systematic learning. From Priestley to Godwin, one might say, there was largely one progressive code to follow on the modern arts and sciences – embrace them, defend them, but accentuate public access to them, promote shared or intersubjective discussion about them, and above all do not disconnect theory from useful practice.

Meanwhile, the fine balance between "knowledge" and "utility" Godwin still tried to maintain in the 1790s would tilt decisively in the early 1800s toward a confrontation between the "literary" politics of the Hunt circle and technoscientific or utilitarian reform movements that crystallized from 1820 to 1830. One growing pressure to note will be the rising authority of the utilitarian "New School of Reform" that increasingly captured not only the sciences and "mechanical arts" as the leading edge of modern knowledges, but also the new institutional forms that it would take to "advance them." From 1823, when the Surrey Institution collapsed under financial pressure, to 1831, when the British Association for the Advancement of the Sciences restructured the disciplinary shape of the sciences by networking the specialist societies (and largely excluding the arts-and-sciences Institutions studied earlier in this book), the Bentham-inspired utilitarians consolidated their Parliamentary reformist programs most institutionally with James Mill's *Westminster Review* (1824) and the founding of the University of London in 1826.[3] Yet as James Chandler and Philip Connell have argued in different ways, "utility" was a question already deeply imbricated in the Hunt circle's debates of the Regency.

Thus several questions can be posed to the Romantic-age Dissenters and reformers who variously struggled with the category "arts and sciences" between the moments of late eighteenth-century Rational Dissent and 1820s and 1830s utilitarianism – between what cultural historians have depicted as a time of inventions and experimental attitudes in the first and a time of measurement, discipline, and calculation in the second. For the Hunt circle and its writers the question would be: why the fine arts (and not the "practical")? What of the sciences, mechanical arts, and the "useful"? What was the meaning of the early modern expression "Republic of Letters" for these writers, editors, institutors, and lecturers, and how was this understanding related to its modern reformulation as a "public sphere"? This was clearly a realm not only of publication, but equally, as

Jon Mee and others have shown, a metropolitan sphere of vigorous "conversations" and sociability that were both like and in important ways unlike their eighteenth-century precursors. If there was a growing division between "arts" and "sciences" among the reformers – articulated especially by the difference between formations like the Hunt circle and the gathering strength of political economy and utilitarianism – was this separation tantamount to a division between "scientific" and "humanist" fields that prefigures the later irreconcilability of those domains as expressed in such landmark debates as that between Thomas Huxley ("Science and Culture") and Matthew Arnold ("Literature and Science") in 1880–83? Given the print-based and aesthetic choices of reformers like the Hunt circle, would it help produce a distinctively *literary* domain or field by the 1820s – or something else?

### History, romance, knowledge

There was not a single kind of history-writing in the eighteenth century, as we have learned from the work of Mark Salber Phillips among others, but an array of historical genres: antiquarian, biographical, political, literary, disciplinary, "conjectural," and philosophical histories. Among these, philosophical and conjectural history, as written by Montesquieu, Hume, Robertson, Ferguson, or Millar, went furthest to encompass the history of nations and particularly of "the history of literature, of the arts and sciences, of manners and customs, even of opinion and sentiment."[4] The category "history" itself had not fit easily into the eighteenth-century encyclopedia's array of arts and sciences. Only in 1777 did a second edition of *Encyclopaedia Britannica* introduce "a new department," history and biography, and the stimulus to do so was the new, close, complex attention devoted to the arts and sciences *as history* by the Scottish philosophical historians.[5] Hume had asked, which forms of governance were historically and politically conducive to the "progress" of arts and sciences, and which impeded them? Far from certain of their inevitable development, Hume and others drew undulating patterns of rise, decline, and recovery depending on the social conditions and political architecture enabling or undercutting them.

At the same time, there was little or no empirical support for such histories; modern historians have distinguished between more or less "pure" forms of conjectural history – citing Millar's *The Origin of the Distinction of Ranks* (1771) and Hume's "Of the Rise and Progress of the Arts and Sciences" (1742) in particular – and those, like Hume's

*History of England* or William Robertson's *History of America*, that alternated between conjectural and more substantively empirical narratives.⁶ The problem was not simply that few histories of particular arts and sciences had yet been written. There was also the methodological question raised by Hume: "What depends on a few persons is, in a great measure, to be ascribed to chance, or secret and unknown causes: What arises from a great number, may often be accounted for by determinate and known causes."⁷ Political and commercial history could be measured in light of the power and politics of large numbers, but "tracing the history of arts and sciences" could only look to small numbers, the "few" of the cultivated and the curious. In that case, "chance ... or secret and unknown causes, must have a great influence on the rise and progress of all the refined arts."⁸ Hence the danger, particularly for a universal history, of "assign[ing] causes which never existed, and reduc[ing] what is merely contingent to stable and universal principles."⁹ Hume's strategy for turning this conundrum on its head would signal a question that would be crucial to all later reflections on how to narrate the history of knowledges. One could choose between two paths. Either one could make the "few" exemplary enough to stand in for the many and the whole (the strategy of canonizing authors and works, one that was under way already in 1742, but was still far from a self-conscious strategy of literary or scientific history). Or one could take the Scottish path: "The question, therefore, concerning the rise and progress of the arts and sciences, is not altogether a question concerning the taste, genius, and spirit of a few, but concerning those of a whole people: and may, therefore, be accounted for, in some measure, by general causes and principles."¹⁰

Writing thirty years before Millar's conjectural history of social institutions, Hume took the "arts and sciences" to school in political history. Thus their "rise and progress" required three premises: "free government," internationalism (or "neighboring and independent states, connected together by commerce and policy"), and then a curiously divided third condition: "A republic is the most favorable to the growth of the sciences, a civilized monarchy to that of the polite arts."¹¹ I shall return to this clearly loaded distinction later in this chapter, since it will figure into early nineteenth-century assessments of how to regard the "arts and sciences" as conducive to a reformer's idea of progress where real political choices are at stake. In 1742, though, Hume's perspective should count as a remarkably prescient way of thinking about how to ground the previously floating modern discourse on the arts and sciences in actual historical and material situations. Putting Millar's chief category *institution* into the picture can only help us see better how long the reach of Hume's problem could become.

It is often remarked that Hume's impact on Godwin changed his political thinking in ways that would turn the second and third editions of *An Enquiry concerning Political Justice* toward accounting for the affects and emotions in his revision of the 1793 first edition's emphatic defense of rationality and necessity. Still, even the 1798 version maintains Godwin's critique of Mandeville and Hume for making "luxury" a precondition of learning rather than its key cultural outcome. Hume's easy way of assuming the "arts" to mean "polite arts" resonates with Mandeville's fiction of the bees, where (in Godwin's summation)

> elegance of taste, refinement of sentiment, depth of penetration, and largeness of science, are among the noblest ornaments of man. But all these, say they, are connected with inequality; they are the growth of luxury ... To this cause we are indebted for the arts of architecture, painting, music and poetry. Art would never have been cultivated if a state of inequality had not enabled some men to purchase, and excited others to acquire the talent which was necessary to sell.[12]

Godwin attributes Rousseau's willingness to renounce the arts and sciences as a whole as a screed against this defense of luxury as the patron of modern knowledges, but his own reply was made (five chapters earlier) in the long, crucial second chapter of Book 8, "Principles of Property." Here Godwin invokes the only legitimate right of private property as property in "the sacred and indefeasible right of private judgment ... the true end of civil institution."[13] Securing the principle of private judgment – Kant's "courage to think for yourself" – is the only way in which the long-trumpeted superiority of "arts and sciences" to the "savage" state can really be salvaged: "why, under the shade of civil society, arts have been invented, sciences perfected and the nature of man, in his individual and relative capacity, gradually developed."[14] Godwin's eighth book of the 1798 *Political Justice* thus might well be marked as the last time in England that an intellectual of the Dissenting legacy could claim the full category of "arts and sciences" as given by the principle of intellectual judgment and politico-moral justice. After this moment, serious Romantic-age reflection by the English left on this matter will increasingly show the obstacles to such a defense by such later admirers and inheritors of Godwinian argument as Hazlitt, Shelley, or Richard Carlile.

Mark Philp's groundbreaking account of how *Political Justice* evolved through three distinctive editions by responding to his sociable networks of discussion through the 1790s has not quite settled, however, the status of *The Enquirer* (1797). For Philp, *The Enquirer* does not mark a break with the 1796 and 1798 editions of *Political Justice*, but emerges instead as a distinct alteration of perspective and method, a supplement to the larger book which turns far more explicitly toward those networks of discussion and the "hints struck out in conversation" that have their own "vivacity" and "richness" unavailable to a more systemic, theoretically framed work like *Political Justice*.[15] Others, like Jon Mee in his important book on Romantic-era conversation, maintain that the cost of *The Enquirer*'s method is too high if conversation seems to be "largely defined against political discourse." Kristen Leaver takes the more extreme position that in this work and *Caleb Williams* (1794), Godwin turns away from the public sphere altogether.[16]

Here I shall instead build on Philp's understanding of *The Enquirer* to see how Godwin's more indirect approach to "political discourse" entails the rich but uneven mediations of private conversation on publicly controversial matters – and often involves dialogues of the author with himself. Godwin's new method of cultural inquiry vows an empirical approach: "incessant recurrence to experiment and actual observation."[17] As filtered through *The Enquirer*, "discussions" emerge as ideas tested in debate, or possibilities of thought tossed into the air, "not as *dicta*, but as the materials of thinking." Hence *The Enquirer* translates the diminishing culture of rational-Dissenter discourse into the printed chapters of a book whose formal organization is marked by intensely serious conversational stops and starts. Many of these essays entail reeducating the educators; or, in the hermeneutic context explored by Tilottama Rajan, of comprehending the complexity of authorial intentions and textual "tendencies" entailed by the construction and reception of meaning in history.

From the many directions taken in *The Enquirer* – questions of conduct, reading, poverty, education, and more – I want to turn to a long-unpublished essay Godwin planned for a second volume of *The Enquirer* that never materialized, "Of History and Romance." Since its first publication in 1990, "Of History and Romance" has been studied for its proleptic yet troubled argument for a new genre, the historical novel. Here I want to accentuate a related question embedded in this essay: the problem of "necessity" and "chance" that would be key to Godwin's maneuvering between historiography and prose fiction. While this essay was an attempt to rethink the genre of historiography as an inquiry into the private, secretive, and politically formative moments of individual lives, it could also not help but reflect on the larger category of history-writing as belonging to the sphere of knowledge itself. Thus I want to read it as a new sort of response to the Scottish conjectural-history case for the "progress of the arts and sciences" raised by Hume in 1742. By challenging Scottish philosophical and conjectural history in 1797 on behalf of a projected historical novel, Godwin also reveals the *analogous* relation between accounting for the arts and sciences on the one hand, and the historical complexity of contemporary literary genres on the other.

The power of Scottish philosophical history had been to grasp the emerging, differentiated spheres of a complex modernity as the outcome of an inexorable historical process, often periodized in the four great stages that culminate in commercial society.[18] As Friedrich Meinecke remarked, its power was also to shake history "violently" out of its comforting remoteness by "plunging it into the present," thereby ensuring that interpretive struggles about the historical past would henceforth "always go hand in hand with all the controversies about the shape of things to come."[19] It was on both counts that Godwin opened his challenge in "Of History and Romance." He contrasts philosophical history's ideological presentism, narrating the past as an inexorable outcome of the birth of commercial society after 1688, with those alternative possibilities of things to come which Godwin will call "the depths of futurity." The Scottish historians' sweeping narratives of how modernity assumed its inevitable shape, Godwin also emphasizes, had since the mid eighteenth century been vigorously campaigning against older testimony of antiquities, as Hume and others steered readers away from "annals" and sources, permitting whole continents of context, by the magic of abridgment, to vanish into the abstract national geographies of the universal historians' narrative machine. Their method, Godwin writes, was the "collation and comparison of successive ages"; their product was the biography of British nationhood – a collective subject called "England" in Hume's case, "America" in William Robertson's, in which "individualities" on the one hand, and the particularity of such moments as the English Civil War on the other, were equally abstracted away. The armature of their method was the ineluctable logic of "probability," the "dull repetition" of a "general history" in which Hume, Robertson, and (implicitly) Burke connive to "furnish us precedents in abundance, ... show us how that which happened in one country has been repeated in another ... that what has occurred in the annals of mankind, may under similar circumstances be produced again."[20] Hume's credo – that "history teaches us nothing new or strange" – had made it scarcely conceivable how history could ever tell the moderns what they did not already know.[21] Universal history's cancellation of possible, unrealized futures prohibits us from conceiving "what it is of which social man is capable," and sentences us, Godwin writes with some Foucauldian flourish, to the institutional order of modernity, where we "dance in fetters," "blight[ed] ... in every grander and more ample development of the soul."[22] Against the probabilizing powers of Scottish philosophical history, Godwin promotes a new kind of historiography focused on agents, motives, and actions. This biographically focused historicism shifts from the abstract subject of the emergent nation to the individual subjects whose public and private acts connive to produce "things as they are." It carries out an investigative agenda designed to follow the agents of history off the public stage and into their closets, to reexamine the "public man" as a private "friend and father of a family," to perform close readings of his works and letters, and suspicious hermeneutics of his public orations and private behaviors. It sets aside enlightened abstraction by grasping the "materials" and "motives," "minute and near," through which history is made. It would replace the ideological trope of probability with the anticipatory figure of "possibility":

> It is thus, and thus only, that we should be enabled to add, to the knowledge of the past, a sagacity that can penetrate into the depths of futurity. We shall not only understand those events as they arise which are no better than old incidents under new names, but shall judge truly of such conjunctures and combinations, their sources and effects, as, though they have never yet occurred, are within the capacities of our nature.[23]

Godwin's anticipatory historicism required an agent capable of linking accounts of the past to yet unrealized projects "within the capacities of our nature." Improbably, he selects the ancient historians who had been vanquished by the moderns – Sallust, Livy, Plutarch – and who would seem a prototype of intellectual agency otherwise unavailable to the Humean or Burkean moderns who groan under the institutional weight of "prejudices and precedents." Despite being downclassed by the moderns as a kind of fabulist, the ancient historian may still serve pragmatically, if not referentially, to produce "a genuine praxis upon the nature of man," a kind of *licentia historica* for imagining possible pasts and futures as something other than probabilistic versions of the world ratified by 1688 and the imposing narratives of philosophical history.[24]

Moreover, the moderns' accusation that the ancients fabricated their histories can be reversed against the moderns themselves: "All history bears too near a resemblance to fable." Hence it is little wonder why "the man of taste," despairing of foundational historiography, might exclaim, "Dismiss me from the falsehood and impossibility of history, and deliver me over to the reality of romance."[25] If we keep in mind that Godwin in *The Enquirer* had often been staging the "hints struck out in conversation" – intriguing ideas, conjectural leaps, the sudden astonishing hunch opening a cascade of possible consequences – the following passage in "Of History and Romance," much quoted in recent Godwin scholarship, should also be taken in this highly conjectural spirit:

> The writer of romance is to be considered as the writer of real history; while he who was formerly called the historian, must be contented to step down into the place of his rival, with this disadvantage, that *he* is a romance writer, without the arduous, the enthusiastic, and the sublime licence of imagination.[26]

Imputing a superior knowledge to the romancer who knows the true motives of his historical characters *because* he has invented them puts in his place the hapless historian who must perpetually mistake the motives of historical characters whose deepest inner lives he has been unable to grasp.

To consider this paradoxical proposal, we need to recall that Godwin's far regions of "romance" were surely not those of Burke's immemorial English antiquity or medieval, aristocratic idealism, but rather the Roman republic and more emphatically the age of Cromwell. So conceived, the true aim of the "historical romance" would be imaginatively to re-open that possibility in English history – the moment of 1642 – which the Scottish philosophical historians, and most notoriously Hume in the first volume of *The History of England* (1763), had been so determined to close. Godwin's later, pessimistic historical novel *Mandeville* would most explicitly return to the Revolution scenarios of the mid seventeenth century to investigate the failures of the historical transformation that produced 1689 rather than the possible worlds of republican imagining.[27] Likewise, his single extended work of political history, *History of the Commonwealth of England* (1824), would open reconstructively with the epigraph, "To attend to the neglected, to remember the forgotten."[28]

In 1797 the deeper subtext of the essay "Of History and Romance" was the unavailability to modern Britain of its own revolutionary moment except as what might be fictionally reconstructed and investigated by the historiographer capable of grasping the multitudinous "conjunctures and combinations" of historical possibility, or what the English revolutionary moment might now look like if narrated by the historical romancer, whose "express stamp of invention" opens investigation of past revolutionary failures and of possible conjunctures of thought and action yet to be made. The republican romance would thereby refute the necessity of British history as the universal historians had narrated it, the better to locate the unrealized futures that proliferated from the mid seventeenth century. It is in this unfamiliar sense – as the regenerator of a historical narrative interrupted by the fate of the 1642 revolution – that Godwin ventures to call "the writer of romance ... the writer of *real* history." To propose the genre of "historical romance" as the ideological alternative to the unacknowledged fictions of universal history was to claim that, through its reflexive awareness of its own fictional status, the novel was empowered to confer upon its authors and readers the constructive "sagacity" to imagine particular futures as well as pasts – to negate the Burkean monopoly on "romance" by reclaiming a reflexive fictionality for politically progressive rather than conservative ends in history.

Godwin's writings from 1796 and 1797 show him increasingly fascinated by contingent possibilities, and with alternative, what-if-this-had-happened histories. He began to imagine the past as a cascade of consequences stemming from little moments occurring other than history stipulates they did. To become fascinated by the contingent was also to imagine that, in some unforeseen way, "everything is connected in the universe," since "every one of these incidents, when it occurred, grew out of a series of incidents that had previously taken place."[29] For authority, Godwin appealed to the scientific. "Natural philosophers," he wrote, argue that "a single grain of sand more or less in the structure of the earth would have produced an infinite variation in its history."[30] The speculations of natural philosophy also helped Godwin further doubt the unqualified assertions of "natural right" in the writings of Thomas Paine. The notion of "necessity," as it will under historical pressure, began to produce in Godwin's revisions of *Political Justice* – and most fully in his project of cultural inquiry and criticism, *The Enquirer* – the complex and chaotic actions of "contingency."

For us, the "contingent" answers to a crisis of historicity in moral philosophy, political theory, literature, and the natural sciences alike – contexts I shall want to invoke for Godwin's moment as well. Among the historical logics Godwin himself investigated in the 1790s – necessity, probability, possibility – there was no precise conceptual equivalent for what today we have seen called "contingency" among a wide range of intellectual discourses: anti-foundational moral philosophy, Marxist rethinking of the problem of historical necessity and causality, revisionary Darwinist evolutionism, or even in the extraordinary postulates of a "radical contingency" in earth's history by comparative planetology or astrogeology.[31] Like these recent articulations of the contingent, Godwin would seek in the concept a means to reconcile his own intellectual and social uncertainty about what is entailed by the reflexive or relative on the one hand, the actual or material on the other. Central to the problem of "contingency" is an uncertainty whether it is an epistemological or an ontological category – whether it designates how things actually happened (or might have happened), or whether it defines the limits of what we know. The Romantic idealist solution to this question is well put by Hegel's provocative interpreter Slavoj Zizek: "Contingency does express the incompleteness of our knowledge, *but this incompleteness also ontologically defines the object of knowledge itself* ... the object itself is not yet ontologically 'realized,' fully actual."[32] There were other solutions to the late eighteenth-century recognition of the problem of "contingency" bred by the Enlightenment category of literature and its difficult legacies of empiricism, skepticism, and mutating genres of knowledge.[33] The conviction Godwin brings to these passages – echoed elsewhere in *The Enquirer* – makes it all the more puzzling why he would retract his proposal for the sagacious historical romance in the final paragraphs of "Of History and Romance." Unexpectedly Godwin ceases to promote the project of literary genre-reform I have just outlined and abruptly forestalls it, as though his own argument for narrative genre-transformation were itself to be read as a "fiction," a thought experiment in both the possibility and the difficulty of changing genres in order to change history. What he had written about the project of philosophical totalization at the beginning of *The Enquirer* – that it is a project "incommensurate to our powers" – must now be said of the reflexive romancer as well: "To write romance is a task too great for the powers of man ... [for it] requires a sagacity scarcely less than divine."[34]

Nearly two decades before *Waverley* (1814), Godwin glimpses and declines, at least in theory, the spectral return of a divine placeholder or surreptitious theologian in the powerful act of authorship that makes things happen in the parallel universe of the British historical novel. Against the powerful act of knowing authorship he has attributed to the historical romancer, Godwin invokes the language of yet another eighteenth-century narrative genre, natural history. His "grain of sand" amounts to the same invocation of contingency as we read in the 1796–98 revisions of *Political Justice*, but now as a principle of what narrative genres can master and what evades them.[35] The most *historical* thing about a narrative genre, romance or historiography, that is to say, is what ultimately escapes it, and what escapes the modern philosophic historian is both motive or "character" and the unpredictable outcomes of "action." Hence, when he invokes the contingent as a means of locating the historicity of narrative genres, Godwin neither returns to the generic hierarchy of the

Enlightenment category of literature (where historiography outranked novels and romances), nor provides the first romantic rationale for fictional narrative's greater symbolic truth of history. Instead, it can be argued, Godwin turns both the empirical historian and the romance-writer into competitors in the universe of narrative genres. The resulting vision of the epistemological and political struggle between genres foretells a literary history something like what Franco Moretti describes as a "Darwinian history of literature, where forms fight one another, are selected by their context, evolve, and disappear like natural species."[36]

If this is the case with genres, or specifically the narrative genres so consequential to Godwin's sense of political history and futurity, could it also be the case for the "arts and sciences" as a whole? In 1742, Hume had conspicuously headed off such a possibility by expanding his historical framework from the "few" and "curious" (the canonizing option) to the many and numerous who make up the nation and Europe as a whole (the sociological option).[37] Yet Godwin neither retreated disappointingly back to accept philosophical history after raising serious doubts, nor did he wisely reject a vision of a historical yet fictional novel that might have led to profound and wider intellectual or literary-history effects. Rather he exposed both historiographic and fictional genres to a principle of contingency that he evokes *from* the sciences (a decidedly anti-Newtonian and, in the spirit of *The Enquirer* as a whole, a Baconian or "experimental" one, or what we now might rather call an aleatory one) – but that could equally have been adopted from one of the "arts" as well, "art" conceived as useful experiment (as Wordsworth and Coleridge would venturesomely describe their poetic experiment in 1798, though Coleridge later demurred) rather than consummate performance.

In "Of History and Romance," Godwin himself seems dislocated by the contingencies that do not permit a generic solution to the ideological effects of modernity's self-justifying "philosophical history." At best, the struggle between historical genres (including the novel) becomes the context of pursuing investigative historical-generic practices that work against the self-assurance of modernity by excavating the "materials" of possible histories that might have been made or might yet be made. Perhaps the key word of *The Enquirer* is "materials": genres are "materials" for use rather than determinate logics. That Godwin would turn out to be premature in this estimate could only be judged from the standpoint of 1814. Godwin himself was for a time suspected to be the anonymous author of *Waverley*; it was Walter Scott who was now proving that the historical romance could very successfully share the probabilist logic and modernizing confidence of Scottish conjectural history.[38] But the exhaustion of "probability" in late modern social theory and political thinking – and in the logic of normative genres as "institutions" – has once again renewed our own urgency to use the generic "materials" that lie ready to hand.

### The Dissenter's London: knowledge and sociability

Rational Dissenters like Godwin could sometimes agonize in the late 1790s about another dimension of their historical moment, the apparent loss of politeness and sociability, the ties that bound them together as a community in the second half of the eighteenth century while also giving them access to wider public and intellectual impact. Godwin devoted *The Enquirer*'s chapter "Of Politeness" to reexamining the Rousseauist association of polite sociability with "a corrupt and vicious mode of society." Dissociated from patrician subterfuge, politeness becomes Godwin's medium of moral conduct grounded in the capacity for intellectual subtlety and a complex awareness of the histories of contemporary argument and dispute.[39] This line of thinking follows from *The Enquirer*'s prefatory judgment that in the past four or five politically combative years, the English progressive left, faced with arrogant and culture-warrior anti-Jacobin rhetorics as well as punitive force and treason trials, had themselves become "too imperious in their tone ... too impatient and impetuous ... The barbarism of our adversaries was no adequate excuse for this."[40] Put differently, this is to say, and not for the last time, that the most aggressive culture-war language from the political right is not necessarily best met by adopting its idioms.

In 1800 the Dissenters' leading journal, the *Monthly Magazine*, enlarged dramatically on the political reformers' embattled position in contemporary cultural production by putting the "arts and sciences" into a startling metropolitan context. From novels and works of history, Dissenters could turn to the least-likely genre of political and cultural criticism, the London guidebook. Beginning in 1802, Richard Phillips, editor of the Dissenting *Monthly Magazine*, began publishing a yearly *The Picture of London*, where he updated in each annual edition the London political and cultural institutions that by 1809 were including guidebook accounts of the new arts-and-sciences Institutions.[41] Surely the most striking chapter in the 1802 *Picture of London* begins by seeming, like most London guidebooks, to celebrate its resplendent cultural achievements. This chapter reprints in its entirety a four-part *Monthly Magazine* essay published in 1800 by an anonymous author later revealed to be the Della Cruscan poet and the close intimate of London's rational Dissenters, Mary Robinson. On her account London, "the mart of literary traffick for the world," appears to all visitors to be the cosmopolitan "centre of attraction for the full exercise of talents, and the liberal display of all that can embellish the arts and sciences." Most important for Mary Robinson, "every man, nay, almost every woman, now reads, thinks, projects, and accomplishes."[42] Her *Monthly Magazine* series seemed to be celebrating an extraordinary and recently achieved degree of social access to London's cultural pleasures in their full scenic bloom: a feast of visual, theatrical, literary, and scientific exhibitions. She depicts a robust print culture that now both illuminated the cosmopolitan, discriminating reader and extended to "the poorest peasant" the ability "to trace the language of truth, in pages calculated by the plainest doctrines and the most rational reasoning, to awaken, enlighten, harmonize, regulate and refine the human understanding."[43] She invokes, at least initially, the Republic of Letters' ethos and practice of an enlightened cosmopolitanism: city-centered and globe-traveling, yet intimately sociable and skilled in arts of conversation; universalizing, yet often philosophically skeptical; tolerant of cultural or religious differences, yet finely discriminating in matters of taste; oriented to particular markets of publication, but writing in broad and unspecialized prose; bowing to no king, yet always well connected, prizing connections over divisions.[44]

But the Londoners or world travelers who read further in Robinson's "Present State of the Manners, Society &c &c of the Metropolis" must have been jarred by the frequently dark, violence-tinged portrait of cultural London that emerged through her fourteen vivid pages. At odds with the fabulous exhibits, theater life, and crowded promenades that stimulated such pleasure in London was the impact that seven years of war on France and suppression of political Dissent by "citizens of the world" was having on metropolitan cultural life, the unpredictable alternations of urban pleasure and stark physical brutality that had become routine in Londoners' daily experience, and above all a punishing kind of emotional and symbolic violence that was altering the character of cultural production in the great metropolis, perhaps irreversibly. Counterrevolutionary politics helped produce over a decade of urban *bouleversement* (as Robinson calls it) – reversals or upheavals of long-maintained cultural and social relationships in the great metropolis.[45] While her detailed account of the cultural pleasures to be experienced or consumed in London is often bright with excitement, it also reminds her readers of what she calls the "spirit of contradiction" that now dominates London life. The nobility are patrician cosmopolitans who "abhor French principles," she observes, while they display a "gusto for foreign dramas, foreign music, and foreign cookery" as well as French domestic maids.[46] Harvesting Gallic cultural distinction while making a costly war on France, London's patrician class has more extensively been turning England's own cultural producers – actors and actresses, poets and novelists, musicians and painters, journalists and natural philosophers – into London's internal exiles. Notwithstanding the enjoyments of consumption in this city, it seems to be Robinson's examination of cultural *production* in London that motivates her rapid and frequent shifts, in "Present State," from delight and appreciation to anger and sometimes grief as she depicts the recent and drastic change in the conditions of its cultural producers: a "*bouleversement* of every thing in the polite world."

As the literary republic had become riven by faction, political repression of dissent, and sectarian violence in the 1790s, what recent scholars have called a "crisis of sociability" cut across the long-cultivated patterns of mutual recognition and polite credibility that had been believed to sustain British and European letters for more than a century.[47] Robinson's essay speaks to this crisis with a palpable sense of shock. In a way that could hardly have been prepared for within the cosmopolitan ethos of the early modern Republic of Letters – where individual complaints about undeserved fame or unrecognized genius had been common in the eighteenth century – Robinson depicts London's most able cultural producers as now, in the later 1790s, unilaterally being cut off and shut out from the urban scenes of exhibition and excitement that their own intellectual and practical labors had done much to produce:

> The pictures of our most celebrated painters are purchased at an inordinate price; and considered as the embellishments of our most magnificent mansions. But the painter is unknown, excepting in his work ... Our nobles make music in their study ... they dedicate whole years to the acquirement of a moderate degree of skill; while their makers, who have attained the utmost altitude of perfection, are considered as unworthy of their friendship and society ... The exalted orders of the community read, approve, admire: the production of the brain is extolled and cherished; but the heart of the writer is a prey to poverty and sorrow ... Women of superior literary endowments are rarely seen at the tables of the wealthy and ennobled ... Men as well as women of talents are shut out from the abodes of the high-born, and rather avoided than courted by the powerfully wealthy in all the gaudy festivity which are annually exhibited in the metropolis ... Even in public they are seldom acknowledged; and if by chance they are recognized, it is by a nod of condescension, which mortifies and degrades the person whom it ostentatiously aims to distinguish.[48]

In these pages Robinson's terms of production and expropriation repeatedly bring into focus the contemptuous and sustained withdrawal of recognition from the metropolitan cultural producers whose finished works England's powerful have made their own treasures and objects of display. What has been steadily unraveling in recent years is the tissue of recognitions that had sustained the older Republic of Letters and that still obtains, she insists, in post-revolutionary as well as pre-revolutionary France. And what in the individual case could be merely the fortunes of the cultural market (some careers rise, some fall) appears in "Present State" to be patrician cosmopolitanism's more systematically realized powers of inflicting a sustained symbolic violence, an anti-intellectualism on an extreme scale, where Robinson goes to the extreme of portraying a London public sphere that is no longer principally argument against argument, nor confrontation face to face, but is now increasingly experienced by many London intellectuals and reformers as an incremental, unprepared for, astonishing process of erasure and disappearance.

After detailing many such instances across the "arts and sciences," Robinson draws a vehement conclusion: "These miserable discriminations are the offspring of the present age: the monsters of this island." It's worth recalling here that, unlike the rational Dissenters, with their relatively stable rites of passage through the Dissenting academies and entry into middle-class occupations, Mary Robinson's early career had been something of a crash-course in London's patrician cosmopolitanism.[49] It took her rapidly, bewilderingly, sometimes rapturously to starring roles on David Garrick's London stage, or to intimate sexual affairs with the Prince of Wales and Charles James Fox, while her very public fall from grace thereafter would turn Robinson into what Pascoe calls the "spectacular *flaneuse*," riding lonely in a carriage around London wearing flamboyant hats and quite likely beginning to grasp the sense in which eighteenth-century cosmopolitanism's professed freedoms of movement and choice had their unstated, locally enforced, harshly administered limits. We might identify here a key contradiction in the posture of those middle-class radicals who now found their cosmopolitan arguments at odds with their long-acculturated expectation of sociable exchange with London's patron class. What had been so recently gained especially by women as cultural producers in Britain – actual entry into the Republic of Letters and recognition as reviewers, poets, political writers, moral philosophers, historians – was now, catastrophically in her view, being abrogated.[50]

As Jon Mee's work shows in persuasive detail, what Gillian Russell and Clara Tuite have called the "collapse of the ideal of sociability" was not absolute and did not affect everyone in the same way; after 1800 other forms of sociability evolved, often in the form of enclaves, sociable "circles," and new social locations for gathering in public in the early nineteenth century.[51] Yet many did not survive the moment Robinson struggles to see beyond in 1800, above all, female cultural producers: "England may enumerate, at the present era, a phalanx of enlightened women, such as no other nation ever boasted. Their writings adorn the literature of the country; they are its ornament, as they ought to be its pride! But they are neglected, unsought, alienated from society; and secluded in the abodes of study." As Craciun points out, Robinson stubbornly held to the hope of a regenerated literary republic driven by journals like the *Monthly Magazine*, even as she could see "no sympathetic association of goal; no genuine impulse of affection, originating in congeniality of mind" and thereby no acting in "union of sentiment and sympathy of feeling" among the "unsought" women writers of her day.[52] Instead, as the national and metropolitan scenes of literary production and institution underwent dramatic change over the next thirty years, so the language of her republican cosmopolitanism became well-nigh unreadable and it remains somewhat difficult to decipher even today.

### From Republic of Letters to literary field

These dialectics of political reform and discourse on "arts and sciences" did not occur in print culture alone, despite the strong investment of the Hunt circle in all manner of print media. Equally important was the intense conversational culture among reformers that, as Mee has recently emphasized, stimulated the reformers' investment in sustaining an ongoing "Republic of Letters."[53] In both ways, the rational Dissenters dispersed after 1800 into a number of important and conflicting cultural formations. The reformers Leigh and John Hunt gathered around the *Examiner* in 1808 have often given the impression of a unified legacy from the earlier century's intellectual Dissent – a picture strengthened by the 1816 Tory assault on the Hunt circle as a collective "Cockney School" of impudent, vulgar pretenders to a place in the literary republic. The designation "Cockney School" itself – though useful for understanding the period's own immediate polemics – has not been an altogether viable term for grasping the complexity of second-generation Romantic progressivism. Philip Connell points to the disparate membership of the Hunt circle and their conflicting social backgrounds and personal alliances (between Keats and Shelley, for one set of reasons, or between Hazlitt and the Hunts for another).⁵⁴ The "Cockney School" was less a unified "cultural formation" (in Raymond Williams's sense of the phrase) than a contradictory assemblage of social and cultural tendencies fused into polemical unity by Tory antagonists.⁵⁵

A related and more persistent problem that I shall pursue in the next few pages is how to assess the continuity, or lack of it, between the late eighteenth century's rational Dissenters and the Hunt circle's dissenting politics – and their differing postures in the British Republic of Letters. It is true that, for instance, Hazlitt, educated at Priestley's Hackney School, took repeated pains to distance himself from the earlier stance of rational Dissent: "A long habit of objecting to everything establishes a monopoly in the right of contradiction," he wrote in "On the Tendency of Sects." For an intellectual culture that submitted "everything to the test of reason," their actions could contradict their doctrines: "The spirit of controversy substitutes the irritation of personal feeling for the independent exertion of the understanding."⁵⁶ And as Connell notes, the later Hazlitt's anti-utilitarian polemics could go so far as to equate the rational Dissenters with the Benthamites themselves.⁵⁷ Yet it would be mistaken to cut the Romantic-age reformers off too cleanly from rational Dissent as well.

We might say that the late eighteenth-century culture of rational Dissent could assume their critical postures *within* a secure sense that they were contributing to, and innovating within, a broad national and international "Republic of Letters." Priestley's own mode of networking and circulating his experimental processes at the laboratory, along with his political and theological writings, still testify to that confidence. For the Hunt circle, Hazlitt, Shelley, and other reformers after 1800, the literary terrain has become so embattled and, like the *Blackwood's* "Cockney School" attack on the reformers, so destructive to their very credibility *as writers* that there must be far more aggressive and self-conscious strategies for staking claims in a literary republic. Hazlitt makes just this distinction by contrasting the "hacking and hewing" intimidation of writers by the *Quarterly Review* or *Blackwood's* – "a serious abuse and a violent encroachment in the republic of letters" – and that "calm, peaceable period with the *Monthly Review*" that "bore 'sole sovereign sway and masterdom' over all literary productions."⁵⁸ More telling for my present purpose is how Hazlitt depicts the *particular* source, besides class-contempt and other weapons, of the current critical press's power to damage the Republic of Letters:

> If the real author is made of so little account by the modern critic, he is scarcely more an object of regard to the modern reader; and it must be confessed that after a dozen close-packed pages of subtle metaphysical

distinction or solemn didactic declamation, in which the disembodied principles of all arts and sciences float before the imagination in undefined profusion, the eye turns with impatience and indifference to the imperfect embryo specimens of them, and the hopeless attempts to realise this splendid jargon in one poor work by one poor author, which is given up to summary execution with as little justice as pity.[59]

If "On Criticism" is a defense of the literary republic against the now-damaging media that dominate it, it's also a critique of the way the *Quarterly* and other leading journals have mobilized the discourse on "arts and sciences" – "disembodying" them in the process – to abstract their principles into a media language of aggressive declamation or "splendid jargon" that reduces the reviewed author to their target rather than their bearer. This is the moment to recall Marilyn Butler's important point about the difference between later eighteenth-century reviewing and what Hazlitt (as well as Coleridge) had been facing since the *Edinburgh Review* brought a media revolution in 1802. Butler showed how earlier reviewing, from the *Monthly* and *Critical Review* (1756) to the *Analytical* (1788), introduced readers to emerging published knowledges in *all* categories by its generous quoting of lengthy passages, framed by brief commentary that usually came from a reviewer with expertise in the author's field.[60]

Far from "oracular theories," Hazlitt adds, such a reviewer offered a claim of some intellectual authority (such as "this is a work of great learning and research," or a different judgment), while treating the author under review with a civil "show of courtesy." Such practices made the review-issue itself an extension of not only the book's argument or information, but also the sociable relations that ideally would sustain all exchanges in the modern Republic of Letters. Hazlitt also means to suggest that in such reviewing, the "arts and sciences" were to the reader embodied in the texts reviewed because of the *way* they were reviewed. This is often not untypical of how Dissenting critics like Hazlitt would come at the question of "arts and sciences," not so much frontally, but within terms of some wider mediatic or political question. Thus, almost casually, Hazlitt makes a fundamental point about how the discursive formation called "arts and sciences" was being transfigured by Britain's leading critical publications by 1818 – from a grounded or embodied *instancing* in the older reviewing apparatus to a print format, established by the *Edinburgh* and *Quarterly* reviews, in which the "disembodied principles of all arts and sciences float before the imagination in undefined profusion." By 1825, Hazlitt would say that all readers were now overpowered by the dazzlement and sense of profusion the journals had been spreading.

## Dissent in the arts

In "On Criticism" Hazlitt revealed that his cultural memory was still, by 1822, somehow embedded in the intellectual norms of rational Dissent. I want to turn now to a larger problem for both Hazlitt and the Hunt circle in grappling with the legacy of "arts and sciences" that the old Dissent both could – and could not – offer them. There is no more telling a discontinuity between the Lunar Society's world and Leigh Hunt's than in the matter of what counts as "arts" that are worthwhile to work and live for. Unlike Priestley, the Wedgwoods, Erasmus Darwin, John Aikin, or for that matter James Watt, Hazlitt and the Hunt circle rarely embraced the sciences, technical inventions, or decorative and "useful" arts so prized among the late eighteenth-century English reformers. The *Examiner* and other Dissenting publications after 1800 seldom speak to what enlivened the heartbeat of rational Dissenters, the lived usefulness of knowledge, pictures, machines, or poems, nor to what William Morris would have to defend seventy years later as the "lesser arts" wrongly demoted. In 1877 Morris pointed, in a marvelous phrase, to the "eventfulness of form" which inhabits *all* the arts, yet which no longer appears visible to us "in those things we are always looking at."[61] On a similar score it is telling that John Landseer, the engraver twice wounded by the Royal Academy and the Royal Institution, found no refuge among the Hunt circle reformers either, but went instead to the Surrey Institution in December 1813 to speak out on his own, engraver's version of "The Philosophy of Art."[62] Meanwhile, William Blake's acid image of the *Examiner* as a "nest of villains" – "we all know that Editors of Newspapers trouble their heads very little about art & science" – points to what seemed to him the contradiction between the *Examiner*'s way of linking the fine arts to Parliamentary reform and public patronage, on the one hand, and following the Royal Academy's practice by attacking engraver-exhibitions like Blake's own in 1808, on the other.[63]

Yet Blake's accusation underestimated what the Hunts very well *did* know about art (setting science aside for the moment). From its earliest issues the *Examiner* tilted strongly and knowledgeably toward the fine arts with Robert Hunt's long-running "Fine Arts" columns, and this tendency was soon evident in the writings of Hazlitt, Roscoe, George Dyer, and Leigh Hunt as well. A key reason for Hazlitt later taking issue with the rational Dissenters' legacy was what he regarded as their Puritan legacy of "distaste for pictures, music, poetry, and the fine arts in general."[64] This reformers' way of accentuating the "fine arts" marked one side of what came to be the signature of the Hunt circle: a "literary politics" that, as it developed from 1808 to the 1820s, became increasingly engaged with, but then finally opposed to, all things utilitarian. Not taking up the rational Dissenters' fascination with sciences, inventions, decorative or "useful" arts would prove to be a costly price for their gains in finer arts. By 1825, as Connell puts it harshly but not inaccurately, the Hunt circle could appear as "an isolated literary rump of metropolitan middle-class reformism." Yet we should not underestimate the depth, complexity, and generosity of the Hunts' and Hazlitt's many-sided engagement with the so-called "fine arts" either.[65]

The post-1800 London Dissenters and reformers could often come into dispute about the positions taken by the *Examiner* toward the English visual arts from 1808 to 1820. Hunt consistently advocated for state patronage of the fine arts, a posture Hazlitt had political reasons to oppose in the age of Pitt and Castlereagh. Toward England's leading art academy, Robert Hunt was far more ambivalent; sometimes indicting the Royal Academy's "cabal of self-seeking and untalented artists" while at other times crowing about its being "a constellation of British genius in painting."[66] Unlike Hazlitt, Hunt would not sustain a critique of the Academy but shifted his stance from column to column, often contesting other art-critical journalists who would follow James Barry in demanding the Academy support and produce what was in the period called painting's highest form, history painting: "We cannot reply in accordance with the opinion of most of the papers, attaching blame to our Artists for the comparatively small show, in the present Exhibition, of Historical talent. It is said, and justly said, that they ought to endeavour to induce and lead an exalted public taste; they ought to try to infuse a public and a philosophical love of Art."[67] The contradiction pointed out by other art critics was that the Royal Academy *advocated* history painting (as part of its broader campaign for the "English School" of art), yet produced mostly commercially profitable portraiture. Hazlitt would increasingly take aim at Hunt's positions in his own art writing, dissenting most polemically from Hunt's embrace of the Academy's program to "improve" the arts by teaching matters of taste and training painters.

But the most unusual difference between the *Examiner*'s politics of art and Hazlitt's lay in their oddly diverging stances toward London's newest authoritative art venue, the British Institution for Promoting the Fine Arts in the United Kingdom. The *Examiner* columns consistently criticized Thomas Bernard's creation for its largely aristocratic tenor and its connoisseurial tastes, which Robert Hunt found especially limiting when the Institution directors promoted "pictures of *pleasing* subjects" rather than "subjects of grandeur" like historical painting.[68] But, even though he had expressed by 1815 a distinct hostility to *all* art institutions in his polemics against the Royal Academy, Hazlitt abruptly turned a corner when the British Institution gave London a surprise in mid 1815 and mounted the city's first public exhibition of early modern Dutch, Italian, and French painting. It was bringing not only the Old Masters and the history of European art into its London galleries, but a number of its more powerful, "gusto"-driven paintings as well.

This moment has something important to do with both the history of Romantic scholarship and the assessment of Hazlitt, since it entails his peculiarly undemocratic view of the fine arts, which remains so seemingly at odds with his well-known political arguments for radical reform. John Barrell has put the most influential case for this view of Hazlitt in *The Political Theory of Painting from Reynolds to Hazlitt*. This argument shows how England had enjoyed a vigorous art discourse accentuating the public function and reach of the fine arts since the *Characteristics* of Shaftesbury (1711), one most decisively institutionalized by Joshua Reynolds's lectures at the Royal Academy from 1770 to 1790. Tracing the vicissitudes of this publicly oriented discourse on painting through Barry, Blake, and Henry Fuseli, Barrell ends with a powerful chapter on Haydon and Hazlitt, which uses Hazlitt's widely circulated *Encyclopaedia Britannica* article "Fine Arts" (1816) to synthesize the critic's art writings from a wide range of earlier texts.[69] By 1816, Barrell argues, Hazlitt managed to cut any remaining tether of visual art with the British public world and make art instead the province of private, intense appreciation that is inaccessible to the common crowd. "The highest efforts of genius, in every walk of art, can never be properly understood by the generality of mankind," Hazlitt wrote in the prose fragment "Why the Arts are not Progressive?"; thus "the fine arts," as John Whale comments, "operate at a distinct remove from the workings of liberal democracy."[70] But as Barrell notes, nearly all Hazlitt's art writing works to this idealizing end except the anomalous essay of the same year, with its punchy argument giving polemical life to its mundane title, "On the Catalogue Raisonné of the British Institution," an essay Barrell sets aside because it is, precisely, at odds with much else Hazlitt wrote on the fine arts.

This article may be idiosyncratic among Hazlitt's other art writings, but it illuminates another side to his more commonly understood postures, such as his sweeping criticisms of "institutions" in general – "On Corporate Bodies" (1823) states the most programmatic version of this case – and the Royal Academy in particular. In fact, contrary to these impressions, Hazlitt seems to have found the new arts-and-sciences Institutions world a convivial, perhaps even importantly useful place to hear an argument or deliver his own. He gave four ten-lecture series at the Russell Institution ("The History of Modern Philosophy" [1812]) and at the Surrey Institution, three consequential lecture series on the drama, the English comic writers, and poetry, first in 1811, then in 1818–19. Hazlitt reportedly attended many more lectures at these Institutions and other London lecture venues. For a drama critic who prized the social experience of London playhouses, the lecturing Institutions' vivid theatricality and sociability had to be a very different experience of literary production than posting a review in the mail. It's true that the British Institution has never been considered part of London's four main lecturing Institutions that were so widely publicized together in the early nineteenth century. The British Institution, rather than lecturing, *modeled* its public outreach, that is, the British Institution modeled European painting and sculpture for an art-impoverished capital city that had only really seen English painters displayed in public places, mostly at Somerset House. (This is also why Mary Robinson's acute criticism that London's art objects remained largely *invisible* to the public of the 1790s has ongoing importance.) From 1805 to 1814, that modeling of the European Old Masters remained on a limited scale: it was an art-student's, not a general public modeling for would-be painters who had to follow restrictive rules when they came to 100 Pall Mall to imitate or copy the Old Masters lent by the Institution's collectors George Beaumont and Julius Angerstein. Only in 1815 did the British Institution's nine directors decide to mount a general public exhibition of Old Masters on a scale to rival the Royal Academy's famous yearly shows of English artists. This 1815 exhibition, it would turn out, was historic. What the British Institution now "introduced to England – and eventually to the world," writes Francis Haskell in *The Ephemeral Museum*, was "a radical innovation which has flourished until our own day: the Old Master exhibition."[71]

To Hazlitt it may have been even more. When he had first seen sixteenth- and seventeenth-century Dutch, Italian, and French painting at the Louvre during the Peace of Amiens in 1802, he was stunned, not only by the European art works he was witnessing for the first time, but surely also by the revolutionary context of the moment and by the fantastic physical domain of the museum itself. "Those masterpieces were the true handwriting on the wall," he had enthused, "which told the great and mighty of the earth that their empire was passed away – that empire of arrogance and frivolity which assumed all superiority to itself, and scoffed at everything that could give a title to it." But though the great moment had long passed by 1815, which was also the year of Napoleon's epic defeat by the British, one part of Hazlitt's memory could still resonate with the revolutionary past, even while standing in the genteel British Institution exhibition room at 100 Pall Mall. "Look around!" he later recalls that moment in the Louvre. "These are my inheritance; this is the class to which I belong!"[72] I am speculating here, but it's unlikely Hazlitt would have missed another telling parallel between the first Old Masters exhibit in London in 1815 and the Louvre in 1802. The British Institution was moving early modern paintings that had long resided in distant country estates, the collectors' homes, to this vibrant and very public metropolitan space, just as the Louvre gave to the public Hazlitt's "inheritance," the formerly private art possessions of the *ancien régime*. Only this time, of course, it was counterrevolutionary 1815, and Britain's wealthy collectors (certainly not all aristocrats) were fully in possession of the exhibit.

This context may help explain one of the most vehement and anomalous of Hazlitt's art writings, his polemic and exposé of a widely circulated but faked art document, "The Catalogue Raisonné of the British Institution" (1815), which Hazlitt reviewed scathingly in the *Examiner*. Far from renouncing art institutions, this essay actively promotes the British Institution, which the anonymously authored Catalogue was attacking. Hazlitt exposes the Catalogue as a ghost-written product of the Royal Academy (the usual suspect for art historians is the painter Robert Smirke), promoting its own "English School" agenda at the expense of the recent exhibition of Old Masters at the British Institution. As Hazlitt read it, the Academy-produced Catalogue made a virulent case against early modern painting and, in a sense, the importance of art history as a whole. Thus, for Hazlitt, the Catalogue's unpardonable besmirching: it calls Flemish painters by their dark name, "the Black Masters," because of their high-contrast, chiaroscuro visual tones; it depicts Vandyke's coloring as "starch and blue"; it turns Rubens's paintings into "brown studies," and Rembrandt's canvases appear as though "dragged ... through the Prince Regent's new sewers."[73] In short, the Old Masters' paintings were *old* in a sense the Catalogue Raisonné vividly revives from the Quarrel of the Ancients and Moderns, but now that Quarrel was being retranslated into a dispute between early modern artists and the British contemporary painters whom the Royal Academy writers were defending and protecting in the eyes of the art-watching public. To Hazlitt the Catalogue Raisonné portrayed art history as a zero-sum game. "All that is taken from the old Masters is so much added to the moderns; the marring of Art is the making of the Academy."[74] Many more choice phrases could be cited from this essay, all to the same effect: Hazlitt is unabashedly siding with the *new* ancients (early modern Italian, French, and Flemish painters) against the Reynolds-influenced moderns. But more important from a social viewpoint, he allies himself here with the connoisseurs, collectors, and administrators of the British Institution in such ways that, on this occasion, Hazlitt's sympathies seem far less "quasi-"aristocratic (as John Kinnaird says in view of his other defenses of high art) than they do, for perhaps the only time in Hazlitt's career, literally aristocratic.[75] Surely he knew that the BI had long been networked with the Royal Institution and with the aristocratic history of connoisseurship against the upstart, low-born painters of the Royal Academy. Yet the broader point, as Peter Funnell points out, is not that Hazlitt had opportunistically turned coat in the contemporary art debate. He was not merely defending an aristocratically supported arts Institution after railing against all other art institutions. It was Hazlitt's unusual willingness to engage in an *intra*-institutional controversy (between the Royal Academy and British Institution) that could reveal how much of an insider he could be to the contemporary art field that he so often professed to stand outside.[76] To picture Hazlitt as projecting himself into the British art field is also to see him as finding ways to use the new division in that field.

For these reasons among others, it was becoming more difficult to comprehend the "arts and sciences" as a whole in the Romantic age without grasping the intensified division into literary, artistic, and scientific fields which these new arts-and-sciences Institutions were provoking and making more complex.[77] It's not that Hazlitt openly acknowledged being a player in the British art field or its unseemly game of power, influence, and commercial snares; it's that writing about art in the public journals, by 1816, had *become* an unavoidable means of making significant moves in that game. This had become possible, I would further suggest, only since the emergence of a consistently public art-critical press around 1806. That press was never far from politics, fashion, or indeed (at some further remove in the art-writing world) religion, Dissenting or otherwise.

I return, then, to the problem of Barrell's strong concept of a "republic of taste" – where a "civic humanist" line of art theory had prevailed in Britain until the breaking point Barrell identifies as "Haydon and Hazlitt" in *The Political Theory of Painting*. Clearly a concept like "republic of taste" belongs with a wider nomenclature of "Republic of Letters" or "commonwealth of learning" in the long eighteenth century, since the same principle of a "political" degree of autonomy from the actual British political state – which is also to say a commitment to "public art" at some fundamental level – is always being asserted in such phraseology. Republics of letters *or* taste, as we know from wide discussion emanating from the reception of Habermas's *Structural Transformation of the Public Sphere*, sought to enjoy that autonomy to the degree they could follow Kant's desideratum, "have the courage to think for yourselves!" Nobody had that courage more than Hazlitt after 1800 (though a significant number of well-known others had comparable degrees of such courage). Yet in breaking from Barrell's "republic of taste," Hazlitt did not retreat into some alternative and uncharacteristically privatized world of individual value or artistic autonomy. My argument is that he rather responded to rapidly changing conditions by siding, in the Catalogue essay that has been my example, with what amounted to factions in another kind of collective world, the "field" or art world as a sociologically articulated perspective that would define such a world and its affiliations. The choice was not between public and private, that is to say, but between *two* versions of a public world of art engagement and contest. One had a historical name – "republic" of some sort – and one had an as-yet unnamed shape in the early nineteenth century. Retrospectively, this alternative shape was the field of artistic production with all its participants and contestants, from art producers like John Northcote to connoisseurs and art historians like R. P. Knight to arts administrators like Thomas Bernard to public art critics like Robert Hunt and William Hazlitt.

### Dissenting vicissitudes: commerce and the "arts and sciences"

The "Catalogue Raisonné" essay of 1816 was also the occasion for one of Hazlitt's brilliantly phrased, trademark principles of a necessary division of interests between commerce and art:

> We do not consume the works of Art as articles of food, clothing, or fuel; but we brood over their *idea*, which is accessible to all, and may be multiplied without end, "with riches fineless" ... The spirit of art is not the spirit of trade: it is not a question between the grower or consumer of some perishable and personal commodity, but it is a question between human genius and human taste, how much the one can produce for the benefit of mankind, and how much the other can enjoy. It is the "link of peaceful commerce 'twixt dividable shores."[78]

This passage is often read as an instance of Hazlitt's privatizing of art-reception, removing it from the public realm and marketplace alike. But it would be more accurate to say that it substitutes one kind of "commerce" for another – the "peaceful commerce" between art producers and their audience, a mode of sociable exchange, for the sphere of consumerism, art markets, premiums, and other prizes offered by the Royal Academy or British Institution, along with all the other "perishables" appearing in the consumer economy.

This passage makes a useful counterpoint, to take another case of dissension among reformers and Dissenters on such matters, to William Roscoe's Dissenting commercial embrace of the "arts and sciences" in a November 1817 inaugural lecture to the Liverpool Royal Institution – an institution that could not have been more different than its namesake London version – by vigorously promoting the marriage of fine arts and commerce under the broader rubric (as published in London) *On the Origin and Vicissitudes of Literature, Science, and Art, and Their Influence on the Present State of Society* (1817).[79] Unlike many London Dissenters of the Regency, the Unitarian, abolitionist Roscoe could also make a case for both sciences and fine arts. The impression given in the *Vicissitudes* that he accentuated the fine arts to the virtual exclusion of the mechanical arts or sciences, which would align him misleadingly with the emphases of the Hunt circle, does not take into account his parallel advocacy for a public science: "The great superiority of a public institution over a private collection, in promoting botanical sciences," he had argued in 1802, is that "the latter depends upon the taste, the finances, or the caprice of an individual" – namely the aristocratic individual who had been botany's prime patron in the eighteenth century.[80] Here, as later in the 1817 *Vicissitudes*, Roscoe makes a characteristically consistent, yet in 1802 still quite unusual, case for middle-class patronage of the arts and sciences by wealthy merchants. As the now-famous historian of the Medicis' art patronage, he was in an authoritative position to distinguish between great-man patronage and the kind of sustained support of the arts only a flourishing commercial center (as he thought) could sustain over historical time. Colonial trade was fundamental to this 1802 vision: "The joint encouragement and patronage of so respectable and numerous a body of proprietors, many of whom have connexions in foreign parts ... afford us the most flattering prospects of success."[81] Roscoe's own Dissenting abolitionism made this a difficult argument to pursue to an audience made up partly of merchants who had profited from the slave trade, but he persisted more emphatically in 1817.

However, I want to cite the part of his 1817 case that would most attract attention among his many London readers:

> If you will protect the arts, the arts will, and ought to remunerate you. To suppose that they are to be encouraged upon some abstract and disinterested plan, from which all idea of utility shall be excluded, is to suppose that

a building can be erected without a foundation. There is not a greater error than to think that the arts can subsist upon the generosity of the public ... What should we think of giving a premium to the author of a worthless poem, by way of encouraging poetry?[82]

What Roscoe rejects is more than aristocratic patronage; it is equally the Royal Academy's and British Institution's pecuniary reward system (contests and premiums) *as well as* the alternative call, like Prince Hoare's, for state patronage of the arts. Rather than take up any posture in the existing London patronage debate, Roscoe has adopted as his own intellectual patron the Scottish common-sense philosopher Dugald Stewart, calling, as John Whale observes, for the rich merchant to be the "man of benevolence." Like both Millar and Hume, furthermore, Roscoe eliminates climate, national character, or some internal motor driving the arts fatefully to "rise" and then "necessarily decline" as keys to the destiny of the arts. Rather "it is to the influence of moral causes, to these dispositions and arrangements in the affairs of mankind, that are particularly within our own power, that we are to seek for the reasons of the progress or decline of liberal studies."[83]

Few Dissenters in London – Hazlitt would be one of the few – would have disagreed that commerce might well be envisioned to have not only a marriageable appeal for sciences, but also a power to sustain the visual arts. Nor was Roscoe's appeal to "utility" in 1817 yet grating to Dissenters' ears; Roscoe had gone to school with Priestley, Aiken, Barbauld, and Fuseli at the Warrington Academy and was still able to speak the language of rational Dissent. Roscoe's principle that any "union of the pursuit of literature with the affairs of the world" will "be effected by establishments in the nature of the present Institution" would have been wholly consistent with what we know of the stance taken by the London and Surrey Institutions, though it would have been at odds with the aristocratically grounded Royal Institution of the years we have thus far noticed, 1800–10, the era of Humphry Davy's and Thomas Bernard's linkage of scientific authority to landed property. Hazlitt himself dismissed Roscoe's case on both its commercial and institutional grounds, we can surmise, and might well have pointed out in some flinty conversational circle with Charles Lamb that William Roscoe might indeed have been the only Englishman to write an ode to an institution.[84] But his 1817 case for the Liverpool arts-and-sciences, along with Roscoe's past ventures in constructing "athenaeums" and botanical institutions, would travel with uncommon directness to the New World, where Thomas Jefferson took his projects and rationale to be a potential model for instituting the University of Virginia.[85] It is therefore not just speculative to think of Roscoe's early nineteenth-century career as a Dissenter's answer to Thomas Bernard, who was equally busy organizing the arts and sciences through forming Institutions (though Bernard wrote no odes) – yet fundamentally divided on the question of class, public, and patronage.

This is why it is significant to find the most challenging review of Roscoe's *Vicissitudes* coming from the Royal Institution in London that Bernard first helped found in 1800, now articulated in its new *Journal of Science and the Arts* in 1818. The *Journal* offers long passages from *Vicissitudes* before coming to its most critical reply. We might expect, given the Royal's origin with aristocratic landholders associated with the Board of Agriculture, that its main objection would be to Roscoe's full-throated advocacy of merchant and commercial patronage for the arts and sciences. Some of the review does point back in that direction. But its most emphatic reply also marks why the Royal Institution in 1818 has become so different from the one that, in Thomas Bernard's time of administrating its lectures, embraced a wide range of "arts and sciences." Unlike 1806, when Bernard invited Coleridge to lecture on "The Principles of the Fine Arts" alongside Davy's chemistry, the Royal Institution *Journal* was now using Roscoe's lecture-book to help it repudiate *any* parallel between the fine arts and sciences. This refusal meant "enforcing" the idea of the distinction

> between such arts and sciences as are matters of taste and amusement, and such as by their effects promote our comfort, and protect or secure our existence ... We are as capricious in our attachments to the means of comfort and the modes of protecting and securing our existence, as to the effects of those arts which form our amusements, our luxury, or pleasure, or are connected with our prejudices or superstitions. The latter arts must ever be subject to fluctuation in their degrees of perfection, from the alteration of our tastes, our love of variety, the natural instability of our wishes, or the proportion of reason with which we happen to be enlightened; and although a change in our desires, inclinations, and understanding, may be too gradual for distinct observation within a very limited period, it must infallibly operate to abate the ardour of improvement and diminish the incentives to excellence in such arts as are ceasing to be the objects of our request or admiration.[86]

Coming as it does in 1818, the Royal Institution's language – and the review seems very much a calculated Institutional reply to Roscoe's widely circulating lecture – now echoes the *Chrestomathia*, which in Bentham's philosophical attempt to make the "arts and sciences" coherent had impolitely dropped the fine arts and poetry to an insulting footnote as "arts of amusement." What the *Journal* of 1818 argues next can make even Bentham seem to have been too soft on the fine and practical arts:

> Painting, sculpture, poetry, music, magic, and astrology, have been peculiarly subject to these alternations of real and sometimes imaginary rise and of decline ... Astronomy, mathematics, chymistry, mechanics, navigation, agriculture, manufactures, have all obtained a gradual or sudden augmentation in their excellence and value since their revival after the fall of the Roman empire, and although great difference may exist in their degrees of perfection in different countries, or in the same country at different times, no person will hesitate to pronounce that the patrimony of such learning is continually improving, and sometimes increasing.[87]

No lecture series of Bernard's day would have put "painting, sculpture, poetry" in league with "magic and astrology," nor would it have drawn the line that now could resonate with Hazlitt telling his own readers in 1816, sharply and without qualification, that the "sciences" always progress while the "arts" never do. Hazlitt's version of the Quarrel of Ancients and Moderns was of course poised to defend the fine arts, particularly from "projects" for the design of a school like Bentham's in 1816. Roscoe himself had not vowed that the fine arts "progress," but he had treated the two domains as equally fundamental to local and national prosperity. Nor would Hazlitt, of course, tolerate the fine arts' "astrological" status as now assigned in 1818 by the Royal Institution. But there was a disturbing symmetry between his own, Dissenting arguments for opposing the sciences and arts and what the now increasingly Benthamite Royal Institution had been confirming on the other side of the divide. At such moments, the "arts" and "sciences" are finding a barrier as much as a connective in the "and" that joins them.

## Parliamentary reform and the knowledges

Thus we need to turn to what become the most deeply divisive questions among those who have spent nearly full lifetimes advocating a sweeping reform of government in Britain, a division that is certainly not only about the knowledges but also about political economy, property, and the emerging discourse later to be institutionalized as the "social sciences." For my purpose here, the question remains how to approach the relationship of "arts and sciences" – what might be called the contradictory relationship of utility and imaginative institution – that would make "1832" a year of both victory and defeat for the British left. For all the dissension I have been noting between the various Romantic-age reformers on the question of "arts and sciences," there stood one arena of shared conviction. Fundamental political and economic reform in Britain, now long delayed from its hopes from the era of rational Dissent, *must* soon come – and when it did, the knowledges *entailed* in the "arts and sciences" must somehow be part of that transformation. In the following pages, I shall take three quite different cases of that shared conviction as shifting alliances and divisions among reformers played out historically and intellectually from 1810 to 1825. The first instance will encompass those rare moments when the post-1800 Dissenters and reformers departed from their reluctance to generalize the "arts and sciences" as a whole – recognizing the now politically compromised character of that very expression – to make some extraordinary propositions.

For twenty years, most of the Hunt circle argued earnestly and pointedly for government patronage of the arts – as we have seen, they usually meant the "fine arts" and rarely addressed the "useful arts" so valued by eighteenth-century rational Dissent. But one version of these arguments could take a more decidedly "literary" and, in the politically dark moment of 1810, a quasi-utopian form in a now little-read *Reflector* prose entry, probably written by Leigh Hunt, in the form of a "dialogue" and "fragment": "THE REFORMERS; or, Wrongs of Intellect. – A fragment of a Political Dialogue," which purports to be recorded at "Utopia Lodge."[88] What's rare about this text for the Hunts is both its spacious embrace of the *wider* category "arts and sciences" and its staging of a dialogue between two wings of the English reform movement which John and Leigh Hunt were themselves straddling around 1810: the constitutionalist reform agitation of Sir Francis Burdett in Parliament, supported in the press by a now-radicalized William Cobbett in the *Political Register* on the one hand, and on the other the *Examiner*'s case for reform as it was still gestating in this inaugural issue of the *Reflector*. The dialogue begins by agreeing on a common ground between the Burdett and the Hunt visions by assessing and roundly rejecting the *Edinburgh Review*'s cautious and commercialist vision of reform that had gained traction by attacking Burdett and Cobbett with abandon. As the dialogue develops, though, increasingly profound disagreements emerge between the Burdett/Cobbett argument for reform and Hunt's still emerging case; the question of the knowledges comes to the forefront of what the whole British reform project should entail. In the following exchanges, "A" speaks for Hunt, and "B" channels Burdett's public speeches. The issues between them are crystallized in "A"'s reply to the Burdett/Cobbett case that "B" has been making:

A. I do not admit the doctrine ... that intellect was, is, and ought to be dependant upon property, and who identifies independence of moral and political principle, with independence of worldly circumstance ... I deny that we ought to go back, or in other words, that a learned and scientific, should implicitly take its political creed from an unlearned and unscientific, age; or limit by the institutions of such an age, its hopes of moral and political amelioration.[89]

If Hunt's modernizing argument rejects the constitutionalist case grounded in 1066 – that "Property would again be made the Basis of Political Right," as "A" puts it – it substitutes an argument no less extreme in its own way. The Burdett argument makes its key error by

> mistaking a secondary for a primary cause. – In your supposing wealth or property to be the cause – whereas it is only a consequence – of the presence of arts and sciences, acting on the national industry, though, when rightly employed, it becomes a reproductive cause in its turn. In every country, the stock of physical and moral strength is in proportion to its real attainments in the arts and sciences, in whose train follow national wealth and happiness.[90]

As we saw in Chapter 2, Humphry Davy had made in 1802 *almost* the same case Hunt does here, though with two signal exceptions: Davy had eliminated the "fine arts" from his otherwise spacious vision of how the "arts and sciences" make modernity, and Davy, like Burdett, also argued for the primacy of (aristocratic) property to ground the arts and sciences. Though not mentioned in the 1810 dialogue, Davy at the Royal Institution must have been on Hunt's mind when he cites "the prime source of our political evils" in his most stinging rebuke to "B." "The arts and sciences, which should have been primary planets and fixed stars in the parliamentary system, are become mere satellites of property, and hence the vortices in which we are whirling to destruction."[91] That Hunt already speaks to a *new* situation in London cultural life probably needs no underscoring by now. Even William Godwin, who had held the political and private-property institutions of the eighteenth century responsible for disturbingly unequal access to modern knowledges, had not gone quite this far or sounded so apocalyptic a note. In the dialogue "B" grows more incredulous at the implications of "A"'s line of argument: "Can you possibly mean that instead of a House of Commons built on property, the third estate, like the groves of an Athenian Academy, should be an assembly of artists and philosophers?"[92] Is this to propose a latter-day Platonic utopia of government by intellectuals? Hunt's character "A" becomes momentarily pragmatic and concedes to Burdett that his reformed Parliament will indeed include "gentlemen of great landed property, or of mercantile property." Hunt's reply then becomes the possible "1832," as we now recall it, that would never take place:

> But [men of property] do not constitute the whole. I want the lower House of Parliament to be a real epitome of the mind of the people of the United Kingdom ... This principle of giving to the country at the seasons of election the full benefit of the actual stock of judgment that each individual in his vocation possessed, should be extended to every art and science – to every species of knowledge, that is susceptible of classification, and that contributes to the welfare of the country; all of which should be represented. I would even have the valuable practical discoveries in Art and Science that may in future be made, provided for – as far as human foresight could make such provision – by ordaining that there shall be an ample representation of such abstract sciences, (mathematics and chemistry for example) as such presumed discoveries must of necessity be connected with, and that every half century, or at other stated periods, a revision should be made of the numbers returned for each art, science, and species of property, with a view to their more harmonious and efficient incorporation.[93]

It was rare for Hunt to put such emphasis on the natural sciences – let alone scientists as Parliamentary representatives of their respective knowledges. But the larger point to make is how materially this vision of reform will differ from the *Examiner*'s repeated calls for government patronage of the fine arts.

To see this, we should now include the third participant in Hunt's dialogue, "C," who has thus far played a minor, quizzical role as a skeptical questioner of the two major reform agendas. Here C tries to extend, and perhaps make absurd, A's plan to turn scientists into MPs: "And would you include poetry, painting, and their sister arts, in your system of representation, as well as astronomy, logic, arithmetic, medicine, with a long *etcetera*?" Or to put C's question in more familiar, yet also somewhat extraordinary terms: poets as *legislators*? "Yes," replies A, "I would have *every* art and science represented, that contributes, or might contribute, to the general prosperity. I can perceive no fairer or more adequate manner in which the essence of the whole of the public mind can be elaborated."[94] This dialogue then takes a somewhat Byronic turn as C responds to this extraordinary Parliamentary vision of poets, painters, sculptors, physicists, botanists, and others making the national laws:

> c. Then we should soon have Coleridge singing his Ode to Liberty, and Mr. Shee his Painter's Remonstrance, instead of making parliamentary orations, in St. Stephen's chapel. Mr. Soane might choose to remodel the

metropolis; Mr. Bell to anatomise our expressions; and Sir Lucas Pepys to purge the constitution, while Doctors Herschel and Maskelin would be *moving* – I suppose, for the moon and stars, in your political hemisphere!⁹⁵

This reference to Coleridge's "Ode to Liberty" may be rather to "Ode to France," which Hunt, Shelley, and others still admired, in ways we might not, as a testament to his former beliefs now in 1810 long renounced. This last jest may also speak to the sober reformer's incapacity to imagine the *arts* legislating at all – as the Burdett character recoils in disbelief – but Hunt's voice turns the astronomical reference into his most telling point for what *kind* of present condition motivates this dialogue, and it serves A's most telling analysis of "the prime source of our political evils. The arts and sciences, which should have been primary planets and fixed stars in the parliamentary system, are become mere satellites of property, and hence the vortices in which we are whirling to destruction."⁹⁶ This 1810 dialogue will in retrospect resonate and seem to look forward to Shelley's more famous and seemingly paradoxical argument for understanding poets as "unacknowledged legislators," but it is still somewhat startling to imagine them as actual legislators debating matters of state and justice in a vastly reformed governmental body. My analysis of Shelley's texts below will tilt that expectation in a somewhat different direction. First, I want to look at what Hunt's character in "The Reformers" proposes from another Dissenting angle, this time Hazlitt's eloquent advocacy of a popular intellect in the powerful reform essay "What Is the People?" (1819). Here the anti-Jacobin question of what or who counts as "legitimate" and what or who doesn't – which has been given a wide and influential press up to the explosive year 1819 – gives Hazlitt the moment to cross a line even most Regency reformers had constantly observed:

> That fine word "Legitimate" never produced any thing but bastard philosophy and patriotism! ... It is thus that the tide of power constantly setting in against the people, swallows up natural genius and acquired knowledge in the vortex of corruption, and then they reproach us with our want of leaders of weight and influence, to stem the torrent. All that has ever been done for society, has, however, been done for it by this intellect, before it was cheapened to be a cat's-paw of divine right. *All discoveries and all improvements in arts, in science, in legislation, in civilization, in every thing dear and valuable to the heart of man, have been made by this intellect* – all the triumphs of human genius over the rudest barbarism, the darkest ignorance, the grossest and most inhuman superstition, the most unmitigated and remorseless tyranny, have been gained for themselves by the people. Great Kings, great law-givers, great founders, and great reformers of religion, have almost all arisen from among the people [my italics].⁹⁷

Hazlitt refers here to a *general* intellect – a version of what Kevin Gilmartin has astutely called the figure of the "popular Leviathan" that appears elsewhere in essays celebrating a robust public sphere in the metropolis[98] – in such a way as to cross every social line that had been earlier assumed or stated by both rational Dissenters in the eighteenth century and the British coalition of reformers, particularly the Hunt circle, in the early nineteenth. It may simply be an intense, indeed a well-nigh sublime moment of *educated* radical rhetoric in these heated years of political debate. Or it may be a breakthrough moment that crosses the line between what E. P. Thompson would later call Hazlitt's middle-class reformist language and Cobbett's popular idioms in *The Making of the English Working Class*.[99]

## Poets and institutors

Hazlitt's popular intellect in "What Is the People?" of 1819 will then pair most antithetically with the increasingly straitened collective intellect taking shape in the 1820s. Though he had been prepared to negotiate the views of the utilitarians before this decade, his writings in the mid 1820s seethe at what have now crystallized as the "arts and sciences" in the *Westminster Review* (1824), where the scientific *Chrestomathia* of 1816 had turned into a serial assault on the fine arts and the literary.

Pointing out that Shelley was "self-consciously working in the Benthamite mode" in the *Philosophical View of Reform*, James Chandler makes a critical distinction between what Shelley could adopt from Bentham and what he would reflexively require for any truly philosophical vision of reform. Shelley surely intended to invoke Bentham in his argument in *A Philosophical View of Reform* that "the establishment of the principle of utility" now promises "the substance, and liberty and equality as the forms according to which the concerns of human life ought to be administered."[100] To agree to Bentham's criterion of "efficiency" in how British institutions should perform, Chandler argues, "suggests a first-order utilitarianism" that nonetheless entails the view Shelley advances – efficiency "betrays an insufficiently 'philosophical' view of reform" as it "involves mechanical or nonreflexive models of political efficacy."[101] Efficiency cannot suffice, one might say, for the same reasons Bentham cannot really be the latter-day Godwin. What radical Dissent had long since shown it did have – a moral and political vision of human possibility – and what Shelley was now, in very different circumstances and with very different resources, renewing for the 1820s was the view that, as Chandler puts it, efficiency "can never finally achieve a normative status" since it "fail[s] to honor the second-order representational project of human perfectibility."

Chandler's term *project* reminds us of the historicity of that term, one Bentham had embraced vigorously in his 1787 tussle with Adam Smith, and the Scottish Enlightenment more broadly, and one he was glad to share with Count Benjamin Rumford's schemes for building new institutions in the 1790s to instruct and habituate the poor to the ways of technological civilization. To speak of the "project of human perfectibility" is to see both what Bentham originally had in common with both Rumford and the rational Dissenters, and to what extent that language has, by 1820, profoundly altered. Efficient and pragmatic programs like the *Westminster Review*'s have displaced "human perfectibility" as a normative horizon, while the term *project* itself would in the long term veer in two directions. One would be the increasingly operational idea of "projects" as a state or moment of every economic, military, or political enterprise: the title "project-director" has over the two centuries since become the *sine qua non* language of modernization in all its organizational forms. The other direction *project* would take after 1820 – and this is the one Chandler draws from its earlier history – would be increasingly ambitious, visionary, and socially transformative, even if today it has fallen into disrepute while the language of "project directors" has spread far and wide. The socially transformative "project," we now can see in hindsight, would appear from Shelley to the utopian socialists and from the visions of Western Marxism in the early twentieth century to the texts of Sartre and even Habermas in the mid to late century.

The question was then whether a public sphere of contested opinion – even Hazlitt's brilliantly abrasive version of that contest – will by itself produce the profoundly transformative aims of "reform" in the early nineteenth century. For Shelley, as Chandler argues, such opinion lacks the "normative" force that he works to find in "poetry" itself. What then carries over from *A Philosophical View of Reform*, by far the more spacious and politically explicit (as well as historical) text, to "A Defence of Poetry," is the ringing claim to poetry's power (if "poetry" is defined well beyond the scope of conventional genre or "verse") to *institute*. Literary history remembers Shelley's resounding finale to the "Defence," that poets are the unacknowledged "legislators" of the world – a language he may well have derived from Hunt-circle writings or discussion topics. But the *View* makes it clearer than does the "Defence" that the more profoundly transformational role is to be grasped as poetry's *instituting* powers. The cognates *institutor, institute,* and *institution* – terms critically enabled by Godwin in the Revolution debate, but ones that Shelley also owes to John Millar's breakthrough Scottish Enlightenment modernizing of those words from their early modern modes – dominate the *View* and the "Defence."

Here is one telling example of Shelley using *institutions*, as he anatomizes the *ancien régime*, in a way that most modern readers have been accustomed to see as a mode of structure:

> The French were what their literature is ...weak, superficial, vain, with little imagination, and with passions as well as judgments cleaving to the external form of things ... Not that their organical differences, whatever they may amount to, incapacitate them from arriving at the exercise of the highest powers to be attained by man. *Their institutions made them what they were*. Slavery and superstition, contumely and the tame endurance of contumely, and the habits engendered from generation to generation out of this transmitted inheritance of wrong, created this thing which has extinguished what has been called the likeness of God in man [my italics].[102]

By rejecting an older topos of national character ("organical differences") to explain why the French acted, thought, and wrote the way they did under centuries of monarchy, Shelley appears to use *institutions* to explain the forces that determined them, and it's a usage so common in the twentieth century – you are what the institutions of power have made you – that it seems almost counterintuitive to read it any other way. Yet Shelley surely meant this in the double and thus rather different sense that so many other passages in the *View* and related writings use. The French were what their *active institutings* (or their "institutions" *as* actions embedded in practices over time) made them, since their acts of institution, over centuries, became the structural institutions which embedded them, by 1789, in their own inescapable histories. Far from the passive subjects of their institutions (which on any given *day* in 1789 they might well have been), the French have made themselves what they were – and here is the moral and political judgment – through what they instituted rightly or wrongly.

There is perhaps no finer balance in English Romantic writing between what Raymond Williams called the active or verbal sense of *institution* – which descends from the early modern usage I have previously associated with the "rites of institution" governing instruction, inheritance, transmission, and founding – and the nominal or structural sense of *institution* which would by the 1830s overtake that early modern sense of action, especially in the emerging social sciences, than in Shelley's texts of 1819–20. A brief sampling among dozens of usages:

> [From *View*:] The great principle of Reform consists in every individual giving his consent to the *institution* and the continuous existence of the social system which is *instituted* for his advantage and for the advantage of others in his situation ... Public happiness is the substance and the end of political *institutions*.
> [From "Defence":] A poet, as he is the author to others of the highest wisdom, pleasures, virtue, and glory ... As to his glory, let time be challenged to declare whether the fame of any other *institutor* of human life be comparable to that of a poet ... Poets, or those who imagine and express this indestructible order, are not only the authors of language and of music, of the dance and architecture, and statuary and painting: they are the *institutors* of laws, and the founders of civil society, and the inventors of the arts of life. (my emphases)[103]

Both passages from the *View* can (and I think should) be read as the earlier text. The further association of "institutor" and "author" in the "Defence" would seem to make this keen verbal balancing of agency and structure an especially *literary* one, even while it works in the opposite way as well: lawmakers and institution-founders are "authors" of civil society and the "arts of life." Also important to notice here is that not only "poetry" itself is granted the force of institutor-ship, so likewise is the necessarily new mode of *defense* of poetry as the nineteenth century's "poetics." It's true that the most powerful past versions of a poetics were "defenses" as well – Aristotle against Plato's state, Sydney against the liturgical utilitarianism of the Church. But Shelley remounts such a "defence" in the age of institutions, as I have been calling the Romantic era, and that makes a crucial difference. In a similar vein of distinction between trivial and profound senses of "criticism" that Shelley's own distinction between verse and poetry surely implies, critical discourse like Shelley's, rather than the array of periodical performances Hazlitt skewers in the essay "On Criticism," belongs to what Shelley calls *poetry*, and thereby must count as a necessarily *instituting* force of the "literary" itself.

In this light, where the Hunt circle and the "philosophical radicals" would constitute two very *real* and tensely related kinds of political reform that likewise entailed important consequences for the arts and sciences in Romantic-age Britain, I want briefly to recall a *third* formation – this one conjectural and counterfactual – as Shelley envisioned it in the *Philosophical View*. Here he paused in the midst of a complex argument to imagine a new kind of collective project: "The poets, philosophers, and artists ought to remonstrate, and ... show the diversity of convictions they entertain of the inevitable connection between national prosperity and freedom, and the cultivation of the imagination and the cultivation of scientific truth and the profound development of moral and metaphysical inquiry." And who would articulate such a cultural formation? Shelley proposed Godwin, Hazlitt, Bentham, and Leigh Hunt projecting a reformist program that would cut across the philosophical differences among the reformers – *and* the "arts and sciences" – to become "worthy of the age and of the cause ... radiating and irresistible like the meridian sun," "strik[ing] all but the eagles who dared to gaze upon its beams, with blindness and confusion."[104] It would have been the most striking confederation of radical reformers to date, certainly the most powerful concatenation of philosophers and political thinkers – meshed closely to poets, novelists, painters, literary critics, and scientists – that England had yet seen join forces in the project of sweeping economic, political, and cultural transformation. This gathering of what might have transfigured the "arts and sciences" in a very different direction than we have thus far seen in the London arts-and-sciences Institutions of 1800 to the 1820s, in making a pointed campaign for sweeping political renovation, would, of course, never take place. As I have suggested above, though, it is not entirely remote from what the *Reflector* had mused so interestingly about in 1811, combined with the more popular depth of intellect Hazlitt was trying to articulate in "What Is the People?" Nor is it entirely removed from what Godwin imagined as a "historical romance" that would counterfactually envision a "futurity" yet to be made – and in fact something quite realizable in a different future than the one that occurred from 1819 to 1832.

# Epilogue: transatlantic crossings

> Night, Gothic night, again may shade the plains
> Where Power is seated, and where Science reigns;
> England, the seat of arts, be only known
> By the gray ruin and the mouldering stone;
> That time may tear the garland from her brow,
> And Europe sit in dust, as Asia now.
> 
> Anna Barbauld, *Eighteen Hundred and Eleven* (1811)

> The Lyceum is the American Theatre. It is the one institution in which we take our nose out of the hands of our English prototypes – the English whom we are always ridiculing and always following – and go alone.
> 
> "Lectures and Lecturing," *Putnam's Monthly* (1857)

In the mid 1820s an end approached for the vibrant "arts-and-sciences" Institutions of the Romantic age as they began losing their central place in London life. In early 1823, the Surrey Institution underwent financial crisis and then sudden, widely discussed collapse. One former administrator called it "a monster of an institution, which, it is hoped, will never again rear its rickety head in this metropolis or any where else."[1] Since 1800, the arts-and-sciences Institutions had all been "rickety" in a sense – often running out of funds, or trying out some odd-duck curricular experiment, they were precarious constructions that might alter a knowledge field, make a sensational splash, or flounder and sputter – but being rickety and unpredictable was arguably part of their impact on the times. These Institutions were constantly changing, often haphazard in their means of cultural invention, yet for the same reasons, unusually interesting to their Romantic-age participants and later cultural historians alike. Just before its breakdown, the Surrey Institution lecturer James Jennings gave a well-publicized talk in late 1822 on the whole Institution-lecturing phenomenon, vividly recalling its stimulating claims to knowledge, its sociability and bright lights, its wide-ranging interfaces with print culture, and the lecturing stars and the eccentrics who had appeared there.[2] Thus it is revealing that when the Scotsman Daniel Brewster began provoking the British "decline of science" debate in 1828, he would evoke a touch of the gothic by writing to Henry Brougham that "nobody is aware of the state of the arts and sciences in this country, of their recent decline, and of the *horrid construction* of all those institutions which are intended to promote them [italics in original]."[3] In 1823 many wanted to believe, with P. G. Patmore, that London's "arts and sciences" Institutions were still so widely influential as to be "giving a tone and character to the age."[4] Jennings's memorial to this world seemed already a sign that they were also now about to be superseded by what would prove, over the next eight years, an institutionally and disciplinarily more powerful configuration of cultural organizing.

This turning point would occur as a period of institutional fission and restructuring from 1823 to 1831. To take these events in rapid order – there was the opening of the National Gallery of Pictures (1824), the founding of the Mechanics' Institute (1824), and the first issues of the utilitarian *Westminster Review* (1824), with its ongoing polemics against the fine arts or those who promoted them. In 1826 came the most far-reaching innovation, the opening of the University of London, which made lecturing its main strategy for public education and hired to teach many of the leading Institution lecturers of the past quarter-century. But perhaps no new institution spoke more pointedly to the question of what counted most as "knowledge" in the emerging domains of art and science than the decisive restructuring of the sciences undertaken by the British Association for the Advancement of Science (BAAS) in 1831. All of these new developments entailed some new level of separation between categories of "art," "science," and mechanical-practical knowledges that were now to be served each by their own institutional domains. All of them also constructed a more durable administrative apparatus for managing the practices or knowledges they had realigned, and all, unlike most of their Romantic "arts and sciences" predecessors, still exist in some form today.

The new centers for fine arts, mechanical arts, disciplinary sciences, and, not least, London's first university of its own promised not only a higher order of structuring and distinguishing various arts and sciences, but the anchoring of those domains in far more discernible and separable fields. Yet they also revealed their origins of one kind or another in the "arts and sciences" Institution world of the past quarter-century. As England's first fully public art museum, the National Gallery of Pictures opened on the West End as a legacy of the British Institution for

Promoting the Fine Arts (whose directors sold it the first collection of Old Masters and British painters), while across town the London Mechanics' Institute resumed the old, unfinished agenda of "useful" and technical learning envisioned by Rumford and Bernard in the late 1790s unrealized prototype for the Royal Institution. The simultaneous founding of the National Gallery and Mechanics' Institute in 1824 – so otherwise far apart in their social, aesthetic, technological, and political agendas – is a reminder of how important a historical conjuncture can be to the building of institutions as well as the changing shape of the "arts and sciences."

Meanwhile, the University of London recruited figures of significant impact from the lecturing platforms, inviting among others Michael Faraday and William Brande of the Royal and London Institutions to professorships at the University.[5] The university worked to put "the spirit of Bentham" into an ambitious institutional shape, while Coleridge noted dyspeptically the continuity between the older lecturing world and the new invention in Bloomsbury as "lecture-bazaars under the absurd name of universities."[6] The British Association for the Advancement of Science, however, organized itself explicitly against the London "arts and sciences" lecturing and exhibition sphere of the Romantic age. By networking the growing number of scientific specialist societies into an administrative pyramid under the direction of the "Gentlemen of Science," the BAAS effectively eclipsed most of the remaining authority for any of the earlier Institutions except for the always-strongest among them, the Royal, where Faraday's electricity would by the mid 1820s prove to be the legitimate, more up-to-date, and professional disciplinary successor to Davy's chemistry.[7] In directing this far-reaching shift of scientific authority from the Romantic-age Institutions' world to the now-coordinated specialist disciplinary sciences, the BAAS also won government funding and chose to meet in various provincial cities, soon to include Cambridge, as a means to avoid centering British sciences in the great metropolis, the commercial and political contexts that for a quarter-century had framed and often energized the "arts and sciences" Institutions as Londoners knew them.[8] These events, well documented elsewhere, also strengthened a growing radical and plebeian movement in London to contest the lines of access to knowledge production and dissemination that "gentlemanly capitalism" (to use again Boyd Hilton's useful expression) at the BAAS was now drawing.

It was in the midst of this cultural realignment that one of the most powerful nineteenth-century portraits of an emerging British modernity appeared in the *Edinburgh Review*. Thomas Carlyle's "Signs of the Times" is still a revealing essay on many counts, but I want to note briefly how it helped alter Britain's picture of its own immediate past. Here Romantic-age "arts and sciences" Institutions appear, this time far less sanguinely than in Charles Lyell's historical sketch of 1826, as among the drivers of a relentless differentiation among modern cultural fields: the Scientific, the Literary, the Religious, the Artistic, the Educational, and the Political fields, all parts of a national culture now at work under what Carlyle called, with an eye to their public emphasis on administrative matters, the "same management."[9] Each field now had its own Humphry Davy wielding some newly authoritative instrument and standing in public at some newly authoritative Institution or Society, spinning out periodicals, staging debates, staging spectacles for London audiences, or burrowing into their scientific specialization. Carlyle's analytic, which I've called elsewhere an "undialectical but potent rhetoric" of cultural criticism, might count here instead as a kind of *faux*-Bourdieu picture of the relentless reproduction, a mechanical picture in its own right, of the emerging modern fields.[10] Modern institutions and their associated print media, now regarded as "mechanisms," could no longer be regarded as *actions*, let alone projects. Carlyle saw only endless cycles of reproduction in such fields and he waited – with an ironically scientific confidence in the probabilities – for a renewed dawn of human agency in a vaguely sensed "dynamic" futurity.

It is still difficult to tell what kinds of transatlantic movement the English institutional reshaping of "arts and sciences" could take in North America, where thus far transatlantic studies have taken the main form of cultural westering to occur in print. No London learning institutions were transplanted into the New World as directly as English books and journals (in the absence of international copyright law) could be reproduced verbatim under a new Philadelphia or New York colophon. While the former colonies may have been instantly "transformed into a provincial center of Anglophone print culture," as Richard Sher puts it,[11] we need to track a far more circuitous process of transatlantic remediation of the sciences and arts through institutional forms – one that has left unclear to this day what European, what English, and what indigenously North American inventions combined to produce the Anglo-American way of framing the arts and sciences as a structured learning order in universities, institutes, and other modes.

But the rise in the late 1820s of American lyceums in New England, and then more explosively across the North American continent, seems to me an unmistakable form of impact by English arts-and-sciences Institutions even if it has been difficult for American cultural historians to trace. The lyceums can also show how difficult it could be for Americans to explain their debt to Britain in matters of the sciences and the arts. We think of the "transatlantic" as a directional movement, yet Americans could assert the transatlantic relation of arts and sciences as a kind of institutional loop. London's Royal Institution was an American brainchild, argued George Ellis in 1877, tracing Count Rumford's Massachusetts birth and Harvard education to the birth of public arts-and-sciences Institutions in London, then demonstrating the reversal of this trajectory to the United States. "The oldest organized institution in this country offering lectures to the community at large for the purposes of a lyceum," Ellis argued, "is that which is still in active operation in the town of Waltham, Massachusetts, and which bears the name of the 'Rumford Institute.'"[12] More straightforwardly, Josiah Holbrook claimed to invent the lyceums himself in 1826, a vision of self-invention questioned by modern American historians who have been unable to tell a more fully convincing story to replace it.[13] According to their major modern historian, Carl Bode, "We cannot find any exact chain of events to connect the American lyceums with their British predecessors."[14] But it will matter that the New England lyceums – outfitted with a lecture hall, library, and laboratory like their London forebears – would mushroom into a far-flung lecturing and (sometimes) research world involving a wide array of intellectuals, activists, controversies, and historical turning points in nineteenth-century America. This phenomenon is well beyond the scope of the present book to investigate, but two points should be noted here. Even more than print distribution, some historians argue, "the lecture system can be said to have created and embodied an American public . . . it transcended the divisions that fragmented the society and culture."[15] Enrolled in this system were all the figures we have met in Romantic-age England: "young and old, male and female, Methodist and freethinker . . . men of letters, science and literature; reformers and conservatives, Unitarians and evangelicals; lawyers, physicians, professors, poets, philosophers, editors and statesmen." Lyceum lectures on the Atlantic seaboard taught chemistry, meteorology, geology, and on the cultural side, the topics of "Defects of Female Education" and, indeed, of Romanticism itself in popular lectures on "The Character of Byron."[16] In the most recent study of the lyceums, Angela Ray notes briefly "the particularities of British American Protestantism" at work in the practices and rules of New England lyceums. There were the same rules imposed on lecturers – they had to refrain from political or religious controversy at the cost of their jobs, above all to refrain, until the 1850s, from even the most indirect allusion to American slavery.[17]

A more explicit case of transatlantic modeling of arts-and-sciences Institutions from England would appear in 1847, when the legal will of James Smithson was read into national knowledge policy. The new Smithsonian Institution was to be based on the whole array of English specialist societies and broader arts-and-sciences Institutions. A trained and independently wealthy chemist in his own right, Smithson had traveled to London in 1784 and, from 1800 to 1814, he paid close attention to the Royal and Surrey Institutions, as well as the specialist knowledge societies, as potential models for an American institutional knowledge-making.[18] As Joseph Henry construed Smithson's will in 1847, all of Britain's learning and research organizations of the early nineteenth century became a relevant framework for shaping an American national center for original research, public diffusion of knowledge, and, not least, "a center of bibliographical knowledge."[19] What Henry reconstructed in the following account of England's post-1800 arts-and-sciences Institution world is strongly inflected by the American situation in which the relation of research to instruction was still trying to be thought out:

> That the terms *increase* and *diffusion* of knowledge are logically distinct, and should be literally interpreted with reference to the will, must be evident when we reflect that they are used in a definite sense, and not as mere synonyms, by all who are engaged in the pursuits to which Smithson devoted his life. In England there are two classes of institutions, founded on the two ideas conveyed by these terms. The Royal Society, the Astronomical, the Geological, the Statistical, the Antiquarian Societies, all have for their object the increase of knowledge; while the London Institution, the Mechanics' Institution, the Surrey Institution, the Society for the Diffusion of Religious Knowledge, the Society for the Diffusion of Useful Knowledge, are all intended to diffuse and disseminate knowledge among men. In our own country, also, the same distinction is observed in the use of the terms by men of science. Our colleges, academies, and common schools, are recognized as institutions partially intended for the diffusion of knowledge, while the express object of some of our scientific societies is the promotion of the discovery of new truths.[20]

As the foregoing chapters have shown, Henry's categorization is curious and certainly inaccurate. It tends to conflate London's arts-and-sciences Institutions of 1800–23, with their configuration of knowledge production and public outreach, with the radically different division of research and instruction that would succeed them: the BAAS world of advanced disciplinary research through specialist societies on the one hand, contrasted with utilitarian societies for disseminating information, or mechanics' institutes teaching technological education on the other. Meanwhile, even if the Smithsonian would most lastingly devolve into a system of museums, the question of a national university capable of standing next to Europe's would emerge from this British legacy as well, and how this matter was resolved would go down in American educational history as "a most decisive moment in the history of humanistic organization – and perhaps of academic organization more generally – in the United States."[21] But that is the topic for another and very different book than the present one.

I have used the term *transfigure* in this book to represent a whole range of actions, ideas, and words used pervasively in the Romantic age in order to reshape the modern discourse of "arts and sciences" as well as the relation of practices and knowledges this expression encompassed. What gave this transfiguring actual material and social *form* in the British early nineteenth century was the coinciding rise of a new kind of institution-building informed by an exceptional self-consciousness in the period concerning what "institutions" are and what powers they can enact. This is why I have tried to avoid reducing this remarkable convergence of "institution" on the one hand, and "arts and sciences" on the other to a simpler formula, something on the order of a claim that "this is how the arts and sciences were institutionalized in the Romantic age." Putting it that way would tend to imply some definitive, long-term trajectory of stable transmission to the future, or might suggest that the Romantic period, in a way Carlyle's analytic seems almost to predict, generated the modern disciplinary system in the university in the late nineteenth century that we still study or teach within today. To resist that way of flattening the complexity and in many ways the uniqueness of what took place in the early nineteenth century, I have been accentuating the contingent, conjunctural, and unpredictable character of these Romantic-age inventions.

That said, I am also claiming that something fundamental changed about the "arts and sciences" in the Romantic age. Distinct and differentiating cultural fields of artistic, literary, scientific, and other modes of cultural production *did* organize themselves out of the far-less defined and negotiated world known to the eighteenth-century discourse of "arts and sciences." Some of these changes cannot surprise us, but I have hoped to render them here in less abstract and more tangibly complex terms than those in which they are often understood. Physical sciences more or less decisively displaced both the older "natural philosophy" and the meaning of "science" as any form of rigorous scholarship. By the end of this period, the scientific field had organized itself into the capacity to make knowledge claims that literary and art producers were now far less able to assert with credibility than Wordsworth could have hoped thirty years before; "science" appeared far more the legitimate claimant to "knowledge" than did either the fine arts, including poetry, or the now well-demarcated and confined territory of the "mechanical" or "practical" arts. Conversely, the fine-arts world had, through a phalanx of new art institutions, publications, and the crystallizing episode of the Elgin Marbles controversy, more firmly and publicly crystallized its answer to the question "what is art?" – and to this extent it became a more distinctively separate field with respect to the sciences and commercial arts by the end of the Romantic age. We can even say that, on the whole, the "fine arts" moved fairly decisively *into* the position formerly occupied in that expression by a confusing mix of artisanal, mechanical, and broadly "useful" arts still being referred to as half of the "arts and sciences." That essential displacement seems to have taken up to another half-century to register across British (and soon American) culture. Both of these generalizations – and I hope they will be tested and revised in future scholarship on the wider question of how the "arts and sciences" became the framework for all organized knowledge production by the end of the nineteenth century – speak in part to what the Romantic-age "arts and sciences" Institutions helped produce themselves, but they also testify to what new conditions of knowledge production and cultural field-formation were created, from the mid 1790s to the mid 1820s, that departed so far from those known to the early modern Republic of Letters or Commonwealth of Learning.

As to literature, I have accentuated the action and self-reflection of particular genres (poetry, novel, and criticism) rather than trying to resolve the still-shifting definition of what "literature" was becoming in this period as what Raymond Williams first called a more "specialized" category of cultural production. But I have also been trying to underscore the essentially "literary" quality of a cultural discourse that constantly, and more urgently in the Romantic age, figured and refigured the specific shapes of that relationship between practices and knowledges called "arts and sciences." To ask "what counted as knowledge?" at a particular historical moment is always also to ask about practices of writing, creating, narrating, lecturing, criticizing, and reflecting – any of which may be at one historical conjuncture or another either excluded or diminished by prevailing standards of what counts as "knowing." Yet *ways* of knowing – and how we judge their organization and means of public access – must always be at issue at times when, as in the Romantic age and indeed in our own, the historical conjuncture seems to put new intellectual and social choices about the "arts and sciences" into the realm of both the possible and the necessary.

# Notes

### Introduction

1 Since I am concerned with both specific, named "Institutions," and also wider institutional discourses and processes in the Romantic period, I shall maintain the capital "I" when referring to any of the formal organizations going by such titles, and the lower-case when I refer to broader institutional questions of the age.
2 On "conservative revolution" in popular discourse, see Kevin Gilmartin, *Writing Against Revolution* (Cambridge University Press, 2006); considered as a top-down "patrician renaissance," see Linda Colley, *Britons* (New Haven: Yale University Press, 1993).
3 Robert Southey, *Letters from England*, 3 vols. (London: Longman, 1808), III: 284.
4 See Adriana Craciun and Luisa Calé, "Introduction" to "The Disorder of Things," a special issue of *Eighteenth Century Studies* 45 (2011): 1–13. I thank Adriana and Luisa for sending me a draft of this text before publication.
5 On the profusion of natural history's objects and methods that made it well-nigh impossible to institutionalize as a discipline, see Noah Heringman, "Natural History in the Romantic Period," in *A Concise Companion to the Romantic Age*, ed. Jon Klancher (New York: Wiley-Blackwell, 2009), pp. 141–67.
6 To speak of "fields" in this period, we should note Ian Duncan's caution about too readily adopting social analytics developed to explain very different historical conditions. "What Bourdieu calls the 'charismatic rupture between art and money' has not yet opened in Edinburgh in the early 1820s," he argues in *Scott's Shadow*; "on the contrary, a newly totalizing convergence of art and money generates charisma" (Ian Duncan, *Scott's Shadow: The Novel in Romantic Edinburgh* [Princeton University Press, 2007], p. xiii). Yet it can be argued that the concept of cultural fields does not require them to take the specific form of art-against-commerce that defines the polarity of what Bourdieu most fully studied in France's late-nineteenth-century (and modernist) literary or art fields. Fields emerge around contests for authority and distinction on any number of grounds, yet what they have most in common are struggles concerted around a particular set of stakes – the

*meaning* of a given field, and the power to define what it stands for. This is the collective interest its participants will have in contesting that meaning, such as the struggle for the right to decide what is scientifically legitimate, or in another domain, "the monopoly of the power to say with authority who are authorized to call themselves writers." See Pierre Bourdieu, *The Field of Cultural Production* (New York: Columbia University Press, 1993), p. 42.

7 Simon Schaffer, "Indiscipline and Interdisciplines: Some Exotic Genealogies of Modern Knowledge" (2010). www.fif.tu-darmstadt.de/media/fif_forum_interdisziplinaere_forschung/sonstigetexte/externe/simonschaffner.pdf, p. 4. (Accessed February 22, 2012.)

8 See Sean Franzel, *Fictions of Dialogue: The Media, Pedagogy, and Politics of the Romantic Lecture* (Evanston, IL: Northwestern University Press, 2013). Franzel accentuates the "intermedial" character of Romantic lecturing in Germany, in relation to print, in a context where German universities and the state both serve to stabilize the conditions of producing and receiving such public scholarship. Given how important these material and institutional conditions become to articulating the range and meaning of "arts and sciences" in each national culture, it is correspondingly difficult to generalize very substantively about that discourse across these national frameworks. For further insight into the English context, I thank Sarah Zimmerman for letting me see her draft introduction to her book project *Romanticism in the Lecturing Room*.

9 Such organizers were wealthy, yet their combination of professional, financial, political, colonial, and landholding interests cannot be easily encompassed by a contrast between simply "aristocratic" and "middle class" social categories. Only in 1823 did manufacturing and lesser-shopkeeper interests invest in the Institutional model at Manchester and then other factory cities. On this stratum of "gentlemanly capitalism," in preference to a term like "upper middle class," see Boyd Hilton, *A Mad, Bad, & Dangerous People? England 1783–1846* (Oxford: Clarendon Press, 2006), pp. 163–67.

10 Thomas Bernard, "Introductory," *Director* 1 (January 24, 1807): 5, 7.

11 Bernard, "On the Art of Good Living," *Director* 1 (1807): 281.

12 See Duncan, *Scott's Shadow* and Paul Keen, *The Crisis of Literature in the 1790s* (Cambridge University Press, 1999).

13 Lord Byron, "Parenthetical Address by Dr. Plagiary," in *The Works of Lord Byron*, ed. Thomas Moore (London: John Murray, 1836), XVII: 243.

14 Hazlitt, "Mr. Coleridge," *The Spirit of the Age* (1825), in *The Selected Writings of William Hazlitt*, ed. Duncan Wu (London: Pickering & Chatto, 1998), VII: 98.

15 [Leigh Hunt], "The REFORMERS; or Wrongs of Intellect – A Fragment of a Political Dialogue," *Reflector* 1 (1811): 28.

16 Samuel Taylor Coleridge, *On the Constitution of Church and State*, ed. John Colmer, vol. X of *The Collected Works of Samuel Taylor Coleridge*, ed. Kathleen Coburn (Princeton University Press, 1976), p. 46.

17 These Romantic critiques or defenses of British institutions are widely known, but it is worth citing here one of the least commented on, but one that explicates the phrase so often used in other writings on political and cultural

institutions of the period, especially in relation to the "arts and sciences": William Hazlitt's "On Corporate Bodies" (1823), in *Selected Writings of William Hazlitt*, ed. Wu, VI: 236–43.

18 Southey, Letter to John Rickman (December 23, 1806), in *The Life and Correspondence of Robert Southey* (London: Longman, 1850), III: 57.

19 Early modern scholars have recently argued that the Renaissance was also "a period of institution-building," and "witnessed a massive growth of institutions designed to shape – and improve – behavior of students, artisans, and many others" (Anne Goldgar and Robert I. Frost, "Introduction," in *Institutional Culture in Early Modern Society*, ed. Goldgar and Frost [Leiden: Brill, 2004], p. xi, and Anthony Grafton, "Afterwords," also in *Institutional Culture*, p. 349). But Grafton also asks a pertinent question: "Were early-modern individuals *aware* of the range of organizations and cultural activities reconstructed here? Where, if anywhere, did they *describe* them?" ("Afterwords," p. 348, my emphasis). One means of depicting these organizations and activities early moderns still lacked was what I am calling here a modern discourse *on* institutions, an analytical language with an increasingly reflexive awareness of their development as understood by historians who inhabited the outcome of that history in an institutional order in the present.

20 The most influential referent for this change from early modern usage of *institution* as "nouns of action and process" to a more decisively modern usage as "nouns of structure" which Raymond Williams located at about the mid eighteenth century, appears in *Keywords* (New York: Oxford University Press, 1983), p. 168. I raise further questions about Williams's historical marker of such change in Chapter 1.

21 For this particular claim, see Jonathan Turner, *Human Institutions: A Theory of Societal Evolution* (Lanham, MD: Rowman & Littlefield, 2003), p. 1.

22 See Peter de Bolla's analysis of Smith's division of labor as a "load-bearing concept" in "Mediation and the Division of Labor," in *This Is Enlightenment*, ed. Clifford Siskin and William Warner (University of Chicago Press, 2010), pp. 87–102.

23 Émile Durkheim, *The Rules of Sociological Method*, ed. Steven Lukes, trans. W. D. Halls (New York: Free Press, 1982), p. 45.

24 For a representative argument, see Talcott Parsons, *Talcott Parsons on Institutions and Social Evolution: Selected Writings*, ed. Leon H. Mayhew (University of Chicago Press, 1982), pp. 117–28; for a useful commentary, see Charles H. Powers, *Making Sense of Social Theory* (Lanham, MD: Rowman & Littlefield, 2010), pp. 151–74.

25 As instances I would cite Thomas Kuhn's institution-based reasoning in *The Structure of Scientific Revolutions* (University of Chicago Press, 1962); Lévi-Strauss's *Structural Anthropology* (London: Penguin, 1958); Raymond Williams's *The Long Revolution* (London: Chatto & Windus, 1961); Habermas's *Structural Transformation of the Public Sphere* (Cambridge, MA: MIT Press, 1962); Foucault's *Birth of the Clinic* (1963; London: Tavistock, 1973) and later works; Bourdieu's thinking on the logic of practice, the work of the habitus, or the

intellectual "fields of cultural production"; and Althusser's reshaping of Marxist categories in the "Ideological State Apparatuses" essay. One of the most striking of these occurs in Jean-Paul Sartre's first volume of *Critique of Dialectical Reason* (1960), a book in which the disappointment or "failure" of modernity's great political revolutions is interpreted as the intervention of a powerfully hypostatized historical figure – Institution, embodied in the Stalin of 1928 or the Robespierre of 1793 – and the power of this "third" actor in the historical process to disrupt and to dominate the first two actors (basically individual and group) to pursue to completion what Sartre philosophically calls their world-historical "project." See Sartre, "The Institution," in *Critique of Dialectical Reason*, vol. 1: *Theory of Practical Ensembles*, trans. Alan Sheridan-Smith (London: Verso, 1976), pp. 576–663.

26 As Jeffrey Williams writes in an astute commentary on recent academic discourse, such language often grasps *institution* as signifying "the structures of regulation and management of contemporary mass society and culture, running in the opposite direction of words like freedom, individuality, or independence." Jeffrey J. Williams, *The Institution of Literature* (Albany: SUNY Press, 2006), p. 2.

27 David Spadafora, *The Idea of Progress in Eighteenth-Century Britain* (New Haven: Yale University Press, 1990), especially Chapter 2, "Ancients and Moderns, Arts and Sciences" (pp. 21–84). Michael McKeon builds on this argument to offer compelling accounts of literary mimesis of the sciences in his "Mediation as Primal Word: The Arts, the Sciences, and the Origins of the Aesthetic," in *This Is Enlightenment*, ed. Siskin and Warner, p. 386.

28 Hazlitt, "Why the Arts are not Progressive? – A Fragment" (1814), in *Selected Writings of William Hazlitt*, ed. Wu, II: 158–62.

29 Benjamin Martin, "Introduction," *The General Magazine of Arts and Sciences, Philosophical, Philological, Mathematical, and Mechanical* 1 (1755): iii.

30 Ephraim Chambers [1729], quoted in Richard Yeo, *Encyclopedic Visions: Scientific Dictionaries and Enlightenment Culture* (Cambridge University Press, 2001), p. 151.

31 As Yeo helps us understand, Chambers promised to define "The THINGS signify'd thereby, In the several ARTS, both LIBERAL and MECHANICAL, And the several SCIENCES, HUMAN and DIVINE," yet the most troubling ambivalences always surfaced in the matter of defining "arts." T. H. Croker's *The Complete Dictionary of Arts and Sciences* (London, 1764), responding to the ongoing blur of arts, vowed to explain "The whole circle of HUMAN LEARNING" in which especially "the DIFFICULTIES attending the Acquisition of EVERY ART, Whether Liberal or Mechanical, are Removed" (quoted in Yeo, *Encyclopedic Visions*, p. 62).

32 Paul Oskar Kristeller, "The Modern System of the Arts" (1951), in *Renaissance Thought and the Arts: Collected Essays* (Princeton University Press, 1990), pp. 163–227. That a notional "system of the [fine] arts" existed after 1750 did not mean it entered easily the realm of "arts and sciences" in the

encyclopedias: even the third edition of the *Encyclopaedia Britannica* (1797) does not unify its lengthy articles on painting, sculpture, poetry, or music by a corresponding entry on "fine arts."

33 Michel de Certeau, "The Arts of Theory," in *The Practice of Everyday Life* (Berkeley: University of California Press, 1984), pp. 65–67. In earlier work, Henri Lefebvre had taken the analytic of "everyday life" in a different direction, now published as *Critique of Everyday Life*, trans. Gregory Elliott and John Moore, 3 vols. (New York: Verso, 2008).

34 See Chapter 5 on the emerging scientific field in the early nineteenth century for a more extended discussion of this question. Niklas Luhmann, adopting a theorem from theoretical biology for social theory, calls this self-structuring process "autopoiesis" in the elaboration of social "systems." Among many works, see for a brief, clarifying explication Luhmann's *Essays on Self-Reference* (New York: Columbia University Press, 1990), pp. 1–20.

35 On the "mechanical" v. "liberal" distinction in eighteenth-century fine arts, see especially John Barrell, *The Birth of Pandora and the Division of Knowledge* (Basingstoke: Macmillan, 1992), pp. 47–49; Morris Eaves, *The Counter-Arts Conspiracy: Art and Industry in the Age of Blake* (Ithaca, NY: Cornell University Press, 1992), p. 173.

36 Speaking of the unformed material of the universe, Schelling in the 1810 Stuttgart Seminars speaks to God's transfiguring the unformed materiality of the universe as "to progressively elevate this excluded and dark [dimension] to clarity, and to transfigure (*hinaufzubilden*) it in the direction of his own consciousness." (Thus this term is quite distinct from the more familiar German expression for transfiguration, *Verklärung*, an illumination of the ground as sign of Christ's "transfiguration" into divinity.) See Friedrich Schelling, *Idealism and the Endgame of Theory*, trans. Thomas Pfau (Albany: State University of New York Press, 1994), p. 207.

37 Friedrich Schelling, *On University Studies*, trans. E. S. Morgan (Athens, OH: Ohio University Press, 1966), p. 132; see also Simon Schaffer: "Genius began to be understood not as a peculiar capacity possessed by a creative artist [or scientist], but as the power which possessed him." (Simon Schaffer, "Genius in Romantic Natural Philosophy," in *Romanticism and the Sciences*, ed. Andrew Cunningham and Nicholas Jardine [Cambridge University Press, 1990], p. 83.)

38 For searching discussions of what remains unsatisfactory about the solution of "relative autonomy," see Fredric Jameson, *Valences of the Dialectic* (New York: Verso, 2009), pp. 315–66; and Pierre Bourdieu, "The Force of Law: Towards a Sociology of the Juridical Field," trans. Richard Terdiman, *Hastings Law Journal* 38 (1987): 805–53.

39 John Guillory, "Literary Critics as Intellectuals: Class Analysis and the Crisis of the Humanities," in *Rethinking Class: Literary Studies and Social Formation*, ed. Wai Chee Dimock and Michael Gilmore (New York: Columbia University Press, 1994), p. 127.

40 See James Chandler, 'Wordsworth's Great Ode: Romanticism and the Progress of Poetry," in *The Cambridge Companion to British Romantic Poetry*, ed. James Chandler and Maureen N. McLane (Cambridge University Press, 2008), pp. 136–54.
41 Saree Makdisi, *William Blake and the Impossible History of the 1790s* (University of Chicago Press, 2003), pp. 78–155.
42 Raymond Williams, "Literature," in *Marxism and Literature* (New York: Oxford University Press, 1977), pp. 45–54.

## Chapter 1 From the age of projects to the age of institutions

1 John Spencer Hill, *A Coleridge Companion* (London: Macmillan, 1983), p. 47.
2 Carl Woodring, *Politics in the Poetry of Coleridge* (Madison: University of Wisconsin Press, 1961), pp. 192–93; William Keach, ed., *Samuel Taylor Coleridge: The Complete Poems* (Harmondsworth: Penguin, 1997), p. 522 at lines 53–60.
3 Martin Gierl's fruitful comparison of Leibniz and Swift – or the Berlin Academy that Leibniz launched and the Lagado Academy that Swift lampooned – runs along analogous lines to those I am pursuing here between Leibniz and Defoe: "Let me tell how Lagado and Berlin invented the concept of the computer and furthered the concept of the modern national state, that universal administrative organizer of social affairs." In the present book, such lines will lead alternatively to the interlinked sphere of conservative "welfare reform" in the 1790s and the emergence of "arts and sciences" administration in the early 1800s. See Martin Gierl, "Science, Projects, Computers and the State: Swift's Lagadian and Leibniz's Prussian Academy," in *The Age of Projects*, ed. Maximillian E. Novak (University of Toronto Press, 2008), p. 299.
4 Daniel Defoe, *An Essay upon Projects* (London: Thomas Cockerill, 1697), p. 12.
5 Defoe, *Essay upon Projects*, p. 29.
6 Maximillian E. Novak, "Introduction," in *Age of Projects*, p. 7.
7 Defoe, *Essay upon Projects*, p. 8.
8 See Mary Poovey, *A History of the Modern Fact* (University of Chicago Press, 1998), pp. 158–66.
9 Defoe, *Essay upon Projects*, p. 11.
10 Joanne Myers, "Defoe and the Project of 'Neighbours' Fare,'" *Restoration: Studies in English Literary Culture, 1660–1700* 35.2 (2011): 2.
11 Myers, "Defoe and the Project of 'Neighbours' Fare'": 8.
12 Defoe, *Essay upon Projects*, pp. 8, 13.
13 Gierl, "Science, Projects, Computers and the State," p. 298.
14 Defoe, *Essay upon Projects*, p. 252.
15 Defoe, *Essay upon Projects*, p. 237.
16 Novak, "Introduction," in *Age of Projects*, p. 7.
17 Gottfried Leibniz, "Precepts for Advancing the Sciences and Arts," in *Leibniz: Selections*, ed. Philip Wiener (New York: Scribners, 1951), pp. 29–46 at p. 29.

18 In this paragraph and the next, I am indebted to the suggestive commentary of Terry Cochran, *The Twilight of the Literary: Figures of Thought in the Age of Print* (Cambridge, MA: Harvard University Press, 2001), pp. 5–30.
19 Leibniz, "Precepts for Advancing the Sciences and Arts," in *Leibniz: Selections*, pp. 39–40.
20 Leibniz, "Precepts," pp. 43–44.
21 Leibniz, "Precepts," pp. 43–45.
22 Leibniz, "Discourse Touching the Method of Certitude, and the Art of Discovery in Order to End Disputes to Make Progress Quickly," in *Leibniz: Selections*, pp. 46–60 at p. 47.
23 Leibniz, "Discourse," p. 48.
24 Cochran, *Twilight of the Literary*, p. 7.
25 Quoted in Cochran, *Twilight of the Literary*, p. 8.
26 I refer to Eisenstein's *The Printing Revolution in Early Modern Europe* (Cambridge University Press, 1983) as well as Adrian Johns's trenchant critique of this argument in *The Nature of the Book: Knowledge in the Making, 1500–1900* (University of Chicago Press, 1998), pp. 10–19. I shall comment further on Johns's side of this argument in Chapter 3, "Wild Bibliography: The Rise and Fall of Book History in the Nineteenth Century," below.
27 Leibniz, "Privilege," quoted in Cochran, *Twilight of the Literary*, p. 8.
28 Cochran, *Twilight of the Literary*, p. 9.
29 Leibniz, "Semestria Literaria," quoted in Cochran, *Twilight of the Literary*, p. 10.
30 Adam Ferguson, *An Essay on the History of Civil Society* (1767), 7th edn. (London: Cadell and Davies, 1814), pp. 204–5.
31 Jeremy Bentham, "To Dr. Smith, On Projects in Arts, etc." (1787), in *The Works of Jeremy Bentham*, ed. John Bowring (Edinburgh: William Tait, 1839), IX: 26, 22.
32 Raymond Williams, "Institution," in *Keywords* (New York: Oxford University Press, 1983), p. 168.
33 "The act of institution is thus an act of communication, but of a particular kind: it *signifies* to someone what his identity is, but in a way that both expresses it to him and imposes it on him by expressing it in front of everyone ... and thus informing him in an authoritative manner of what he is and what he must be." Any such action, "through education, leads to durable dispositions, habits and usages." See Pierre Bourdieu, "The Rites of Institution," in *Language and Symbolic Power*, trans. Gino Raymond and Matthew Adamson (Cambridge, MA: Harvard University Press, 1991), pp. 121–23.
34 Karl Marx, *The Grundrisse*, trans. Martin Nikolaus (New York: Vintage, 1975), pp. 85–93, 105–6. The concept of "simple abstraction" has been persuasively extended by Michael McKeon to explain the emergence of the novel as a "simple abstraction" encompassing innumerable narrative instances before the mid eighteenth century, in *The Origins of the English Novel, 1600–1740* (Baltimore: Johns Hopkins University Press, 1987), pp. 15–19.
35 Bergin and Fisch, "Introduction," in *The New Science of Giambattista Vico*, trans. Thomas Goddard Bergin and Max Harold Fisch (Ithaca, NY: Cornell University Press, 1968), pp. lxiii–lxv.

36 Bergin and Fisch, "Introduction," p. xliv.
37 See James Chandler, *England in 1819* (University of Chicago Press, 1998), pp. 128–30.
38 John Millar, *The Origin of the Distinction of Ranks* (1771), 4th edn. (Edinburgh: Blackwood, 1806), p. 318.
39 Millar, *Origin*, p. 6. Millar's introduction also refutes the determinist climate theory of national origins, probably in response to Montesquieu. But this will prove easier to show than to rethink the problem of institutional and national founding. For extended discussion, see Christopher J. Berry, *The Social Theory of the Scottish Enlightenment* (Edinburgh University Press, 1997), pp. 82–88.
40 Millar, *Origin*, p. 7.
41 Ferguson, *Essay on the History of Civil Society*, p. 205.
42 Millar, *Origin*, pp. 6–7.
43 Francis Jeffrey, "Millar's *View of the English Government*," *Edinburgh Review* 3 (1803): 157.
44 I draw here on McClellan's detailed histories of learned academies and societies in *Science Reorganized: Scientific Societies in the Eighteenth Century* (New York: Columbia University Press, 1985), esp. pp. 1–40; and his update, "Scientific Institutions and the Organization of Science," in *The Cambridge History of Science*, ed. Roy Porter (Cambridge University Press, 2003), IV: 87–106. I have also profited from Martha Ornstein's older but still useful *The Role of Scientific Societies in the Seventeenth Century* (University of Chicago Press, 1938).
45 McClellan, "Scientific Institutions," pp. 92–94.
46 *Prospectus of the Royal Institution of Great Britain* (London: Royal Institution, 1800), p. 5.
47 See, for further details, the *Scholarly Societies Project*. www.lib.uwaterloo.ca/society/history/1714asib.html.
48 McClellan, *Science Reorganized*, pp. 101–2.
49 Richard Sher, "Commerce, Religion, and the Enlightenment in Eighteenth-Century Glasgow," in *Glasgow: Beginnings to 1830*, ed. T. M. Devine and Gordon Jackson (Manchester University Press, 1995), I: 350.
50 For the importance of its opening to women as lecture-goers, see Arianne Chernock's brief account in *Men and the Making of Feminism in Britain* (Stanford University Press, 2010), pp. 49–51.
51 Sher, "Commerce, Religion, and the Enlightenment," p. 350.
52 On this point, see R. J. Morris, "Clubs, Societies, and Associations," in *The Cambridge Social History of Britain, 1750–1950*, ed. F. M. L. Thompson (Cambridge University Press, 1990), III: 395–444.

### Chapter 2 The administrator as cultural producer: restructuring the arts and sciences

1 For the most polemical of Romantic arguments indicting the administrator, see William Hazlitt, "On Corporate Bodies," in *Selected Writings of William Hazlitt*, ed. Duncan Wu (London: Pickering & Chatto, 1998), VI: 236–43.

2 Richard Baxter, *Catholick Theologie: Plain, Pure, Peaceable* (London: Nevill Simmons, 1677), p. 177.
3 Bernard was credited with founding twenty-three new institutions, among them the Cancer Institution, School for the Indigent Blind, the African Institution, London Fever Hospital, Fish Association, and the Association for the Relief of the Manufacturing Poor. See Jonathan Fowler, "The Adventures of an 'Itinerant Institutor': The Life and Philanthropy of Thomas Bernard," Ph.D. dissertation (Department of History, University of Tennessee, 2003). Fowler usefully stresses Bernard's multifarious interest in founding societies and institutions, but for unclear reasons largely bypasses Bernard's fundamental role in the Royal Institution's formative period; the only previous biography of Bernard, published shortly after his death, is James Baker, *Life of Thomas Bernard, Baronet* (London: John Murray, 1819).
4 Isaac D'Israeli observed how coffee-house socializing seemed by 1817 "a custom which has declined within our recollection, since institutions of a higher character, and society itself, has improved so much of late." D'Israeli, "Introduction of Tea, Coffee, and Chocolate," in *Curiosities of Literature* (London: John Murray, 1817), III: 378.
5 On the new lecture-hall sociability in London, see Gillian Russell, "Spouters or Washerwomen? The Sociability of Romantic Lecturing," in *Romantic Sociability: Social Networks and Literary Culture in Britain, 1770–1840* (Cambridge University Press, 2002), pp. 123–44.
6 The telling comment on the personal presence of star intellectuals among London audiences, noted many times in the period, was made by James Jennings in *A Lecture on the History and Utility of Literary Institutions* (1823), quoted in Geoffrey Carnall, "The Surrey Institution and Its Successor," *Adult Education* 26 (1953): 199.
7 [Peter George Patmore], *Letters on England by Victoire, Count de Saligny* (London: Henry Colburn, 1823), I: 232.
8 [Patmore], *Letters on England*, I: 228.
9 George Jacob Holyoake, *Self Help a Hundred Years Ago*, 3rd edn. (London: Swan Sonnenschein, 1891), p. 37. Holyoake added, "Thirty years later Robert Owen, who ... had doubtless read [Bernard's] papers, began to write on the 'Science of Society'. Seventy and more years elapsed before Lord Brougham, who knew all about Mr. Bernard's views, became the President of the 'Social Science Association.'"
10 Fowler, "'Itinerant Institutor,'" pp. 67–68.
11 Robert Southey, "The Poor," *Quarterly Review* 15 (1816): 215. Kevin Gilmartin shows why "it was through such publications [as Bernard's *Reports*] rather than his own experience that Southey's prose accrued the moral reformer's usual stock of improving facts and exemplary cases": see *Writing against Revolution* (Cambridge University Press, 2007), p. 240.
12 Leonard Schwarz and Jeremy Poulton, "Parish Apprenticeship in Eighteenth Century and Early Nineteenth-Century London," research.ncl.ac.uk/pauperlives/ehspapersummary.pdf.

13 [Thomas Bernard], *Reports of the Society for Bettering the Condition of the Poor* (London: W. Bulmer, 1799), 11: 27–28.
14 For this brief account of a complex debate in the 1780s and 1790s, I have drawn upon Joanna Innes, "The State and the Poor: Eighteenth-Century England in European Perspective," in *Rethinking Leviathan: The Eighteenth-Century State in Britain and Germany*, ed. John Brewer and Eckhart Hellmuth (London: Oxford University Press, 1999), pp. 225–80; Donna Andrew, *Philanthropy and Police: London Charity in the Eighteenth Century* (Princeton University Press, 1989); Lynn Hollen Lees, *The Solidarities of Strangers: The English Poor Laws and the People 1770–1948* (Cambridge University Press, 1998); Joanna Innes and Hugh Cunningham, eds., *Charity, Philanthropy and Reform: From the 1690s to 1850* (New York: St. Martin's Press, 1998); Sandra Sherman, *Imagining Poverty* (Columbus: Ohio State University Press, 2001); J. R. Poynter, *Society and Pauperism: English Ideas on Poor Relief, 1795–1834* (London: Routledge and Kegan Paul, 1969).
15 Thomas Bernard, *The Barrington School ... or the New System of Instruction in Facilitating the Religious and Moral Instruction of the Poor* (London: W. Bulmer, 1812), pp. 47–48.
16 Thomas Bernard, "Twelve True Old Golden Rules," *Reports of the Bettering Society* 2 (1800): 282–85.
17 Boyd Hilton, *A Mad, Bad, and Dangerous People? England 1783–1846* (Oxford: Clarendon Press, 2006), p. 183. Note also Michael Warner's insight that evangelicals of this period were not opposed to the "secular" as such, but rather opposed competing religious authorities who sought to restrict knowledge production and/or activist efforts to abolish slavery. See Warner, *The Evangelical Public Sphere in Eighteenth-Century America* (Philadelphia: University of Pennsylvania Press, 2013).
18 Boyd Hilton, *The Age of Atonement: The Influence of Evangelicalism on Social and Economic Thought, 1795–1865* (Oxford: Clarendon Press, 1988), pp. 18–19, 13.
19 Hilton, *A Mad, Bad, and Dangerous People*, p. 167.
20 Bernard, "Preface," in *Of the Education of the Poor* (London: W. Bulmer, 1809), pp. 38–39.
21 Bernard, *Reports of the Bettering Society*, 1: iii–iv.
22 Jeremy Bentham, "To Dr. Smith, On Projects in Arts, etc." (1787), in *Defense of Usury*, in *The Works of Jeremy Bentham*, ed. John Bowring, 9 vols. (Edinburgh: William Tait, 1839), IX: 22–26.
23 See Charles Bahmueller, *The National Charity Company: Jeremy Bentham's Silent Revolution* (Berkeley: University of California Press, 1981), p. 73.
24 Coleridge, "Review of Count Rumford's Essays" (1796), in *The Watchman*, ed. Lewis Patton, vol. 2 of *The Collected Works of Samuel Taylor Coleridge* (Princeton University Press, 1970), p. 175.
25 Charles Lamb, "Count Rumford," in Letter to Rickman, January 14, 1802, *Letters of Charles Lamb*, ed. E. V. Lucas (London: J. M. Dent, 1935), 1: 294.
26 Morris Berman, *Social Change and Scientific Organization: The Royal Institution 1799–1844* (Ithaca, NY: Cornell University Press, 1978), pp. 12–13.

My own account draws partly on Berman, but substantively on the Bence Jones history he rejected. Despite idealizing Benjamin's Rumford role as "founder" and demonizing Thomas Bernard as selling out science to "fashion" – both judgments are unsupportable, though they make for a fascinating melodrama – Bence Jones's history has the considerable strength of its wealth of documentary detail and original sources for these years; his history also convincingly demonstrates Rumford's credibility to contemporaries in the sciences and even suggests why he would have a longer-term effect on certain levels of American research as well. Berman corrects Bence Jones by showing the aristocratic dominance of the Institution's first years, but his account can too often make Humphry Davy appear as a puppet of the Board of Agriculture. Though following Berman's account broadly, Jan Golinski has since persuasively altered this view of Davy by grasping his powers of scientific-field shaping to make chemistry a scientific discipline, in *Science as Public Culture* (Cambridge University Press, 1992).

27 See Sandra Sherman, *Imagining Poverty* (Columbus: Ohio State University Press, 2001), pp. 294–98. Tim Fulford has given a similar picture of Rumford focused on Blake's campaign against the exploitation of children as chimney sweeps; see "Britain's Little Black Boys and the Technologies of Benevolence," in Tim Fulford, Debbie Lee, and Peter J. Kitson, *Literature, Science, and Exploration in the Romantic Era: Bodies of Knowledge* (Cambridge University Press, 2004), pp. 228–70.

28 Sherman, *Imagining Poverty*, p. 298.

29 Benjamin Thompson, Count Rumford, "An Account of an Establishment for the Poor at Munich" (1796), in *Collected Works of Count Rumford*, ed. Sanborn C. Brown (Cambridge, MA: Harvard University Press, 1970), v: 58–59; see also Sherman, *Imagining Poverty*, p. 141.

30 Quoted in Henry Bence Jones, *The Royal Institution: Its Founder and Its First Professors* (London: Longman, 1871), pp. 138–39.

31 Rumford, "Proposals for Forming By Subscription in the Metropolis of the British Empire a Public Institution" (1799), in *Collected Works*, ed. Brown, v: 441–42.

32 The courts settled the copyright case *Beckett* v. *Donaldson* in 1774 with long-lasting results we still struggle to understand today. But Boulton's and Watt's defense of patent rights – even after their patent expired shortly before the launching of the RI in March 1799 – has been less appreciated. See Adrian Johns, *Piracy: The Intellectual Property Wars from Gutenberg to Gates* (University of Chicago Press, 2009), pp. 250–58.

33 Matthew Robinson Boulton to Matthew Boulton, February 28, 1800, cited in Berman, *Social Change and Scientific Organization*, p. 76.

34 Bence Jones, *Royal Institution*, p. 222.

35 Thomas Bernard, Report to the Proprietors of the Royal Institution on May 2, 1803, quoted in Bence Jones, *Royal Institution*, p. 203.

36 "Review of Thomas Young's *Lectures*," *Critical Review*, 3rd series, 12.1 (Sept. 1807): 1–2.

37 Letter to Marcel Pictet, July 5, 1800, quoted in Sanborn Brown, *Benjamin Thompson, Count Rumford* (Cambridge, MA: MIT Press, 1979), p. 230.
38 Banks, letters to Rumford in April and June 1804, quoted in Bence Jones, *Royal Institution*, pp. 261, 263. John Gascoigne points out that William Wilberforce, with the now considerable force of the evangelical Clapham Sect, came to Bernard's defense, claiming Banks and Rumford had "almost ruined" the institution before Bernard saved it. The dispute was partly religious; the Deist Banks openly disdained Bernard's profession of evangelical zeal and Wilberforce's "clerical meddling." See John Gascoigne, *Joseph Banks and the English Enlightenment* (Cambridge University Press, 1994), pp. 222–23; 43–48.
39 Thomas Frognall Dibdin, *Reminiscences of a Literary Life* (London: John Major, 1836), 1: 226. By 1836, memories of Bernard's career as an institutor and administrator of major London cultural institutions had long since faded, if they were known publicly at all. Dibdin's pages, written as his collaborator on the *Director*, give the most vivid personal profile of him I have found anywhere in this period.
40 Ann Bermingham, "Urbanity and the Spectacle of Art," in *Romantic Metropolis*, ed. James Chandler and Kevin Gilmartin (Cambridge University Press, 2005), pp. 160–61.
41 Dibdin, *Reminiscences*, 1: 229–30.
42 Bernard's portrait, painted by William Ward in 1804, hangs in the National Portrait Gallery. www.npg.org.uk/collections/search/portraitLarge/mw125272/Sir-Thomas-Bernard-2nd-Bt.
43 Sophie Elizabeth Higgins, *The Bernards of Abington* (London: Longman, 1846), pp. 142–43.
44 Thomas Young, quoted in Bence Jones, *Royal Institution*, p. 211.
45 Robert Southey, *Letters from England*, 2nd edn. (London: Longman, 1808), III: 285.
46 "On the Rise and Progress of the Royal Institution," *Journal of Science and Art* 3 (1817): xiv.
47 Jan Golinski, "Humphry Davy's Sexual Chemistry," *Configurations* 7 (1999): 15–41.
48 Quoted in Bence Jones, *Royal Institution*, pp. 241–42. Arianne Chernock shows in more detail how the Anderson Institution, in breaking away from the University of Glasgow, strategically changed the audience for scientific lectures by inviting women in significant numbers. See Chernock, *Men and the Making of Modern British Feminism* (Stanford University Press, 2010), pp. 49–51. Only in London, though, did women's lecture-going seem to become a matter of polemical discussion in the media.
49 Francis Horner to John Murray, November 15, 1804, *Memoirs and Correspondence of Francis Horner, M.P.* (London: John Murray, 1843), 1: 275. Sydney Smith, quoted in Bence Jones, *Royal Institution*, p. 264.
50 *The British Critic* n.s. 7 (1817): 163–64. For a skeptical view of claims by the Institutions and modern historians that this scientific domain had really

opened itself to women's acting or writing, see Saba Bahar, "Jane Marcet and the Limits to Public Science," *British Journal for the History of Science* 34 (2001): 29–49.
51 Gillian Russell, *Romantic Sociability*, pp. 123–44.
52 J. N. Hays, "Science in the City: The London Institution 1805–1850," *British Journal for the History of Science* 7 (1974): 146–62.
53 Dibin, *Reminiscences*, 1: 238–39.
54 William Brande, *An Introductory Address Delivered in the Amphitheater of the London Institution* (London: printed by Richard and Arthur Taylor, 1819), p. 34. For local reasons, the London Institution's public lecturing did not begin until 1819 though it had been open to the public for its library and other functions since 1806. For the continued resistance of business interests to science in Victorian Britain, see Thomas Huxley, "Science as Culture," in Thomas Huxley, *Science and Culture, and Other Essays* (London: Macmillan, 1882), pp. 3–5.
55 *A Catalogue of the Library of the London Institution* (London, 1835), p. v; "An Account of the London Institution," *Monthly Magazine* 23 (1807): 309–14.
56 [William Combe], "The Surrey Institution," in *The Microcosm of London*, ed. Rudolph Ackermann (London: Ackermann, 1809), III: 154–60. The present book's cover shows a very different Rowlandson picture of Frederick Accum lecturing on chemistry at the Surrey, far less formal than the Ackermann version and suggesting more of the vibrant energy and startled onlookers often reported by the press.
57 Davy's remark is quoted in Golinski, *Science as Public Culture*, p. 246.
58 See the vivid attack on Methodist "love feasts," for instance, in "Nightingale's Portraiture of Methodism," *Anti-Jacobin Review* 33 (1809): 236–47.
59 It is not entirely clear whether the full Surrey Institution or control of its library is at issue in Adam Clarke's account of the struggle that appears in James Everett, *Adam Clarke Portrayed* (London: Hamilton, Adams, 1844), II: 260–61. But Clarke is vehement about the struggle and suggests it goes to the top of the Institution.
60 Geoffrey Carnall, "The Surrey Institution and Its Successor," *Adult Education* 26 (1953): 198. The more admiring view, which a reading of John Mason Good's volume *The Book of Nature* supports, is taken by Frederick Kurzer, "A History of the Surrey Institution," *Annals of Science* 57 (2000): 131.
61 John Mason Good, *The Book of Nature*, 3 vols. (London: Longman, 1826).
62 John Mason Good, ed. and trans., *The Nature of Things: A Didactic Poem Translated from the Latin of Titus Lucretius Carus, Accompanied with the Original Text, and Illustrated with Notes Philological and Explanatory*, 2 vols. (London: Longman, 1805). His Latin source text was Gilbert Wakefield's edition, *T. Lucretii Cari de Rerum Natura*, 3 vols. (London: Bibliopolis, 1796–97). Both Unitarians, Good and Wakefield formed a collaboration lasting a decade; see, for their versions of Lucretius, Michael Vicario, *Shelley's Intellectual System and Its Epicurean Background* (New York: Routledge, 2007), pp. 120–52.
63 Michael Vicario, *Shelley's Intellectual System*, p. 125.

64 Colin Kidd, *The Forging of Races: Race and Scripture in the Protestant Atlantic World 1600–2000* (Cambridge University Press, 2006), p. 119.
65 For a brief account see David Hopkins, "The English Voices of Lucretius from Lucy Hutchinson to John Mason Good," in *The Cambridge Companion to Lucretius*, ed. Philip Gillespie and Stuart Hardy (Cambridge University Press, 2007), p. 256.
66 Frederick Miller, *St. Pancras, Past and Present* (London: Heywood, 1874), pp. 138–39.
67 See Uttara Natarajan, *Hazlitt and the Reach of Sense* (Oxford: Clarendon Press, 1998). For a brief account of Hazlitt's Russell Institution lectures, which he may have given four times, see Augustine Birrell, *William Hazlitt* (London: Macmillan, 1902), pp. 192–94.
68 See Linda Colley, *Britons* (New Haven: Yale University Press, 1993), pp. 176–77, for the British Institution as a key exhibit in her case for the patrician renaissance.
69 On Angerstein's role and contributions at the BI, see Francis Haskell, *The Ephemeral Museum* (New Haven: Yale University Press, 2000), p. 49; Thomas Smith, *Recollections of the British Institution* (London: Simpkin & Marshall, 1860), pp. 40, 202.
70 See John Brewer, *The Pleasures of the Imagination* (University of Chicago Press, 1997), pp. 252–87.
71 Haskell, *Ephemeral Museum*, p. 48.
72 This chart of two years' lectures at the Royal was drawn up by Bence Jones, *Royal Institution*, p. 276. These lecture programs would change from year to year, as would the proportion of subject-matters, and they varied between Institutions, but overall they generally seem to have followed the model Bernard devised around 1804. The smaller Surrey Institution, by contrast, featured four to six lecture series each year.
73 Of the fifteen lecturers, we might add, only four – Davy and Landseer soon, Opie and Smith posthumously – published versions of their talks, making the print trail of such public performances difficult to follow, even for the Romantic-age Institution that has otherwise left by far the fullest record of its work.
74 Evidence for the content of Dibdin's "English Literature" lectures appears most fully in the recurring "Bibliographiana" section of Thomas Bernard's 1807 journal, the *Director* 1 (1807): 80–87 and *passim*.
75 Morton Paley, *Coleridge and the Fine Arts* (New York: Oxford University Press, 2008), pp. 25–66. His doubts about publicly professing the fine-arts also show in this letter to Davy: "I would require references and illustrations not suitable to a public Lecture Room … I ought not to reckon upon spirits enough to seek about [for] books of Italian Prints, &c." (*The Collected Letters of Samuel Taylor Coleridge*, ed. Earl Leslie Griggs [Oxford: Clarendon Press, 1956], III: 29).
76 The painter Prince Hoare's account of Opie's Royal Institution lectures appears in *Lectures on Painting, Delivered at the Royal Academy by the Late John Opie*, ed. Amelie Opie (London: Longman, 1809), pp. 57–69 at p. 66.

77 See Alan Richardson's account of the controversy in *Literature, Education, and Romanticism: Reading as Social Practice, 1780–1832* (Cambridge University Press, 1994), pp. 91–103.
78 I have learned most about these remarkable commercial ventures in art production from Luisa Calé, *Fuseli's Milton Gallery: "Turning Readers into Spectators"* (Oxford: Clarendon Press, 2006); Morris Eaves, *The Counter-Arts Conspiracy: Art and Industry in the Age of Blake* (Ithaca, NY: Cornell University Press, 1992); and especially Thora Brylowe, "Romantic Arts and Letters: British Print, Paint, Engraving, 1770–1830," Ph.D. dissertation, Carnegie Mellon University, 2008.
79 I am indebted to Brylowe's important insight on this critical moment in her paper "*Sculpsit*: John Landseer's Lectures and Engraving as Mediation," North American Society for Studies in Romanticism Annual Conference, Vancouver, BC (August 2010).
80 John Landseer, *Lectures on the Art of Engraving, Delivered at the Royal Institution* (London: Longman, 1807), p. xxiv. Landseer almost certainly refers to Bernard's own arts-and-sciences journal the *Director*, published from January to July 1807, but the Institutional context can be confusing. No administrator of the Royal Institution (where Landseer was fired) held the title "Director" (they were "managers"); it was the British Institution for Promoting the Fine Arts in the United Kingdom, founded by Bernard in 1805, that appointed "Directors" to administrate the new art institution, and on behalf of which Bernard launched the *Director* in 1807. Thus Landseer could only have meant Bernard in this passage, the cross-over administrator between Institutions.
81 Landseer, *Lectures*, p. xxiii.
82 On Renaissance patronage practices, see especially F. W. Kent and Patricia Simons, eds., *Patronage, Art, and Society in Renaissance Italy* (New York: Oxford University Press, 1987).
83 Theodor Adorno, "Culture and Administration" (1961), in *The Culture Industry*, ed. J. M. Bernstein (New York: Routledge, 1991), p. 108.
84 Landseer, *Lectures*, p. xxxiv. For Bayle's principle, see *The Dictionary Historical and Critical of Mr. Peter Bayle* (1684), trans. Pierre des Maizeaux, 2nd edn. (London: printed for J. J. and P. Knapton, et al., 1735), II: 388–89.
85 "Memoirs of Sydney Smith," *Quarterly Review* 97 (1855): 116–17.
86 Francis Horner, *Memoirs and Correspondence of Sir Francis Horner, M.P.*, ed. Leonard Horner (London: John Murray, 1843), I: 298.
87 The "electrical" remark appears in Cockburn's account of the *Edinburgh*'s sudden impact in 1802 – "It was an entire and instant change of every thing that the public had been accustomed to in that sort of composition." See Henry Cockburn, *The Life of Lord Jeffrey* (Edinburgh: A. & C. Black, 1852), p. 106.
88 [Henry Brougham], "Bakerian Lecture on Light and Colors," *Edinburgh Review* 1 (1803): 450–56.
89 *Edinburgh Review* 11 (1807): 390.

90 Humphry Davy, "A Discourse Introductory to a Course of Lectures on Chemistry" (1802), in *The Collected Works of Humphry Davy*, ed. John Davy, 9 vols. (London: Smith, Elder, 1839), II: 309–26.
91 Golinski, "Humphry Davy's Sexual Chemistry," p. 25.
92 For the best account of this *habitus clivé*, see Pierre Bourdieu, *Sketch for a Self-Analysis*, trans. Richard Nice (University of Chicago Press, 2008); and for the relation of habitus and field more broadly, Bourdieu, *The Logic of Practice*, trans. Richard Nice (Stanford University Press, 1990), pp. 52–65.
93 Golinski, *Science as Public Culture*, p. 187.
94 See Berman, *Social Change and Scientific Organization*, pp. 54–70.
95 Richard Carlile, *An Address to Men of Science* (London: R. Carlile, 1821). See Chapter 5 for an extended discussion of Carlile's critique, which perhaps counts as the first version, however different in its epistemological bearings, of what arose more widely in the late twentieth century as the social critique of the sciences.
96 Golinski, *Science as Public Culture*, pp. 203–18.
97 John C. Adams, "Epideictic and Its Cultured Reception," in *Rhetorics of Display*, ed. Lawrence J. Prelli (Columbia: University of South Carolina Press, 2006), pp. 294–95. I have also drawn on Robert Danisch's excellent account of epideictic's socially galvanizing effects in *Pragmatism, Democracy, and the Necessity of Rhetoric* (Columbia: University of South Carolina Press, 2007), pp. 120–28. More generally, I have benefited from the work on epideictic rhetoric at work in Romantic essayists by Katie Homar in her Ph.D. dissertation "'Prose Declaimers': British Romantic Prose Authors and Rhetoric in the Romantic Era," Department of English, University of Pittsburgh (in progress).
98 Wordsworth, "Preface to *Lyrical Ballads*" (1802), in *The Prose Works of William Wordsworth*, ed. Alexander Grosart (London: Edward Moxon, 1876), II: 91. Catherine E. Ross updates the circumstantial but compelling case for linking Davy's January 1802 lecture to Wordsworth's somewhat agonized language on the poet and the "man of science" in this extended section of the "Preface." See "'Twin Labourers and Heirs of the same Hopes': The Professional Rivalry of Humphry Davy and William Wordsworth," in *Romantic Science*, ed. Noah Heringman (Albany: SUNY Press, 2003), pp. 28–29.
99 Davy, *Collected Works*, II: 319.
100 Davy, *Collected Works*, II: 327.
101 Humphry Davy, "Parallels between Science and Art" (1807), in *Collected Works of Humphry Davy*, ed. John Davy (London: Smith, Elder, 1839), IX: 306, 308.
102 Davy, *Collected Works*, IX: 307.

**Chapter 3 Wild bibliography: the rise and fall of book history in the nineteenth century**

1 Leah Price, "Introduction: Reading Matter," *The History of the Book and the Idea of Literature*, special issue of *PMLA*, ed. Leah Price and Seth Lehrer (January 2006): 9–16.

2 "Bibliographia," *Encyclopaedia Britannica*, 3rd edn. (1791–97); Thomas Hartwell Horne, *An Introduction to the Study of Bibliography*, 2 vols. (London: Cadell, Davies, 1814). On the importance and scope of the phrase "bibliographical codes," see Jerome McGann, *The Textual Condition* (Princeton University Press, 1991), pp. 13–16, 57–61.

3 Thomas Frognall Dibdin, "Preface" to Joseph Ames, *Typographical Antiquities; or the History of Printing in England, Scotland, and Ireland*, 3rd edn. (London: William Miller, 1812), II: 3.

4 Luigi Balsamo, one of the few historians of early modern bibliography, credits Naude with the first subject-centered bibliography when Naude compiled all works on political philosophy and statecraft in a single ordered system. Luigi Balsamo, *Bibliography: History of a Tradition*, trans. William A. Pettas (Berkeley: Bernard Rosenthal, 1990), pp. 92–93. On the "bibliographical" as a broader hermeneutic for the Romantic age, see Andrew Piper, *Dreaming in Books: The Making of the Bibliographical Imagination in the Romantic Age* (University of Chicago Press, 2009).

5 Quoted in Balsamo, *Bibliography*, p. 73.

6 David McKitterick, "Bibliography, Bibliophily, and the Organization of Knowledge," in *The Foundations of Scholarship: Libraries and Collecting 1650–1750*, ed. David Vaisey and David McKitterick (Los Angeles: William Andrews Clark Memorial Library, University of California, 1992), p. 48; Richard Yeo, *Encyclopedic Visions: Scientific Dictionaries and Enlightenment Culture* (Cambridge University Press, 2001).

7 Dibdin, "Bibliographiana," *Director* 3 (January 1807): 1.84.

8 Philip Connell, "Bibliomania: Book Collecting, Cultural Politics, and the Rise of Literary Heritage in Romantic Britain," *Representations* 71 (Summer 2000): 24–47; Ina Ferris, "Bibliographic Romance: Bibliophilia and the Book Object," and Deidre Lynch, "'Wedded to Books': Bibliomania and the Romantic Essayists," both in "Romantic Libraries," ed. Ina Ferris, *Praxis: An Online Journal of Romantic Circles* (posted February 2004). www.rc.umd.edu/praxis/libraries/toc.html.

9 Connell accentuates their power to disturb when he points to the "vertiginous sense of the arbitrariness of economic value" they helped induce that "threatened to destabilize the more legitimate criteria of textual appreciation implied by the notions of learning and taste." Connell, "Bibliomania," pp. 25, 28.

10 See Adrian Johns, *The Nature of the Book: Print and Knowledge in the Making* (University of Chicago Press, 1998), and his debate with Eisenstein in "How to Acknowledge a Revolution," *American Historical Review* 107 (2002): 106–25. Johns's brilliant account of the unstable character of the book throughout the early modern period has inspired my own thinking about the status of books in the early nineteenth century. In viewing this problem from my own disciplinary vantage point in literary and cultural studies, I am in one sense extending the problem Johns raises from the perspective of "literary" history.

11 Gustave Peignot, *Dictionnaire raisonée bibliographie* (1802), quoted in Balsamo, *Bibliography*, p. 147. Also still useful for the history of early European

bibliography work is Rudolf Blum, *Bibliographia: An Inquiry into its Definition and Designations* (1969), trans. Mathilde V. Rovelstad (Folkestone: Dawson House, 1980).

12 Samuel Paterson's admiring obituary appeared in *Monthly Magazine* 15 (1803): 44. See also Paul Keen's account of an earlier, late eighteenth-century, far less gaudy wave of bibliomania taking the form of an obsession with books, and showing the disruptive powers of commercial energy on existing orders of knowledge, in *Literature, Commerce, and the Spectacle of Modernity, 1750–1800* (Cambridge University Press, 2012), pp. 82–91.

13 Between 1800 and 1810, essays, reviews, or brief notices of the new interest in bibliography appeared in the *Monthly Review*, the *Monthly Magazine*, the *Anti-Jacobin Review*, the *Quarterly Review*, the *British Critic*, and especially the essays and books cited below: *A Bibliographical Dictionary*, the *Director*, *Censuria Bibliographica*, *Typographical Antiquities*, and *The Bibliomania: or Book-Madness*.

14 Adam Clarke, *A Bibliographical Dictionary: In all Departments of Literature* (London: W. Baynes, 1802–6).

15 Clarke published these last two volumes separately as *The Bibliographical Miscellany*, 2 vols. (London: W. Baynes, 1806). For his detailed comparison of bibliographical systems, see *Miscellany*, II: 146–218.

16 For an in-depth study of late nineteenth-century specialist scientific journals that bore little resemblance to Romantic-age scientific print, see Alex Csiszar, "Seriality and the Search for Order: Scientific Print and its Problems during the Late Nineteenth Century," *History of Science* 48.3/4 (September/December 2010): 399–434.

17 See McKitterick's excellent account of this search for a scientific library, "Bibliography," pp. 58–61.

18 Charles Lyell, "Scientific Institutions," *Quarterly Review* 34 (1826): 154–59; see also my discussion of this key essay for the history of science in Chapter 5.

19 Thomas Astle, *The Origins and Progress of Writing*, 2nd edn. (London: White, 1803); Charles Burney, ed., *A Catalogue of the Library of the Royal Institution of Great Britain*, 2nd edn. (London: Payne and Foss, 1821).

20 Thomas Frognall Dibdin, *The Bibliomania, or Book-Madness: A Bibliographical Romance* (1811; London: Chatto & Windus, 1876), p. 551. This "new and improved edition" – the fourth since Dibdin's original, short version published in 1809 – is now the most widely available in a contemporary reprint (Bristol: Thoemmes Press, 1997); like the 1842 and 1856 editions before it, the 1876 edition combines the early 1809 text with the expanded, arch dialogues of the 1811 revision that is referred to in most scholarship on Dibdin, along with the 1811 subtitle "A Bibliographical Romance." Fittingly, every edition of *The Bibliomania* differs significantly from the others; tracking the editions in comparative detail would itself add something useful to the history of "book history."

21 For the substance of these lectures, see Dibdin, *Reminiscences of a Literary Life* (London: John Major, 1836), 1: 233–45; and reports in the *Director*, passim.

22 John Payne Collier's remark was one of the more memorable: "I felt myself more humble than the meanest worm before the Almighty." Transcript of November 21, 1811, in Coleridge, *Lectures 1808–1819 On Literature*, ed. Reginald Foakes, vol. 5 of *The Collected Works of Samuel Taylor Coleridge* (Princeton University Press, 1987), 1: 203.
23 Ina Ferris, "Book Fancy: Bibliomania and the Literary Word," *Keats-Shelley Journal* 58 (2009): 33–52.
24 Dibdin, *Bibliomania*, pp. 539–40.
25 It is also clear that Dibdin's lectures and *Director* essays were having an impact on new print projects by publishers like Longman and men of letters like Robert Southey. Corresponding with Longman in August 1807, Southey considers the scope of Longman's proposed *Bibliotheca Britannica*, then defers to Dibdin: "There is a sort of title-page and colophon knowledge – in one word, bibliology – which is exactly what is wanted for this purpose, and in which he is very much my superior." Robert Southey, letter to Longman, September 20, 1807, in *The Life and Correspondence of Robert Southey*, ed. Charles Cuthbert Southey (New York: Harper & Brothers, 1855), p. 225.
26 Dibdin, *Director*, 1: 84.
27 Clarke, *Bibliographical Miscellany*, 1: v.
28 Coleridge, *Collected Letters*, 1: 412; also cited in Albert Boehm's important account of publishing the volume in "The 1798 *Lyrical Ballads* and the Poetics of Late Eighteenth-Century Book Production," *ELH* 63 (1996): 457.
29 Paul Gutjahr and Megan L. Benton, "Introduction," in *Illuminating Letters: Typography and Literary Interpretation* (Amherst: University of Massachusetts Press, 2001), p. 1.
30 [Thomas James], *The Pursuits of Literature*, 7th edn. (London: Longman, 1798), p. 135.
31 For good treatments of the black letter's cultural impact, see Sarah A. Kelen, "*Peirs Plouhman* (sic) and the 'Formidable Array of Blackletter' in the Early Nineteenth Century," and Paul Gutjahr, "The Letter(s) of the Law: Four Centuries of Typography in the King James Bible," in *Illuminating Letters*, ed. Gutjahr and Benton, pp. 47–67 and 17–43 respectively. Unlike the black-letter King James prized by Anglican bibliophiles like Dibdin, the Geneva Bible of 1560 used by many Dissenters was printed entirely in roman.
32 Dibdin, *Reminiscences*, 1: 236.
33 "Review of *The Works of Edmund Spenser*, with the principal Illustrations of various Commentators, ed. Rev. Henry John Todd," *Anti-Jacobin Review* 25 (1806): 1. See also Francis Douce, *Illustrations of Shakespeare, and of Ancient Manners* (London: Longman, 1807) and John Ferriar, *Illustrations of Sterne* (London: Cadell and Davies, 1798).
34 Samuel Egerton Brydges, *Censura Literaria* (London: Longman, 1808), IX: 1–3.
35 For the following discussion, I have learned much from Robert Shaddy, "Grangerizing; 'One of the Unfortunate Stages of Bibliomania,'" *Book Collector* 49 (2000): 536–46; Marcia Pointon, "Illustrious Heads," in *Hanging the Head: Portraiture and Social Formation in Eighteenth-Century England*

(New Haven: Yale University Press, 1993); and Lucy Peltz, "The Extra-Illustration of London: The Gendered Spaces and Practices of Antiquarianism in the Late Eighteenth Century," in *Producing the Past: Aspects of Antiquarian Culture and Practice, 1770–1850*, ed. Martin Myrone and Lucy Peltz (Aldershot: Ashgate, 1999), pp. 115–34.

36 Luisa Calé, "Dickens Extra-Illustrated: Heads and Scenes in Monthly Parts (The Case of *Nicholas Nickleby*)," *Yearbook of English Studies* (2011): 8–32 at p. 8. By the 1840s, Calé shows, extra-illustrating was being incorporated into commercial publishing, at least for Dickens, as her selection of rather extraordinary visual plates shows in this remarkable essay.

37 Herbert Henry Edmund Craster, *History of the Bodleian Library, 1845–1945* (Oxford: Clarendon Press, 1952), p. 113.

38 Robert Southey, quoted in Lucy Peltz, "Facing the Text: The Amateur and Commercial Histories of Extra-Illustration ca. 1770–1840," in *Owners, Annotators, and the Signs of Reading*, ed. Robin Myers et al. (New Castle, DE: Oak Knoll, 2006), p. 94.

39 John Hill Burton, *The Book Hunter*, quoted in Shaddy, "Grangerizing," p. 543.

40 Holbrook Jackson, *The Anatomy of Bibliomania*, 2nd edn. (Urbana: University of Illinois Press, 2001), p. 579.

41 Though wealthy aristocrats are commonly identified as infected with the Romantic book-madness, the occasionally extravagant libraries of eighteenth-century Dissenters and the historical interests of nineteenth-century plebeian journalists like Hone, author of *The Political House That Jack Built* (1816), suggest otherwise. Hone's black-letter reading shows him to be a student of Douce and others writing in this antiquarian mode: *Ancient Mysteries Described, Especially the English Miracle Plays* (London: Wm. Hone, 1823).

42 See Connell, "The Bibliomania," for a claim that the bibliophiles and bibliomaniacs were driven by a Burkean conservatism. As Tories they may have deferred casually to such politics, but to a surprising degree they were actually recurring targets of anti-Jacobin spleen (see n. 33 above).

43 Linda Colley, *Britons* (New Haven: Yale University Press, 1993).

44 Quoted in J. B. B. Burns, ed., *An Account of the Religious and Literary Life of Adam Clarke*, 2 vols. (New York: Mason and Lane, 1837), i: 394; see pp. 96–100 on the broader "sonship" controversy; n.a., *The Life and Labours of Adam Clarke, to which is added an Historical Sketch of the controversy concerning the Sonship of Christ* (London: John Stephens, 1834), pp. 462–66. The multivolume work commonly called Clarke's *Commentary on the Bible* was first published as Adam Clarke, *The New Testament of Our Lord and Saviour Jesus Christ* (London: A. Paul, 1825) and republished in many British and American editions since, most recently in electronic format as "Adam Clarke's Bible Commentary," www.godrules.net/library/clarke/clarke.htm.

45 For useful distinctions among the modes of British Dissent in this moment, see Daniel White, *Early Romanticism and Religious Dissent* (Cambridge University Press, 2006); Kevin Gilmartin, "Romanticism and Religious Modernity: From Natural Supernaturalism to Literary Sectarianism," in *The Cambridge History of*

*English Romanticism*, ed. James Chandler (Cambridge University Press, 2008), pp. 621–47; Michael Watts, *The Dissenters*, vol. II (Oxford: Clarendon Press, 1995); Robert Maniquis, "Transfiguring God: Religion, Romanticism, Revolution," in *The Blackwell Concise Companion to Romanticism*, ed. Jon Klancher (Oxford: Wiley-Blackwell, 2009), pp. 14–35.

46 Dibdin, *Bibliomania*, pp. 473–79. First published in the final issue of the *Director* in July 1807, this curious dream-passage reappears in later editions of *The Bibliomania, or Book-Madness* from 1811 to 1903; it was almost certainly the result of Dibdin's being awed by both the Anglican evangelical social vision of Thomas Bernard and the emerging arts-and-sciences Institutions the Royal had afforded him. It is hardly the same world of the book-warrior antiquarian collectors whom Dibdin would increasingly cultivate after 1807.

47 On Hannah More's version of modernizing evangelicalism, see Gilmartin, *Writing Against Revolution*, chapter 2.

48 This Richard Watson (1781–1833) should not be confused with the same-named but Anglican Bishop of Llandaff whom Wordsworth criticized in the 1790s. By the time Watson challenged Clarke's argument for the human birth of Christ, he was facing a distinguished scholar, bibliographer, and practitioner of the Higher Criticism in Clarke.

49 "Nightingale's Portraiture of Methodism," *Anti-Jacobin Review* 33 (1809): 236–47.

50 William Gifford's last word against bibliography and bibliomania alike came in the damaging review "Mr. Dibdin's Library Companion," *Quarterly Review* 32 (June 1825): 152–60.

51 For the only scholarly attempt to assess Clarke's work, see Francesco Cordasco, "Adam Clarke's *Bibliographical Dictionary* (1802–1806)," *Studies in Bibliography* 4 (1951–52): 189–92.

52 For an overview of the new scholarly bibliographical scholarship at mid-century and beyond, which largely overlooks the historical bibliography coming before it, see Thomas Tanselle, "Bibliographical History as a Field of Study," *Studies in Bibliography* 41 (1988): 33–58.

53 On the "social text" and the relationship between editing texts and books, see Jerome McGann, "From Text to Work: Digital Tools and the Emergence of the Social Text," *Romanticism on the Net* 41–42 (February–May 2006), www.erudit.org/revue/RON/2006/v/n41/013153ar.html; and D. F. McKenzie, *Bibliography and the Sociology of Texts* (Cambridge University Press, 1986).

54 Joseph Lowenstein, *The Author's Due: Printing and the Prehistory of Copyright* (University of Chicago Press, 2002), p. 252.

55 A. W. Ward and A. R. Waller, eds., *The Cambridge History of English Literature* (Cambridge University Press, 1915), XII: 362.

56 For a skeptical view of the claim to science from a later advocate of the New Bibliography, see Thomas Tanselle, "Bibliography and Science," *Studies in Bibliography* 27 (1974): 55–89; and "Bibliographical History as a Field of Study," *Studies in Bibliography* 41 (1988): 33–58.

57 Price, "Introduction: Reading Matter," pp. 10–11.

58 This question paraphrases but also repurposes a similar question asked by Adrian Johns (*The Nature of the Book*, p. 623) by asking what wider aim and purpose, beyond its own disciplinary aims, does it hope to achieve? See Johns, *The Nature of the Book*, p. 623.
59 McKenzie, *Bibliography and the Sociology of Texts*, pp. 9–11.
60 The black-boxing process, Latour remarks, "makes the joint production of actors and artifacts entirely opaque." Bruno Latour, *Pandora's Hope: An Essay on the Reality of Science Studies* (Cambridge, MA: Harvard University Press, 1999), p. 183.

**Chapter 4 Print and institution in the making of art controversy**

1 Prince Hoare, *Inquiry into the Requisite Cultivation and Present State of the Arts of Design in England* (London: Richard Phillips, 1806), p. 211.
2 Clark Olney, *Benjamin Robert Haydon: Historical Painter* (Atlanta: University of Georgia Press, 1952), p. 97.
3 James Elmes, "Preface," in *Annals of the Fine Arts* 1 (1816): iii. A number of art historians have taken Elmes's claim to heart, e.g. Holger Hoock, *The King's Artists* (New York: Oxford University Press, 2005), p. 132.
4 For the late eighteenth-century art press focused on Royal Academy exhibitions, see Mark Hallett, "The Business of Criticism," in *Art on the Line*, ed. David Solkin (New Haven: Yale University Press, 2001), pp. 65–76; Hoock, *The King's Artists*, pp. 129–32. For Germany, where an arts-interested press seems to have flourished throughout the second half of the eighteenth century, see Trevor Fawcett and Clive Phillpot, eds., *The Art Press: Two Centuries of Art Magazines* (London: Art Book Company, 1976).
5 The exception is Andrew Hemingway's trenchant survey in *Landscape Imagery and Urban Culture in Early Nineteenth-Century Britain* (Cambridge University Press, 1992), pp. 105–54.
6 Michael Kammen, *Visual Shock: A History of Art Controversies in American Culture* (New York: Knopf, 2006), pp. xi–xii.
7 Richard Howells, "Controversy, Art, and Power," in *Outrage: Art, Controversy, and Society*, ed. Richard Howells, Andreea Ritivoi, and Judith Schachter (New York: Palgrave, 2012), pp. 19–46.
8 The phrase "art controversy" or its variants tended to appear in non-specialist print media for a broadly intellectual readership, especially the *Athenaeum* 1371 (February 4, 1854): 155; Philip Gilbert Hamerton, "Amateurship: A Conversation," *Macmillan's Magazine* 14 (1866): 432; John Robert Seeley, "Elementary Principles in Art," *Macmillan's Magazine* 16 (1867): 1, and not long afterward in broad-audience American magazines like *Appleton's Journal* 10 (1881): 92.
9 Pierre Bourdieu, *The Field of Cultural Production: Essays on Art and Literature*, ed. Randall Johnson (New York: Columbia University Press, 1993).
10 Howard Becker, *Art Worlds* (Berkeley: University of California Press, 1982), p. x.

11 C. W. Moulton, *Queries: Devoted to Literature, Art, Science, Education* (Buffalo, NY: C. L. Sherill, 1885), 1: 3, 59.
12 Kate FitzGibbon, *Who Owns the Past? Cultural Policy, Cultural Property, and the Law* (New Brunswick, NJ: Rutgers University Press, 2009), p. 109.
13 For updates on the debate, see Christopher Hitchens, *The Elgin Marbles: Should They Be Returned to Greece?* (London: Chatto & Windus, 1987); William St. Clair, *Lord Elgin and the Marbles*, 2nd edn. (New York: Oxford University Press, 1998).
14 Trevor Fawcett, *The Rise of English Provincial Art* (Oxford: Clarendon Press, 1974).
15 Holger Hoock, "Reforming Culture: National Art Institutions in the Age of Reform," in *Rethinking the Age of Reform: Britain 1780–1850*, ed. Arthur Burns and Joanna Innes (Cambridge University Press, 2003), pp. 254–55.
16 William Hazlitt, "An Inquiry, whether the Fine Arts are Promoted by Academies and Public Institutions?" (1816), in *The Complete Works of William Hazlitt*, ed. P. P. Howe (London: J. M. Dent, 1930–34), XVIII: 37–51.
17 Henry Fuseli, "On the Present State of the Art" (1825), in *Lectures on Painting by the Royal Academicians: James Barry, John Opie, Henry Fuseli*, ed. Ralph Wornum (London: Henry G. Bohn, 1848), p. 559.
18 John Brewer, *The Pleasures of the Imagination* (University of Chicago Press, 1997), p. 244.
19 Jonathan Richardson, *A Discourse on the Dignity, Certainty, Pleasure, and Advantage of the Science of a Connoisseur* (London: W. Churchill, 1719).
20 Jay Robert Bolter and Richard Grusin, *Remediation: Understanding New Media* (Cambridge, MA: MIT Press, 2000).
21 Prince Hoare, *Artist* 1.1 (March 14, 1807): 3 (issues individually paginated).
22 Hoare, *Artist* 1.1 (March 14, 1807): 10–11.
23 For the quantitative comparison, I have used Joshua Reynolds, *Seven Discourses Delivered in the Royal Academy by the President* (London: T. Cadell, 1778), which runs to 338 pages. The 21 editions of the *Artist* published in 1807 by Prince Hoare, at 16 pages per issue, run to 336 pages.
24 James Northcote, 'Decipit Exemplar,' *Artist* 1.9 (May, 9 1807): 3, 5.
25 John Flaxman, *Artist* 1.12 (1807): 3.
26 On the painters' acid views of Payne Knight, see Joseph Farington, *The Diary of Joseph Farington*, ed. Kenneth Garlick and Angus Macintyre (New Haven: Yale University Press, 1978–), VIII: 2968.
27 The expression "dare to think for yourself" had been, of course, the challenge of Enlightenment to Europeans most memorably posed by Kant in the 1784 essay "What Is Enlightenment?" But the phrase "thinking for yourself [or ourselves, etc.]" had been widespread across Europe, and always in relation to print culture's power to make one an "author," since the emergence of the print-based Republic of Letters around 1700. See my account of this process in "The Vocation of Criticism and the Crisis of the Republic of Letters," in *The Cambridge History of Literary Criticism*, vol. V: *Romanticism*, ed. Marshall Brown (Cambridge University Press, 2000), pp. 296–320.

28 Especially in Clement Greenberg, "Towards a Newer Laokoon" (1940), in *Collected Essays and Criticism*, ed. John O'Brian (University of Chicago Press, 1993), 1: 23–37. On the "ideology of modernism" in Greenberg and modern formalism, see the acute commentary by Fredric Jameson, *A Singular Modernity* (New York: Verso, 2002), pp. 169–77.
29 Morris Eaves, *The Counter-Arts Conspiracy: Art and Industry in the Age of Blake* (Ithaca, NY: Cornell University Press, 1992), pp. 33–91; Thora Brylowe, "Romantic Art and Letters: British Print, Paint, Engraving 1770–1830," Ph.D. dissertation (Carnegie Mellon University Department of English, 2008), chapters 3–4; Luisa Calé, *Fuseli's Milton Gallery: "Turning Readers into Spectators"* (Oxford: Clarendon Press, 2006).
30 Pierre Bourdieu, *The Rules of Art: Genesis and Structure of the Literary Field* (Stanford University Press, 1996), p. 224.
31 Hoare's sister made the formal request: Mary Hoare to Elizabeth Inchbald, February 24, 1807, in *Memoirs of Mrs. Inchbald*, ed. James Boaden, 2 vols. (London: Richard Bentley, 1833), II: 361–62.
32 These comments are all recorded in Farington, *Diary*, VIII: 3084.
33 Northcote, *Artist* 1.9 (1807): 7.
34 Farington, *Diary*, VIII: 3061.
35 Adrian Johns, *The Nature of the Book: Print and Knowledge in the Making* (University of Chicago Press, 1998).
36 Prince Hoare, *Artist* 1.1 (1807): 11.
37 Linda Colley makes the 1805 British Institution a key exhibit in her argument that British aristocrats took over the discourse of nationalism by making their own private holdings in art and rare books the "public" property of the nation by way of limited exhibition in spaces like the British Institution or in great public libraries. See Colley, *Britons* (New Haven: Yale University Press, 1993), p. 176.
38 Farington, *Diary*, VIII: 2962.
39 Coleridge deferred the offer until January 1808 and insisted on changing the topic to "Principles of Poetry." See Reginald Foakes's clarifying account in Coleridge, *Lectures 1808–1819 on Literature*, vol. 5 of *The Collected Works of Samuel Taylor Coleridge* (Princeton University Press, 1987), 1: 5–8, 11–12.
40 Adolf Michaelis, *Ancient Marbles in Great Britain*, trans. C. A. M. Fennell (Cambridge University Press, 1882), p. 149.
41 For a penetrating discussion of "Romantic classicism" and the debate on its status in the period, see Theresa Kelley, "Keats, Ekphrasis, and History," in *Keats and History*, ed. Nicholas Roe (Cambridge University Press, 1998), pp. 212–37.
42 On definitions of *ekphrasis*, see James Heffernan, *Museum of Words: The Poetics of Ekphrasis from Homer to Ashbery* (University of Chicago Press, 1993), p. 1.
43 Robert Hunt began a weekly "Fine Arts" column in the second issue of the *Examiner* in January 1808, doubtless having a shelf of *Artist* issues to help him think about the larger question of how the Royal Society itself was part of the "old corruption" that public art patronage could help rectify.

44 "Elegant and Imitative Arts," *La Belle Assemblée*, n.s. 2 (1811): 358.
45 "Opinions of Eminent Artists Respecting the Elgin Marbles," *New Monthly Magazine* 5 (1816): 249. It's also true that Prince Hoare saw his larger case for national or state patronage lost with the Marbles decision – private patronage and commercial art-buying would continue to govern the field of art production until long after World War II. England thus avoided what we would *now* call "public art" in the early nineteenth century by using the state to symbolically empower the artist rather than to support the production of art works. The British state remained wary of sponsoring public patronage of the arts even after its interventions of 1816, 1824, and 1835–36.

### Chapter 5 History and organization in the Romantic-age sciences

1 For an account of why the history of science has, since the 1990s, won disciplinary standing while "science studies" remains inchoate, see Lorraine Daston, "Science Studies and the History of Science," *Critical Inquiry* 35 (2009): 798–813.
2 Robin Valenza, *Literature, Language, and the Rise of the Intellectual Disciplines in Britain, 1680–1820* (Cambridge University Press, 2009). On natural history's resistance to discipline, see Noah Heringman, "Natural History in the Romantic Period," in *A Concise Companion to the Romantic Age*, ed. Jon Klancher (Malden, MA: Wiley-Blackwell, 2009), pp. 141–67.
3 Schaffer, "Indisciplines and Interdisciplines: Some Exotic Genealogies of Modern Knowledge" (2010) at www.fif.tu-darmstadt.de/media/fif_interdisziplinaere_forschung/sonstigetexte/externe/simonschaffner.pdf, p. 2 (February 2, 2012).
4 Charles Gillispie, *The Edge of Objectivity: An Essay in the History of Scientific Ideas* (Princeton University Press, 1960), pp. 196–201.
5 For prototypes of this influential plotline, see Northrop Frye, *Fearful Symmetry: A Study of William Blake* (1947) (Princeton University Press, 1969) and Harold Bloom, *Blake's Apocalypse: A Study in Poetic Argument* (Ithaca, NY: Cornell University Press, 1970).
6 Joel Black, "Newtonian Mechanics and the Romantic Rebellion," in *Beyond the Two Cultures: Essays on Science, Technology, and Literature*, ed. Joseph W. Slade and Judith Yaross Lee (Iowa City: Iowa University Press, 1990), pp. 131–40.
7 Noah Heringman, "Introduction," in *Romantic Science: The Literary Forms of Natural History* (Albany: State University of New York Press, 2003), p. 2.
8 Richard Carlile, *An Address to Men of Science* (London: R. Carlile, 1821), p. 7. Carlile is also referring to William Lawrence, whose lectures on physiology and zoology in 1816 and 1817 Carlile himself was about to republish as proof of the materialist turn in sciences of life (William Lawrence, *Lectures on Physiology, Zoology, and the Natural History of Man* [London: Richard Carlile, 1822]). But Davy's discourse on chemistry had succeeded in making *all* scientific thinking ultimately responsive to its powerful pictures of chemical process at the basis of every natural knowledge.

9 Carlile, *Address*, p. 9.
10 Carlile, *Address*, pp. 6–7.
11 Priestley to Rotheram (May 31, 1774), in *Science, Medicine, and Dissent: Joseph Priestley 1733–1804*, ed. R. G. W. Anderson (London: Wellcome Trust/Science Museum, 1987), p. 50.
12 Golinski, *Science as Public Culture*, p. 76. This paragraph broadly follows Golinski's comparisons of Priestley's and Davy's methods and intellectual frameworks.
13 Foucault also regarded the "specific intellectual" as arising, in the mid twentieth century, upon a wide "extension of technico-scientific structures in the economic and strategic domain" which "gave him his real importance." Michel Foucault, "Truth and Power," in *Power/Knowledge: Selected Interviews and Other Writings, 1972–77*, ed. Colin Gordon (New York: Pantheon, 1980), pp. 129–30.
14 Carlile, *Address*, p. 8.
15 Carlile, *Address*, p. 28.
16 Edmund Burke, *Reflections on the Revolution in France* (1790), ed. Conor Cruise O'Brien (Harmondsworth: Penguin, 1969), p. 163.
17 Burke, *Reflections*, p. 106.
18 Thomas Malthus, *An Essay on the Principle of Population* (London: Joseph Johnson, 1798), p. 4; on Malthus's way of amplifying this sense of scientific complexity to his argument in the 1803 revision of *Population*, see Marilyn Butler, "Telling It Like a Story: The French Revolution as Narrative," *Studies in Romanticism* 28 (1989): 354–55.
19 These debates have been discussed in a wide range of scholarship; for the essential texts and modern commentaries, see especially John Thelwall, "Essay on Animal Vitality" (1793), rpt. in Nicholas Roe, *The Politics of Nature: William Wordsworth and Some Contemporaries* (New York: Palgrave, 2002), pp. 96–119; John Abernethy, *The Surgical Works* (London: Longman, 1811); Samuel Taylor Coleridge, "Theory of Life" (1816), in *Shorter Writings and Fragments*, vol. 11 of *The Collected Works of Samuel Taylor Coleridge*, ed. Kathleen Coburn et al. (Princeton University Press, 1969–), part 1, pp. 481–557; Marilyn Butler, "The Shelleys and Radical Science," in *Frankenstein, or the Modern Prometheus*, ed. Marilyn Butler (New York: Oxford University Press, 1994), pp. xv–xxi; Karl M. Figlio, "The Metaphor of Organization: An Historiographic Perspective on the Bio-Medical Sciences of the Early Nineteenth Century," *History of Science* 14 (1976): 17–53; Trevor Levere, *Poetry Realized into Nature: Samuel Coleridge and Early Nineteenth-Century Science* (Cambridge University Press, 1981), pp. 46–52, 205–12. For an incisive recent treatment of these issues, see James Robert Allard, *Romanticism, Medicine, and the Poet's Body* (Aldershot: Ashgate, 2007), pp. 66ff.
20 Coleridge, *Biographia Literaria*, ed. James Engell and W. Jackson Bate, vol. 7 of *The Collected Works of Samuel Taylor Coleridge*, 2 vols. (Princeton University Press, 1973), 11: 29. See also Robert Maniquis, "The Book in the Text of the *Biographia Literaria*," in *On the Biographia Literaria*, ed. Frederick Burwick (Oklahoma City: University of Oklahoma Press, 1988).

21 William Blizard and Thomas Chevalier, quoted in Christopher Fox, "Introduction," in *Inventing Human Science: Eighteenth-Century Domains*, ed. Christopher Fox, Roy Porter, and Robert Wokler (Berkeley: University of California Press, 1995), p. 11.
22 Coleridge, *The Collected Letters of Samuel Taylor Coleridge*, ed. Earl Leslie Griggs (Oxford: Clarendon Press, 1956), 1: 349.
23 Saree Makdisi, *William Blake and the Impossible History of the 1790s* (University of Chicago Press, 2003), pp. 85–87.
24 See L. C. Jacyna, "Images of John Hunter in the Nineteenth Century," *History of Science* 21 (1983): 85–108; and "Immanence or Transcendence: Theories of Life and Organization in Britain, 1790–1835," *Isis* 74 (1983): 311–29.
25 Lawrence, *Lectures*, p. 53; see also Adrian Desmond, *The Politics of Evolution* (University of Chicago Press, 1989), pp. 117–21. Coleridge identified Lawrence's claim to life's self-organization as "republicanism"; what Coleridge ignored was the politics of Lawrence's anthropology, which as Londa Schiebinger has detailed, identified life's self-organization with the supremacy of Caucasian racial lines in physiological development. Londa Schiebinger, *Nature's Body: Gender in the Making of Modern Science* (Boston: Beacon Press, 1993), pp. 133, 139–40, 185.
26 Coleridge, *The Friend*, ed. Barbara E. Rooke, vol. 4 of *The Collected Works of Samuel Taylor Coleridge*, ed. Kathleen Coburn (Princeton University Press, 1969), 1: 493n.
27 Coleridge, *The Friend*, 1: 474.
28 *Hysteron proteron* here means "the last first." Coleridge, "Theory of Life," in *Shorter Works and Fragments*, ed. H. J. Jackson and J. R. de J. Jackson, vol. 11 of *The Collected Works of Samuel Taylor Coleridge* (Princeton University Press, 1995), part 2, pp. 501–2. In a "Philosophical Lecture" of March 15, 1819, Coleridge repeated this argument, adding, "To say that life is the result of organization . . . is assuredly what I before said, to affirm a thing to be its own parent or to determine the parent to be the child of his own child" (*Lectures 1818–1819 on the History of Philosophy*, ed. J. R. de J. Jackson, vol. 8 of *The Collected Works of Samuel Taylor Coleridge* [Princeton University Press, 2000], part 2, pp. 524–25).
29 Niklas Luhmann, "The Autopoiesis of Social Systems" and "Complexity and Meaning," in *Essays on Self-Reference* (New York: Columbia University Press, 1990), pp. 1–20, 80–85. Luhmann follows the theoretical biology of Humberto Maturana and Francisco Varela, who define autopoietic systems as "networks of productions of components that recursively, through their interactions, generate and realize the network that produces them and constitute, in the space in which they exist, the boundaries of the network as components that participate in the realization of the network" (Maturana and Varela, quoted in Luhmann, *Essays*, p. 3).
30 Coleridge, *Biographia Literaria*, ed. James Engell and W. Jackson Bate, vol. 7 of *The Collected Works of Samuel Taylor Coleridge* (Princeton University Press, 1983), 11: 62–63.

31 Coleridge, *Aids to Reflection*, ed. John Beer, vol. 9 of *The Collected Works of Samuel Taylor Coleridge* (Princeton University Press, 1995), pp. 395–96.
32 Roger Chartier, *The Order of Books* (Stanford University Press, 2004), p. 53.
33 See Marjorie Levinson's reading of the poem in *Keats's "Life of Allegory": The Origins of a Style* (Cambridge, MA: Blackwell, 1988); and Daniel Watkins, *Keats's Poetry and the Politics of the Imagination* (Rutherford, NJ: Fairleigh Dickinson University Press, 1989), pp. 26–31.
34 See Simon Schaffer's account of what it could take to turn claims into discoveries in this period in "Scientific Discoveries and the End of Natural Philosophy," *Social Studies of Science* 16 (1986): 387–420.
35 Jan Golinski dates the first use of the phrase to Thomas Kuhn; see Jan Golinski, "Humphry Davy: The Experimental Self," *Eighteenth Century Studies* 45 (2011): 15; Thomas Kuhn, *The Essential Tension: Selected Studies in Scientific Tradition and Change* (University of Chicago Press, 1977), pp. 147, 220.
36 See Michael Rectenwald, "The Publics of Science: Periodicals and the Making of British Science, 1820–1860," Ph.D. dissertation (Carnegie Mellon University, Department of English, 2005), pp. 169–75. Rectenwald gives an illuminating account of Lyell's *Quarterly Review* essays on pp. 169–81. From its early chapters on Lyell's evolutionism, Rectenwald goes on to make an incisive study of George Holyoake's contradictory leadership and writing for the Secularist movement in mid-Victorian Britain.
37 Simon Schaffer, "Priestley and the Politics of Spirit," in *Science, Medicine, and Dissent: Joseph Priestley (1733–1804)*, ed. Robert Anderson and Christopher Lawrence (London: Wellcome Trust, 1987), p. 43.
38 Charles Lyell, "Scientific Institutions," *Quarterly Review* 34 (1826): 160.
39 Lyell, "Scientific Institutions," p. 156.
40 Lyell, "Scientific Institutions," p. 154.
41 Jonathan Sawday, *Engines of the Imagination: Renaissance Culture and the Rise of the Machine* (New York: Routledge, 2007), p. 279.
42 Lyell, "Scientific Institutions," p. 179.
43 Lyell, "Scientific Institutions," p. 175.
44 Lyell, "Scientific Institutions," p. 176.
45 Lyell, "Scientific Institutions," p. 177.
46 Lyell, "Scientific Institutions," p. 176.
47 Thomas De Quincey, "Letters to a Young Man, Whose Education Has Been Neglected" (1823), in *The Collected Writings of Thomas De Quincey*, ed. David Masson (Edinburgh: Black, 1897), XI: 48.

## Chapter 6 The Coleridge Institution

1 Anthony Grafton ventures 1417 as the earliest discernible date of the modern *respublica*'s appearance in "A Sketch Map of a Lost Continent: The Republic of Letters," *Republics of Letters: A Journal for the Study of Knowledge, Politics, and the Arts* 1.1 (May 1, 2009): http://rofl.stanford.edu/node/34. The historiography on this topic is now enormous, but among the most widely cited

pictures of the Republic are Anne Goldgar, *Impolite Letters: Conduct and Community in the Republic of Letters 1680–1750* (New Haven, CT: Yale University Press, 1995); and Dena Goodman, *The Republic of Letters: A Cultural History of Enlightenment* (Ithaca, NY: Cornell University Press, 1993).
2 Lorraine Daston, "The Ideal and the Reality of the Republic of Letters in the Enlightenment," *Science in Context* 4 (1991): 367–85.
3 See Paul Keen, *The Crisis of Literature in the 1790s: Print Culture and the Public Sphere* (Cambridge University Press, 1999), chapter 1; Ian Duncan, *Scott's Shadow: The Novel in Romantic Edinburgh* (Princeton University Press, 2007), pp. 49–58; and my essay "The Vocation of Criticism and the Crisis of the Republic of Letters," in *The Cambridge History of Literary Criticism*, vol. 5: *Romanticism*, ed. Marshall Brown (Cambridge University Press, 2000), pp. 296–320.
4 [Thomas Christie], "To the Public," *Analytical Review* 1 (1788): i–iv.
5 Samuel Taylor Coleridge, *Table Talk*, ed. Carl Woodring, vol. 14 of *The Collected Works of Samuel Taylor Coleridge*, ed. Kathleen Coburn (Princeton University Press, 1990), 1: 285.
6 Coleridge, *The Statesman's Manual* (1816), in *Lay Sermons*, ed. R. J. White, vol. 6 of *The Collected Works of Samuel Taylor Coleridge*, p. 107; Coleridge, *Biographia Literaria*, ed. James Engell and Walter Jackson Bate, vol. 7 of *The Collected Works of Samuel Taylor Coleridge*, ed. Kathleen Coburn (Princeton University Press, 1976), 1: 54.
7 Byron's remarks on Coleridge's lecturing are too little cited: "Coleridge has attacked the *Pleasures of Hope*, and all other pleasures whatsoever. Mr. [Samuel] Rogers was present, and heard himself indirectly *rowed* by the lecturer. We are going in a party to hear the new Art of Poetry by this reformed schismatic; and were I one of these poetical luminaries, or of sufficient consequence to be noticed by the man of lectures, I should not hear him without an answer." Letter to Francis Hodgson, December 8, 1811, in *Byron's Letters and Journals*, vol. 11: *"Famous in my time": 1810–1812*, ed. Leslie Marchand (Cambridge, MA: Harvard University Press, 1973), pp. 140–41.
8 Coleridge, *Biographia Literaria*, 1: 220–21.
9 Coleridge, Letter to William Collins, December 6, 1818, in *Collected Letters*, IV: 992–93. See also Sarah Zimmerman, "Coleridge the Lecturer, A Disappearing Act," in *Spheres of Action: Speech and Performance in Romantic Culture*, ed. Alexander Dick and Angela Esterhammer (University of Toronto Press, 2009), p. 59.
10 Coleridge, *The Collected Letters of Samuel Taylor Coleridge*, ed. Earl Griggs (Princeton University Press, 1956), III: 385, 392, 409. Bernard is frequently visible in this and other roles through all Coleridge's letters from 1808 to 1814.
11 See Robin Valenza, *Literature, Language, and the Rise of the Intellectual Disciplines in Britain, 1680–1820* (Cambridge University Press, 2009).
12 Coleridge, *Biographia Literaria*, II: 105.

13 Priestley's chapters in *Disquisitions relating to Matter and Spirit* (London: J. Johnson, 1777) included "Of the Seat of the Sentient Principle in Man," and the word appeared frequently in his work to designate a version of spirit animating matter.
14 Peter Manning, "Manufacturing the Romantic Image: Coleridge and Hazlitt Lecturing," in *Romantic Metropolis: The Urban Scene of British Culture, 1780–1840*, ed. James Chandler and Kevin Gilmartin (Cambridge University Press, 2005), p. 232.
15 From an 1812 lecture at Willis's Rooms on *Romeo and Juliet* in Coleridge, *Lectures 1808–1819 On Literature*, ed. Reginald Foakes, vol. 5 of *Collected Works* (Princeton University Press, 1987), 1: 494.
16 The most influential case in *Biographia Literaria* comes at the end of Chapter 14 with its sequence of "opposites" that reconcile in a single organized form: *Biographia Literaria*, 11: 15–18.
17 On this point see also my *The Making of English Reading Audiences, 1790–1832* (Madison: University of Wisconsin Press, 1987), pp. 164–70.
18 Valenza, *Literature and the Intellectual Disciplines*, p. 219.
19 Valenza, *Literature and the Intellectual Disciplines*, pp. 139–46.
20 Coleridge, *Biographia Literaria*, 11: 54.
21 John Bender, "Novel Knowledge: Judgment, Experience, Experiment," in *This Is Enlightenment*, ed. Clifford Siskin and William Warner (University of Chicago Press, 2010), p. 284.
22 Bender, "Novel Knowledge," p. 291.
23 Michael McKeon, "Mediation as Primal Word: The Arts, the Sciences, and the Origins of the Aesthetic," in *This Is Enlightenment*, ed. Siskin and Warner, pp. 389–97.
24 Coleridge, *Biographia Literaria*, 11: 13.
25 Richard Holmes, *Coleridge: Darker Reflections, 1804–1834* (New York: Pantheon, 1998), p. 461.
26 For a representative case, see Robert Flint, *Philosophy as "Scienta Scientarum": A History of Classifications of the Sciences* (Edinburgh: William Blackwood, 1904).
27 John Stuart Mill, *On Bentham and Coleridge*, ed. F. R. Leavis [1950] (New York: Harper, 1962), pp. 8, 40.
28 Mill, *On Bentham and Coleridge*, p. 130.
29 Leavis, "Introduction" to *On Bentham and Coleridge*, p. 2.
30 Leavis, "Introduction," p. 7.
31 Raymond Williams, *Culture and Society, 1780–1950* [1958] (New York: Oxford University Press, 1983), pp. 49–70. Michel Foucault's important reading of Bentham's Panopticon writings has if anything widened the opposition of Coleridgean and Benthamite legacies further since the publication of *Discipline and Punish* (New York: Pantheon, 1977).
32 Mill, *On Bentham and Coleridge*, p. 40.
33 Mill, *On Bentham and Coleridge*, p. 101; Jeremy Bentham, *Chrestomathia* (London: Payne and Foss, 1816), p. 148.

34 "Prospectus to the *Encyclopaedia Metropolitana*" (1817), in Samuel Taylor Coleridge, *The Shorter Works and Fragments*, ed. H. J. and J. R. de J. Jackson, vol. II of *The Collected Works of Samuel Taylor Coleridge* (Princeton University Press, 1995), part I, pp. 586–87.
35 Bentham, *Chrestomathia*, p. 11.
36 Bentham's association with the University of London is of course legendary, yet rarely examined. For a searching analysis of Bentham's theoretical work as a university model, see Robert Young, "The Idea of a Chrestomathic University," in *Logomachia: The Conflict of the Faculties*, ed. Richard Rand (Lincoln: University of Nebraska Press, 1992), pp. 99–126.
37 Coleridge, "Treatise on Method," in *Shorter Works*, part I, pp. 683–84.
38 Bentham, *Chrestomathia*, pp. 8–9.
39 Bentham, *Chrestomathia*, pp. 9–10.
40 See Frances Ferguson, "The Sublime and Education: Educational Rationalization/Sublime Reason," *Praxis: An Online Journal of Romantic Circles*. www.rc.umd.edu/praxis/sublime_education/ferguson/ferguson.html. Paragraph 6.
41 Bentham, *Chrestomathia*, p. 10.
42 Bentham, *Chrestomathia*, pp. 9–10.
43 Bentham, *Chrestomathia*, p. 10. In addition to texts cited in Chapter 1, see Gottfried Wilhelm Leibniz, *New Essays concerning the Human Understanding* (1704), trans. Alfred Gideon Langley (Chicago: Open Court Press, 1916), pp. 474–77. See also Jacques Derrida's provocative pages on Leibniz and invention, practices, and method, in senses that also bear on the questions raised in *Chrestomathia*, in *Psyche: Inventions of the Other*, ed. Peggy Kamuf (Stanford University Press, 2007), pp. 30–41.
44 Ellen Messer-Davidow and David Shumway give a definition of disciplinarity (still a term of uncertain range and meaning in 1993) in terms that bring forward from Bentham's and Coleridge's moment the elements of disciplinarity that must be made to "cohere": "disciplinarity is about the coherence of a set of otherwise disparate elements: objects of study, methods of analysis, scholars, students, journals, and grants, to name a few." Ellen Messer-Davidow, David R. Shumway, and David J. Sylvan, *Knowledges: Historical and Critical Studies in Disciplinarity* (Charlottesville: University Press of Virginia, 1993), p. 3.
45 See Alan Richardson, *Literature, Education, and Romanticism: Reading as Social Practice, 1780–1832* (Cambridge University Press, 1994).
46 Bentham, *Chrestomathia*, p. 9. For a clarifying synopsis of the logic of autopoiesis, see Niklas Luhmann, *Essays on Self-Reference* (New York: Columbia University Press, 1990), pp. 1–20.
47 Bentham, *Chrestomathia*, pp. 9–11.
48 Mill, *On Bentham and Coleridge*, p. 140.
49 Bentham, *Chrestomathia*, p. 11.
50 Quoted in Larry Stewart, *The Rise of Public Science* (Cambridge University Press, 1992), p. 169.
51 Bentham, *Chrestomathia*, p. 243.

52 Ferguson, "The Sublime and Education," paragraphs 10 and 29.
53 Coleridge, *The Friend*, I: 479.
54 Coleridge, *The Friend*, I: 479–81.
55 Coleridge, *The Friend*, I: 471. This is, of course, the signature relationship between poetry and chemistry that Trevor Levere influentially expanded into a bond between Romantic literature and sciences in his *Poetry Realized into Nature: Samuel Taylor Coleridge and Early Nineteenth-Century Science* (Cambridge University Press, 1981).
56 Coleridge, *Collected Letters*, IV: 816.
57 See James Chandler, "The Politics of Sentiment: Notes toward a New Account," *Studies in Romanticism* 49 (2010): 567–72.
58 Coleridge, *The Friend*, I: 464–65.
59 Coleridge, *Biographia Literaria*, I: 38.
60 Coleridge, *The Friend*, I: 463.
61 Coleridge, *The Friend*, I: 457.
62 Coleridge, *The Friend*, I: 455.
63 J. R. de J. Jackson, *Method and Imagination in Coleridge's Criticism* (London: Routledge & Kegan Paul, 1969), p. 40; Jerome Christensen, *Coleridge's Blessed Machine of Language* (Ithaca, NY: Cornell University Press, 1981), p. 233.
64 Coleridge, *The Friend*, I: 455.
65 Coleridge, *The Friend*, I: 488–49.
66 Quoted in Rob Iliffe, "Material Doubts: Hooke, Artisan Culture, and the Exchange of Information in 1670s London," *British Journal for the History of Science* 28 (1995): 286.
67 Robert Hooke, "A General Scheme, or Idea of the Present State of Natural Philosophy and How Its Defects May be Remedied" (1666), in *Posthumous Works of Robert Hooke*, ed. Robert Waller [1705] (New York: Frank Cass, 1971), pp. 23–24.
68 Coleridge gives (and mangles) this passage from Hooke in a long footnote. Coleridge, *The Friend*, I: 484.
69 Trevor Levere, *Poetry Realized into Nature*, p. 74.
70 Coleridge, *Biographia Literaria*, II: 52–57.
71 Humphry Davy, "A Discourse Introductory to a Course of Lectures on Chemistry" [1802], in *The Collected Works of Humphry Davy*, ed. John Davy (London: Smith, Elder, 1839), II: 316–17.
72 Humphry Davy, "Introductory Lectures for the Courses of 1805," in Davy, *Collected Works*, VIII: 163.
73 Davy, *Collected Works*, II: 312.
74 In a recent essay on disciplinary histories, Lorraine Daston makes a compelling case for why historians of science "have become self-consciously disciplined by submitting to the discipline of history and archival research" rather than, like science studies, taking their home disciplines in the social sciences for granted. In this process, science studies have remained "interdisciplinary" in a way that relies on the solidity of their own social-scientific authority in its disciplinary history, while history of science has become all the more disciplinary in its *own*

right by submitting to self-schooling in the discipline of historiography and its archival methods. Equally paradoxical, from the present book's viewpoint, is that by learning the discipline and methods of history, these historians of science have been led back to a history of the *arts*. These are not, in the modern sense, "fine" or aesthetic arts, but the "arts" that can appear when the effort to understand "highly technical procedures" used now might lead historians of science to find why they "stem from cultural competences (for example, brewing beer)." Robert Hooke's vast catalogue may have left out brewmasters, but it was this kind of search for long-embedded practices and practical knowledges that makes him the rejected but necessary antitype for Coleridge's "English Plato." See Lorraine Daston, "Science Studies and the History of Science," *Critical Inquiry* 35 (2009): 798–813 at p. 808.

75 Jeremy Bentham, *The Rationale of Reward* (1825), in *The Works of Jeremy Bentham*, ed. John Bowring (Edinburgh: William Tait, 1839), II: 253. The *Rationale* reprints along with this now-rigid distinction between "arts and sciences" of utility and those of "amusement" the part of *Chrestomathia* I have been reading in this chapter. The "rationale of reward" meant urging the British government to provide funding only for the latter. The British literary and visual arts would continue to remain without state support.

76 Bentham, *Works*, ed. Bowring, VIII: 21.
77 Coleridge, *The Friend*, I: 176.
78 Coleridge, *On the Constitution of Church and State*, ed. John Colmer, vol. 10 of *The Collected Works of Samuel Taylor Coleridge*, ed. Kathleen Coburn (Princeton University Press, 1972), p. 61.
79 Coleridge, *Biographia Literaria*, II: 29.
80 Philip Connell, *Romanticism, Economics, and the Question of "Culture"* (New York: Oxford University Press, 2001), p. 143.
81 Coleridge, *On the Constitution of Church and State*, p. 46.
82 Thomas Kuhn, *The Essential Tension* (University of Chicago Press, 1977), p. 220.
83 Coleridge, *Lay Sermons*, ed. R. J. White, vol. 6 of *The Collected Works of Samuel Taylor Coleridge*, ed. Kathleen Coburn (Princeton University Press, 1972), p. 33.
84 Coleridge, *Church and State*, pp. 42–43.
85 Coleridge, *Church and State*, p. 47.
86 Max Weber, *Economy and Society: An Outline of Interpretive Sociology* [1920], ed. Günther Roth and Claus Wittich, 2 vols. (Berkeley: University of California Press, 1978), I: 714.
87 See Pierre Bourdieu's account of the conceptual origin of his own theory of fields of cultural production in "Legitimation and Structured Interests in Weber's Sociology of Religion," in *Max Weber, Rationality and Modernity*, ed. Scott Lash and Sam Whimster (London: Allen & Unwin, 1987), pp. 119–36.

## Chapter 7 Dissenting from the "arts and sciences"

1 John Barrell, *The Political Theory of Painting from Reynolds to Hazlitt: "The Body of the Public"* (New Haven: Yale University Press, 1986), pp. 314–41.

2 Ian Duncan, *Scott's Shadow: The Novel in Romantic Edinburgh* (Princeton University Press, 2007), pp. 9–18.
3 See e.g. "Prospectus to the University of London," *London Magazine* n.s. 5 (August 1826): 554–58.
4 Mark Salber Phillips, *Society and Sentiment: Genres of Historical Writing in Britain, 1740–1820* (Princeton University Press, 2000), p. 17.
5 Conjectural history distinguished itself by making modernity's emergence depend on the category "arts and sciences" to measure "human society, in its infancy, making the first faint essays toward the arts and sciences," as Hume put it. See David Hume, "On the Study of History" (1741), in *Essays Moral, Political, and Literary*, ed. Eugene F. Miller (Indianapolis: Liberty Fund, 1985), p. 585. Phillips usefully distinguishes "philosophical" and "conjectural histories," the latter as a more critical model of the older narrative political histories. See Phillips, *Society and Sentiment*, pp. 171–90.
6 See especially H. M. Hopfl, "From Savage to Scotsman: Conjectural History in the Scottish Enlightenment," *Journal of British Studies* 17 (1978): 19–41 at 20–23; and Phillips, *Society and Sentiment*, pp. 48–49.
7 David Hume, "Of the Rise and Progress of the Arts and Sciences" (1742), in *Essays*, p. 112.
8 Hume, "Rise and Progress," p. 114.
9 Hume, "Rise and Progress," p. 113.
10 Hume, "Rise and Progress," p. 114.
11 Hume, "Rise and Progress," p. 124.
12 William Godwin, *An Enquiry concerning Political Justice* (1798), ed. Isaac Kramnick (Baltimore: Penguin, 1985), p. 750.
13 Godwin, *Political Justice*, p. 722.
14 Godwin, *Political Justice*, p. 723.
15 William Godwin, "Preface" to *The Enquirer* (London: Robinson, 1797), p. vii; Mark Philp, *Godwin's Political Justice* (London: Duckworth, 1986), pp. 202–5. Making this point also requires me to revise my own earlier claim that "Godwin renounced the theoretical ambition of *Political Justice* – the task of philosophical totalization that by 1797 he was calling 'incommensurate to our powers'" (Jon Klancher, "Godwin and the Genre Reformers: On Necessity and Contingency in Romantic Narrative Theory," in *Romanticism, History, and the Possibilities of Genre*, ed. Tilottama Rajan and Julia M. Wright [Cambridge University Press, 1998], p. 28). Godwin surely points to the inherent liability of a large-scope systematic work – but I no longer think he meant his own book, but rather *any* version of such an inquiry, and even so, he was by no means certain of this question: "*it is perhaps* a method of investigation incommensurate to our powers," he wrote (p. vi). *The Enquirer* entails a different genre of critical discourse and a cautionary note, not a renunciation, really, of anything.
16 Jon Mee, *Conversable Worlds: Literature, Contention, and Community, 1762–1830* (Oxford University Press, 2011), p. 156; Kristen Leaver, "Pursuing Conversations: *Caleb Williams* and the Romantic Construction of the Reader," *Studies in Romanticism* 33 (1994): 589–610.

17 Godwin, *The Enquirer*, p. vii. In *Godwin's Political Justice*, p. 216, Philp remarks that "Godwin wrote as if a republic of virtue was possible because he lived in a community which attempted to realize the basic principles of such a republic" – see also Philp's mapping of these communities and their memberships, pp. 231–52. In this chapter, the next ten pages (thirteen paragraphs) are adapted and revised from my earlier essay "Godwin and the Genre Reformers: On Necessity and Contingency in Romantic Narrative Theory," in *Romanticism, History, and the Possibilities of Genre*, ed. Tilottama Rajan and Julia M. Wright (Cambridge University Press, 1998), pp. 27–35; a previous version of the 1998 article also appeared, and was acknowledged, in my essay "Godwin and the Republican Romance: Genre, Politics, and Contingency in Cultural History," *Modern Language Quarterly* 56 (1995): 145–65.

18 Mark Phillips challenges the widespread understanding of a central role for the "stadial" paradigm in Scottish historiography in *Society and Sentiment*, pp. 171–73. Stadial history as such is not especially important to my account of Godwin here, but the useful distinction between "conjectural history" and "philosophical history" certainly is.

19 Friedrich Meinecke, *Historism* (1959), trans. J. E. Anderson (New York: Herder and Herder, 1972), p. 62.

20 William Godwin, "Of History and Romance" (1797), in William Godwin, *Things as They Are, or The Adventures of Caleb Williams*, Appendix D, ed. Maurice Hindle (Baltimore: Penguin, 1988), p. 362.

21 David Hume, *An Enquiry Concerning Human Understanding*, ed. Eric Steinberg (Indianapolis: Hackett, 1977), pp. 54–55.

22 Godwin, "Of History and Romance," pp. 363, 365.

23 Godwin, "Of History and Romance," pp. 364, 363.

24 Godwin, "Of History and Romance," p. 367.

25 Godwin, "Of History and Romance," p. 371. These arguments are revived from early eighteenth-century debates that have been well explored by Michael McKeon, *The Origins of the English Novel, 1600–1740* (Baltimore: Johns Hopkins University Press, 1987), pp. 47–65.

26 Godwin, "Of History and Romance," p. 372.

27 Pamela Clemit usefully reads *Mandeville: A Tale of the Seventeenth Century in England* (1817) in relation to Godwin's lengthy meditations on the English Revolution, in *The Godwinian Novel: The Rational Fictions of Godwin, Brockden Brown, Mary Shelley* (Oxford: Clarendon Press, 1993), pp. 70–104. Most recently, Tilottama Rajan makes a challenging case for the novel's quizzical and indeterminate judgment on the historical novel's project in "The Disfiguration of Enlightenment: War, Trauma, and the Historical Novel in Godwin's *Mandeville*," in *Godwinian Moments: From Enlightenment to Romanticism*, ed. Robert M. Maniquis and Victoria Myers (University of Toronto Press, 2011), pp. 172–93.

28 Godwin, *History of the Commonwealth of England* (London, 1824–28); see also John Morrow, "Republicanism and Public Virtue: William Godwin's *History of the Commonwealth of England*," *The Historical Journal* 34 (1991): 645–64.

29 Godwin, *Political Justice*, p. 193.
30 Godwin, "Of History and Romance," p. 372.
31 Moral philosophy: Richard Rorty, *Contingency, Irony, and Solidarity* (Cambridge University Press, 1989); paleontology: Stephen J. Gould, *Wonderful Life: The Burgess Shale and the Nature of History* (New York: Norton, 1989); political philosophy: Slavoj Zizek, *Tarrying with the Negative* (New York: Verso, 1993); comparative planetology: Herbert Shaw, *Craters, Cosmos, and Chronicles: A New Theory of the Earth* (Stanford University Press, 1994).
32 Zizek, *Tarrying*, pp. 153–54.
33 On early eighteenth-century questions of contingency and fiction, see the useful discussion of Lois Chaber, "'This Intricate Labyrinth': Order and Contingency in Eighteenth-Century Fictions," *Studies in Voltaire and the Eighteenth Century* 212 (1992): 185–209.
34 Godwin, "Of History and Romance," p. 372.
35 This surprising, much-commented-on conclusion to "Of History and Romance" has often been read as a moment of Godwin coming to his senses: no fictional history can really substitute for the knowledge production actual historiography can give us, even with its ideological blinders on. For this reading, see Phillips, *Society and Sentiment*, pp. 118–21.
36 Franco Moretti, "The Moment of Truth," and "On Literary Evolution," in *Signs Taken for Wonders* (New York: Verso, 1989), pp. 254, 262–78. For the most recent version of this argument, which suggests placing Godwin's essay, along with his later historical novels, into a wider generic process, see Moretti, *Graphs, Maps, and Trees* (London: Verso, 2007).
37 Although Hume could write a conjectural-history essay about the arts and sciences, it is important to note that history-writing itself often had no legible place in that continuum.
38 Anna Barbauld's long and innovative introduction to her fifty-volume edition *The British Novelists* (London: Rivington, 1810) ends by vowing, "Let me make the novels of a country, and let who will make the systems." Yet this kind of wide purview and claim to "stable and universal principles" would also enable historiography to begin claiming disciplinary authority even as, in Ian Duncan's words, it "revoked its membership in the general category of 'literature' – formerly inclusive of all kinds of written discourse." Walter Scott's invention of the historical novel in 1814 would thus make the novel itself a "correspondent in that divorce" between history-writing and the Enlightenment's category of literature, giving the novel itself a proto-disciplinary force to define, as "fiction," the fundamental authority of imaginative literature in the nineteenth century and beyond. Duncan, *Scott's Shadow*, p. 126.
39 Godwin, *The Enquirer*, pp. 327–35.
40 Godwin, *The Enquirer*, p. ix.
41 Richard Phillips, ed., *The Picture of London for 1802* (London: R. Phillips, 1803).
42 In the following analysis I cite from this essay in its original form: M[ary] R[obinson], "Present State of the Manners, Society &c &c of the Metropolis

of England," *Monthly Magazine* 10 (1800): 35–38, 138–40, 218–22, 305–6. This complex, important essay has been republished as an important "lost document" by Adriana Craciun in *PMLA* 119.1 (2004): 103–17, along with an illuminating introduction. The next five pages of this chapter (seven paragraphs) are adapted from my essay "Discriminations, or Romantic Cosmopolitanisms in London," in *Romantic Metropolis*, ed. James Chandler and Kevin Gilmartin (Cambridge University Press, 2005), pp. 65–72.

43 Robinson "Present State," p. 35.
44 For a broad and still useful account, see Thomas Schlereth, *The Cosmopolitan Ideal in Eighteenth-Century Thought* (Notre Dame University Press, 1977).
45 On the "art of the state" as a political and periodical genre, see James Chandler, *England in 1819: The Case of Romantic Historicism and the Politics of Literary Culture* (University of Chicago Press, 1998), pp. 120–30.
46 Robinson, "Present State," pp. 306, 139. On the mid eighteenth-century aristocratic imitation of the French, in a very different political context, see John Brewer, *The Pleasures of the Imagination* (University of Chicago Press, 1997), pp. 83–85.
47 Paul Keen, *The Crisis of Literature in the 1790s* (Cambridge University Press, 1999); Gillian Russell and Clara Tuite, eds., *Romantic Sociability* (Cambridge University Press, 2002).
48 Robinson, "Present State," pp. 36–37, 138, 219–20.
49 For an extended biographical analysis of her social history, and an illuminating comparison with Anna Barbauld's Dissenting work, see Anne Janowitz, *Women Romantic Poets: Anna Barbauld and Mary Robinson* (Tavistock: Northcote House, 2010).
50 Judith Pascoe, *Romantic Theatricality: Gender, Poetry, and Spectatorship* (Ithaca, NY: Cornell University Press, 1997), pp. 130–62.
51 Jon Mee, *Romantic Conversability* (Oxford University Press, 2011).
52 Robinson, "Present State," p. 220; Craciun, "Mary Robinson," p. 14.
53 Mee's account shows the long-lasting commitment to vigorous, flinty conversation among Romantic progressive circles well into the 1820s. His focal point is often Hazlitt, for whom no promise of "consensus" could mitigate the need for all-out argument on deeply felt points of contest. He attributes this against-the-odds will to serious conversation, in one of Britain's most repressive periods, to the ongoing vitality of a "Republic of Letters," which my own account (more in agreement with Duncan and Keen) sees rather as having already lost its normative authority after the 1790s. In my view, it's precisely the 1790s decline of the "Republic of Letters," as a legitimate institutional and social grounding of knowledge-exchange, that helps make the "public sphere" of combustible argument even more remarkable in the period 1800–20. That sphere is no longer contained within the polite limits of the eighteenth-century Republic of Letters, and so becomes rambunctiously – if only for a short period – "open to all," including the plebeian radical voices of Cobbett, Wade, and Carlile.
54 See Philip Connell, *Romanticism, Economics, and the Question of "Culture"* (New York: Oxford University Press, 2001), pp. 188–90. For the relevant

context of this point, see Jeffrey Cox, *Poetry and Politics in the Cockney School: Keats, Shelley, Hunt, and their Circle* (Cambridge University Press, 1998).
55 On Williams's concept of the "cultural formation," see *Marxism and Literature* (New York: Oxford University Press, 1977), pp. 117–27.
56 Hazlitt, "On the Tendency of Sects" (1815), in *Selected Writings of William Hazlitt*, ed. Duncan Wu (London: Pickering & Chatto, 1998), II: 48–49.
57 Connell, *Romanticism*, p. 229 n. 131.
58 Hazlitt, "On Criticism" (1822), in *Selected Writings of William Hazlitt*, ed. Wu, VI: 193.
59 Ibid., p. 192.
60 Marilyn Butler, "Culture's Medium: The Role of the Reviews," in *The Cambridge Companion to British Romanticism*, ed. Stuart Curran (Cambridge University Press, 1993), pp. 120–47.
61 William Morris, "The Lesser Arts" (1877), in *News from Nowhere and Other Writings*, ed. Clive Wilmer (Baltimore: Penguin, 1993), pp. 231–54. In this lecture Morris remarks, "it is only in latter times, and under the most intricate conditions of life, that [the fine arts and decorative or practical arts] have fallen apart from one another; and I hold that, when they are so parted, it is ill for the Arts altogether; the lesser ones become trivial, mechanical, unintelligent, incapable of resisting the changes pressed upon them" (p. 233).
62 The only report of that lecture we have comes from Crabb Robinson, the diarist and frequent lecture-goer who made little of Landseer's philosophical engraver-aesthetics, but noted instead the speaker's rhetoric, an "indulgence in sarcasms and in emphatic diction. He pronounces his words in *italics*." Henry Crabb Robinson, *Diaries, Reminiscences, and Correspondence*, ed. Thomas Sadler, 3 vols. (London: Macmillan, 1869), I: 505–6.
63 William Blake, "Public Address," in *The Complete Poetry and Prose of William Blake*, ed. David Erdman (New York: Random House, 1965), p. 572.
64 Hazlitt, *Selected Writings*, ed. Wu, II: 46–47.
65 Connell, *Romanticism*, p. 229.
66 Quoted in Andrew Hemingway, *Landscape Imagery and Urban Culture in Early Nineteenth-Century Britain* (Cambridge University Press, 1992), p. 119.
67 "R. H.," "Fine Arts," *Examiner* 9 (May 7, 1815): 301.
68 Quoted in Hemingway, *Landscape Imagery*, p. 119.
69 Barrell, *Political Theory of Painting*, pp. 314–41. By breaking ranks with the "republic of taste" elaborated through the eighteenth century, Barrell argues, Hazlitt's posture in the 1816 "Fine Arts" encyclopedia article (and many others that share its view) signals a decisive turn toward a kind of liberalism that assigns the domain of art to one realm of human cultural production, but commerce, economics, and politics to others (*Political Theory of Painting*, pp. 336–37).
70 Hazlitt, "Why the Arts are not Progressive? – A Fragment," in *Selected Writings of William Hazlitt*, II: 158; John Whale, *Imagination Under Pressure, 1789–1832: Aesthetics, Politics and Utility* (Cambridge University Press, 2000), p. 129.

71 Francis Haskell, *The Ephemeral Museum: Old Master Paintings and the Rise of the Art Exhibition* (New Haven: Yale University Press, 2000), p. 63.
72 Hazlitt, *Life of Napoleon Bonaparte* (1830), in *The Complete Works of William Hazlitt*, ed. P. P. Howe (London: Dent, 1930–34), XIII: 212.
73 Hazlitt, "On the Catalogue Raisonné of the British Institution," in *Selected Writings of William Hazlitt*, ed. Wu, II: 144–45.
74 Hazlitt, "On the Catalogue Raisonné," in *Selected Writings of William Hazlitt*, II: 141.
75 See John Kinnaird, *William Hazlitt, Critic of Power* (New York: Columbia University Press, 1978), p. 126.
76 Peter Funnel, "William Hazlitt, Prince Hoare, and the Institutionalization of the British Art World," in *Towards a Modern Art World*, ed. Brian Allen (New Haven: Yale University Press, 1995), pp. 153–54.
77 Barrell, *Theory of Painting*, pp. 336–37.
78 Hazlitt, *Selected Writings*, ed. Wu, II: 143.
79 In the following pages I have benefited especially from the work of John Whale, "The Making of a City of Culture: William Roscoe's Liverpool," *Eighteenth-Century Life* 29.2 (2005): 91–107, and Arline Wilson, *William Roscoe: Commerce and Culture* (Liverpool University Press, 2008).
80 William Roscoe, *An Address, Delivered Before the Proprietors of the Botanic Garden in Liverpool* (Liverpool: printed by J. M'Creery, 1802), p. 29. As Wilson notes, Roscoe had read his own botany papers to the Linnean Society from 1804 to 1810, where he got to know Joseph Banks and proved himself no stranger to English sciences well after the Priestley debacle in 1791 (Wilson, *William Roscoe*, p. 86). On the arts side of Roscoe's work, however, Wilson's account is oddly skewed. Roscoe, she suggests, "questioned the idea of 'art for art's sake' and attempted to justify his thesis that literature and art could and should not be dissociated from commerce" (p. 92). Since no such notion as "art for art's sake" existed in this era, Wilson must mean the opposite – art for aristocracy's sake – that Roscoe was at pains to dispute.
81 Roscoe, *Botanic Garden*, p. 30.
82 William Roscoe, *On the Origin and Vicissitudes of Literature, Science, and Art and Their Influences on the Present State of Society* (London: Cadell and Davies, 1817), p. 21.
83 Roscoe, *Origin and Vicissitudes*, p. 26.
84 *Ode on the Institution of a Society in Liverpool: For the Encouragement of Designing, Drawing, Painting, Etc.* (Liverpool: printed for William Roscoe, 1774).
85 John Whale, "The Making of a City of Culture," pp. 102–3.
86 Review of William Roscoe, *Journal of Science and the Arts* 5 (1818): 21–23.
87 Review of William Roscoe, *Journal of Science and the Arts* 5 (1818): 22.
88 [Leigh Hunt], "THE REFORMERS; or Wrongs of Intellect – A Fragment of a Political Dialogue," *The Reflector* 1 (1811): 17–28 at 28.
89 Hunt, "Reformers," 1: 22.
90 Hunt, "Reformers," 1: 24.

91 Hunt, "Reformers," 1: 28.
92 Hunt, "Reformers," 1: 26.
93 Hunt, "Reformers," 1: 27.
94 Hunt, "Reformers," 1: 27.
95 Hunt, "Reformers," 1: 27–28. Sir Lucas Pepys, an Oxford-educated physician, was Hester Piozzi's personal doctor; Neville Maskelyne was still the Royal Astronomer in 1810. St. Stephen's Chapel had been the House of Commons' meeting place since the 1540s, and had long since become a general metaphor for the Commons in public usage. Hunt may have also in mind its powerful association with the Commons' declaration, on March 2, 1629, of the "assertion of the privilege of free speech and of the absolute control of Parliament over its own proceedings." See *Fortnightly Review* 108 (1920): 754.
96 Hunt, "Reformers," 1: 28.
97 Hazlitt, "What Is the People?" (1819), in *Complete Works of William Hazlitt*, ed. Howe, VII: 269.
98 Kevin Gilmartin, "Hazlitt's Visionary London," in *Repossessing the Romantic Past*, ed. Paul Hamilton and Heather Glen (Cambridge University Press, 2007), pp 40–62.
99 See E. P. Thompson, *The Making of the English Working Class* (New York: Vintage, 1963), pp. 745–49.
100 Shelley, *A Philosophical View of Reform* (1819), in *Shelley's Prose*, ed. David Lee Clark (New York: Fourth Estate, 1988), pp. 229–60.
101 James Chandler, *England in 1819* (University of Chicago Press, 1998), p. 516.
102 Shelley, *Philosophical View*, p. 236.
103 Shelley, *Shelley's Prose*, pp. 253, 247 ("View"); pp. 295, 279 ("Defence").
104 Shelley, *Shelley's Prose*, p. 259.

### Epilogue: transatlantic crossings

1 Letter signed "A. D." to *The Literary Chronicle for the Year 1823* (London: Davidson, 1823), pp. 314–15.
2 James Jennings, *A Lecture on the History and Utility of Literary Institutions* (London: Sherwood, Jones, 1823). See also "Jennings' Lectures on Literary Institutions," *British Critic* 20 (1823): 424.
3 Daniel Brewster, letter to Henry Brougham, March 10, 1828, quoted in Jack Morrell and Arnold Thackray, *Gentlemen of Science: Early Years of the British Association for the Advancement of Science* (Oxford: Clarendon Press, 1981), p. 41.
4 [Peter George Patmore], *Letters on England by Victoire, Count de Saligny*, 2 vols. (London: Henry Colburn, 1823), 1: 228–32.
5 Negley Harte, *The University of London, 1836–1986* (London: Athlone Press, 1986); see also F. M. L. Thompson, ed., *The University of London and the World of Learning, 1836–1986* (London: Hambledon Press, 1986), pp. ix–xvii.

6 Coleridge, *Church and State*, p. 69. As Coleridge would have known well, the poet and *New Monthly Magazine* editor Thomas Campbell both lectured on poetry at the Royal Institution in 1812 and became the most widely quoted proponent of a new London University in 1825.
7 For this ranking, see Morrell and Thackray, *Gentlemen of Science*, pp. 26–29.
8 As Morrell and Thackray comment, the BAAS cultivated a "nonsectarian, inclusive, and non-political public image" for British science, but no Dissenters, evangelicals, Utilitarians, Methodists, or "die-hard Tories" were part of their number: "the idea of science that they urged was that of the moderate, latitudinarian, Anglican centre." *Gentlemen of Science*, p. 26.
9 [Thomas Carlyle], "Signs of the Times," *Edinburgh Review* 49 (1829): 438–59.
10 See my *The Making of English Reading Audiences, 1790–1832* (Madison: University of Wisconsin Press, 1987), p. 73. Some of Bourdieu's less perceptive readings by literary critics see only diagrams of reproduction as relentless as Carlyle's mechanical fields; for an acute assessment of the earlier American literary reception of Bourdieu along these lines, see John Guillory, "Bourdieu's Refusal," in *Pierre Bourdieu: Fieldwork in Culture*, ed. Nicholas Brown and Imre Szeman (Lanham, MD: Rowman & Littlefield, 2000), pp. 19–42.
11 Richard Sher, "Transatlantic Books and Literary Culture," in *Transatlantic Literary Studies, 1660–1830*, ed. Eve Tavor Bannet and Susan Manning (Cambridge University Press, 2012), p. 10.
12 George Ellis, *Memoir of Sir Benjamin Thompson, Count Rumford* (Boston: American Academy of Arts and Sciences, 1871), p. 650. In an interesting if neglected history of urban universities, W. H. G. Armytage similarly proposed that Rumford forged "the architectural embodiment of American ideas on higher education" in the Royal Institution. W. H. G. Armytage, *Civic Universities: Aspects of a British Tradition* (London: Ernest Benn, 1955), pp. 162–65. Rumford had, of course, learned his own skills at educational engineering in the hothouse politics of Germany in the 1790s, though this was far from the reformed University of Berlin that usually appears decisive for American educational ancestry.
13 See for the manifesto that helped to create many more lyceums across the US, Josiah Holbrook, *American Lyceum* (Boston: Perkins & Marvin, 1829).
14 Carl Bode, *The American Lyceum: Town Meeting of the Mind* (Carbondale: Southern Illinois University Press, 1968), p. 24.
15 Donald M. Scott, "The Popular Lecture and the Creation of a Public in Mid-Nineteenth-Century America," *Journal of American History* 66 (1980): 791–809 at 808. See for an instance, "Lyceums and Lecturing in America," *All the Year Round* n.s. 5 (1871): 317–21.
16 Angela Ray, *The Lyceum and Public Culture in the Nineteenth-Century United States* (East Lansing: Michigan State University Press, 2005), pp. 29 and 45. As slavery and abolition became unavoidable topics in these arenas, Ray shows briefly the rise of African-American lyceums in northern cities, *The Lyceum*, pp. 30–32.

17 Bode, *American Lyceum*, p. 9.
18 Heather Ewing, *The Lost World of James Smithson: Science, Revolution, and the Birth of the Smithsonian Institution* (New York: Bloomsbury, 2007), pp. 202–4, 260–65.
19 Joseph Henry, "Programme of the Organization of the Smithsonian Institution" (1847), in *Scientific Writings of Joseph Henry* (Washington, DC: Smithsonian Institution, 1886), pp. 263–82 at p. 272.
20 Henry, "Programme," p. 272.
21 Laurence Veysey, "The Plural Organized Worlds of the Humanities," in *The Organization of Knowledge in Modern America, 1860–1920*, ed. Alexandra Oleson and John Voss (Baltimore: Johns Hopkins University Press, 1979), p. 67.

# Bibliography

## PRIMARY SOURCES

"An Account of the London Institution." *Monthly Magazine* 23 (1807): 309–14.
Ackermann, Rudolph, ed. *The Microcosm of London*. 3 vols. London: Ackermann, 1809.
Ames, Joseph. *Typographical Antiquities, or The History of Printing in England, Scotland, and Ireland*. 1749. 3rd edn. Ed. Thomas Frognall Dibdin. 4 vols. London: William Miller, 1810–19.
*Annals of the Fine Arts* (1816–20).
*The Anti-Jacobin Review* (1798–1821).
*The Artist* (1807, 1809).
Astle, Thomas. *The Origins and Progress of Writing*. 1783. 2nd edn. London: J. White, 1803.
Baker, James. *Life of Thomas Bernard, Baronet*. London: John Murray, 1819.
Barbauld, Anna Laetitia. *Eighteen Hundred and Eleven*. London: J. Johnson, 1812.
"An Essay on the Origin and History of Novel Writing." In *The British Novelists*. Ed. Anna Barbauld. 50 vols. London: F. C. & J. Rivington, 1810. 1: 3–62.
Baxter, Richard. *Catholick Theologie: Plain, Pure, Peaceable*. London: Nevill Simmons, 1677.
Bayle, Pierre. *The Dictionary Historical and Critical of Mr. Peter Bayle*. 1684. Trans. Pierre Des Maizeaux. London, 1735.
Beiser, Frederick, ed. *The Early Political Writings of the German Romantics*. Cambridge University Press, 1996.
Bence Jones, Henry. *The Royal Institution: Its Founder and Its First Professors*. London: Longmans, 1871.
Bentham, Jeremy. *Chrestomathia: Being a Collection of Papers Explanatory of the Design of an Institution Proposed to be Set on Foot Under the Name of the Chrestomathic Day School*. London: Payne and Foss, 1816.
*The Works of Jeremy Bentham*. Ed. John Bowring. 9 vols. Edinburgh: William Tait, 1839.
Bernard, Thomas. *The Barrington School*. London: W. Bulmer, 1812.
*Of the Education of the Poor*. 1809. London: W. Bulmer, 1839.
"Twelve True Old Golden Rules." *Reports of the Bettering Society* 2 (1800): 282–85.

[Bernard, Thomas, ed.] *The Reports of the Society for Bettering the Condition and Increasing the Comforts of the Poor.* London: W. Bulmer, 1797–99. Vols. I–II.
"Bibliographia." In *Encyclopaedia Britannica.* 3rd edn. Edinburgh, 1797.
Blake, William. *The Complete Poetry and Prose of William Blake.* Ed. David Erdman. New York: Random House, 1965.
Boaden, James, ed. *Memoirs of Mrs. Inchbald.* 2 vols. London: Richard Bentley, 1833.
Brande, William. *An Introductory Address Delivered in the Amphitheater of the London Institution.* London: printed by Richard and Arthur Taylor, 1819.
*The British Critic* (1792–1843).
[Brougham, Henry.] "Bakerian Lecture on Light and Colors." *Edinburgh Review* 1 (1803): 450–56.
Brown, James Duff. *A Manual of Practical Bibliography.* London: Routledge, 1906.
Brydges, Samuel Egerton. *The British Bibliographer.* 2 vols. London: R. Triphook, 1812.
   *Censura Literaria.* 10 vols. London: Longmans, 1805–9.
Bulloch, John Malcolm. *The Art of Extra-Illustration.* London: Treherne, 1903.
Burke, Edmund. *Reflections on the Revolution in France.* 1790. Ed. Conor Cruise O'Brien. Harmondsworth: Penguin, 1969.
Burney, Charles, ed. *A Catalogue of the Library of the Royal Institution of Great Britain.* 2nd edn. London: Payne and Foss, 1821.
Burns, J. B. B., ed. *An Account of the Religious and Literary Life of Adam Clarke.* 2 vols. New York: Mason and Lane, 1837.
Byron, George Gordon, Lord. *Byron's Letters and Journals.* Vol. 11: *"Famous in My Time": 1810–12.* Ed. Leslie Marchand. Cambridge, MA: Harvard University Press, 1973.
   *The Works of Lord Byron.* Ed. Thomas Moore. 18 vols. London: John Murray, 1836.
*The Cambridge History of English and American Literature.* Vol. XII: *The Nineteenth Century.* Ed. Adolphus Ward. Cambridge University Press, 1915.
Carlile, Richard. *An Address to Men of Science.* London: R. Carlile, 1821.
[Carlyle, Thomas.] "Signs of the Times," *Edinburgh Review* 49 (1829): 438–59.
   *On Heroes, Hero-Worship and the Heroic in History.* 1841. New York: AMS Press, 1969.
*A Catalogue of the Library of the London Institution.* London, 1835.
[Christie, Thomas.] "To the Public." *Analytical Review* 1 (1788): i–iv.
Clarke, Adam. *A Bibliographical Dictionary: In All Departments of Literature.* 6 vols. London: J. Baynes, 1802–6.
   *The Bibliographical Miscellany.* 2 vols. London: J. Baynes, 1806.
   *The Life and Labours of Adam Clarke, to which is added an Historical Sketch of the controversy concerning the Sonship of Christ.* London: John Stephens, 1834.
   *The New Testament of Our Lord and Saviour Jesus Christ.* London: A. Paul, 1825.
Cockburn, Henry. *Life of Lord Jeffrey.* Edinburgh: A. & C. Black, 1852.

Coleridge, Samuel Taylor. *The Collected Letters of Samuel Taylor Coleridge*. Ed. Earl Leslie Griggs. 6 vols. Oxford: Clarendon Press, 1956.
*The Collected Works of Samuel Taylor Coleridge*. Gen. ed. Kathleen Coburn. Princeton University Press, 1969–.
*Samuel Taylor Coleridge: The Complete Poems*. Ed. William Keach. Harmondsworth: Penguin, 1997.
*The Critical Review* (1756–1817).
Davy, Humphry. *The Collected Works of Humphry Davy*. Ed. John Davy. 9 vols. London: Smith, Elder, 1839.
Defoe, Daniel. *An Essay upon Projects*. London: Henry Cockerill, 1697.
De Quincey, Thomas. *The Collected Writings of Thomas De Quincey*. Ed. David Masson. 15 vols. London: A. & C. Black, 1897.
Dibdin, Thomas Frognall. *The Bibliographical Decameron*. 3 vols. London, 1817.
*The Bibliomania; or Book-Madness*. London: Longman, 1809.
*The Bibliomania: or Book-Madness: A Bibliographical Romance in Six Parts: a New and Improved Edition*. 1811. London: Chatto & Windus, 1876.
*Reminiscences of a Literary Life*. 2 vols. London: J. Major, 1836.
*Director: A Weekly Literary Journal* (1807).
D'Israeli, Isaac. *Curiosities of Literature: Consisting of Anecdotes, Characters, Sketches, and Observations, Literary, Critical, and Historical*. 3 vols. London: John Murray, 1817.
Douce, Francis. *Illustrations of Shakespeare, and of Ancient Manners*. London: Longman, 1807.
*Eclectic Review* (1805–68).
*Edinburgh Review* (1802–1929).
Ellis, George E. *Memoir of Sir Benjamin Thompson, Count Rumford*. Boston: American Academy of Arts and Sciences, 1871.
Everett, James. *Adam Clarke Portrayed*. 2 vols. London: Hamilton, Adams, 1844.
The *Examiner* (1808–86).
Farington, Joseph. *The Diary of Joseph Farington*. 16 vols. Ed. Kathryn Cave. New Haven: Yale University Press, 1978–.
Ferguson, Adam. *An Essay on the History of Civil Society*. 1767. 7th edn. London: Cadell and Davies, 1814.
Ferriar, John. *Illustrations of Sterne*. London: Cadell and Davies, 1798.
Flint, Robert. *Philosophy as Scienta Scientarum: A History of Classifications of the Sciences*. Edinburgh: William Blackwood, 1904.
Fuseli, Henry. "On the Present State of the Art." 1825. In *Lectures on Painting by the Royal Academicians: James Barry, John Opie, Henry Fuseli*. Ed. Ralph Wornum. London: Henry G. Bohn, 1848.
*The General Magazine of Arts and Sciences, Philosophical, Philological, Mathematical, and Mechanical* (1755).
Godwin, William. *The Enquirer: Reflections on Education, Manners, and Literature*. London: J. Robinson, 1797.
*An Enquiry concerning Political Justice*. 1793. Ed. Isaac Kramnick. London, 1798. Rpt. Baltimore: Penguin, 1985.

"Of History and Romance." 1797. Appendix D in *Things as They Are, or The Adventures of Caleb Williams*. Ed. Maurice Hindle. Baltimore: Penguin, 1988. Pp. 359–73.
*History of the Commonwealth of England*. London, 1824–28.
Goethe, Wolfgang. *Theory of Colours [Farbenlehre]*. 1810. Trans. Charles Locke Eastlake. London: John Murray, 1840.
Goldsmith, Oliver. *A Citizen of the World*. 1760. In *The Collected Works of Oliver Goldsmith*. 5 vols. Ed. Arthur Friedman. Oxford: Clarendon Press, 1966.
Good, John Mason. *The Book of Nature*. 3 vols. London: Longman, 1826.
Good, John Mason, trans. *Lucretius on the Nature of Things*. 2 vols. London: Longman, 1805.
Gregory, Olinthus. *Of the Life, Writings, and Character, Literary, Professional, and Religious, of the Late John Mason Good, M. D.* London: Henry Fisher, 1828.
Hamerton, Philip Gilbert. "Amateurship: A Conversation." *Macmillan's Magazine* 14 (1866): 426–32.
Hazlitt, William. *The Complete Works of William Hazlitt*. Ed. P. P. Howe. 21 vols. London: J. M. Dent, 1930–34.
*The Selected Writings of William Hazlitt*. Ed. Duncan Wu. 9 vols. London: Pickering & Chatto, 1998.
Henry, Joseph. "Programme of the Organization of the Smithsonian Institution." 1847. In *Scientific Writings of Joseph Henry*. Washington, DC: Smithsonian Institution, 1886. Pp. 263–82.
Higgins, Sophia Elizabeth. *The Bernards of Abington and Nether Winchenden: A Family History*. 4 vols. London: Longmans, 1904.
Hoare, Prince. *Inquiry into the Requisite Cultivation and the Present State of the Arts of Design in England*. London: Richard Phillips, 1806.
[Holbrook, Josiah.] *American Lyceum, or Society for the Improvement of Schools*. Boston: Perkins & Marvin, 1829.
Holyoake, George Jacob. *Self-Help A Hundred Years Ago*. 3rd edn. London: Swan Sonnenschein, 1891.
Hone, William. *Ancient Mysteries Described; especially the English Miracle Plays*. London: W. Hone, 1823
Hooke, Robert. "A General Scheme, or Idea of the Present State of the Present State of Natural Philosophy" (1666). In *Posthumous Works of Robert Hooke*. 1705. Ed. Robert Waller. New York: Frank Cass, 1971.
Horne, Thomas Hartwell. *An Introduction to the Study of Bibliography*. 2 vols. London: Cadell & Davies, 1814.
Horner, Francis. *Memoirs and Correspondence of Sir Francis Horner, M.P.* Ed. Leonard Horner. 2 vols. London: John Murray, 1843.
Hume, David. *An Enquiry Concerning Human Understanding*. 1751. Ed. Eric Steinberg. Indianapolis: Hackett, 1977.
*Essays Moral, Political, and Literary*. 1777. Ed. Eugene Miller. Indianapolis: Liberty Fund, 1985.
[Hunt, Leigh.] "THE REFORMERS: or Wrongs of Intellect – A Fragment of a Political Dialogue," *The Reflector* 1 (1811): 17–28.

Huxley, Thomas. *Science and Culture, and Other Essays*. London: Macmillan, 1882.
Jeffrey, Francis. *Contributions to the Edinburgh Review*. 4 vols. London: Longman, 1844.
Jennings, James. *A Lecture on the History and Utility of Literary Institutions*. London: Sherwood, Jones, 1823.
*Journal of Science and the Arts* (1816–19).
*La Belle Assemblée* (1806–37).
Lamb, Charles. *The Letters of Charles Lamb*. Ed. E. V. Lucas. 3 vols. London: J. M. Dent, 1935.
Landseer, John. *Lectures on the Art of Engraving: Delivered at the Royal Institution of Great Britain*. London: Longman, 1807.
 ed. *The Review of Publications of Art*. London: Samuel Tipper, 1808.
Lawrence, William. *Lectures on Physiology, Zoology, and the Natural History of Man*. 1816. London: Richard Carlile, 1822.
Leibniz, Gottfried Wilhelm. *Leibniz: Selections*. Ed. Philip Wiener. New York: Scribners, 1951.
 *New Essays Concerning the Human Understanding*. 1704. Trans. Alfred Gideon Langley. Chicago: Open Court Press, 1916.
*The Life and Labours of Adam Clarke*. London: John Stephens, 1834.
[Lyell, Charles.] "Scientific Institutions." *Quarterly Review* 34 (1826): 153–79.
Malthus, Thomas. *An Essay on the Principle of Population*. London: Joseph Johnson, 1798.
Mathias, Thomas James. *The Pursuits of Literature*. 1794. Seventh edn. London: T. Becket, 1798.
"Memoirs of Sydney Smith." *Quarterly Review* 97 (1855): 106–42.
Michaelis, Adolf. *Ancient Marbles in Great Britain*. Trans. C. A. M. Fennell. Cambridge University Press, 1882.
Mill, John Stuart. *On Bentham and Coleridge*. 1838–40. Ed. F. R. Leavis. New York: Harper, 1962.
Millar, John. *A Historical View of the English Government*. 4 vols. London: J. Mawning, 1803.
 *The Origin of the Distinction of Ranks: An Inquiry into the Circumstances which Give Rise to the Influence and Authority in the Different Members of Society*. 1771. 4th edn. Edinburgh: William Blackwood, 1806.
Miller, Frederick. *St. Pancras, Past and Present*. London: Heywood, 1874.
*Monthly Magazine* (1796–1843).
*Monthly Review* (1749–1845).
Morris, William. "The Lesser Arts." 1877. In *News from Nowhere and Other Writings*. Ed. Clive Wilmer. Baltimore: Penguin, 1993. Pp. 231–54.
Moulton, C. W. *Queries: Devoted to Literature, Art, Science, Education*. Buffalo, NY: C. L. Sherill, 1885.
*New Monthly Magazine* (1814–44).
"Nightingale's *Portraiture of Methodism*." *Anti-Jacobin Review* 33 (1809): 236–47.
Northcote, James. "Decipit Exemplar." *Artist* 1.9 (May 9, 1807): 3, 5.

Opie, John. *Lectures on Painting, Delivered at the Royal Academy by the Late John Opie*. Ed. Amelie Opie. London: Longman, 1809.
Paris, J. A. *The Life of Humphry Davy*. London: Henry Coburn, 1831.
[Patmore, Peter George]. *Letters on England by Victoire, Count de Saligny*. 2 vols. London: Henry Colburn, 1823.
*The Picture of London, for 1802*. London: R. Phillips, 1803.
Priestley, Joseph. *Disquisitions relating to Matter and Spirit*. London: J. Johnson, 1777.
    *Experiments and Observations on the Different Kinds of Air*. 1774. 3rd edn. London: J. Johnson, 1781.
    *The History and Present State of Electricity*. London: J. Johnson, 1767.
*Prospectus of the Royal Institution of Great Britain, The*. London: Royal Institution, 1800.
*Putnam's Magazine* (1853–1910).
*The Quarterly Review* (1809–).
*The Reflector* (1810–11).
Reynolds, Joshua. *Discourses on Art*. 1790. Ed. Robert Wark. 3rd edn. New Haven: Yale University Press, 1997.
    *Seven Discourses Delivered in the Royal Academy by the President*. London: T. Cadell, 1778.
Richardson, Jonathan. *A Discourse on the Dignity, Certainty, Pleasure, and Advantage of the Science of a Connoisseur*. London: W. Churchill, 1719.
Robinson, Henry Crabb. *Diaries, Reminiscences, and Correspondence*. Ed. Thomas Sadler. 3 vols. London: Macmillan, 1869.
Robinson, Mary. *Memoirs of the Late Mrs. Robinson*. Philadelphia: T. and W. Bradford, 1802.
R[obinson], M[ary]. "Present State of the Manners, Society &c &c of the Metropolis of England." *Monthly Magazine* 10 (1800): 35–38, 138–40, 218–22, 305–6.
Roscoe, Henry. *The Life of William Roscoe, by His Son*. 2 vols. London: Cadell and Blackwood, 1833.
Roscoe, William. *An Address, Delivered Before the Proprietors of the Botanic Garden in Liverpool*. Liverpool: printed by J. M'Creery, 1802.
    *On the Origin and Vicissitudes of Literature, Science and Art, and Their Influence on the Present State of Society*. Liverpool: Cadell and Davies, 1817.
Rumford, Count Benjamin. *Collected Works of Count Rumford*. Ed. Sanborn C. Brown. 5 vols. Cambridge, MA: Belknap Press of Harvard University, 1970.
Schelling, Friedrich. *Idealism and the Endgame of Theory*. Trans. and ed. Thomas Pfau. Albany: State University of New York Press, 1994.
    *On University Studies*. 1803. Trans. E. S. Morgan. Ed. Norbert Guterman. Athens, OH: Ohio University Press, 1966.
Seeley, John Robert. "Elementary Principles in Art." *Macmillan's Magazine* 16 (1867): 1–12.
Shelley, Percy Bysshe. *Shelley's Prose, or A Trumpet of a Prophecy*. 1954. Ed. David Lee Clark. New York: Fourth Estate, 1988.

Smith, Adam. *The Wealth of Nations*. 1776. Ed. R. A. Seligman. 2 vols. New York: Dutton, 1964.
Smith, Thomas. *Recollections of the British Institution*. London: Simpkin & Marshall, 1860.
South, Robert. "All Contingencies under the Direction of God's Providence." 1684. In *Sermons Preached upon Several Occasions*. Philadelphia: Sorin & Ball, 1844. 1: 121–36.
Southey, Robert. *Letters from England*. 1807. 2nd edn. London: Longman, 1808.
  *The Life and Correspondence of Robert Southey*. Ed. Charles Cuthbert Southey. New York: Harper & Bros., 1855.
Thelwall, John. "Essay on Animal Vitality." 1793. In *The Politics of Nature: William Wordsworth and Some Contemporaries*. Ed. Nicholas Roe. New York: Palgrave, 2000. Pp. 96–119.
Vico, Giambattista. *The New Science of Giambattista Vico*. 1745. Trans. Thomas Goddard Bergin and Max Harold Fisch. Ithaca, NY: Cornell University Press, 1968.
*Westminster Review* (1824–1914).
Whewell, William. *History of the Inductive Sciences: From the Earliest to the Present Times*. 3 vols. London: John W. Parker, 1837.
Wordsworth, William. *The Prose Works of William Wordsworth*. Ed. Alexander Grosart. 3 vols. London: Edward Moxon, 1876.

## SECONDARY SOURCES

Adams, John C. "Epideictic and Its Cultured Reception." In *Rhetorics of Display*. Ed. Lawrence J. Prelli. Columbia: University of South Carolina Press, 2006. Pp. 293–310.
Adorno, Theodor. "Culture and Administration." In *The Culture Industry*. Ed. J. M. Bernstein. New York: Routledge, 2001. Pp. 107–31.
Allard, James Robert. *Romanticism, Medicine, and the Poet's Body*. Aldershot: Ashgate, 2007.
Allen, Brian, ed. *Towards a Modern Art World*. New Haven: Yale University Press, 1995.
Anderson, Amanda, and Joseph Valente, eds. *Disciplinarity at the Fin de Siecle*. Princeton University Press, 2002.
Andrew, Donna. *Philanthropy and Police: London Charity in the Eighteenth Century*. Princeton University Press, 1989.
Armytage, W. H. G. *Civic Universities: Aspects of a British Tradition*. London: Benn, 1955.
Bahar, Saba. "Jane Marcet and the Limits to Public Science." *British Journal for the History of Science* 34 (2001): 29–49.
Bahmueller, Charles. *The National Charity Company: Jeremy Bentham's Silent Revolution*. Berkeley: University of California Press, 1981.
Balsamo, Luigi. *Bibliography: History of a Tradition*. Trans. William A. Pettas. Berkeley: Bernard Rosenthal, 1990.

Barrell, John. *The Birth of Pandora and the Division of Knowledge*. Basingstoke: Macmillan, 1992.
  *The Political Theory of Painting from Reynolds to Hazlitt: The "Body of the Public."* New Haven: Yale University Press, 1986.
Becker, Howard. *Art Worlds*. Berkeley: University of California Press, 1982.
Bender, John. "Novel Knowledge: Judgment, Experience, Experiment." In *This Is Enlightenment*. Ed. Clifford Siskin and William Warner. University of Chicago Press, 2010. Pp. 284–300.
Berman, Morris. *Social Change and Scientific Organization: The Royal Institution 1799–1844*. Ithaca, NY: Cornell University Press, 1978.
Bermingham, Ann. "Urbanity and the Spectacle of Art." In *Romantic Metropolis*. Ed. James Chandler and Kevin Gilmartin. Cambridge University Press, 2005. Pp. 151–76.
Berry, Christopher. *The Social Theory of the Scottish Enlightenment*. Edinburgh University Press, 1997.
Birrell, Augustine. *William Hazlitt*. London: Macmillan, 1902.
Black, Joel. "Newtonian Mechanics and the Romantic Rebellion." In *Beyond the Two Cultures: Essays on Science, Technology, and Literature*. Ed. Joseph W. Slade and Judith Yaross Lee. Iowa City: Iowa University Press, 1990. Pp. 131–40.
Bloom, Harold. *Blake's Apocalypse: A Study in Poetic Argument*. Ithaca, NY: Cornell University Press, 1970.
Blum, Rudolf. *Bibliographia: An Inquiry into its Definition and Designations*. 1969. Trans. Mathilde V. Rovelstad. Folkestone: Dawson House, 1980.
Bode, Carl. *The American Lyceum: Town Meeting of the Mind*. Carbondale: Southern Illinois University Press, 1968.
Boehm, Alan D. "The 1798 *Lyrical Ballads* and the Poetics of Late Eighteenth-Century Book Production." *ELH* 63 (1996): 453–87.
Bolter, Jay Robert, and Richard Grusin. *Remediation: Understanding New Media*. Cambridge, MA: MIT Press, 2000.
Bourdieu, Pierre. *The Field of Cultural Production*. Ed. Randall Johnson. New York: Columbia University Press, 1993.
  *Language and Symbolic Power*. Trans. Gino Raymond and Matthew Adamson. Ed. John B. Thompson. Cambridge, MA: Harvard University Press, 1991.
  "Legitimation and Structured Interests in Weber's Sociology of Religion." Trans. Chris Turner. In *Max Weber, Rationality and Modernity*. Ed. Scott Lash and Sam Whimster. London: Allen & Unwin, 1987. Pp. 119–36.
  *The Rules of Art: Genesis and Structure of the Literary Field*. Trans. Susan Emanuel. Stanford University Press, 1996.
Brannigan, Augustine. *The Social Basis of Scientific Discoveries*. Cambridge University Press, 1981.
Brewer, John. *The American Leonardo: A Tale of Obsession, Art and Money*. New York: Oxford University Press, 2009.
  *The Pleasures of the Imagination*. University of Chicago Press, 1997.

Brockliss, Laurence. *Calvet's Web: Enlightenment and the Republic of Letters in Eighteenth-Century France*. New York: Oxford University Press, 2002.
"The European University in the Age of Revolution, 1789–1850." In *The History of the University of Oxford*. Vol. 6: *Nineteenth-Century Oxford*. Ed. M. G. Brock and Mark C. Curthoys. New York: Oxford University Press, 2002. 1: 77–133.
Brown, Sanborn. *Benjamin Thompson, Count Rumford*. Cambridge, MA: MIT Press, 1979.
Brylowe, Thora. "Romantic Art and Letters: British Print, Paint, Engraving 1770–1830." Ph.D. dissertation, Department of English, Carnegie Mellon University, 2008.
"Sculpsit: John Landseer's Lectures and Engraving as Mediation." Conference Paper, North American Society for the Study of Romanticism, Vancouver, BC (August 2010).
Butler, Marilyn. "Culture's Medium: The Role of the Review." In *The Cambridge Companion to British Romanticism*. Ed. Stuart Curran. Cambridge University Press, 1993. Pp. 120–47.
*Romantics, Rebels, and Reactionaries*. New York: Oxford University Press, 1981.
"The Shelleys and Radical Science." In *Frankenstein, or the Modern Prometheus*. Ed. Marilyn Butler. New York: Oxford University Press, 1994. Pp. xv–xxi.
Calé, Luisa. "Dickens Extra-Illustrated: Heads and Scenes in Monthly Parts (The Case of *Nicholas Nickleby*)." *Yearbook of English Studies* 40 (2010): 8–32.
*Fuseli's Milton Gallery: "Turning Readers into Spectators."* Oxford: Clarendon Press, 2006.
Calé, Luisa, and Adriana Craciun. "The Disorder of Things." *Eighteenth-Century Studies* 45 (2011): 1–13.
Cardwell, D. S. L. *The Organization of Science in England*. London: Heinemann, 1972.
Carnall, Geoffrey. "The Surrey Institution and Its Successor." *Adult Education* 26 (1953): 197–208.
Certeau, Michel de. *The Practice of Everyday Life*. Berkeley: University of California Press, 1984.
Chaber, Lois. "'This Intricate Labyrinth': Order and Contingency in Eighteenth-Century Fictions." *Studies in Voltaire and the Eighteenth Century* 212 (1992): 185–209.
Chandler, James. *England in 1819: The Case of Romantic Historicism and the Politics of Literary Culture*. University of Chicago Press, 1998.
"The Politics of Sentiment: Notes toward a New Account." *Studies in Romanticism* 49 (2010): 553–75.
"Wordsworth's Great Ode: Romanticism and the Progress of Poetry." In *The Cambridge Companion to British Romantic Poetry*. Ed. James Chandler and Maureen McLane. Cambridge University Press, 2008. Pp. 136–54.
Chandler, James, and Kevin Gilmartin, eds. *Romantic Metropolis: The Urban Scene of British Culture, 1780–1840*. Cambridge University Press, 2005.

Chartier, Roger. *The Order of Books*. Trans. Lydia G. Cochrane. Stanford University Press, 1994.
Chernock, Arianne. *Men and the Making of Modern British Feminism*. Stanford University Press, 2010.
Christensen, Jerome. *Coleridge's Blessed Machine of Language*. Ithaca, NY: Cornell University Press, 1981.
Clark, William. *Academic Charisma and the Origins of the Research University*. University of Chicago Press, 2006.
Clemit, Pamela. *The Godwinian Novel: The Rational Fictions of Godwin, Brockden Brown, Mary Shelley*. Oxford: Clarendon Press, 1993.
Cochran, Terry. *Twilight of the Literary: Figures of Thought in the Age of Print*. Cambridge, MA: Harvard University Press, 2001.
Coleman, Dierdre. *Coleridge and "The Friend."* Oxford: Clarendon Press, 1988.
Colley, Linda. *Britons: Forging the Nation, 1707–1837*. New Haven: Yale University Press, 1993.
Connell, Philip. "Bibliomania: Book Collecting, Cultural Politics, and the Rise of Literary Heritage in Romantic Britain." *Representations* 71 (Summer 2000): 24–47.
  *Romanticism, Economics and the Question of "Culture."* New York: Oxford University Press, 2001.
Cordasco, Francesco. "Adam Clarke's *Bibliographical Dictionary* (1802–1806)." *Studies in Bibliography* 4 (1951–52): 189–92.
Cox, Jeffrey N. *Poetry and Politics in the Cockney School: Keats, Shelley, Hunt, and their Circle*. Cambridge University Press, 1998.
Craciun, Adriana. "Mary Robinson, the *Monthly Magazine*, and the Free Press." In *Romantic Periodicals and British Culture*. Ed. Kim Wheatley. New York: Frank Cass, 2003. Pp. 17–36.
Craciun, Adriana, intro. "Present State of the Manners, Society &c &c of the Metropolis of England." By Mary Robinson. *PMLA* 119.1 (2004): 103–17.
Craster, Herbert Henry Edmund. *History of the Bodleian Library, 1845–1945*. Oxford: Clarendon Press, 1952.
Csiszar, Alex. "Seriality and the Search for Order: Scientific Print and its Problems during the Late Nineteenth Century." *History of Science* 48 (2010): 399–434.
Cunningham, Andrew, and Nicholas Jardine, eds. *Romanticism and the Sciences*. Cambridge University Press, 1990.
Danisch, Robert. *Pragmatism, Democracy, and the Necessity of Rhetoric*. Columbia: University of South Carolina Press, 2007.
Daston, Lorraine. "The Ideal and Reality of the Republic of Letters in the Enlightenment." *Science in Context* 4 (1991): 367–85.
  "Science Studies and the History of Science." *Critical Inquiry* 35 (2009): 798–813.
De Bolla, Peter. "Mediation and the Division of Labor." In *This Is Enlightenment*. Ed. Clifford Siskin and William Warner. University of Chicago Press, 2010. Pp. 87–102.
Derrida, Jacques. *Psyche: Inventions of the Other*. Ed. Peggy Kamuf. Stanford University Press, 2007.

Desmond, Adrian. *The Politics of Evolution*. University of Chicago Press, 1989.
Duncan, Ian. *Scott's Shadow: The Novel in Romantic Edinburgh*. Princeton University Press, 2007.
Durkheim. Émile. *The Rules of Sociological Method*. Ed. Steven Lukes. Trans. W. D. Halls. New York: Free Press, 1982.
Eaves, Morris. *The Counter-Arts Conspiracy: Art and Industry in the Age of Blake*. Ithaca, NY: Cornell University Press, 1992.
Epstein, James. *Radical Expression: Political Language, Ritual, and Symbol in England, 1790–1850*. New York: Oxford University Press, 1994.
Ewing, Heather. *The Lost World of James Smithson: Science, Revolution, and the Birth of the Smithsonian Institution*. New York: Bloomsbury, 2007.
Fawcett, Trevor. *The Rise of English Provincial Art: Artists, Patrons, and Institutions outside London, 1800–1830*. Oxford: Clarendon Press, 1974.
Fawcett, Trevor, and Clive Phillpot, eds. *The Art Press: Two Centuries of Art Magazines*. London: Art Book Company, 1976.
Ferguson, Frances. "Coherence and Changes in the Unknown World." *New Literary History* 35 (2004): 303–19.
"Envy Rising." *ELH* 69 (2002): 889–905.
"The Sublime and Education: Educational Rationalization/Sublime Reason." *Praxis: An Online Journal of Romantic Circles*. www.rc.umd.edu/praxis/sublime_education/ferguson/ferguson.html.
Ferris, Ina. "Bibliographic Romance: Bibliophilia and the Book Object." In *Romantic Libraries*. Ed. Ina Ferris. *Praxis: An Online Journal of Romantic Circles*. Posted February 2004. www.rc.umd.edu/praxis/libraries/toc.html.
"Book Fancy: Bibliomania and the Literary Word." *Keats-Shelley Journal* 58 (2009): 33–52.
Figlio, Karl M. "The Metaphor of Organization: An Historiographic Perspective on the Bio-Medical Sciences of the Early Nineteenth Century." *History of Science* 14 (1976): 17–53.
FitzGibbon, Kate. *Who Owns the Past? Cultural Policy, Cultural Property, and the Law*. New Brunswick: Rutgers University Press, 2009.
Foucault, Michel. *The Birth of the Clinic*. 1963. London: Tavistock, 1973.
*Discipline and Punish: The Birth of the Prison*. Trans. Alan Sheridan. New York: Pantheon, 1977.
*The Order of Things: An Archaeology of the Human Sciences*. 1966. New York: Random House, 1970.
*Power/Knowledge: Selected Interviews and Other Writings, 1972–77*. Ed. Colin Gordon. New York: Pantheon, 1980.
Fowler, Jonathan. "Adventures of an 'Itinerant Institutor': The Life and Philanthropy of Thomas Bernard." Ph.D. dissertation, Department of History, University of Tennessee, 2003.
Fox, Christopher, et al., eds. *Inventing Human Science: Eighteenth-Century Domains*. Berkeley: University of California Press, 1995.
Franzel, Sean. *Fictions of Dialogue: The Media, Pedagogy, and Politics of the Romantic Lecture*. Evanston, IL: Northwestern University Press, 2013.

Frye, Northrop. *Fearful Symmetry: A Study of William Blake*. 1947. Princeton University Press, 1969.
Fulford, Tim, Debbie Lee, and Peter J. Kitson. *Literature, Science and Exploration in the Romantic Era: Bodies of Knowledge*. Cambridge University Press, 2004.
Fullerton, Peter. "Patronage and Pedagogy: The British Institution in the Early Nineteenth Century." *Art History* 5 (1982): 59–72.
Funnell, Peter. "The London Art World and Its Institutions." In *London – World City, 1800–1840*. Ed. Celina Fox. New Haven: Yale University Press, 1992. Pp. 155–66.
  "William Hazlitt, Prince Hoare, and the Institutionalization of the British Art World." In *Towards a Modern Art World*. Ed. Allen. Pp. 145–56.
Gascoigne, John. *Joseph Banks and the English Enlightenment: Useful Knowledge and Polite Culture*. Cambridge University Press, 1994.
Gillispie, Charles Coulson. *The Edge of Objectivity: An Essay in the History of Scientific Ideas*. Princeton University Press, 1960.
Gilmartin, Kevin. "Hazlitt's Visionary London." In *Repossessing the Romantic Past*. Ed. Heather Glen and Paul Hamilton. Cambridge University Press, 2006. Pp. 40–62.
  "Romanticism and Religious Modernity: From Natural Supernaturalism to Literary Sectarianism." In *The Cambridge History of English Romanticism*. Ed. James Chandler. Cambridge University Press, 2008. Pp. 621–47.
  *Writing Against Revolution: Literary Conservatism in Britain, 1790–1832*. Cambridge University Press, 2007.
Goldgar, Anne. *Impolite Letters: Conduct and Community in the Republic of Letters 1680–1750*. New Haven: Yale University Press, 1995.
Goldgar, Anne, and Robert I. Frost. "Introduction." In *Institutional Culture in Early Modern Society*. Ed. Anne Goldgar and Robert I. Frost. Leiden: Brill, 2004.
Golinski, Jan. "Humphry Davy's Sexual Chemistry." *Configurations* 7 (1999): 15–41.
  "Humphry Davy: The Experimental Self." *Eighteenth-Century Studies* 45 (2011): 15–28.
  *Science as Public Culture: Chemistry and Enlightenment in Britain, 1760–1820*. Cambridge University Press, 1992.
Goodman, Dena. *The Republic of Letters: A Cultural History of Enlightenment*. Ithaca, NY: Cornell University Press, 1993.
Gould, Stephen J. *Wonderful Life: The Burgess Shale and the Nature of History*. New York: Norton, 1989.
Grafton, Anthony. "Afterwords." In *Institutional Culture in Early Modern Society*. Ed. Goldgar and Frost. Pp. 348–49.
  "A Sketch Map of a Lost Continent: The Republic of Letters." *Republics of Letters: A Journal for the Study of Knowledge, Politics, and the Arts* 1 (May 2009). http://rofl.stanford.edu/node134.
  *Worlds Made by Words: Scholarship and Community in the Modern West*. Cambridge, MA: Harvard University Press, 2009.
Greenberg, Clement. "Towards a Newer Laokoon" (1940). In *Collected Essays and Criticism*. Ed. John O'Brian. University of Chicago Press, 1993.

Guillory, John. "Bourdieu's Refusal." In *Pierre Bourdieu: Fieldwork in Culture.* Ed. Nicholas Brown and Imre Szeman. Lanham, MD: Rowman & Littlefield, 2000. Pp. 19–42.

"Literary Critics as Intellectuals: Class Analysis and the Crisis of the Humanities." In *Rethinking Class: Literary Studies and Social Formation.* Ed. Wai-Chee Dimock and Michael Gilmore. New York: Columbia University Press, 1994. Pp. 107–28.

"Literary Study and the Modern System of the Disciplines." In *Disciplinarity at the Fin de Siecle.* Ed. Anderson and Valente. Pp. 19–43.

Gutjahr, Paul. "The Letter(s) of the Law: Four Centuries of Typography in the King James Bible." In *Illuminating Letters: Typography and Literary Interpretation.* Ed. Paul Gutjahr and Megan Benton. Amherst: University of Massachusetts Press, 2001. Pp. 17–43.

Gutjahr, Paul, and Megan Benton, eds. *Illuminating Letters: Typography and Literary Interpretation.* Amherst: University of Massachusetts Press, 2001.

Habermas, Jürgen. *The Structural Transformation of the Public Sphere: An Inquiry into a Category of Bourgeois Society.* 1962. Trans. Thomas Burger. Cambridge, MA: MIT Press, 1989.

Hallett, Mark. "The Business of Criticism." In *Art on the Line: The Royal Academy Exhibitions at Somerset House 1780–1836.* Ed. David Solkin. New Haven: Yale University Press, 2001. Pp. 65–75.

Hamilton, Paul. *Coleridge's Poetics.* Stanford University Press, 1983.

Harte, Negley. *The University of London, 1836–1986.* London: Athlone Press, 1986.

Haskell, Francis. *The Ephemeral Museum: Old Master Paintings and the Rise of the Art Exhibition.* New Haven: Yale University Press, 2000.

Hays, J. N. "The London Lecturing Empire 1800–1850." In *Metropolis and Province Science in British Culture 1780–1850.* Ed. Ian Inkster and Jack Morrell. Philadelphia: University of Pennsylvania Press, 1983. Pp. 91–119.

"Science in the City: The London Institution 1819–40." *British Journal for the History of Science* 7 (1974): 146–62.

Heffernan, James. *Museum of Words: The Poetics of Ekphrasis from Homer to Ashbery.* University of Chicago Press, 1993.

Hemingway, Andrew. *Landscape Imagery and Urban Culture in Early Nineteenth-Century Britain.* Cambridge University Press, 1992.

Hemingway, Andrew, and Richard Vaughan, eds. *Art in Bourgeois Society, 1790–1850.* Cambridge University Press, 1998.

Heringman, Noah. "Introduction." In *Romantic Science: The Literary Forms of Natural History.* Ed. Noah Heringman. Albany: State University of New York Press, 2003.

"Natural History in the Romantic Period." In *A Concise Companion to the Romantic Age.* Ed. Jon Klancher. Malden, MA: Wiley-Blackwell, 2009. Pp. 141–67.

Hilton, Boyd. *The Age of Atonement: The Influence of Evangelicalism on Social and Economic Thought, 1795–1865.* Oxford: Clarendon Press, 1988.

*A Mad, Bad, and Dangerous People? England 1783–1846*. Oxford: Clarendon Press, 2006.
Hitchens, Christopher. *The Elgin Marbles: Should They Be Returned to Greece?* London: Chatto & Windus, 1987.
Holmes, Richard. *Coleridge: Darker Reflections, 1804–1834*. New York: Pantheon, 1998.
Hoock, Holger. *The King's Artists: The Royal Academy of Arts and the Politics of British Culture, 1760–1840*. Oxford: Clarendon Press, 2005.
  "Reforming Culture: National Art Institutions in the Age of Reform." In *Rethinking the Age of Reform: Britain 1780–1850*. Ed. Arthur Burns and Joanna Innes. Cambridge University Press, 2003. Pp. 254–70.
Hopfl, H. M. "From Savage to Scotsman: Conjectural History in the Scottish Enlightenment." *Journal of British Studies* 17 (1978): 19–41.
Hopkins, David. "The English Voices of Lucretius from Lucy Hutchinson to John Mason Good." In *The Cambridge Companion to Lucretius*. Ed. Philip Gillespie and Stuart Hardy. Cambridge University Press, 2007. Pp. 254–73.
Howells, Richard. "Controversy, Art, and Power." In *Outrage: Art, Controversy, and Society*. Ed. Richard Howells, Andreea Ritivoi, and Judith Schachter. New York: Palgrave, 2012. Pp. 19–46.
Iliffe, Rob. "Material Doubts: Hooke, Artisan Culture, and the Exchange of Information in 1670s London." *British Journal for the History of Science* 28 (1995): 285–318.
Innes, Joanna. "The State and the Poor: Eighteenth-Century England in European Perspective." In *Rethinking Leviathan: The Eighteenth-Century State in Britain and Germany*. Ed. John Brewer and Eckhart Hellmuth. London: Oxford University Press, 1999. Pp. 225–80.
Innes, Joanna, and Hugh Cunningham, eds. *Charity, Philanthropy and Reform: From the 1690s to 1850*. New York: St. Martin's Press, 1998.
Jackson, Holbrook. *The Anatomy of Bibliomania*. 1930. Urbana: University of Illinois Press, 2001.
Jackson, J. R. de J. *Method and Imagination in Coleridge's Criticism*. London: Routledge & Kegan Paul, 1969.
Jacyna, L. C. "Images of John Hunter in the Nineteenth Century." *History of Science* 21 (1983): 85–108.
  "Immanence or Transcendence: Theories of Life and Organization in Britain, 1790–1835." *Isis* 74 (1983): 311–29.
Jameson, Fredric. *A Singular Modernity*. New York: Verso, 2002.
Janowitz, Anne. *Women Romantic Poets: Anna Barbauld and Mary Robinson*. Tavistock: Northcote House, 2010.
Johns, Adrian. "How to Acknowledge a Revolution." *American Historical Review* 107 (2002): 106–25.
  *The Nature of the Book: Print and Knowledge in the Making*. University of Chicago Press, 1998.
  *Piracy: The Intellectual Property Wars from Gutenberg to Gates*. University of Chicago Press, 2009.

Kammen, Michael. *Visual Shock: A History of Art Controversies in American Culture*. New York: Knopf, 2006.
Keach, William. *Arbitrary Power: Romanticism, Language, Politics*. Princeton University Press, 2004.
Keen, Paul. *The Crisis of Literature in the 1790s: Print Culture and the Public Sphere*. Cambridge University Press, 1999.
  *Literature, Commerce, and the Spectacle of Modernity, 1750–1800*. Cambridge University Press, 2012.
Kelen, Sarah A. "*Peirs Plouhman* (sic) and the 'Formidable Array of Blackletter' in the Early Nineteenth Century." In *Illuminating Letters*. Ed. Gutjahr and Benton. Pp. 47–67.
Kelley, Theresa M. "Keats, Ekphrasis, and History." In *Keats and History*. Ed. Nicholas Roe. Cambridge University Press, 1995. Pp. 212–37.
Kenny, Neil. "Books in Space and Time: Bibliomania and Early Modern Histories of Learning and 'Literature' in France." *MLQ: A Journal of Literary History* 61 (2000): 253–86.
Kent, F. W., and Patricia Simons, eds. *Patronage, Art, and Society in Renaissance Italy*. New York: Oxford University Press, 1987.
Kidd, Colin. *The Forging of Races: Race and Scripture in the Protestant Atlantic World. 1600–2000*. Cambridge University Press, 2006.
Kiernan, V. G. "Evangelicalism and the French Revolution." *Past and Present* 1 (February 1952): 44–56.
Kinnaird, John. *William Hazlitt, Critic of Power*. New York: Columbia University Press, 1978.
Klancher, Jon. "Discriminations, or Romantic Cosmopolitanisms in London." In *Romantic Metropolis*. Ed. James Chandler and Kevin Gilmartin. Cambridge University Press, 2005. Pp. 65–72.
  "Godwin and the Genre Reformers: On Necessity and Contingency in Romantic Narrative Theory." In *Romanticism, History, and the Possibilities of Genre*. Ed. Tilottama Rajan and Julia M. Wright. Cambridge University Press, 1998. Pp. 21–38.
  "Godwin and the Republican Romance: Genre, Politics, and Contingency in Cultural History." *Modern Language Quarterly* 56 (1995): 145–65.
  *The Making of English Reading Audiences, 1790–1832*. Madison: University of Wisconsin Press, 1987.
  "Transmission Failure: From the London Lecturing Empire to the *Collected Coleridge*." In *Theoretical Issues in Literary History*. Ed. David Perkins. Cambridge, MA: Harvard University Press, 1991. Pp. 77–95.
  "The Vocation of Criticism and the Crisis of the Republic of Letters." In *The Cambridge History of Literary Criticism*. Vol. 5: *Romanticism*. Ed. Marshall Brown. Cambridge University Press, 2000. Pp. 296–320.
Koselleck, Reinhart. *Critique and Crisis: Enlightenment and the Pathogenesis of Modern Society*. 1959. Cambridge, MA: MIT Press, 1988.
Kristeller, Paul Oskar. "The Modern System of the Arts." 1951. In *Renaissance Thought and the Arts: Collected Essays*. Princeton University Press, 1990. Pp. 163–227.

Kuhn, Thomas. *The Essential Tension: Selected Studies in Scientific Tradition and Change*. University of Chicago Press, 1977.
*The Structure of Scientific Revolutions*. University of Chicago Press, 1962.
Kurzer, Frederick. "A History of the Surrey Institution." *Annals of Science* 57 (2000): 109–41.
Latour, Bruno. *Pandora's Hope: An Essay on the Reality of Science Studies*. Cambridge, MA: Harvard University Press, 1999.
*Science in Action: How to Follow Scientists and Engineers through Society*. Cambridge, MA: Harvard University Press, 1987.
Leaver, Kristen. "Pursuing Conversations: *Caleb Williams* and the Romantic Construction of the Reader." *Studies in Romanticism* 33 (1994): 589–610.
Lees, Lynn Hollen. *The Solidarities of Strangers: The English Poor Laws and the People 1770–1948*. Cambridge University Press, 1998.
Levere, Trevor. *Poetry Realized into Nature: Samuel Taylor Coleridge and Early Nineteenth-Century Science*. Cambridge University Press, 1981.
Lévi-Strauss, Claude. *Structural Anthropology*. London: Penguin, 1958.
Levinson, Marjorie. *Keats's "Life of Allegory": The Origins of a Style*. Cambridge, MA: Blackwell, 1988.
Lowenstein, Joseph. *The Author's Due: Printing and the Prehistory of Copyright*. University of Chicago Press, 2002.
Luhmann, Niklas. *Essays on Self-Reference*. New York: Columbia University Press, 1990.
Lynch, Deidre. "'Wedded to Books': Bibliomania and the Romantic Essayists." In *Romantic Libraries*. Ed. Ina Ferris. *Praxis: An Online Journal of Romantic Circles*. www.rc.umd.edu/praxis/libraries/toc.html.
McCalman, Iain. "Popular Irreligion in Early Victorian England: Infidel Preachers and Radical Theatricality in 1830s London." In *Religion and Irreligion in Victorian Society: Essays in Honor of R. K. Webb*. Ed. R. W. Daus and R. J. Helmstadter. New York: Routledge, 1992. Pp. 51–67.
McClellan III, James. *Science Reorganized: Scientific Societies in the Eighteenth Century*. New York: Columbia University Press, 1985.
"Scientific Institutions and the Organization of Science." In *The Cambridge History of Science*. Ed. Roy Porter. Cambridge University Press, 2003. IV: 87–106.
McGann, Jerome. "From Text to Work: Digital Tools and the Emergence of the Social Text." *Romanticism on the Net* 41–42 (February–May 2006). www.erudit.org/revue/RON/2006/v/n41/013153ar.html.
*The Textual Condition*. Princeton University Press, 1991.
McKenzie, D. F. *Bibliography and the Sociology of Texts*. Cambridge University Press, 1986.
McKeon, Michael. "Mediation as Primal Word: The Arts, the Sciences, and the Origins of the Aesthetic." In *This Is Enlightenment*. Ed. Siskin and Warner. Pp. 384–412.
*The Origins of the English Novel, 1600–1740*. Baltimore: Johns Hopkins University Press, 1987.

McKitterick, David. "Bibliography, Bibliophily, and the Organization of Knowledge." In *The Foundations of Scholarship: Libraries and Collecting 1650–1750*. Ed. David Vaisey and David McKitterick. Los Angeles: William Andrews Clark Memorial Library, University of California, 1992. Pp. 31–61.
Makdisi, Saree. *William Blake and the Impossible History of the 1790s*. University of Chicago Press, 2003.
Malcolm, Noel. *Aspects of Hobbes*. New York: Oxford University Press, 2002.
Maniquis, Robert M. "The Book in the Text of the *Biographia Literaria*." In *On the "Biographia Literaria."* Ed. Frederick Burwick. University of Oklahoma Press, 1988.
  "Transfiguring God: Religion, Romanticism, Revolution." In *The Blackwell Concise Companion to Romanticism*. Ed. Jon Klancher. Oxford: Wiley-Blackwell, 2009. Pp. 14–35.
Maniquis, Robert M., and Victoria Myers, eds. *Godwinian Moments: From the Enlightenment to Romanticism*. University of Toronto Press, 2011.
Manning, Peter. "Manufacturing the Romantic Image: Coleridge and Hazlitt Lecturing." In *Romantic Metropolis: The Urban Scene of British Culture, 1780–1840*. Ed. Chandler and Gilmartin. Pp. 227–45.
Mee, Jon. *Conversable Worlds: Literature, Contention, and Community, 1762–1830*. Oxford University Press, 2011.
  *Romanticism, Enthusiasm, and Regulation: Poetics and the Policing of Culture in the Romantic Period*. New York: Oxford University Press, 2003.
Meinecke, Friedrich. *Historism*. 1959. Trans. J. E. Anderson. New York: Herder and Herder, 1972.
Messer-Davidow, Ellen, David R. Shumway, and David J. Sylvan, eds. *Knowledges: Historical and Critical Studies in Disciplinarity*. Charlottesville: University Press of Virginia, 1993.
Moretti, Franco. *Graphs, Maps, Trees: Abstract Models for Literary History*. London: Verso, 2007.
  "On Literary Evolution." In *Signs Taken for Wonders*. New York: Verso, 1989. Pp. 254–78.
Morrell, Jack. "London Institutions and Lyell's Career: 1820–41." *British Journal for the History of Science* 9 (1976): 132–46.
Morrell, Jack, and Arnold Thackray. *Gentlemen of Science: Early Years of the British Association for the Advancement of Science*. Oxford: Clarendon Press, 1981.
Morris, R. J. "Clubs, Associations, and Institutions." In *The Cambridge Social History of Britain 1750–1950*. Ed. F. M. L. Thompson. 3 vols. Cambridge University Press, 1990. III: 395–443.
Morrow, John. "Republicanism and Public Virtue: William Godwin's *History of the Commonwealth of England*." *Historical Journal* 34 (1991): 645–64.
Myers, Joanne. "Defoe and the Project of 'Neighbours' Fare.'" *Restoration: Studies in English Literary Culture, 1660–1700* 35.2 (2011): 1–19.
Natarajan, Uttara. *Hazlitt and the Reach of Sense*. Oxford: Clarendon Press, 1998.
Novak, Maximilian, ed. *The Age of Projects*. University of Toronto Press, 2008.

O'Brien, Karen. *The Uses of History in Early Modern Britain*. Ed. Paulina Kemes. San Marino: Huntington Library Press, 2006.
Olney, Clark. *Benjamin Robert Haydon: Historical Painter*. Atlanta: University of Georgia Press, 1952.
Ornstein, Martha. *The Role of Scientific Societies in the Seventeenth Century*. University of Chicago Press, 1938.
Paley, Morton. *Coleridge and the Fine Arts*. New York: Oxford University Press, 2008.
Pascoe, Judith. *Romantic Theatricality: Gender, Poetry, and Spectatorship*. Ithaca, NY: Cornell University Press, 1997.
Peltz, Lucy. "The Extra-Illustration of London: The Gendered Spaces and Practices of Antiquarianism in the Late Eighteenth Century." In *Producing the Past: Aspects of Antiquarian Culture and Practice, 1770–1850*. Ed. Martin Myrone and Lucy Peltz. Aldershot: Ashgate, 1999. Pp. 115–34.
  "Facing the Text: The Amateur and Commercial Histories of Extra-Illustration ca. 1770–1840." In *Owners, Annotators, and the Signs of Reading*. Ed. Robin Myers et al. New Castle, DE: Oak Knoll, 2006. Pp. 91–135.
Phillips, Mark Salber. *Society and Sentiment: Genres of Historical Writing in Britain, 1740–1820*. Princeton University Press, 2000.
Philp, Mark. *Godwin's Political Justice*. London: Duckworth, 1986.
Piper, Andrew. *Dreaming in Books: The Making of the Bibliographical Imagination in the Romantic Age*. University of Chicago Press, 2009.
Pointon, Marcia. *Hanging the Head: Portraiture and Social Formation in Eighteenth-Century England*. New Haven: Yale University Press, 1993.
Poovey, Mary. *A History of the Modern Fact: Problems of Knowledge in the Sciences of Wealth and Society*. University of Chicago Press, 1998.
Poynter, J. R. *Society and Pauperism: English Ideas on Poor Relief, 1795–1834*. London: Routledge & Kegan Paul, 1969.
Price, Leah. "Introduction." In *The History of the Book and the Idea of Literature*. Special issue of *PMLA* 121 (January 2006): 9–16.
Pullan, Ann. "Public Society or Private Interests? The British Institution in the Early Nineteenth Century." In *Art in Bourgeois Society*. Ed. Hemingway and Vaughan. Pp. 27–44.
Rajan, Tilottama. "The Disfiguration of Enlightenment: War, Trauma, and the Historical Novel in Godwin's *Mandeville*." In *Godwinian Moments*. Ed. Maniquis and Myers. Pp. 172–93.
  *The Supplement of Reading: Figures of Understanding in Romantic Theory and Practice*. Ithaca, NY: Cornell University Press, 1990.
Rasch, William. "Theories of Complexity, Complexities of Theory: Habermas, Luhmann, and the Study of Social Systems." *German Studies Review* 14 (1991): 65–83.
Ray, Angela. *The Lyceum and Public Culture in the Nineteenth-Century United States*. East Lansing: Michigan State University Press, 2005.

Rectenwald, Michael. "The Publics of Science: Periodicals and the Making of British Science, 1820–1860." Ph.D. dissertation, Department of English, Carnegie Mellon University, 2005.
Richardson, Alan. *Literature, Education, and Romanticism: Reading as Social Practice, 1780–1832*. Cambridge University Press, 1994.
Roper, Derek. *Reviewing before the "Edinburgh," 1788–1802*. London: Methuen, 1978.
Rorty, Richard. *Contingency, Irony, and Solidarity*. Cambridge University Press, 1989.
Ross, Catherine E. "'Twin Labourers and Heirs of the Same Hopes': The Professional Rivalry of Humphry Davy and William Wordsworth." In *Romanticism and Science*. Ed. Heringman. Pp. 23–49.
Rothblatt, Sheldon. "London: A Metropolitan University?" In *The University and the City*. Ed. Thomas Bender. Oxford: Clarendon Press, 1996. Pp. 119–49.
Russell, Gillian. "Spouters or Washerwomen? The Sociability of Romantic Lecturing." In *Romantic Sociability*. Ed. Gillian Russell and Clara Tuite. Cambridge University Press, 2002. Pp. 123–44.
St. Clair, William. *Lord Elgin and the Marbles*. New York: Oxford University Press, 1998.
  *The Reading Nation in the Romantic Period*. Cambridge University Press, 2004.
Sartre, Jean-Paul. *Critique of Dialectical Reason*. 1: *Theory of Practical Ensembles*. Trans. Alan Sheridan-Smith. London: Verso, 1976.
Sawday, Jonathan. *Engines of the Imagination: Renaissance Culture and the Rise of the Machine*. New York: Routledge, 2007.
Schaffer, Simon. "Genius in Romantic Natural Philosophy." In *Romanticism and the Sciences*. Ed. Cunningham and Jardine. Pp. 82–98.
  "Indiscipline and Interdisciplines: Some Exotic Genealogies of Modern Knowledge." 2010. www.fif.tu-darmstadt.de/media/fif_interdisziplinaere_forschung/sonstigetexte/externe/simonschaffner.pdf.
  "Priestley and the Politics of Spirit." In *Science, Medicine, and Dissent: Joseph Priestley (1733–1804)*. Ed. Robert Anderson and Christopher Lawrence. London: Wellcome Trust, 1987. Pp. 39–53.
  "Scientific Discoveries and the End of Natural Philosophy." *Social Studies of Science* 16 (1986): 387–420.
Schiebinger, Londa. *Nature's Body: Gender in the Making of Modern Science*. Boston: Beacon Press, 1993.
Schlereth, Thomas. *The Cosmopolitan Ideal in Eighteenth-Century Thought*. Notre Dame University Press, 1977.
Shaddy, Robert. "Grangerizing; 'One of the Unfortunate Stages of Bibliomania.'" *Book Collector* 49 (2000): 536–46.
Shapin, Steven. *Never Pure: Historical Studies of Science as if It Was Produced by People with Bodies, Situated in Time, Space, Culture, and Society and Struggling for Credibility and Authority*. Baltimore: Johns Hopkins University Press, 2010.
Shaw, Herbert. *Craters, Cosmos, and Chronicles: A New Theory of the Earth*. Stanford University Press, 1994.

Sher, Richard. "Commerce, Religion, and the Enlightenment in Eighteenth-Century Glasgow." In *Glasgow: Beginnings to 1830*. Ed. T. M. Devine and Gordon Jackson. Manchester University Press, 1995. 1: 312–59.
"Transatlantic Books and Literary Culture." In *Transatlantic Literary Studies, 1660–1830*. Ed. Eve Tavor Bannet and Susan Manning. Cambridge University Press, 2012. Pp. 10–27.
Sherman, Sandra. *Imagining Poverty: Quantification and the Decline of Paternalism*. Columbus: Ohio State University Press, 2001.
Siskin, Clifford, and William Warner, eds. *This Is Enlightenment*. University of Chicago Press, 2010.
Snow, C. P. *The Two Cultures and the Scientific Revolution*. Cambridge University Press, 1960.
Spadafora, David. *The Idea of Progress in Eighteenth-Century Britain*. New Haven: Yale University Press, 1990.
Stewart, Larry. *The Rise of Public Science: Rhetoric, Technology, and Natural Philosophy in Newtonian Britain*. Cambridge University Press, 1992.
Tanselle, G. Thomas. "Bibliographical History as a Field of Study." *Studies in Bibliography* 41 (1988): 33–58.
"Bibliography and Science." *Studies in Bibliography* 27 (1974): 55–89.
Thompson, E. P. *The Making of the English Working Class*. New York: Vintage, 1963.
Thompson, F. M. L., ed. *The University of London and the World of Learning, 1836–1986*. London: Hambledon Press, 1986.
Turner, Jonathan H. *Human Institutions: A Theory of Societal Evolution*. New York: Rowman & Littlefield, 2003.
Valenza, Robin. *Literature, Language, and the Rise of the Intellectual Disciplines in Britain, 1680–1820*. Cambridge University Press, 2009.
Veysey, Laurence. "The Plural Organized Worlds of the Humanities." In *The Organization of Knowledge in Modern America, 1860–1920*. Ed. Alexandra Oleson and John Voss. Baltimore: Johns Hopkins University Press, 1979. Pp. 51–106.
Vicario, Michael A. *Shelley's Intellectual System and its Epicurean Background*. New York: Routledge, 2007.
Warner, Michael. *The Evangelical Public Sphere in Eighteenth-Century America*. Philadelphia: University of Pennsylvania Press, 2013.
Watkins, Daniel. *Keats's Poetry and the Politics of the Imagination*. Rutherford, NJ: Fairleigh Dickinson University Press, 1989.
Watts, Michael. *The Dissenters: From the Reformation to the French Revolution*. Oxford: Clarendon Press, 1978.
*The Dissenters: The Expansion of Evangelican Nonconformity*. Oxford: Clarendon Press, 1995.
Weber, Max. *Economy and Society*. 1920. Ed. Guenther Roth and Claus Wittich. 2 vols. Berkeley: University of California Press, 1978.
Whale, John. *Imagination Under Pressure, 1789–1832: Aesthetics, Politics and Utility*. Cambridge University Press, 2000.

"The Making of a City of Culture: William Roscoe's Liverpool." *Eighteenth Century Life* 29.2 (2005): 91–107.
White, Daniel. *Early Romanticism and Religious Dissent*. Cambridge University Press, 2006.
Wiener, Joel H. *Radicalism and Freethought in Nineteenth-Century Britain: The Life of Richard Carlile*. Westport, CT: Greenwood Press, 1983.
Williams, Jeffrey J. "Introduction: Institutionally Speaking." In *The Institution of Literature*. Albany: State University of New York Press, 2006. Pp. 1–18.
Williams, Raymond. *Culture and Society, 1780–1950*. 1958. New York: Oxford University Press, 1983.
  *Keywords: A Vocabulary of Culture and Society*. 2nd edn. New York: Oxford University Press, 1983.
  *The Long Revolution*. London: Chatto & Windus, 1961.
  *Marxism and Literature*. New York: Oxford University Press, 1977.
Wilson, Arline. *William Roscoe: Commerce and Culture*. Liverpool University Press, 2008.
Woodring, Carl. *Politics in the Poetry of Coleridge*. Madison: University of Wisconsin Press, 1961.
Yeo, Richard. "Classifying the Sciences." In *The Cambridge History of Science*. Ed. Roy Porter. Cambridge University Press, 2004. IV: 241–66.
  *Encyclopedic Visions: Scientific Dictionaries and Enlightenment Culture*. Cambridge University Press, 2001.
Young, Robert. "The Idea of a Chrestomathic University." In *Logomachia: The Conflict of the Faculties*. Ed. Richard Rand. Lincoln: University of Nebraska Press, 1992. Pp. 99–126.
Zimmerman, Sarah. "Coleridge the Lecturer, A Disappearing Act." In *Spheres of Action: Speech and Performance in Romantic Culture*. Ed. Alexander Dick and Angela Esterhammer. University of Toronto Press, 2009. Pp. 46–72.
Zizek, Slavoj. *Tarrying with the Negative*. New York: Verso, 1993.

# Index

academies and learned societies *See also:* names of individual academies and societies
  arts and sciences in, 1660–1800, 13
  compared as institutional forms, 45–46
  compared with English arts-and-sciences Institutions, 19, 30, 44–47
  how specialist societies displaced arts-and-sciences Institutions in England, 1830s, 225
  opposition to in British art field, 112
  role of specialist societies in second scientific revolution, 140–43
*Accademia delle Scienze dell'Istituto di Bologna*, 47
Accum, Frederick, 68, 244
Ackermann, Rudolph, 68
  *Microcosm of London, The*, 64, 67, 71, 92
  *Repository of the Arts*, 108
administration and administrators, 2, 102
  at arts-and-sciences Institutions, 5, 52–53
  at British Institution, 71, 119
  at London Institution, 66–67
  at Royal Institution, 64–65
  at Surrey Institution, 68
  contrasted to Renaissance patronage, 77
  impact on lecturers and lecturing programs, 72–77
  in second scientific revolution, 147–48
  in the modern university, 52
  organizing of culture by, 51, 226
  print media's attention to, 67
  terminology of, 51–52
Adorno, Theodor, 12, 51, 77
adult education, 48
Althusser, Louis, 12
Ames, Joseph, 94
  *Typographical Antiquities*, 94
*Analytical Review*, 155, 184
Anderson Institution (Glasgow), 66, 243
  as precursor of Royal Institution, 47–48
Anderson, John, 47
Angerstein, John Julius, 71, 143, 206

*Annals of the Fine Arts*, 7, 108
  and British art field, 124
  and Elgin Marbles controversy, 122
*Anti-Jacobin Review*, 7, 68, 103
antiquarianism
  and rise of bibliographical study in England, 86, 96–98
  in the visual arts, 113
Arnold, Matthew
  "Literature and Science," 186
art periodicals, 6, 108–9, 123
*Artist*, 6, 116
  and art-critical press, 108
  and British art field, 118–21
  and broadening definition of liberal arts in, 116–17
  and mediation of art disputes, 122–24
  audiences of, 116–18
  claims to autonomy of artists in, 113–16
  contributors to, 113
  critiques of, 117
  impact on British art field, 111
  remediating visual arts into print authorship, 112–13
  role in preparing Elgin Marbles controversy, 110–11, 121–24
arts *see* fine arts, mechanical arts, arts and sciences
arts and sciences, 119
  and political reform, 9, 23, 156, 176, 182–86, 213–19
  and religious controversy, 8
  and rise of bibliographical study in England, 85–88
  and secularism, 178
  as a meta-disciplinary category, 121
  as disciplinary system of modern university, 2, 121, 124, 167
  as disciplinary system of the modern university, 229
  as literary expression, 153–54
  dialectical relation of, 5, 183

arts and sciences (cont.)
  early modern relation of, 13–16
  in dream vision, 102, 252
  relation of practices to knowledges within, 16–17, 148–49
  temporality and progress of, 13, 18–19, 147–48, 166, 186–87
  theorizing of, by Bentham and Coleridge, 162–63
  transfiguring of, definition, 16–19
arts-and-sciences Institutions, 1–4
  and their public impact, 52–54
  as stimulating the field of bibliography and book history, 85–86
  compared to academies and societies, 4, 44–47, 52
  in English provinces, 45, 128, 145–46
  *See also: names of individual institutions*
Astle, Thomas
  *Origins and Progress of Writing, The*, 91
Astronomical Society, 141
audiences
  of lecturing, 3, 74–75
  of women at lectures, 66
authorship, 88, 104
  artists' claims to, 107–8, 112–14, 123
  expertise and, 153
  extra-illustration as, 98–99
  of novels and histories, 194–95
  study of bibliography and, 87, 97, 101, 104
autonomy
  and relative autonomy of sciences in nineteenth century, 144
  historical degrees of, 16–17
  of the artist as producer, 114–16

Bacon, Francis, 35, 79, 172, 183
  *Novum Organum*, 113, 173
Baillet, Adrien, 86
Banks, Joseph, 3, 48, 59, 72, 91
  and crisis of Royal Institution, 63, 80
  and origins of Royal Institution, 48, 59–60
Barbauld, Anna, 223, 267
Baring, Francis, 66
Barrell, John, 183
  *Political Theory of Painting from Reynolds to Hazlitt, The*, 205, 208–9
Barry, James, 107, 111, 204
Bayle, Pierre, 37, 77, 153
Beaumont, George, 206
Becker, Howard, 110
Beddoes, Thomas, 79
Beloe, William, 90, 94
Bence Jones, Henry, 62, 242
  *Royal Institution: Its Founder and First Professors, The*, 60
Bender, John, 160
Bentham, Jeremy, 3
  and University of London, 225
  arts and sciences redefined by, 165–68
  *Chrestomathia*, 7, 153, 156, 162, 164–69, 176, 183
  and Royal Institution, 176
  discipline-formation and, 166–67
  on joint-tenancy of art and science, 165
  on method, 162–68
  on practices of knowledge, 166–67
  on projecting, 39
  *Rationale of Reward*, 176, 264
  Royal Institution, critique of, 176
  Rumford and, 58–59
  social scientific in, 168
  v. Coleridge on "method," 164–66
  v. Coleridge on the "arts and sciences," 163
Berlin Academy of the Sciences, 34, 45
Berman, Morris, 59, 80, 242
Bermingham, Ann, 64
Bernard, Thomas, 3, 54
  administrator of arts and sciences, as, 52, 64–65, 121
  American origins of, 54
  and Anglican evangelicalism, 48, 57, 102
  and career of Humphry Davy, 79
  and evangelicalism, 243
  and libraries, 91
  and meta-disciplinary logic of the "arts and sciences," 120–21
  and origin of the *Director*, 120–21
  and Samuel Taylor Coleridge, 49
  and Society for Bettering the Condition of the Poor, 55–58
  and the *Director*, 6, 246
  and visual arts, 119–21
  as director of the British Institution, 121
  as institution-builder, 240
  as manager of lectures, 72
  as organizer of Royal Institution lecture curriculum, 72–77
  as reformer of English poor law, 55–56
  Coleridge's lectures managed by, 157
  collaboration with projectors, 58, 65
bibliography, 4, 6
  and "arts and sciences," 85–87
  and bibliographical codes, 85, 88
  as "English Literature" at Royal Institution, 73
  as bibliographical literary history, 73, 90
  bibliographical theory in the Enlightenment, 89–90
  bibliographical v. encyclopedic models of knowledge, 90

contradictory relation with Bibliomania, 99
  emerging study of in England, 85
  historical, and the New Bibliography, 104–5
  in religious controversy, 101–3
  making a scientific print culture in England, 90–92 *See also:* book history
Bibliomania, 86–87
  and rise of English bibliographical studies, 86–88
  black-letter and black-letter reading, 96–98
  contradictory relation with bibliographical studies, 95–96
  extra-illustration in, 98–100
  showing instability of the modern book, 100
Black, Joel, 126
black-letter
  in religious controversy, 101
black-letter mania, 96, 104
  method of "black-letter reading," 96–98
*Blackwood's Magazine*, 55
Blades, William, 104
Blake, William, 9, 126
  "Annotations to Reynolds," 46
  "Holy Thursday," 9
  and the Hunt Circle, 203
  social and biological organization in, 134
Bloom, Harold, 126
Bode, Carl, 227
book history, 4 *See also:* Bibliography
  and knowledge claims, 149
  and media archeology, 105
  as "English Literature" at Royal Institution, 73
  as historical bibliography, 20
  contemporary aims of, 105
  debate between Adrian Johns and Elizabeth Eisenstein, 88
  nineteenth century compared to late twentieth, 85, 105–6
  role in the humanities, 61, 84
Boulton, Matthew
  and intellectual property, 62
Bourdieu, Pierre, 115
  and question of autonomy in cultural fields, 16–17
  concept of institutions in, 12
  definition of fields, 115, 144, 149, 232
    as embedded controversies, 110
  on rites of institution, 40, 238
  on the Republic of Letters, 45
  origin of theory of fields in, 264
Boydell, John, 76, 115
Bradshaw, Henry, 104
Brande, William, 67, 225
Brewer, John, 71, 112

Brewster, Daniel, 224
British Association for the Advancement of Science, 147, 185, 224
  and the arts-and-sciences Institutions, 225
*British Critic*, 7, 66
British Institution for Promoting the Fine Arts in the United Kingdom, 1, 64, 205, 225
  administration of, 70–72, 77, 119
  and display of European visual art, 71
  as attacked by the "Catalogue Raisonné of the British Institution," 207
  as precursor to the National Gallery, 103
  Hazlitt and the *Examiner* on, 204–8
  in British art field, 107, 119–21
  role in the "patrician renaissance" of, 71
  Thomas Bernard's founding of, 52
British Library, 91
British Museum, 122–23, 143
Brougham, Henry, 78, 224
Brydges, Egerton, 87, 94
  and black-letter reading, 97
Brylowe, Thora, 76, 115
Burke, Edmund, 32, 46, 101
  and idea of complexity, 132
  on institutions, 9
  *Reflections on the Revolution in France*, 132
Burton, John Hill, 99
Butler, Marilyn, 202
Byron, George Gordon, Lord, 3, 8, 123, 126, 156, 227, 260

Calé, Luisa, 4, 98, 115, 251
*Cambridge History of English Literature, The*, 104
Campbell, Thomas, 3, 53
Carlile, Richard, 3, 127
  *Address to Men of Science*, 80, 128–32
  compared to Lyell's history of Romantic science, 145
  critique of Humphry Davy in, 128–29
  and definition of "knowledge," 148
  and printing press v. Davy's lecturing institution, 132
  and William Godwin, 188
Carlyle, Thomas, 133
  "Signs of the Times," 225–26
Chambers, Ephraim, 37
  *Cyclopaedia*, 14, 35, 182
*Champion*, 108
Chandler, James, 41, 170, 185, 218–19
Chartier, Roger, 30, 85, 91, 106
*Chemist*, 80
Christensen, Jerome, 172
Clarendon, Lord Henry
  *History of the Rebellion and Civil Wars in England*, extra-illustrated, 99

Clarke, Adam, 69, 89, 94, 138, 184
  and *Anti-Jacobin Review*, 103
  and bibliographical studies in England, 90
  and bibliographical systems, 90
  and Methodism, 104
  and Methodist controversy, 101–2
  and Thomas Frognall Dibdin, 102
  at the Surrey Institution, 103
  *Bibliographical Dictionary*, 90, 101
  on typography, 95
clerisy, 158
  and distinction between "cultivation" and "civilization," 180
Cobbett, William, 100
Cochran, Terry, 36–37
Cockney School, 123, 200
Coleridge, Samuel Taylor, 2–3, 65, 126, 144
  "Aeolian Harp," 134
  "Fears in Solitude," 28–29, 48–50, 158
  "Ode to France," 217
  "Prospectus to the *Encyclopaedia Metropolitana*," 163
  "Treatise on Method," 162, 170, 172
  *Aids to Reflection*, 137, 181
  and discourse of organization, 133
  and *Encyclopaedia Metropolitana*, 162, 170
  and expression "arts and sciences," 158
  and language of *institution*, 48–50
  and publishing of *Lyrical Ballads*, 95
  and Romantic science, 128, 133–39
  and the "fine arts," 245
  and Thomas Bernard, 121
  and typography, 95
  as historian of the Republic of Letters, 155
  as literary lecturer, 27, 74, 93, 156–57, 161
  *Biographia Literaria*, 7, 94, 133, 137, 155, 162–63, 171
  and problem of method, 172
  and religious field, 178
  compared to Bentham on "method," 164–65
  compared to Bentham on the "arts and sciences," 162–63
  distinction of "method" and "theory" in, 169
  fine arts and problem of "method," 169
  *Friend, The*, 7, 153, 156, 161, 170–75, 183
  *Lay Sermons*, 180
  on bibliographical codes, 138
  on distinction between "method" and "theory," 173
  on institutions, 39
  on language of *institution*, 28–29
  on organization and self-organization, 135–37
  on print editions and scientific instruments, 137–38
  *On the Constitution of Church and State*, 9, 156, 158, 177–81
  on the University of London, 225
  Rumford and, 59
  *Theory of Life*, 7, 137, 258
  *Watchman*, 59
collectors and collecting, 2
  of books, 86, 94
  of visual arts, 71
Colley, Linda, 119, 255
  and concept of "patrician renaissance," 70, 87, 101, 103
Colquhoun, Patrick, 55, 58
commerce
  and fine arts, Hazlitt on, 209–10
  and fine arts, in William Roscoe, 210–12
  and science at the London Institution, 67
  in public art galleries, 209–10
Commonwealth of Learning *see* Republic of Letters
Connell, Philip, 87, 178, 185, 200, 204, 251
connoisseurs, 122
  and discipline of art history, 123
  at the British Institution, 71, 208
  dispute with painters and sculptors, 21, 71, 112
  in the Elgin Marbles controversy, 123
contingency
  and chance in the formation of sciences, 144–45
  and historical fiction in Godwin, 193–95
  in concept and history of institutions, 12
controversies
  as embedded in fields of cultural production, 8, 66
  in art field
    and print media, 121–24
  in the making of institutions, 8
  mediation of, in print and institutions, 121–24
  on Bibliomania, 93
  on museums and galleries, 143
  on the visual arts, 108–11, 253
cosmopolitanism, 183, 197–99
Cottle, Joseph, 95
Craciun, Adriana, 4, 200
criticism, Romantic literary and cultural, 7, 17
  and concept of "institutions," 12–13
Cromwell, Oliver, 192
Cumberland, James, 116

D'Israeli, Isaac, 240
Dance, George, 117
Darnton, Robert, 85, 106
Darwin, Erasmus
  *Zoonomia*, 158
Daston, Lorraine, 154, 263
Davy, Humphry, 3, 27, 53, 95, 127

"Parallels between Science and Art," 82–84
and epideictic rhetoric, 81–82, 247
and Friedrich Schelling on "genius," 17
and inaugural lecture of 1802, 77–78, 82
and Jeremy Bentham, 164
and Romantic science, 128
and social relation to audience, 79
and steam engine, 62
and technology, mechanical arts, 84
and the discourse on "arts and sciences," 80–84
and Thomas Bernard, 121
and women in audience, 65
at Royal Institution, 62, 65
Coleridge on science of, 169
Coleridge's lectures managed by, 74, 157
compared to Joseph Priestley, 80–82
*Edinburgh Review* response to, 78
radical critics of, 80, 129
scientific authority of, 79–80
Wordsworth's response to 1802 lecture of, 77–78, 81–82, 247
Dawkins, Richard, 125
de Bolla, Peter, 10
de Bure, Guillaume, 90
de Certeau, Michel, 35
  on arts and sciences, 14
De Quincey, Thomas
  compared to Coleridge on "literature," 161
  on literature of knowledge, 149
  on literature of power v. literature of knowledge, 161
Defoe, Daniel
  as projector, compared to Leibniz, 30
  *Essay upon Projects, An*, 27, 29–33
  on private advantage and public good, 31–32
  project for languages in, 33
Dennett, Daniel, 125
Dibdin, Thomas Frognall, 3, 65, 89–90
  and Adam Clarke, 102
  and bibliographical studies, 85
  and Bibliomania, 87
    black-letter reading, 96
  and historical bibliography, 105
  as editor of *Typographical Antiquities*, 94
  as lecturer, 73, 92–93
  *Bibliographical Decameron, The*, 94
  *Bibliomania, or Book-Madness, The*, 87, 93–94, 99, 103, 249
  editions of, 249
  *Bibliophobia, The*, 87
Diderot, Denis
  *Encyclopedie*, 35, 37
differentiation
  of autopoietic systems, 148
  of cultural fields, 5, 226

of knowledge genres, 7
of nations and knowledges, 127, 146–47
of scientific disciplines, 128
*Director*, 6, 82, 102, 120
and administrative position of "director," 246
as linking the Royal and British Institutions, sciences and fine arts, 93
disciplinarity, 5
and Coleridge on method, 173
and concept of institution, 12
and disciplinary histories, 147
and history of sciences, 125–26, 263
and indisciplines, 4
and knowledge categories in arts-and-sciences Institutions, 72–74, 77
and poetry, 165–68
and predisciplinarity, 165–68
the case of book history, 105–6
and predisciplinarity in the sciences, 143
and the Republic of Letters, 154
definitions of, 262
in Bentham's *Chrestomathia*, 165–68
in Coleridge's writing on, 22, 165–68
discovery, 172
and "method" in Coleridge, 172
as an "art" in Leibniz, 35
in fine arts v. sciences, 82–83
in poetry and astronomy, 138–39
Dissenters
and administration of "arts and sciences," 67
and arts-and-sciences Institutions, 184
and bibliographical controversy, 101
and projects, 33
and Russell Institution, 70
and the "arts and sciences," 23
as audience in arts-and-sciences Institutions, 3, 66, 68
on systems of the "arts and sciences," 156
Dissenters, Rational
and discourse of "arts and sciences," 183–85, 200–1
in relation to the Hunt Circle, 203
Douce, Francis
*Illustrations of Shakespeare*, 97
drama
and mimesis of the sciences, 160
Duncan, Ian, 7, 154, 184, 232
Durkheim, Émile, 11, 40
*Rules of Sociological Method*, 11
Dyer, George, 203

East India Company, 66
Eaves, Morris, 115
Edinburgh Philosophical Society, 141
*Edinburgh Review*, 7, 44, 55, 77, 202, 225

*Edinburgh Review* (cont.)
  and art-critical press, 108
  and involvement in London arts-and-sciences world, 70, 77–79
education
  and controversy on monitorial schools, 75, 167
  as adult education, 48
  at University of London, methods of, 224
  in Coleridge's plan for National Church, 178–81
  in eighteenth-century charity schools, 57
  in Godwin's *Enquirer*, 189
  of artisans and mechanics, 54
  of the poor
    at early Royal Institution, 60–62
    Thomas Bernard on, 56–57
  of women in arts-and-sciences Institutions, 27, 65–66
  plans of in Bentham, *Chrestomathia*, 166
  study of literature and liberal education, 163
Eisenstein, Elizabeth, 85, 88
*ekphrasis*, 122
Elgin Marbles controversy, 72, 108, 112, 114, 230
  and print media, 121–24
Ellis, George, 227
Emerson, Ralph Waldo, 27
*Encyclopaedia Britannica*, 165, 186
encyclopedias of arts and sciences, 13–14, 35
  and biannual *semestria*, 34
  and debate on progress, 16
  and tree of knowledge, 60
encyclopedism, Enlightenment
  critique of in Bentham and Coleridge, 163, 165–66
  v. bibliographical models of knowledge, 89–90
English Revolution, 190, 192–93
engraving, 3
  and Royal Academy of Arts, 16
  as controversial topic at Royal Institution, 75–77
  as lecturing topic at arts-and-sciences Institutions, 72
  in mechanics' education, 61
  v. the fine arts, 75–76
Enlightenment, 55, 254
  and Republic of Letters, 154
  and Romantic-age arts and sciences, 7–8
  concept and language of "institution" in, 1, 11, 44
  concept of "literature" in, 73, 157, 195
  discourse on "arts and sciences" in, 82, 156
  forms of historiography in, 156, 186–87
  projects and institutions in, 19
evangelicalism
  and bibliographical controversy, 101
  and bifurcation of Scottish Enlightenment, 48

  and book history, 103
  and institution-building, 103
  and modernity, 102
  and political economy, 56–58
  Anglican
    relation to arts and sciences, 102
*Examiner*, 6–7, 203
  and art-critical press, 108
  and British art field, 124
  and Rational Dissent, 200
  and reform of British art field, 123
  on the fine arts, 203–5
extra-illustration, 98–100
  and modern visual media, 100
  methods of, 98–99

Faraday, Michael, 27, 225
Farington, Joseph, 118, 120
fashion and fashionability
  and female audience of "arts and sciences," 65
  and lecturing curriculum at Royal Institution, 72
  in British art world, 123
  in the "arts and sciences," 63
Ferguson, Adam, 10, 42, 186
  *Essay on the History of Civil Society, An*, 39
  on institutions, 42
Ferguson, Frances, 166, 168
Ferriar, John
  *Illustrations of Sterne*, 97
Ferris, Ina, 87, 94
fields of cultural production
  and religious field, 177–78, 181
  as conjunctures of disputes, 124
  as knowledge fields, 4
  in Thomas Carlyle, "Signs of the Times," 225–26
  relation to publics, 124
fine arts
  and sciences, compared by Humphry Davy, 83
  and scientific drawings, 169–72
  as mediating pure and mixed sciences, 169–72
  relation to practical or mechanical arts, 14, 230
  relation to the literary, 148–49
Flaxman, John, 113–14
Foucault, Michel, 4, 12
  *Discipline and Punish*, 261
  on specific intellectuals, 130, 257
Fox, Charles James, 199
Franklin, Ben, 171
Franzel, Sean, 5, 233
French Revolution, 54, 88
Frye, Northrop, 126
Funnell, Peter, 119, 208
Fuseli, Henry, 112, 115, 117

Galileo, 132
Garrick, David, 199
genres, 195
  and the "arts and sciences," 190
  in work of Dissenters, 184
  of Enlightenment historiography, 186
Geological Society, 141
Gierl, Martin, 33, 237
Gifford, William, 97, 103
Gillispie, Charles, 126
Gilmartin, Kevin, 55
  *Writing Against Revolution*, 178
Godwin, William, 3, 116, 193
  "Of History and Romance," 189–96
  and conservative language of complexity, 133
  and critique of institutions, 9, 39, 184
  and Leigh Hunt, 215
  *Caleb Williams*, 189
  contingency as historical principle in, 193–95
  *Enquirer, The*, 185, 188–89, 195
  *Enquiry concerning Political Justice, An*, 49, 133, 185, 188–89, 193–94
  *History of the Commonwealth of England*, 192
  *Mandeville*, 192
  natural philosophy in, 193
Goethe, Wolfgang, 126
  and history of science, 125
Golinski, Jan, 65, 79–80, 242
Good, John Mason, 69, 184
  *The Book of Nature*, 68
Gould, Stephen Jay, 125
Granger, James, 98
Greenberg, Clement, 115
Guillory, John, 17, 272

Habermas, Jürgen, 12
  *Structural Transformation of the Public Sphere, The*, 209
Hallam, Henry, 69
Haskell, Francis
  *Ephemeral Museum, The*, 206
Haydon, Benjamin, 71, 108, 123
  *Judgment of Connoisseurs upon Works of Art Compared with That of Professional Men*, 123
Hazlitt, William, 2–3, 53, 108, 123, 200
  "Fine Arts," 205
  "On Corporate Bodies," 205
  "On Criticism," 201–2
  "On the Catalogue Raisonné of the British Institution," 205–9
  "On the Tendency of Sects," 201
  "What Is the People?," 218, 222
  "Why the Arts are not Progressive?," 13, 205
  and critique of institutions, 9, 39, 111
  and Jeremy Bentham, 39
  and William Godwin, 188
  as literary lecturer, 27
  at the Louvre, 206–7
  *Essays on the Principles of Human Action*, 70
  in the Republic of Letters, 201
  lectures at Russell Institution, 70, 206
  lectures at Surrey Institution, 206
  on "arts and sciences," 182–83, 202
  on Rational Dissenters, 201
  *Spirit of the Age, The*, 7, 9, 182
Heringman, Noah, 128, 232
Herschel, William, 128
  and discovery of Uranus, 139
Hippisley, Sir John, 63
historical romance *see* novel
historicism
  in William Godwin, 191
  Romantic
    and concept of "institution," 11–13
historiography
  and conjectural history, 38, 186–88, 190, 265
  and romance, 191–95
  in the Enlightenment, 186–87
history of books *see:* book history
history of sciences, 263
  and Romantic age, 125–26
  discipline-formation and, 125–26
  role of practical knowledges in, 174
Hoare, Prince
  and crisis of British art field, 107–8
  and professionalism of fine arts, 118
  and widening of concept of artist, 116–17
  as editor of the *Artist*, 107–8
  *Inquiry into the Requisite Cultivation and Present State of the Arts of Design in England*, 107
  on artists as authors, 107, 118–19
  on professionalism in the fine arts, 113
  v. Thomas Bernard
    founding of the *Artist*, 120
Hodgskin, Thomas, 80
Hogarth, William, 64
Holbrook, Josiah, 227
Holcroft, Thomas, 116
Holmes, Richard, 162
Holyoake, George, 55, 240
Homer, editions of, 137
Hone, William
  *Ancient Mysteries Described*, 100, 251
Hoock, Holger, 111, 119
Hooke, Robert, 18, 35
  "A General Scheme, or Idea of the Present State of Natural Philosophy," 173–74

Hooke, Robert (cont.)
  and Coleridge on history of sciences, 173–75
  and histories of science, 264
  on artisan and mechanical knowledges, 168
Hoppner, John, 113–14
Horne, Thomas Hartwell
  *Introduction to the Study of Bibliography*, 85
Horner, Francis, 66, 69, 78–79
Howells, Richard, 109
Hume, David, 141, 183, 188
  "Of the Rise and Progress of the Arts and Sciences," 44, 186–88, 190, 195
  and conjectural history, 186, 190
  *History of England*, 186, 192
Hunt, Leigh, 3, 87, 123, 200, 203
  and Rational Dissenters, 203
  on the "arts and sciences" and Parliamentary reform, 217, 222
  "The REFORMERS," 215
  *Reflector, The*, 9
Hunt, Robert, 200
  and fine-arts criticism, 123
  on the fine arts, 203–4
Hunter, John, 22
  and "second scientific revolution," 127
  and Coleridge on "method," 169
  role in idea of second scientific revolution, 142–43
  role in vitalist/materialist debate on "organization," 133–36
Huxley, Thomas
  "Science and Culture," 186

Inchbald, Elizabeth, 116
*Institut National*, 49
institutions
  and book history, 37
  and projects, 30
  and the word *institution*, 29
  as organized complexity in Burke, 133
  Coleridge's modernizing of the concept of, 176–77
  discourse and language of, 38–44, 234
  ecclesiastical orign of term, Max Weber on, 181
  historical meanings of *institute* and *institution* in Raymond Williams, 39–40
  meanings of the words *institute* and *institution*, 39
    in Millar, 44
    in Vico, 40–41
  naming of, 4
  of arts and sciences, 27
  Romantic attitudes toward, 11, 132–33
  Romantic discourse on, 11, 50
  scientific v. historicist concepts of, 11
  transatlantic impact, 27

intellectual property, 61–62
  and "arts and sciences" at Royal Institution, 84
  and copyright, 88
intellectuals
  as scientists, role of, 131
  definition of, 127
  specific and universal, 257

Jackson, Holbrook
  *Anatomy of Bibliomania, The*, 100
Jackson, J. R. de J., 172
Jeffrey, Francis, 44, 77–78
Johns, Adrian, 88, 106, 118
Johnson, Joseph, 129

Kammen, Michael, 109
Keach, William, 29
Keats, John, 3, 108, 123, 200
  "Ode on a Grecian Urn," 122
  "On First Looking into Chapman's Homer," 138–39
Keen, Paul, 7, 154, 249
Kidd, Colin, 69
Kinnaird, John, 208
Knight, Richard Payne, 114, 209
Kristeller, Paul Oskar, 14
Kuhn, Thomas, 12, 126
  and concept of second scientific revolution, 140, 179

*La Belle Assemblée*, 108
  and British art field, 123–24
Lamb, Charles, 3, 59, 87
Landseer, John, 16
  and Leigh Hunt circle, 203
  and Thomas Bernard, 246
  as critic of arts-and-sciences administration, 75–77, 246
  *Lectures on Engraving at the Royal Institution*, 76
Latour, Bruno, 105, 253
Lawrence, William, 128
  debate on John Hunter legacy, 134–37
Leaver, Kristen, 189
Leavis, F. R., 163
lecturing and lectures, 5
  and celebrity, 20, 53
  and disciplinary categories, 72–74
  at the Royal Institution, 73–76, 79
  at the Russell Institution, 70
  at the Surrey Institution, 67–69
  at the University of London, 225
  audiences of, 3
  of Samuel Taylor Coleridge, 93, 156–59
  of Thomas Frognall Dibdin, 92–93
  on moral philosophy, 72

on physics, 69
Romantic, English v. German, 5
to mechanics and artisans, 61
to women, 66
topical curriculum of Royal Institution, 73
Leibniz, Gottfried Wilhelm, 19, 29, 45
  "On an Academy of Arts and Sciences," 27
  "Precepts for Advancing the Arts and Sciences," 33–34
  and information overload, 34
  and knowledge projects, 38
  arts-and-sciences projects of, 29
  as projector, compared to Defoe, 30
  on hidden practices of knowledge, 35–36
  on practices, 36
  reform of encyclopedias in, 34–35
Levere, Trevor, 174
Lévi-Strauss, Claude, 12
libraries
  and French Revolution, 89
  and publishing industry, 36
  circulating, 92
  in arts-and-sciences Institutions, 6, 91–92
Linnean Society, 45, 141–42
literature
  and definitions of knowledge, 148–49, 230–31
  and rise of English bibliography, 85–87
  as defined by Enlightenment, 91, 157
  as defined in relation to "arts and sciences," 1
  as literature of power v. literature of knowledge, 149
  disciplinary history of, 3, 12, 23, 155
  impact of arts-and-sciences Institutions on meaning of, 156–57
  in analogy of scientific and literary instruments, 137–40
Lockhart, John Gibson, 140
London, 64
  as commercial center, 5
London Institution, 1, 27, 66–67, 244
London Magazine, 108
Lucretius, 68–69
  De Rerum Natura, 68
Luhmann, Niklas, 148
  and logic of autopoiesis, 136, 258
  systems concept compared to Bentham's, 167
Lunar Society, 62
lyceums, American, 223
  and English arts-and-sciences Institutions, 1, 27, 226–28
Lyell, Charles, 3, 149
  "Scientific Institutions," 91, 140–48
  and narrative of second scientific revolution, 127–28, 140
  on arts-and-sciences Institutions, 143–44
  on complexity of discipline-formation and history of nations, 141
  on debate over John Hunter legacy, 142–43
  Principles of Geology, 140
Lynch, Deidre, 87

Macklin, James, 115
Makdisi, Saree, 134
Malthus, Thomas, 133
Mandeville, Bernard, 31, 188
Manning, Peter, 158
Marcet, Jane
  Conversations on Chemistry, 27, 66
Marnier, Jean, 90
Marsigli, Luigi Ferdinando, 47
Marx, Karl
  Grundrisse, The, 40
Marxism
  and concept of institution, 11
  and concept of relative autonomy, 17
  and idea of project in history, 219
materialism and vitalism debate, 133–34
Mathias, Thomas James, 97, 103
  Pursuits of Literature, The, extra-illustrated, 99
McClellan, James, 45–47
McGann, Jerome, 85, 104, 106
McKenzie, D. F., 104, 106
  Bibliography and the Sociology of Texts, 105
McKeon, Michael, 160, 235
  The Origins of the English Novel, 238
mechanical arts
  ambivalent relation to "arts and sciences" of, 14, 16, 230
  among Rational Dissenters, 182
  and utilitarianism, 185
  as practices of knowledge, 148
  Coleridge on, 164
  education in, 54, 60, 63
  engraving as, 16
  Humphry Davy on, 81, 83–84
  in first version of Royal Institution, 61–62
  of printing and publishing, 73, 90
  v. fine arts in the Artist, 114
Mechanics' Institute, 61, 147, 224–25
media
  as institution, 6
Mee, Jon, 186, 189, 200, 268
Meinecke, Friedrich, 190
method See also: Bentham, Jeremy; Coleridge, Samuel Taylor
  Francis Bacon on, 113
Methodism, 8, 68–69
  and bibliographical studies, 101–2
Metropolitan Literary Institution, 1, 44
Mill, John Stuart, 156, 176

Mill, John Stuart (cont.)
  comparison of Bentham and Coleridge in, 162–63
Millar, John, 10, 183, 186
  *Historical View of the English Government*, 44
  on the concept of "institution," 187, 220
  *Origin of the Distinction of Ranks, The*, 41–44, 186
Milton, John, 144–45
  *Paradise Lost*, 145
models and modeling
  and lectures, 61
  of the visual arts, 71
Montesquieu, 186
*Monthly Magazine*, 184, 196, 200
Moray, Robert, 173
Moretti, Franco, 195
*Morning Chronicle*, 122
Murray, John, 66
music
  and harmonizing of the "arts and sciences," 170–71
Myers, Joanne, 32

National Church
  and "arts and sciences," 179–81
  and Church of England, 178
National Gallery of Pictures, 103, 143, 147, 224
nations and division of knowledges, 145–47
natural philosophy, 27, 144 *See also:* history of sciences
*Naturphilosophie*, 126
Naude, Gabriel, 86, 248
*New Monthly Magazine*, 108
  and British art field, 123–24
Newton, Isaac, 125, 173
Northcote, James, 113–15, 117
Novak, Maximillian, 31
novel
  and British art field, 123
  and the sciences, 160

Opie, John, 74, 113, 116
organization
  and "method" in Coleridge and Bentham, 165
  and language of complexity in political discourse, 132–33
  and self-organization, 135–37
  as biological and national in John Hunter debate, 133–37
  as concept in Coleridge, 133
  in work of Coleridge, 159
  of institutions, sciences, and nations in Romantic age, 142–47
  of scientific disciplines, 128
Oxford University, 63

Paine, Thomas, 62, 193
Paris Academy, 45
Parsons, Talcott, 11, 148
Pascoe, Judith, 199
Paterson, Samuel, 89, 94
Patmore, Peter George, 53, 224
patronage, 111, 113
  and Parliamentary reform, 203
  and public art in Britain, 256
Peignot, Gustave, 89
Phillips, Mark Salber, 186, 266
Phillips, Richard, 196
Philomathic Institution, 44
*Philosophical Transactions*, 45, 118
Philp, Mark, 188–89
Piper, Andrew, 86
Pneumatic Institute, 79
poetry
  and "verse" in Shelley, 50
  and painting compared to science by Humphry Davy, 83
  and poet as institutor, 39
  as lecturing category, 73
  as situated among disciplines, 159–60
  Coleridge on, 159–61
poets as legislators
  in Leigh Hunt, *Reflector*, 216
Poovey, Mary, 31
Porden, Eleanor
  *Veils, or the Triumph of Constancy, The*, 66
Porson, Richard, 90
Poussin, Nicolas, 117
Price, Leah, 105
Priestley, Joseph, 33, 128, 132, 141, 184
  and Rational Dissenters, 201
  and Romantic science, 129
  *Disquisitions Relating to Matter and Spirit*, 158
  *History and Present State of Electricity*, 125
  methods of, 129–30
Prince of Wales, 199
print media
  and "media time," 38
  and art controversy, 109, 121–24
  and projects, 38
  and relations to arts-and-sciences institutions, 118–19
  in transatlantic studies, 226
progress
  in Coleridge's concept of method, 171–72
  of arts and sciences, 13, 147
projects and projectors, 2
  critique of in Scottish Enlightenment, 42–44

knowledge-organizing projects in Europe, Leibniz on, 34–38
project as agenda of social transformation in Shelley, 219
social wefare projects in Britain, Defoe on, 30–33 *See also:* Defoe, Daniel; Leibniz, Gottfried Wilhelm
Protestantism
bibliography and "religion of the book," 100–3
public sphere, 189
and crisis of sociability, 199

Quarrel of Ancients and Moderns
and modern Enlightenment history, 191–92
and Romantic art controversy, 207
arts and sciences in, 13
place of mechanical and practical arts, 13
*Quarterly Journal of Science and the Arts*, 7, 108
*Quarterly Review*, 7, 55, 77, 103–4, 127
and scientific institutions, 140

Rajan, Tilottama, 189
Ray, Angela, 227
Rectenwald, Michael, 140
*Reflector*, 222
remediation, 112
of art producers, 122
of visual arts into print authorship, 112–13
Republic of Letters, 44, 77, 86, 119, 153, 158
and "second scientific revolution," 146
and arts-and-sciences Institutions, 7, 53
and category of "literature," 73
and crisis of sociability, 198–99
and disciplinary specialization, 154
and disciplines, 157
and Dissenters, 185
and learned societies, 141
and Rational Dissenters, 201
and *respublica literaria*, 34, 37, 178
crisis and failure of, 7, 154–55
history of, 154–56
periodizing of, 154–56
societies and academies in, 45
Reynolds, Joshua, 113
*Discourses on Art*, 45, 113, 118
Robertson, William, 186, 190
*History of America*, 187
Robinson, Henry Crabb, 3
Robinson, Mary, 3, 184
"Present State of the Manners, Society, &c &c of the Metropolis of England," 196–99
and Rational Dissenters, 197, 199
cosmopolitanism celebrated in, 197
on women as cultural producers, 200
Romantic classicism, 122

Romantic science
co-production of by scientific and literary writers, 128
gendering of, 126
politics and materialism of, 129
Romilly, Samuel, 69
Roscoe, William, 53, 184, 203, 270
*On the Origin and Vicissitudes of Literature, Science, and Art*, 210–13
Rousseau, Jean-Jacques, 188
Rowlandson, Thomas, 92, 244
Royal Academy, 6, 13, 46, 108, 111, 113, 116, 119, 203
and British Institution, 70, 120
and the *Artist*, 122
compared to Royal Society, 45
exhibitions of, compared to the British Institution's, 206
Hazlitt's critique of, 205
Royal College of Surgeons, 133, 135, 142
Royal Institution, 1, 66, 77, 93, 148
administration of, and Thomas Bernard, 62–65, 76–77
and Bentham's *Chrestomathia*, 176
and middlebrow taste for knowledge, 65
and Royal Society, 103
and welfare projects, 29
art lectures at, 116
historiography of, 59
impact of, since 1800, 28
lecturing programs at, 72–76 *See also:* Davy, Humphry; Coleridge, Samuel Taylor; Landseer, John; Opie, John; Smith, Sydney
library of, 91–92
naming of, 19, 44, 46–48
origins of
as institute for artisans and mechanics, 60–62
in evangelicalism, 57
transatlantic impact of, 227
transformed into upper-class arts-and-sciences Institution, 63
women in audiences of, 65–66
Royal Society, 6, 35, 45–46, 51, 63, 118, 173
and inarticulate practical knowledges, 168
and Royal Institution, 103
compared to Royal Academy, 45
Robert Hooke's critique of, 173–74
Rumford, Count Benjamin, 3, 48, 62, 79, 227
American origins of, 54
and Joseph Banks, 63
as projector and co-founder of Royal Institution, 58–63
*Essays, Political, Economical, and Philosophical*, 60
on concept of institutions, 60

Ruskin, John, 114
Russell Institution, 1, 27, 70, 79, 182
Russell, Gillian, 53

Sartre, Jean-Paul, 12
Sawday, Jonathan, 145
Schaffer, Simon, 5, 125
 on interdisciplinarity, 126
Schelling, Friedrich, 16, 236
Schlegel, August, 158
Schlegel, Friedrich, 126
scientific and literary instruments, 127, 132, 153
 in work of Coleridge and Keats, 137–40
scientific print culture
 and libraries of arts-and-sciences Institutions, 91–92
 and rise of bibliography in England, 90–91
scientific revolution, second, 4, 22, 126
 as institutional differentiation of modern scientific disciplines, 140–47
 in Thomas Kuhn, 179
Scott, Walter
 *Waverley*, 194–95
Scottish Enlightenment, 48
 and evangelicalism, 48
 and historical concept of, 29
 and historiography, 190–91
 and modern discourse on institutions, 39, 41–44
 critique of projectors in, 38–39, 219
Secord, James, 125
Shakespeare Gallery, 75, 115
Shakespeare, William, 157
 and logic of Coleridge's "method," 169, 172
 Coleridge's lectures on, 161
 *Hamlet*, 172
Shapin, Steven, 125
Sharp, Richard, 184
Shelley, Percy Bysshe, 3, 123, 200
 and critique of institutions, 9
 and Lucretius' materialism, 69
 and the language of *institution*, 39, 219–21
 and utilitarianism, 218–20
 and William Godwin, 188
 *Defence of Poetry, A*, 183, 219–22
 on poet as "institutor," 11
 *Philosophical View of Reform, A*, 183, 218–22
 poetry as act of institution in, 220–22
Sher, Richard, 48, 226
slave trade, 28, 228
Smellie, William
 *Encyclopaedia Britannica*, 37
Smith, Adam, 10, 39, 42, 55, 57
 on harmony in arts and society, 170
Smith, Sydney, 65, 79
 as Royal Institution lecturer on moral philosophy, 78
Smithson, James, 228
Smithsonian Institution
 and London arts-and-sciences Institutions, 228–29
Snow, C. P.
 *Two Cultures, The*, 126
Soane, John, 113–15
sociability, 66
 and projects, 32
 Godwin and crisis of, 196
social sciences
 and view of modernity as differentiation, 148
 role in building arts-and-sciences Institutions, 20, 55
societies, learned *see:* academies and learned societies
Society for Bettering the Condition of the Poor, 55–58
Society of Antiquaries, 6
South, Robert, 177
Southey, Robert, 3, 10, 56, 65, 99
 and institution-building, 10
Southwark Institution, 44
Spadafora, David, 13
Spencer, Herbert, 148
Surrey Institution, 1, 27, 53, 69, 157, 244
 and political controversy, 68, 103
 as commercial, 68
 collapse of, 5, 185
 in religious controversy, 69

Thelwall, John, 134
Thompson, Benjamin *see:* Rumford, Count Benjamin
Thompson, E. P., 135
 *Making of the English Working Class, The*, 218
*Times, The* (London), 122
transatlantic relation of arts and sciences, 27, 155, 226–29
transfiguring of knowledges, 16–19, 147
 and modern discipline formation, 229–31
 in Coleridge's theory of method, 175–76
tree of knowledge, 180
typography, 90
 and bibliographical codes, 94–95
 and science, 94

universities
 and arts-and-sciences Institutions, 44
 and disciplinary system, 11
 and lecturing in Germany v. England, 5
 Cambridge University, 27, 63, 163

compared to arts-and-sciences Institutions, 63
Harvard University, 54
history of, 2
Oxford University, 27
University of Bologna, 47
University of Edinburgh, 63
University of Glasgow, 48
University of London, 147, 224–25
utilitarianism, 224
    and Hunt-circle reformers, 204
    and Rational Dissenters, 185, 201
    Percy Shelley and, 218–20 *See also:* Bentham, Jeremy

Valenza, Robin, 125, 157, 159–60
Vicario, Michael, 69
Vico, Giambattista
    and the language of *institution*, 41
    discourse on institutions in, 40–41
    *Nuovo Scienza*, 40
Volta, Alessandro, 131, 169, 171

Wakefield, Gilbert, 68
Warner, Michael, 241
Watson, Richard, 103
Watt, James, 61
    and intellectual property, 61, 84
Weber, Max, 181
Webster, James, 61

*Westminster Review*, 185, 218, 224
Whewell, William
    *History of the Inductive Sciences*, 125, 140
Wilberforce, William, 56, 243
Williams, Raymond, 12, 180
    *Keywords* (on *institution*), 39–40
    on cultural formations, 201
    on culture and civilization, 178
    on Mill, Bentham, and Coleridge, 163
women
    and the Republic of Letters, 199
    as cultural producers in England, 200
    education of, 3, 27, 31, 65–66
    in arts-and-sciences libraries, 92
Woodring, Carl, 29
Wordsworth, William, 126
    "Ode: Intimations of Immortality," 19
    "Preface to *Lyrical Ballads*," 50, 78, 137, 158
    and disciplinarity, 159–60, 230
    *Lyrical Ballads*, 95, 137
        and norms of sciences, 160
    on institutions, 39
    response to Humphry Davy, 78, 81–82

Yeo, Richard, 14, 235
Young, Thomas, 66, 242

Zizek, Slavoj, 194

CAMBRIDGE STUDIES IN ROMANTICISM

*General editor*
JAMES CHANDLER, *University of Chicago*

1. Romantic Correspondence: Women, Politics and the Fiction of Letters
   MARY A. FAVRET
2. British Romantic Writers and the East: Anxieties of Empire
   NIGEL LEASK
3. Poetry as an Occupation and an Art in Britain, 1760–1830
   PETER MURPHY
4. Edmund Burke's Aesthetic Ideology: Language, Gender and Political Economy in Revolution
   TOM FURNISS
5. In the Theatre of Romanticism: Coleridge, Nationalism, Women
   JULIE A. CARLSON
6. Keats, Narrative and Audience
   ANDREW BENNETT
7. Romance and Revolution: Shelley and the Politics of a Genre
   DAVID DUFF
8. Literature, Education, and Romanticism: Reading as Social Practice, 1780–1832
   ALAN RICHARDSON
9. Women Writing about Money: Women's Fiction in England, 1790–1820
   EDWARD COPELAND
10. Shelley and the Revolution in Taste: The Body and the Natural World
    TIMOTHY MORTON
11. William Cobbett: The Politics of Style
    LEONORA NATTRASS
12. The Rise of Supernatural Fiction, 1762–1800
    E. J. CLERY
13. Women Travel Writers and the Language of Aesthetics, 1716–1818
    ELIZABETH A. BOHLS
14. Napoleon and English Romanticism
    SIMON BAINBRIDGE
15. Romantic Vagrancy: Wordsworth and the Simulation of Freedom
    CELESTE LANGAN

16. Wordsworth and the Geologists
   JOHN WYATT

17. Wordsworth's Pope: A Study in Literary Historiography
   ROBERT J. GRIFFIN

18. The Politics of Sensibility: Race, Gender and Commerce in the Sentimental Novel
   MARKMAN ELLIS

19. Reading Daughters' Fictions, 1709–1834: Novels and Society from Manley to Edgeworth
   CAROLINE GONDA

20. Romantic Identities: Varieties of Subjectivity, 1774–1830
   ANDREA K. HENDERSON

21. Print Politics: The Press and Radical Opposition: in Early Nineteenth-Century England
   KEVIN GILMARTIN

22. Reinventing Allegory
   THERESA M. KELLEY

23. British Satire and the Politics of Style, 1789–1832
   GARY DYER

24. The Romantic Reformation: Religious Politics in English Literature, 1789–1824
   ROBERT M. RYAN

25. De Quincey's Romanticism: Canonical Minority and the Forms of Transmission
   MARGARET RUSSETT

26. Coleridge on Dreaming: Romanticism, Dreams and the Medical Imagination
   JENNIFER FORD

27. Romantic Imperialism: Universal Empire and the Culture of Modernity
   SAREE MAKDISI

28. Ideology and Utopia in the Poetry of William Blake
   NICHOLAS M. WILLIAMS

29. Sexual Politics and the Romantic Author
   SONIA HOFKOSH

30. Lyric and Labour in the Romantic Tradition
   ANNE JANOWITZ

31. Poetry and Politics in the Cockney School: Keats, Shelley, Hunt and their Circle
   JEFFREY N. COX

32. Rousseau, Robespierre and English Romanticism
   GREGORY DART

33. Contesting the Gothic: Fiction, Genre and Cultural Conflict, 1764–1832
   JAMES WATT

34. Romanticism, Aesthetics, and Nationalism
   DAVID ARAM KAISER

35. Romantic Poets and the Culture of Posterity
   ANDREW BENNETT

36. The Crisis of Literature in the 1790s: Print Culture and the Public Sphere
   PAUL KEEN

37. Romantic Atheism: Poetry and Freethought, 1780–1830
   MARTIN PRIESTMAN

38. Romanticism and Slave Narratives: Transatlantic Testimonies
   HELEN THOMAS

39. Imagination under Pressure, 1789–1832: Aesthetics, Politics, and Utility
   JOHN WHALE

40. Romanticism and the Gothic: Genre, Reception, and Canon Formation, 1790–1820
   MICHAEL GAMER

41. Romanticism and the Human Sciences: Poetry, Population, and the Discourse of the Species
   MAUREEN N. MCLANE

42. The Poetics of Spice: Romantic Consumerism and the Exotic
   TIMOTHY MORTON

43. British Fiction and the Production of Social Order, 1740–1830
   MIRANDA J. BURGESS

44. Women Writers and the English Nation in the 1790s
   ANGELA KEANE

45. Literary Magazines and British Romanticism
   MARK PARKER

46. Women, Nationalism and the Romantic Stage: Theatre and Politics in Britain, 1780–1800
   BETSY BOLTON

47. British Romanticism and the Science of the Mind
   ALAN RICHARDSON

48. The Anti-Jacobin Novel: British Conservatism and the French Revolution
   M. O. GRENBY

49. Romantic Austen: Sexual Politics and the Literary Canon
   CLARA TUITE

50. Byron and Romanticism
   JEROME MCGANN AND JAMES SODERHOLM

51. The Romantic National Tale and the Question of Ireland
   INA FERRIS

52. Byron, Poetics and History
   JANE STABLER

53. Religion, Toleration, and British Writing, 1790–1830
   MARK CANUEL

54. Fatal Women of Romanticism
   ADRIANA CRACIUN

55. Knowledge and Indifference in English Romantic Prose
   TIM MILNES

56. Mary Wollstonecraft and the Feminist Imagination
   BARBARA TAYLOR

57. Romanticism, Maternity and the Body Politic
   JULIE KIPP

58. Romanticism and Animal Rights
   DAVID PERKINS

59. Georgic Modernity and British Romanticism: Poetry and the Mediation of History
   KEVIS GOODMAN

60. Literature, Science and Exploration in the Romantic Era: Bodies of Knowledge
   TIMOTHY FULFORD, DEBBIE LEE, AND PETER J. KITSON

61. Romantic Colonization and British Anti-Slavery
   DEIRDRE COLEMAN

62. Anger, Revolution, and Romanticism
   ANDREW M. STAUFFER

63. Shelley and the Revolutionary Sublime
   CIAN DUFFY

64. Fictions and Fakes: Forging Romantic Authenticity, 1760–1845
   MARGARET RUSSETT

65. Early Romanticism and Religious Dissent
   DANIEL E. WHITE

66. The Invention of Evening: Perception and Time in Romantic Poetry
   CHRISTOPHER R. MILLER

67. Wordsworth's Philosophic Song
   SIMON JARVIS

68. Romanticism and the Rise of the Mass Public
   ANDREW FRANTA

69. Writing against Revolution: Literary Conservatism in Britain, 1790–1832
   KEVIN GILMARTIN

70. Women, Sociability and Theatre in Georgian London
   GILLIAN RUSSELL

71. The Lake Poets and Professional Identity
   BRIAN GOLDBERG

72. Wordsworth Writing
   ANDREW BENNETT

73. Science and Sensation in Romantic Poetry
   NOEL JACKSON

74. Advertising and Satirical Culture in the Romantic Period
   JOHN STRACHAN

75. Romanticism and the Painful Pleasures of Modern Life
   ANDREA K. HENDERSON

76. Balladeering, Minstrelsy, and the Making of British Romantic Poetry
   MAUREEN N. MCLANE

77. Romanticism and Improvisation, 1750–1850
   ANGELA ESTERHAMMER

78. Scotland and the Fictions of Geography: North Britain, 1760–1830
   PENNY FIELDING

79. Wordsworth, Commodification and Social Concern: The Poetics of Modernity
   DAVID SIMPSON

80. Sentimental Masculinity and the Rise of History, 1790–1890
   MIKE GOODE

81. Fracture and Fragmentation in British Romanticism
   ALEXANDER REGIER

82. Romanticism and Music Culture in Britain, 1770–1840: Virtue and Virtuosity
   GILLEN D'ARCY WOOD

83. The Truth about Romanticism: Pragmatism and Idealism in Keats, Shelley, Coleridge
   TIM MILNES

84. Blake's Gifts: Poetry and the Politics of Exchange
   SARAH HAGGARTY

85. Real Money and Romanticism
   MATTHEW ROWLINSON

86. Sentimental Literature and Anglo-Scottish Identity, 1745–1820
   JULIET SHIELDS

87. Romantic Tragedies: The Dark Employments of Wordsworth, Coleridge, and Shelley
   REEVE PARKER

88. Blake, Sexuality and Bourgeois Politeness
   SUSAN MATTHEWS

89. Idleness, Contemplation and the Aesthetic
   RICHARD ADELMAN

90. Shelley's Visual Imagination
   NANCY MOORE GOSLEE

91. A Cultural History of the Irish Novel, 1790–1829
   CLAIRE CONNOLLY

92. Literature, Commerce, and the Spectacle of Modernity, 1750–1800
   PAUL KEEN

93. Romanticism and Childhood: The Infantilization of British Literary Culture
   ANN WEIRDA ROWLAND

94. Metropolitan Art and Literature, 1810–1840: Cockney Adventures
   GREGORY DART

95. Wordsworth and the Enlightenment Idea of Pleasure
   ROWAN BOYSON

96. John Clare and Community
   JOHN GOODRIDGE

97. The Romantic Crowd
   MARY FAIRCLOUGH

98. Romantic Women Writers, Revolution and Prophecy
   ORIANNE SMITH

99. Britain, France and the Gothic, 1764–1820
   ANGELA WRIGHT

100. Transfiguring the Arts and Sciences
    JON KLANCHER